DIMAGGIO

DIMAGGIO
SETTING THE RECORD STRAIGHT

MORRIS ENGELBERG
MARV SCHNEIDER

FOREWORD BY DR. HENRY A. KISSINGER

MBI

First published in 2003 by MBI Publishing Company, Galtier Plaza, Suite 200, 380 Jackson Street, St. Paul, MN 55101-3885 U.S.A.

The information in this book is true and complete to the best of our knowledge. All recommendations are made without any guarantee on the part of the author or Publisher, who also disclaim any liability incurred in connection with the use of this data or specific details.

Library of Congress Cataloging-in-Publication Data Available

ISBN 0-7603-1482-9

Front jacket photographs: main image, Joe DiMaggio portrait by David M. Spindel; background image, DiMaggio during the 1949 World Series, courtesy AP/Wide World Photos. Used by permission.
Back jacket photograph, DiMaggio at Yankee Stadium in 1941, courtesy AP/Wide World Photos. Used by permission.
Frontispiece photograph, DiMaggio portrait from 1941, courtesy AP/Wide World Photos. Used by permission.

Edited by Josh Leventhal
Book design by Peregrine Graphics
Jacket design by Tom Heffron

In grateful remembrance of
Pauline Engelberg and Rosalie DiMaggio
Two very special mothers

MORRIS ENGELBERG

To Anna Burris, my wife, more valuable than rubies

MARV SCHNEIDER

CONTENTS

FOREWORD
Dr. Henry A. Kissinger

I HAD JUST TURNED SIXTEEN and had been in this country for less than a year when I first fell under the spell of Joe DiMaggio. I had arrived in New York in 1938 with my parents and younger brother, escaping the increasingly dangerous environment in Nazi Germany. We settled in Washington Heights in upper Manhattan, a haven for many other German Jewish refugees, and I enrolled in a local high school. But times were tough during the Depression, especially for those without a ready command of the language, and the next year I switched to night school in order to work at a cousin's shaving brush factory during the day.

My coworkers at the factory were mostly second-generation Italian-Americans, who seemed to have a passionate interest in a game called baseball and particularly in a player named Joe DiMaggio. Many things about America were still new and strange to me and, although I had been an avid sports fan in Germany, baseball was something about which I knew nothing. My lack of knowledge must have seemed equally strange to my new Italian friends, for one Sunday one of them invited me to go with him to a doubleheader at Yankee Stadium. We sat in the fifty-five-cent bleachers, where we couldn't see much of what was going on at home plate but had a good view of the great DiMaggio. His graceful fielding and the soaring fly balls he hit deep into left field astonished me, and I was hooked. From then on I was a rabid fan, and every Sunday when the Yankees were playing a home game, I would walk forty-five minutes to the stadium to watch my hero work his magic. I had become an American in my heart, if not yet in the eyes of the Bureau of Naturalization.

At that time, the idea that I would one day be the secretary of state of my adopted country was no more unlikely a dream than that one day I would meet and become a friend of Joe DiMaggio's. But many years later, a foot problem brought me to the office of Dr. Rock Positano, a well-known podiatrist and sports medicine specialist. Another of his patients was DiMaggio, who happened to be there at the same time, and Dr. Positano introduced us. I admit to feeling like a star-struck adolescent again, but Joe was gracious and easy to chat with. It turned out that our appointments were often at the same hour, so we saw each other with some frequency, and a friendship developed. We found we had much to talk about, for Joe was very interested in and knowledgeable about current affairs, and I loved hearing his baseball stories.

I remained a fan until the end of his life. When he died, I felt not only a personal bereavement at the loss of a close friend but the sorrow of a nation, which had lost an authentic American hero. By his example, Joe had taught two generations of youngsters the meaning of excellence, to do their best but to accept defeat with good sportsmanship, and that tomorrow was another day and another game in which to try again.

One of those kids had been me.

PREFACE
Marv Schneider

FOR MORE THAN A HALF CENTURY, Joe DiMaggio was one of the most revered and beloved sports figures of his time. More than just a famous athlete, DiMaggio was a great figure of American culture. As a result, some thirty biographies of this American icon have been published since Joltin' Joe burst onto the national scene with the New York Yankees baseball team in 1936. For the most part, these biographies were written by people who never met DiMaggio, or to quote Joe D., "Guys I never even had a cup of coffee with."

Joe DiMaggio shared much more than a cup of coffee with Morris Engelberg. There were many days when the two had breakfast, lunch, dinner, and a late-night snack together. Engelberg was DiMaggio's close friend and adviser. He was the attorney who negotiated the ventures that made DiMaggio a multimillionaire, and yet he refused any fee, because he couldn't take money from his boyhood idol. According to Joe's granddaughter Kathie DiMaggio Stein, "for sixteen years Morris was my grandfather's best friend. Nobody knew Big Joe like Morris did."

They shared countless hours in front of the TV sets in each other's den, watching sports, news, and movies, or just talking. They sat side by side on flights to DiMaggio's public appearances and memorabilia shows, with DiMaggio offering his thoughts on Ted Williams, Mickey Mantle, his brother Dom, and the presidents he had met.

They lounged in their backyards, which were only yards apart on the Intracoastal Waterway in Florida, and DiMaggio spoke of things that were deep in his soul. He recounted his love for Marilyn Monroe, and his anguish about how she died; his anger at John and Bobby Kennedy, and about being betrayed by Frank Sinatra, who had been a friend; his feelings about his only son, with whom he was estranged for many years; and his concern about how he would be remembered in history.

Engelberg was at DiMaggio's bedside during Joe's battle against lung cancer. He was there to say goodbye and to hear his friend's final words, "I'll finally get to see Marilyn again."

There were light moments, to be sure, such as DiMaggio's story of the time he and Yogi Berra occupied the same piece of Yankee Stadium grass under a fly ball, and his parody of Jose Canseco getting conked on the head by a ball he should have caught.

This is not a baseball book. It is not about games, seasons, and statistics—although these are brush strokes in a portrait of one of the greatest center fielders ever to play the game. Rather, this is a profile of a man who forever will be part of our memory of the twentieth century. It offers something none of the other books could: an insider's intimate view of Joe DiMaggio.

Engelberg at one time insisted he would take his recollections of those conversations to his grave. But then something changed his mind—he felt DiMaggio was being maligned in death. Engelberg felt that he owed his friend one last favor, and that was to challenge the untruths that had besmirched the memory of the man who was America's number one sports hero, and to set the record straight.

I wrote the story as Engelberg told it to me, in the first person. I hoped this would convey the depth of feeling that Engelberg had for the man he wished had been his father. I first met Engelberg when I covered DiMaggio's final illness and death for the Associated Press, where I worked for forty-three years as a sportswriter and editor. His fascinating devotion to DiMaggio was to have been the subject of this book, but the more interviews and research I did, the broader the book became. For more than a year, I spoke with DiMaggio's old friends, former teammates, and others whose paths had crossed with his. I interviewed members of DiMaggio's family, including his grandchildren, who would never before discuss Joe's private life. Their trust in Engelberg opened doors for me. Through frank discussions with people who knew Marilyn Monroe, including an ex-lover, and fifty-year-old letters written by a close friend to both Joe and Marilyn, I was able to discover new insights into what was once the world's most famous romance.

DiMaggio himself contributed to *Setting the Record Straight* with excerpts from a diary he kept in the latter part of his life. Joe may not have liked everything in this book, but even as critical as he was, he would have agreed that this book tells the real story of his life.

◆ ◆ ◆

Thank you, Morris, for your trust in sharing those memories of Joe and his family that you once told me were locked in your heart as secrets forever. After more than four decades of reporting, editing, and writing sports stories, this was the biggest story of all, and you let me tell it the way it was, blemishes and all.

My grateful thanks are also due to Joe Nachio, who opened his lips, heart, and soul as never before to reminisce about his old buddy; and to Paula and Jim Hamra and Kathie and Roger Stein for talking so openly about their grandfather. To other members of the DiMaggio family, including nephew Joe, and his wife, Marina, and to Sue DiMaggio: thank you for your faith and frankness.

My appreciation for the cooperation and memories contributed by DiMaggio's teammates Yogi Berra, Dr. Bobby Brown, Jerry Coleman, Whitey Ford, Tommy Henrich, Gil McDougald, and Phil Rizzuto; and other major leaguers, including Hank Aaron, Eldon Auker, Jeff Conine, and Ted Williams.

Bob Solotaire was more than generous with his recollections and heirloom letters from his father, George, who played so important a role in DiMaggio's adult life. Bob Slatzer was of extraordinary help for sharing the story of his love and adventures with Marilyn Monroe and his memories of Joe. Dr. Rock Positano, who knew Joe so well, graciously probed his memory and freely shared his knowledge and insights.

Thanks, too, for the valuable information provided by Maury Allen, Marty Appel, Dr. Earl Barron, Hal Bock, Norman Brokaw, Donald Burris, Jerald Cantor, Pellegrino D'Acierno, Scott DiStefano, Mario Faustini, Mike Fernandez, Dr. Salvatore Ferrera, Joe Franco, Rob Gloster, Eddie Jaffe, Bernie Kamber, Dr. Henry Kissinger, John Klobucar, Frank LaBono, Marty Lederhandler, Martha Lee, Seymour Levy, Leonard Lewin, Dan McGonigle, Harland McPhun Jr., Laurie Milgrim, Myles Malman, Luciano Pavarotti, Otto Perl, Sy Presten, George Randazzo, Arthur Richman, Karen Ritch (RN), Irwin Rosee, Stanley Rubens, Charles L. Ruffner, Rocky Russo, Frank Sacco, Kathleen Salvo, Russell Schneider, Louis Schwartz, Frank Simino, Paul Sirmons, Rita Sokoloff, Lee Solters, Sam Spear, William Stadiem, Gerald Stern, Bert Sugar, Fay Vincent, Norman Werksman, and Bill Williams.

My gratitude to Judith Joseph, whose tireless and diligent efforts as our agent brought special success to this project.

Special thanks to those who provided some of the research and background material, including Sheila and Dr. Allen Burris, Alan Perzley, David Greenberg, and the understanding staff at the Teaneck, New Jersey, Public Library. To Robert Geller, my gratitude for his wise guidance and direction.

This project could not have been successfully completed without the technical assistance and patience of Glenie Marie Byrd and my wife, Anna Burris, who provided the intelligent counsel and encouragement that kept me on the right track.

————•————

JOE, MY IDOL

WHEN I WAS EIGHT YEARS OLD, I shocked my mother by telling her that I wished Joe DiMaggio was my father.

"Morris, don't even think such a thing," she said. "DiMaggio? He's Italian. You're an orthodox Jewish boy."

But I was a Jewish boy without a father. At least, not one I ever knew. My father, Morris, died of an aneurysm three months before I was born. Pauline, my mother, did a marvelous job of raising two sons, but I desperately wanted a dad, like everyone else in the apartment house in Brooklyn where we lived, and like everyone in the yeshiva, the parochial school I attended. Someone of whom to be proud, someone about whom to brag.

Who better than Joe DiMaggio, the greatest baseball player in the world? The Joe DiMaggio who glided across the 11-inch TV screen in our Boro Park apartment to the outermost regions of Yankee Stadium, where he effortlessly caught fly balls. The DiMaggio whose heroics were lavishly described on the sports pages of seven newspapers on the racks at the corner candy store. I read every story about the Yankees every day.

My mother's four brothers rooted for the Yankees and Giants, even though they too lived in Brooklyn, because they were raised on Manhattan's Lower East Side. Their discussions of DiMaggio's heroics made a great impression on a five-year-old. "Nobody, and I mean nobody in the entire world, can cover so much ground like

Joe DiMaggio," my uncle Leo would say. "And," his brother Morris contributed, "he makes it look so easy, it's like he floats across the grass." "Never mind his fielding, what about his hitting? That's what he's known for," Uncle Mac insisted. "He's got a perfect swing," Uncle Harry added. "When he hits the ball, goodbye Charlie. It's gone." Their opinions became great truths to me. There was no question about it, No. 5, Joe's uniform number, was number one in my family. Even the name "Joltin' Joe DiMaggio" had a nice ring to it. I proudly pasted No. 5 on my T-shirts and jackets.

It was not easy being a Yankees fan where I lived, only 3 miles from Ebbets Field, where the Dodgers played. Everyone in the neighborhood was caught up in Dodger fervor all summer, and when the Dodgers made it to the World Series in 1947, there was no other subject for discussion.

Forever burned into my memory is the sixth game of that classic Yankee-Dodger confrontation, the first Series to be televised nationally. It was the end of the Jewish holiday of Sukkoth, and in my religious home it was forbidden to turn on the television set or anything else requiring electricity. But five blocks away was Red's saloon, where I knew the TV would be tuned to the Series.

A seven-year-old could not get into Red's, but I pushed a milk bottle crate up to the window and stood on it to watch the whole game. The smells of beer and cigars and the sound of men cheering created an ambience I can recall even today.

With the Yankees leading the Series three games to two, the Dodgers scored four runs in the bottom of the sixth inning to take an 8–5 lead in the sixth game. In the bottom half of the inning, DiMaggio came to bat with two Yankees on base. A home run by Joe would tie the score. In an instant, it appeared that my silent prayer had been answered. DiMaggio took a mighty swing at a pitch from Joe Hatten and drove the ball 400 feet toward the left-field corner at Yankee Stadium. But Brooklyn's Al Gionfriddo raced to the waist-high fence in front of the bullpen, reached up, and made the catch.

The guys at the bar let out a shout of joy and threw their arms into the air. DiMaggio was almost at second base by the time Gionfriddo made the catch. When he saw that the ball had been caught, Joe kicked the dirt in the base path. It was a rare display, if not his only display, of emotion on the baseball field. I got off my crate and kicked it. The Yankees lost the game, 8–6. It was a long, sad walk home, and once I got there, I could turn to no one for solace. I couldn't tell anyone what I had seen because they would know I was off watching a game through a saloon window on a holiday. I wasn't sad for long, though, because the Yankees won the Series the next day.

The following year, I had a day never to be forgotten. My uncles took me to Yankee Stadium for the first time, and I saw him, Joltin' Joe DiMaggio. No one has ever seen God, not even Moses, who had to settle for a burning bush. But I saw Joe DiMaggio taking batting practice, running out to the greenest grass outfield I had ever seen, and poised at the plate waiting for a pitch in a game against the Detroit Tigers. There he was, live and in person: that picture-book wide stance, that perfect swing, and that all-out sprint to first base.

What I saw that day intensified my worship of my idol in a pin-stripe uniform. As I grew older, I copied his batting stance, his running style, and the way he caught a ball—even the way he combed his hair into a pompadour.

Toward the end of the 1949 season, I watched Joe DiMaggio Day on TV. Joe was presented with a Cadillac, a speedboat, two television sets, and much more. His mother was there, and because the Yankees were playing the Red Sox, so was his younger brother Dom, then Boston's center fielder. But what I remembered most was DiMaggio's son, Joe Jr., who was eight years old, a year younger than I. He was on the field with his father. How I wished I were in his place.

◆ ◆ ◆

After DiMaggio retired, it became my mission to keep his style alive, on the baseball diamond and off. Along with copying his batting stance, as I grew older and went to college and law school, I emulated his style of dress. Conservative three-button dark suits, white shirt, red or blue tie. I grew to 6-foot-5, even taller than DiMaggio. I moved to southern Florida in 1969, but I was still the Brooklyn kid who never forgot his idol.

By the time I reached forty, I had accomplished a great deal, but one thing was missing. I had never met DiMaggio, who by then was spending a lot of time in southern Florida. Not that I didn't try. Clients who might have had any possible links to my hero were asked to help me in my quest. It became a joke among my friends and office staff.

Then, Cal Kovens, who had retained me for a legal project, came through. "DiMaggio?" asked Kovens. "That *schmaggegie*? We just took a steam bath together this morning. He's staying at a place I own. He'll call you tonight, and you can set up an appointment to meet. What's a good time for him to call?" I never really expected that he would call, but half-jokingly I replied, "Around eight o'clock."

Precisely at 8:00 P.M. on January 31, 1983, the phone rang. My wife, Stephanie, put her hand over the mouthpiece and whispered, "It's Joe DiMaggio." This was the moment I had envisioned and rehearsed in my mind for thirty-six years, and now, like in a nightmare, I was paralyzed. I couldn't move to the phone, and if I could have I wouldn't have been able to speak. All I managed to get out was, "Tell him I'll call him back. Take a message."

DiMaggio's message was that he would meet me for breakfast at 8:00 A.M. the next morning in the coffee shop at Kovens' Boca Teeca Hotel and Country Club.

I was up at 4:00 A.M. and left my home at 5:15 for the twenty-five-minute ride on I-95 to Boca Raton. I told Stephanie to be prepared to rush out of the house if I should call to say that my car had broken down. It never had before, but who knew what might happen? I took my portable phone, which in those days was a foot long and weighed about five pounds.

It was barely 5:45 when I drove up to Boca Teeca. I was dressed in my DiMaggio uniform: dark blue three-buttoned suit, white button-down shirt, red tie, and Allen-Edmonds black wingtips, polished to a mirror-like shine.

I sat on a leather couch in the empty lobby to wait out the two hours. My emotions wavered between worry and anticipation. How could I be certain that it was actually DiMaggio on the phone with Stephanie? Suppose someone was playing a practical joke? If Joe DiMaggio did indeed walk into that lobby, how would I react? What would I say? I began to sweat and I felt my clothes sticking to me. What would DiMaggio think of a man in a wrinkled shirt?

The clock in the lobby reached a quarter to eight when I heard the man at the front desk talking with DiMaggio on the phone. I was certain Joe was canceling the appointment, especially when the hotel manager approached me. Thankfully, I was wrong. Mr. DiMaggio wanted me to know he had overslept and would be five minutes late.

I had no way of knowing then, but when I got to know DiMaggio, I realized that I had no cause for worry. With him, an appointment made was an appointment kept. I never knew him to cancel a meeting, including one that he kept just thirty minutes after learning he had lung cancer.

At exactly 8:05, Joe DiMaggio came into the lobby wearing a white shirt, red tie, a wine-colored sweater, and a dark blue blazer. I introduced myself. His facial expression was stern and he said, "Mr. Engelberg, I am sorry that I am five minutes late." "Mr. DiMaggio," I replied, "I waited nearly forty years to meet you, and I would have waited five more hours to shake your hand." He smiled. He told me later that he got a big kick from that remark, a 6-foot-5 well-dressed lawyer acting like a little boy.

I never carried my business cards, not from the first day I went into practice. But on this day, I took one with me and extended it to Joe. "Mr. DiMaggio, I would really appreciate it if you would acknowledge that I met you by signing the back of my card. Otherwise, no one will ever believe I shook your hand."

He completely ignored my outstretched hand, put his arm around my shoulder, and invited me in to breakfast. Certainly no one was going to believe this! We were joined by Nick Nicolosi, an aide of Kovens' who was a buffer and companion for DiMaggio. As we crossed the road to the restaurant, a car sped toward us, and we had to hurry to get out of the way. DiMaggio broke into a run, and even at the age of sixty-nine, he exhibited that same graceful stride with which he used to chase down fly balls.

As we walked into the restaurant, the golfers who were having breakfast stood up and gave DiMaggio an ovation. We made our way to the table, and he was greeted with handshakes and pats on the back. That was my introduction to what it was like to be with DiMaggio in a public setting, something I would experience often over the next sixteen years. Just being around DiMaggio made you feel important. In our years together, I saw that no matter where we went or what other celebrities were there, DiMaggio's presence was overpowering. All eyes were on him. This was true no matter who was watching him. Doctors, lawyers, diplomats, construction workers on a sidewalk site, or guys in a restaurant kitchen washing dishes all became kids again, awed by his presence.

The breakfast that day, which should have lasted forty-five minutes, continued for nearly five hours.

DiMaggio was amazed by how much I knew about him, including his neck and shoe size. We talked about games he had played when I was a youngster. He was astonished at how many details I remembered.

Aside from being able to quote most of his statistics, I told him that I had used his Yankees uniform number on my basketball jerseys at Brooklyn College, and I used two significant years of his career as the numbers for the combination locks on my lockers: 1936, when he made his big league debut, and 1941, the year of his 56-game hitting streak.

Throughout that first meeting, DiMaggio called me Mr. Engelberg. It was his practice to use Mr., Miss, or Mrs. at least for the first two or three meetings. This was his way of saying, "You're not my friend or buddy, yet." It was a wall he put up to keep out those who would invade his privacy.

When we left the restaurant, DiMaggio put his arm around my shoulder and invited Nicolosi and me to his room. There he opened a huge Samsonite suitcase. The case had long since gone out of style and was held together with tape, but he traveled with that same suitcase until his final trip in 1998. He took out two 8-by-10 photographs, one depicting his famed swing and the other a promotional portrait from the Bowery Savings Bank of New York in which he wore a blue suit, white shirt, and red tie, similar to what I was wearing that morning. Without hesitation, I selected the portrait. "Good choice," he said.

DiMaggio took the photo I selected, sat down, and using a dark blue Sharpie pen, wrote "Morris — A real pleasure to sit and have a lengthy conversation with an old-time fan. Best always, Joe DiMaggio."

I drove back to my office with that photo on the front seat next to me, and glanced at it from time to time as if to convince myself that I really did have that meeting. That night, I invited my brother and a crowd of cousins and neighbors to my home to see the autographed photo and to hear the story of how Joe and I trotted across the road together, then sat and talked for so long. I spared them no detail, even describing his broad shoulders and powerful wrists, and, of course, what he wore.

The blue ink of DiMaggio's autograph has since faded to green, but the memory of Joe giving me that very special photo remains as it was on that magical day in 1983. It was a day that changed my life and the life of my family. Not even in my most optimistic fantasy did I imagine the friendship that would grow from that meeting. Nor could I imagine that sixteen years into the future, this American legend, my childhood hero, would die with me grasping his hand.

1

THE EARLY YEARS

No one is quite sure when or where Joe DiMaggio first swung a bat at a ball. That moment is lost among the myths, half-truths, and facts that grew with the Joe D. legend in San Francisco's North Beach neighborhood. There was a story, but not from Joe, that he and his friends used a boat paddle to hit a cloth ball tied with string. There was no question in the neighborhood, though, that when the DiMaggio kid did get a bat in his hands, he could hit. He regularly put the ball over the fence at the North Beach playground. "Hit the car," the other kids urged whenever the Powell Street cable car clanged by as Joe was at bat. Supposedly, he did hit it at least once. He later played at the Funston playground, which had a bigger outfield and there was less danger of losing those precious baseballs.

Joe talked about playing in the rocky lots where a dairy kept the horse-drawn wagons that delivered milk door-to-door each morning. He said he played in the infield because he didn't have a good enough arm or strong enough legs to play in the outfield. He had no glove because he couldn't afford to buy one; if he couldn't borrow someone else's, he played barehanded. "I had a real scatter-arm," he said. "Even later on, when I was trying to play shortstop for the San Francisco Seals, I had a strong arm, but I made a lot of throwing errors. My teammates kidded me that it was dangerous to sit behind first base when I played short. I actually broke a seat behind first base with one of my throws. After a while, my arm got better, and my legs came around, too." He also said he had some kind of a problem with his legs that forced him to wear braces on his knees as a youngster. By the time Joe was in Francisco Junior High, and had grown taller and stronger, that problem no longer bothered him.

DiMaggio's jump from the sandlot to minor league ball was accomplished with the help of his brother Vince, who was two years older and playing for the San Francisco Seals, of the Pacific Coast League (PCL). The money that Vince brought home convinced their father, Giuseppe DiMaggio, that there might be something worthwhile in baseball after all. Vince's real contribution to Joe's baseball career, in addition to showing Poppa the money, was in recommending his brother to Seals manager Ike Caveney.

Joe acknowledged that his brother helped launch his pro career, but he said he was not an unknown to the Seals. "A fellow named Spike Hennessey had seen me play at Funston, and he was friendly with Charlie Graham, who owned the Seals," DiMaggio said. "He told Mr. Graham about me, and took me to see him. So when Vince told Ike about me, Mr. Graham knew who I was." That fateful recommendation took place just before the last weekend of the 1932 season. Augie Galan, who later became a major leaguer, was the Seals shortstop at the time, and he had an opportunity to play some exhibition games in Hawaii. Since the Seals were in last place in the PCL and only three games remained on their schedule, Galan was given permission to leave. That's when Vince said he had a brother who was playing shortstop with semipro teams in town and could fill in for Galan.

Joe was a couple of months from his eighteenth birthday when he made his pro debut on a Saturday afternoon at Seals Stadium. He hit a triple in his first at-bat, loping around the bases in that long stride for which he became famous. That hit and a couple of outstanding running catches in short left field were the extent of DiMaggio's heroics that day and in Sunday's doubleheader, but the experience left him with a lasting memory: "I didn't get paid."

Galan came back to the Seals in 1933 and again won the short-stop job, but the Seals invited Joe to try out in preseason work-outs. They were impressed enough to offer him a contract. It had to be Joe's hitting that caught Caveney's attention, because according to Joe, his throwing still was atrocious. Also, Hennessey was a big DiMaggio booster, and Graham valued him as an exceptional judge of talent.

Enter Tom DiMaggio, the oldest of the brothers and "the brains" of the family. He negotiated for Joe, and since his brother was only eighteen, a member of the family had to witness the contract signing. Tom did that, too, but not very well. He didn't notice that Joe signed the document as "De Maggio." More important to Tom were the numbers on the agreement: $225 a month, which was about two times more than what most PCL rookies were getting.

"Tom did pretty well on that deal," Joe remembered years later. "He put in a bonus clause calling for two suits, both of which went to him. I didn't even get reimbursed for the carfare to the stadium and back. It cost me thirty cents."

Joe started the season on the bench, but he wasn't there for long. He was sent in as a pinch hitter for the right fielder in a game early in the season, and he walked. When the inning ended, Caveney told him, "Go out to right." DiMaggio was jolted. "I had never played the outfield before."

◆ ◆ ◆

The future Hall of Famer was no overnight sensation in his first foray in professional baseball. He actually was little more than a green, overanxious teenager during the first two months of the season. But on May 28, DiMaggio began what would be a 61-game hitting streak, the likes of which had never been seen before or since in the PCL.

Looking back at that streak, Joe said it was very different from his major league record 56-game hitting streak in 1941. "No pressure, no big crowds, no reporters following me around."

Yet, newspapers in PCL cities did report that fan interest grew after the streak reached 40 games. Crowds were larger than usual, especially in San Francisco, where many Italian-Americans who had never been to a baseball game turned out to see their *paisan*. To most of the writers, he was still "De Maggio," and that's the way his name appeared in stories and box scores. In July he signed a bat endorsement contract with the Hillerich & Bradsby Co., and his signature was Joe Di Maggio—not Joseph, and with a space between Di and Maggio. (A psychologist might suggest that the odd signature was Joe's attempt to separate himself from his family and declare his independence.) Seals owner Charlie Graham was confused. When the streak ended, he asked Joe for the correct spelling so that the name could be engraved on a watch that was to be presented to him to commemorate the feat. "You can spell it any old way," DiMaggio told him.

PCL seasons were seemingly endless in those days. Joe played 187 games that first year, during which he batted .340 and drove in a league-leading 169 runs. In the process of becoming the team's right fielder, he pushed Vince out of a job. That probably didn't bother Joe because he was even more competitive against his brothers than he was against everyone else.

The publicity from the hitting streak and DiMaggio's stellar statistics had major league scouts poised for the 1934 season, and it couldn't come fast enough for the Seals. The club was on the verge of bankruptcy. Graham needed a big offer for DiMaggio from a major league team. The figure he had in mind was $75,000. Tom DiMaggio had his own visions of sugarplums for his brother, and he told Graham that Joe would have to be cut in before agreeing to any deal. The New York Yankees and Boston Red Sox were among those interested. After a Sunday doubleheader early in the season, however, Joe got out of a jitney van on his way to dinner at the home of one of his sisters, and he stepped on everybody's dreams. He tore cartilage in his left knee.

That might have been enough to scare off any potential big league suitors. DiMaggio's reputation was so great, however, that the Yankees decided he was worth the gamble. Joe always credited a scout named Bill Essick with maintaining the Yankees' interest in him. Essick had lived in North Beach, and he learned of the hero of the neighborhood rock lots even before Joe's sensational rookie year with the Seals. Together with Joe Devine, who scouted the Bay Area for the Yankees, Essick convinced General Manager Ed Barrow and owner Colonel Jacob Ruppert that the kid was young enough to bounce back from the injury. The Yankees had doctors check the knee, and they agreed. Barrow whined about damaged goods, and he drove down the price to $25,000 plus five players from the Yankees farm system. Graham felt he should get something extra in return for taking so little money, and he asked that the Seals be allowed to hold onto DiMaggio for one more year. Joe's hitting streak had made him a West Coast celebrity, someone who could pull people into parks and keep the financially shaky Seals afloat.

DiMaggio said that the last part of the deal was a big break for him, because the Seals hired Lefty O'Doul as their new manager that season. O'Doul had come out of San Francisco in the 1920s to become a major league star, and his name was legend among the kids in the city, including Joe DiMaggio. More important, O'Doul proved to be an excellent batting instructor. DiMaggio said that O'Doul taught him a lot about hitting that year and in the years that followed, when Joe would come home after a season with the Yanks. DiMaggio gave O'Doul and Lefty's friend, Ty

Cobb, a lot of credit for his success. Cobb, who lived in Burlingame, California, was around Seals Stadium often, and he always had hitting advice for the kid. Joe hit .398 in his final year and led San Francisco to the pennant.

In addition to the on-field instruction, Cobb also helped DiMaggio negotiate his first big league contract. As Joe Nachio, DiMaggio's longtime friend and confidante, explained, "Remember, Joe quit high school in his first year. He wasn't what you would call a literary giant. He wanted to include a letter when he sent back the unsigned contract, but he didn't know what words to use. So, Cobb dictated a letter and told Joe to put it in his own handwriting. When Barrow received Joe's rejection, he sent another contract, but it still wasn't what Joe wanted, so he went back to Cobb and Cobb dictated a stronger letter."

That got the salary up to $8,000, from the initial offer of about $5,500, but Cobb told him he was sure he could get an additional $500 with another letter. "We better leave it at that," Joe said, "or they're liable to trade me to the St. Louis Browns." (The lowly Browns were perennial last-place finishers.) Within a few days, Barrow called Joe and told him, "I'm going to give you a good raise, but you tell that sonofabitch Cobb to stop writing your letters."

◆ ◆ ◆

A couple of months later, DiMaggio headed for spring training with the Yankees in St. Petersburg, Florida. The journey would provide him with an after-dinner speech topic for the rest of his life. The Yankees' double-play combination of Frank Crosetti and Tony Lazzeri lived in San Francisco, and Essick prevailed on them to take the rookie to camp in Lazzeri's new Ford. Crosetti and Lazzeri sat up front and shared the driving, while the twenty-one-year-old rookie sat in the back seat taking in the sights on his first trip east of the Rockies. DiMaggio said virtually nothing, except to respond to questions, and Lazzeri wasn't much of a talker, so it was a rather silent trip. As DiMaggio told it through the years, after breakfast one morning, Crosetti said that he was tired of driving. "Me, too," said Lazzeri, and they agreed that it was time for the rookie to drive. "I told them I would be happy to drive, but I didn't know how, and had no license," DiMaggio said.

The trio arrived at camp ahead of schedule, with the pitchers and catchers, and DiMaggio was assigned to share Room 819 with Crosetti in the St. Petersburg Hotel. Crosetti told the rookie that women usually were not allowed to visit in the room, but if Joe should find himself in there with one, he was to slip the "Do Not Disturb" sign under the door to let Crosetti know. "The kid blushed, and told me, 'You bet,'" Crosetti recalled.

A photo displayed on the wall of my office shows Joe leaning against a fence with Lazzeri and Crosetti. DiMaggio told me that the photo was taken soon after the three had arrived at training camp that spring. The young rookie looked relaxed in the photo, as if he belonged. I asked him, those many decades later, how he could have looked so at ease as a rookie in camp. His expression grew very serious and he said, "Morris, I knew I could hit major league pitching." That was an unusual bit of braggadocio for DiMaggio, who almost never boasted about his talent.

Soon after he arrived at his first major league spring training, DiMaggio was assigned a nickname. "We called him Dago," teammate Tommy Henrich said. Lazzeri and Crosetti were "Big Dago" and "Little Dago," so DiMaggio became just "Dago." Political correctness had not yet been invented, and Henrich insisted that the rookie did not seem offended. "Hell, they called me Kraut-head." Fourteen years later, when Billy Martin joined the Yankees, DiMaggio called him Dago.

The press made a big deal about DiMaggio's Italian heritage and mentioned it in ways that today would prompt letters of protest. DiMaggio's family was described as the "San Francisco DiMaggios by way of Sicily." Dan Daniel, who covered DiMaggio and the Yankees for the *World Telegram*, called him Giuseppe in stories. Joe was the "olive-skinned Italian," the "Italian sensation," the "San Francisco Italian," and at least once in a New York newspaper, the "Big Wop." Despite the seemingly offensive monikers, most Italian-Americans were proud that the new sensation was one of their own.

The feelings that Americans of Italian heritage had about DiMaggio was explored by Pellegrino D'Acierno, a scholarly authority on such matters. D'Acierno, professor of comparative literature at Hofstra University and visiting professor of Italian at Columbia University, wrote, "Although a number of Italian-Americans (Ping Bodie, Tony Lazzeri, and Frank Crosetti) and other hyphenated American ballplayers, most notably Hank Greenberg, had preceded him into the big leagues, [DiMaggio] was the primary force in the demolition of the 'ethnic line' in baseball." In his treatise, *Deconstructing the Great DiMaggio: The Biographer as Evil Eye*, D'Acierno said that DiMaggio, with his bearing, the elegant way he dressed, and his almost regal attitude, represented the aristocracy of his class, shattering the "Dago" image much of the American media had assigned to Italians. He was an American Italian, rather than Italian-American. (D'Acierno also authored *The Italian American Heritage: A Companion to Literature and the Art.*)

Mario Cuomo, former governor of New York, recalled the pride that he and others in the community took in DiMaggio shattering the stereotype. "He looked like an American," Cuomo said. "He was a symbol of what Italian-American kids like me could accomplish."

Dan Daniel was among the first to learn that the Italian kid from San Francisco had more going for him than just his baseball skills. He had something called integrity. Soon after Joe arrived, he was approached by the sportswriter, who told him his editor at the *World Telegram* wanted to run a series of stories on him. "It's OK with me," Joe said, and the newspaper began to promote the upcoming series on page one. Another paper then offered Joe $3,000 to do the stories. Daniel said that since he couldn't pay for the interviews, he would understand if DiMaggio backed out. "You were first," said Joe, who passed up what would have been a much-needed bonus.

The press had been waiting for this "next Babe Ruth," and they found him a wonderful source for training-camp stories. Phenoms that grow in the spring, tra la, fade when the pitchers start throwing curves—but not this one, the writers promised. As shy as he was, DiMaggio proved to be a good interview. He spoke in the clichés in which his interviewers wrote, although some writers did not restrict their prose by using exact quotes and made even their most inarticulate subjects sound like eloquent statesmen. But the microphone told it like it was, and DiMaggio responded to a newsreel interviewer: "Yes, one day I hope to break Babe Ruth's record of 60 home runs."

During the season, DiMaggio managed to get a compliment from the Babe himself. The retired Yankee legend was at a game in which Joe hit two home runs. As DiMaggio headed for the dugout after the second homer, Ruth nodded at him from a box seat and said, "Nice going, Joe." The rookie was pleased that Ruth called him by name. "He usually called guys 'kid,'" Joe said. What he didn't know was that Ruth also used "Joe" as a fits-all salutation.

Everything was going well for the rookie at spring training until—as would happen often throughout his career—injury intervened. Someone stepped on his left foot in an exhibition game. "I thought I was spiked, but there was no blood, just a bruise," DiMaggio said. "The next morning the foot was swollen so I went to see Doc Painter." Earle Painter, the Yankees trainer, put Joe's damaged foot into a diathermy machine, and went about his other business. "I felt it burning, but I thought that's what it was supposed to feel like," DiMaggio said. "Then it really began to hurt, but I didn't want to complain." By his silence (he wanted to be the macho Italian Stallion), the shy rookie let Doc Painter cook his foot. That was on March 22, and the treatment ended Joe's exhibition season.

Joe DiMaggio limped into New York not quite the conquering rookie hero the writers had portrayed him to be. The team still was making its way up the Atlantic coast, and DiMaggio arrived alone. He made it to the Hotel New Yorker, two blocks from Penn Station, and waited for the team to arrive and for his foot to heal. Joe took the subway to the Bronx to see Yankee Stadium for the first time, but never went in. He traveled with the team to Washington, D.C., where President Roosevelt threw out the first ball, but he did nothing more than take batting practice. Even that was too much, as he reinjured his left foot and had to wait until May 3 to play in his first big-league game. About 30,000 fans showed up for that Sunday game against the St. Louis Browns, the largest crowd at Yankee Stadium since Opening Day.

Manager Joe McCarthy put DiMaggio in left field, batting third. He wore No. 9 on his flannel uniform jersey. If he was nervous, he didn't show it. He began his career with a single, triple, and single, and the Yankees won, 14–5.

DiMaggio did very well in those opening weeks, and won rave reviews at home and away. In Detroit, the Tigers player-manager, Mickey Cochrane, said he had never seen a batter with a better free swing. New York Giants Manager Bill Terry predicted the kid would be the best of the Yankees, if he wasn't already. (Don't forget, Lou Gehrig was on the team.) And umpire George Moriarty declared that DiMaggio was the most remarkable rookie he had seen in thirty years. The message got across to the ticket-buying public, and they chased each other through the turnstiles. True,

Italian flags showed up in the stands in cities like Boston and Chicago, and a band of Italian funeral musicians in Detroit serenaded DiMaggio with tarantellas—but most of the spectators drawn to the parks wouldn't know a cannoli from a calzone. They were there to see the rookie sensation for themselves, and DiMaggio put on a good show for his growing audience, at the plate and in the field.

As great a team as the 1936 Yankees were, with six future Hall of Famers, the players had to adhere to McCarthy's strict code of dress and conduct, which included a smoking ban during games. But the manager, himself a Hall of Famer, granted special dispensations to his superstars, DiMaggio and Gehrig. Because he didn't want them "flipping their lids," they were allowed to smoke in the runway between the dugout and the clubhouse, and since they batted third and fourth, they usually went back there together. What did those two baseball greats talk about during those intimate moments? "Not much. We just smoked," said DiMaggio, a three-pack-a-day man. Gehrig was not much on talk, either.

The two would sit in the clubhouse after a loss and suffer silently over coffee, dragging on their cigarettes and staring into space. Each would blame himself for the Yankees loss, even though that was very rarely true.

Early in June, a trade opened the way for DiMaggio's move to center field. Ben Chapman, who had been the center fielder, was sent to the Washington Senators. McCarthy insisted it had nothing to do with his desire to move Joe to center, but rather Chapman's attitude, which McCarthy found surly and disruptive. "Chapman did not like Jews, and the Yankees were nervous about that getting out," DiMaggio told me. "Too many Jewish and Italian fans." McCarthy tried DiMaggio in left field and then right field for a while before finally moving him to the position for which he became famous.

"He never would have become the great outfielder he was if I hadn't moved him there," McCarthy told sportswriter Maury Allen, author of *Where Have You Gone, Joe DiMaggio? The Story of America's Last Hero.* McCarthy was an old man and long since retired when he recalled his decision to make DiMaggio a center fielder, and he cherished the memory of it as a significant contribution to the history of baseball. "He needed that room to roam in Yankee Stadium. Only the really great ones can play out there. It was the toughest center field in baseball."

Joe agreed that it was no picnic playing in the vast expanses of that piece of Bronx real estate. In those days it was nearly 500 feet to Yankee Stadium's center-field wall. DiMaggio said the shadows, especially in September, and smoke that blew from the stands often made it very difficult to pick up the ball as it headed toward him. That may have been the reason Joe played shallow, preferring to turn his back to the plate and race to catch up with the ball rather than play deep and run in to make the catch. Former Commissioner Fay Vincent said DiMaggio told him he patterned that style of play after Tris Speaker. Speaker, who retired in 1928, was considered the best center fielder ever to play the game. "He said he was determined to be the new Tris Speaker," Vincent recalled.

DiMaggio's fame took a big jump forward later that month in Chicago, and Colonel Ruppert was there to see it. The precocious rookie hit two home runs in one inning and had two doubles against the White Sox. By then, DiMaggio was leading all American League outfielders in voting for the All-Star Game, a remarkable feat for a rookie.

DiMaggio started in right field and batted third, in front of Gehrig, in that All-Star Game, which was played in Boston. As far as he was concerned, the less said about that day, the better. He went 0-for-5, failing even to hit the ball out of the infield. He also made an error and played a single into a triple. "I was overconfident, and I embarrassed myself," he said. His best memory? "Joe

McCarthy tapped me on the shoulder in the locker room and said, 'Don't let it get you down.'"

Obviously, it didn't. DiMaggio went on a hitting tear right after the All-Star break, and finished the season with a .323 batting average and 125 runs batted in. The Yankees won 102 games that year and claimed the pennant by 19½ games over the second-place Tigers. It was their first pennant in four years, and while DiMaggio's presence played a major role, he would laugh whenever someone said they won because of him. "That was the greatest team I ever played on," he would remark whenever he studied a picture of the 1936 Yankees on my office wall, and he looked at it often. More than once, I saw the supposedly unemotional DiMaggio get teary eyed when he looked at the photo. "There's Gehrig, [Bill] Dickey, Tony [Lazzeri], Goofy [Lefty Gomez]. What a great bunch of guys. Look at all those Hall of Famers on one team." Six of the regular starters batted over .300, led by Dickey at .362, and five of them drove in more than 100 runs, led by Gehrig's 152.

The Yankees played the Giants in the Nickel World Series—so called for the five cents it cost to take the subway in those days (compared with $1.50 during the 2000 Subway Series)—and the American League champions won it in six games. Joe got the first of his nine World Series rings, and it was the one he cherished most until the very end. He made the cover of *Time* magazine, and later was a cover boy for *Life* and *Liberty*. If there had been a *Pursuit of Happiness* magazine, he would have made that, too. When he returned home to San Francisco, DiMaggio used his World Series share for a down payment on a house he bought for his parents on Beach Street.

◆ ◆ ◆

DiMaggio spent his first big league off-season being a celebrity, speaking to youth clubs, Rotary Clubs, and to his buddies in the

North Beach pubs. But he also listened, getting advice from O'Doul and Cobb. Although Cobb had the reputation for being the angriest man ever to play big league ball, he was also without question one of the greatest hitters in baseball history. Infielders cursed Cobb for coming at them with spikes high on the base paths. He had few friends, if any, and he was a racist. But he won the American League batting title twelve times in a stretch of thirteen years. Cobb had a twenty-four-year career batting average of .367, the highest ever, and he was a tough guy to strike out. He was a good person for a young, up-and-coming ballplayer to listen to.

"Don't be too anxious on a 3-2 pitch," he told Joe. "If it's not good, lay off it."

He also recommended that DiMaggio start the season with a 40-ounce bat and switch to a 37- or 38-ounce bat after August 1. "Because," he said, "you'll be tired by then." Also, Cobb told him that at the height of summer, it was ridiculous to waste energy under a hot sun shagging fly balls. "You already know how to catch, so quit after a couple and sit in the shade."

Cobb, who was fifty-one years old that winter, showed up at spring training in 1937 with some more hints. He told DiMaggio to take his time leaving the park after a game. "Cool down good before you take your shower, and then sit around after your shower. If you are still sweating when you leave the park, you could catch cold." DiMaggio, throughout his career, usually was the last player to leave the ballpark.

Cobb's advice continued through the years, but after that winter, his lectures were given over lunch or dinner at Joe DiMaggio's Grotto, a seafood restaurant on Fisherman's Wharf. Cobb very likely was the one who gave Joe the idea that he didn't have to pay for restaurant meals.

Even after his sensational year, DiMaggio was offered the same salary he received as a rookie. The Yankees quickly bumped it up to $10,000. Joe asked for $17,500. He signed for $15,000.

The Yankees' 1937 season began as had the previous year: without Joe DiMaggio. He developed a sore arm during the exhibition season, and doctors determined that his problem was in his throat. His enlarged tonsils were removed, and he was in bed eating ice cream when he should have been in center field. His right arm still bothered him when he got into the lineup on May 1, but he was OK at the plate. At the All-Star break, DiMaggio was hitting .346 and had 20 home runs. He finished the season batting .346 and led the league with 46 homers.

It was in 1937 that DiMaggio first faced Bob Feller, an eighteen-year-old Iowa farm boy with a 100-mile-per-hour fastball. Joe introduced himself at Cleveland's Municipal Stadium by hitting a single, a double, and a bases-loaded homer—and that set the pattern for their head-to-head matchups throughout their careers. "I put him in the Hall of Fame," said the Indians' right-hander, who was himself a legendary Hall of Fame pitcher. Ted Williams regarded Feller as the toughest pitcher he ever faced, and he marveled at the way DiMaggio hit him.

DiMaggio revealed to Joe Nachio the secret of his success against Feller. "I counted the stitches. When it was a curve, the stitches and the ball revolved. When it was a straight fastball, the stitches didn't revolve, so I knew what was coming." Joe had a wide stance and strong wrists, so he could swing late, giving him time to see if he was getting a fastball or a curve, and he hit curves better than fastballs. "I never guessed what pitch was coming no matter who was pitching," DiMaggio said. "I always looked for a fastball, and if it was something else, I adjusted."

DiMaggio, like Williams, had exceptional eyesight. "We were across the street from a movie theater one night and I wondered how much the admission was," Nachio recalled. "'It's seventy-five cents,' Joe told me. He had read the sign in the box office window. I just barely made out that there was a sign in the window. I said, 'Joe, look through the wall and tell me what the movie is about.'"

DiMaggio played in his second straight World Series in 1937, and his father was there to watch him bop his first Series home run. In the final game of that year's Fall Classic, DiMaggio drove a ball onto the left-field roof at the Polo Grounds. "That was a special thrill," Joe said. "When I was a kid, they used to put a big board on one of the newspaper buildings in San Francisco to show what was happening at the World Series. Light bulbs would show men on base and what the batter did. I used to stand there and dream of hitting a home run in the Series at Yankee Stadium or the Polo Grounds, where the Yankees played before the Stadium was built. My dream came true that year."

◆ ◆ ◆

That year was special for another reason. DiMaggio got a bit part in a movie, *Manhattan Merry-Go-Round.* On the set he met Dorothy Arnold, a beautiful blonde dancer with white, smooth skin, whom he wooed and married two years later.

He also met Joe Gould, a Broadway character and manager of heavyweight champion Jimmy Braddock. Gould is credited with first showing Joe the joys of New York nightlife, although DiMaggio had many willing tutors when it came to that. George Solotaire, Broadway's top ticket broker, was one, and publicist Bernie Kamber was another. All were said to have introduced Joe to "Broadway Broads," who meant it when they told him they were delighted to make his acquaintance.

Kamber laughed when asked about that, some sixty years later. "He did all right with the ladies; he didn't need any help. He would get the women, and the ones he didn't want, he would give to George." One of Kamber's buddies at the Friars Club described DiMaggio as one of the hungriest guys in New York when it came to sexual appetite.

Gould, a slightly built dynamo who sometimes wore a beret for effect, introduced Joe to Toots Shor even before New York's most famous saloonkeeper opened the restaurant that Joe helped make famous, or as Toots would say, "vice-worsa." That two-story brick building across 51st Street from the stage door at Radio City Music Hall became a sports bar before there were such things. But its clientele was not beer-and-pretzel types. Rather, the place attracted baseball and football players, jockeys, actors, press agents, sports gamblers, and the big byline sportswriters. Joe quickly became the prime attraction. He was seated where he could see who was there but not be seen by too many who were there. It became a ritual among the regulars to check out his table when they arrived, just to see if Joe was cutting into a steak. It made them feel good as they pressed into the highly polished dark-wood bar just to know he was in the house. DiMaggio's aura even pierced the bricks and penetrated into Hamburger Mary's next door, where the less affluent dined, including Associated Press reporters and photographers, whose offices were across the street. "He's in there with Dorothy Arnold," or "Joe just went in with Hemingway," were among the updated bulletins that circulated in Mary's on any given night.

It was in Shor's place that DiMaggio and George Solotaire began a friendship that lasted until Solotaire's death in 1965. Solotaire, the 5-foot-5 son of impoverished Russian-Jewish immigrants (Soltaroff was their name), came out of the Brooklyn Hebrew Orphan Asylum to become a major player on the New York scene. He was king of the ticket brokers during the golden age of Broadway musicals, the man to see when you needed tickets to *Oklahoma!, Annie Get Your Gun, South Pacific, Guys and Dolls*, or any of the other mega-hits that were sold out night after night. He also managed to acquire excellent tickets to Yankees and Giants games and the big prizefights. Solotaire's clients ranged from members of President Roosevelt's cabinet (Harry Hopkins, for one) to big-time mobsters, and a lot of people in between. If celebrity mobsters Frank Costello, Longy Zwillman, and Owney Madden, and America's prime bookmaker, Frank Erickson, did not want to be at opening nights, they had friends and family who did. DiMaggio became a regular Mr. First Nighter, tuxedo and all. Solotaire rated the prime table at the Stork Club, the Colony, Gallagher's, Lindys, and all the other "in places," and often Joe was with him.

Joe and George's long-lasting friendship served a purpose for each of them. Although it didn't need much polishing, Solotaire's image was bolstered further by being seen with the famous ballplayer. For Joe, the relationship allowed him to live the good life, which he certainly couldn't have afforded if he had to reach for his own wallet. Through the witty, cheerful Solotaire, Joe met some very attractive young ladies, before, during, and after his marriage to Dorothy. He provided upscale settings for Joe to entertain his friends. The two men shared suites at the Elysee and Madison Hotels for years. When DiMaggio wanted to buy an apartment in the Madison, Solotaire advanced him the money for a down payment.

In addition to the financial benefits, "Gentleman George" was eleven years older than DiMaggio, and he saw himself as Joe's protector, serving as the buffer that Joe always looked for to keep away the pests. "DiMaggio was not very sophisticated or wise in the ways of Broadway when he first came to New York," said George's son, Robert Solotaire. "My father could spot a mile away someone who wanted something for nothing from Joe, and he kept them away from him."

At the end, DiMaggio returned the favor. The two were in Hawaii when Solotaire suffered a stroke, and Joe flew with him to California, where George was hospitalized.

Solotaire was as close as anyone to DiMaggio for those thirty years, as I was for the last sixteen years of Joe's life, yet Joe never once mentioned Solotaire's name to me. He kept his life compartmentalized. He had friends in San Francisco, Chicago, New York, and Florida, but other than a few exceptions, he rarely if ever mingled them.

◆ ◆ ◆

As famous as Solotaire was with the Broadway crowd, when the two were together he became "that guy with DiMaggio," as was true for everybody in Joe's company. DiMaggio had become a full-fledged celebrity, and he dressed the part. For most of his years in baseball and for years afterward, he made the "Best Dressed" lists of the magazines that chronicled such things. "There are three things I would not want to be," Nachio declared. "His tailor, his barber, or his driver. He drove those people nuts with his demands."

"Yes, he was very exacting, but he was really no trouble at all," said Otto Perl, who began making suits for DiMaggio soon after opening his tailoring business at the end of 1949. He remembered every detail about his star customer. "He was about 6-foot-2, 200 pounds with very broad shoulders. He wanted the straight-line look. Everything had to be perfect. He would stand in the three-sided mirror and study the suit. He knew what he wanted, and if you listened and did what he told you, he was easy to get along with."

Perl's favorite memory was a walk he took with DiMaggio down Fifth Avenue. "I had a good collection of fine material, but he couldn't find anything he liked. So, I took him to a woolen house in the mid-50s off Fifth. My place was on Madison Avenue and 60th Street. We walked those few blocks, and it was like he was running for office. Men reached out to shake his hand, people on the other side of the street were calling his name, cars were honking their horns, cab drivers were shouting at him. And he was walking along with his big stride, smiling and acknowledging people. I had a hard time keeping up with him," said the 5-foot-6 Perl.

A $300 suit resulted from that walk, and DiMaggio wanted to know why he paid more than his friends. "You want the best, you have to pay," Perl said. That was good enough for Joe. Perl's customers were a roster of New York elite, from major business-men to sports figures. The multimillionaire brothers Cecil and Louis Wolfson were the ones who brought DiMaggio into the shop for the first time. Those were the kind of high-powered friends he had. Of course, DiMaggio's presence in the shop sent the customers and Perl's twelve tailors into a tizzy. One of the tailors told Perl to ask for free tickets to a game, and the boss said, "Absolutely not. I don't want him to ask for a free suit."

Not only was the gentleman an expert tailor, he obviously was also a great judge of DiMaggio's personality. Some forty years later, DiMaggio confided to his diary his displeasure with a tailor named Mukrem, who had made six pairs of slacks for Joe. Mukrem had asked DiMaggio to autograph four baseballs for him. "That annoyed me, as I pay for all my obligations," Joe fumed.

Perl, who had escaped from the Holocaust in Europe and was more familiar with soccer than baseball, did ask DiMaggio for something: to tell him what it took to be a good player. Joe responded, "You have to be hungry."

◆ ◆ ◆

Toots Shor's place remained DiMaggio's hangout during his career and into retirement, and through two wives. Whether he was with Dorothy Arnold or Marilyn Monroe, depending on the year, the couple was put at a table with a bottle of expensive champagne, where Toots could protect them from those who would intrude on their privacy. Both women were disparaged at various times by the uncouth Shor, a heavyset man with a round face and a big mouth. The latter eventually led to fractures in his relationship with DiMaggio. "But he never got booed in my joint," Shor reflected years later, after Joe stopped showing up.

That was a reference to the boos Joe heard after his infamous holdout in 1938. There had been holdouts before, but none that attracted as much attention as DiMaggio's that year. The Yankees were coming off back-to-back World Series championships, ending a three-year run without a pennant, and DiMaggio had just put together two first seasons unlike anything anyone had seen before. He batted .335 and drove in 292 runs over those two years. Those were solid negotiating points for DiMaggio. On the minus side for him and every other player was the reserve clause, which protected the owners and gave players two options: play for the team that owns your rights for life, or stay home and milk the cows or work in a factory. The problem was, there was very little work in factories or anyplace else in 1938. The Great Depression still had America by the throat.

So, when DiMaggio asked for a raise that would boost his salary from $15,000 to $40,000, while men were selling apples on street corners for a nickel just to earn enough for something to eat, he had a tough sell. The Yankees knew it. Reportedly, it was Gould who devised the strategy that Joe should ask for $40,000 and then magnanimously agree to play for $30,000. In their opening discussion, general manager Barrow was simply amazed at DiMaggio's demand. "You know, young man, it took Lou Gehrig fifteen years to earn the salary you are asking for, and you have been with the Yankees only two seasons. What would you say if I told you that Lou Gehrig is not making $40,000?" Joe said he looked Barrow straight in the eye and told him, "I would say Lou Gehrig is highly underpaid."

DiMaggio also was being advised by his brother Tom, and while this was going on, Joe worked in the restaurant. He posed in a chef's hat for newsreel cameras, stirring pots of pasta and vowing to spend the baseball season in the kitchen. Finally, on April 20, DiMaggio capitulated in a telegram, which read, "Your terms accepted." Beer baron owner Ruppert continued to play hardball, and he told the press that DiMaggio's salary would not begin until manager McCarthy deemed him in condition to play.

As the writers quaffed beer and ate corned beef sandwiches in the barroom at Ruppert's brewery on Manhattan's Upper East Side, their host told them, "I hope this young man has learned his lesson. His pay will be $25,000, no more, no less." So, Joe did get a $10,000 raise, but he missed another Opening Day, and he incurred the wrath of the fans.

When he made his 1938 debut 12 games into the season in Washington, DiMaggio was booed. He also wound up in the hospital after colliding with the club's new second baseman, Joe Gordon, as they converged under a pop up. Both were knocked out and bruised. DiMaggio's ego was bruised for a long time afterward because he continued to be booed at Yankee Stadium and on the road. He never forgot that. He told Joe Williams of the *World Telegram*, "I woke up in the middle of the night hearing the boos. I got up, smoked a cigarette, and walked the floor." He said the booing made his insides turn over. "You keep saying you will get used to it, but you never do. I stuffed my ears with cotton, but nothing helped."

What amazed me was that despite the booing, which hurt him deeply, he never lost his affection for his fans. Even in his final days, DiMaggio talked about how much the fans meant to his career.

While the 1938 holdout was the most bitter, others followed. DiMaggio's whole personality was to be a holdout. When I first started negotiating Joe's business deals in his later years, I convinced him that he was selling himself short and should get more than what he was getting. Forever after, he always thought he was being shortchanged. If I would say, "Joe, we've got $3 million" in a memorabilia venture, he would say, "Another $200,000?" His first reaction was to say "no," and then after he thought about it, he said "OK," but he always wanted more money.

◆ ◆ ◆

The Yankees won their third straight pennant in 1938 and their third straight World Series. It was another big year for DiMaggio, as well. In 145 games, he batted .324, drove in 140 runs, and hit 32 homers.

Joe made up his mind that winter that he was going to change his image and smile more. "I didn't like being called a sourpuss," he said. "I wanted to put that holdout and the boos behind me, and the injuries, too."

As for his conditioning, Cobb had told him that walking was the best exercise he could do in the off-season, so he put on hunting boots and walked up and down the hills of San Francisco. He also spent a lot of time in the restaurant, where business was very good. Once when Cobb was there he watched Joe dip a piece of freshly baked sourdough bread into a dish of olive oil. "You should try soaking your bats in that stuff for a couple of weeks during the winter," Cobb said, pointing to the olive oil. "Then hang them up to dry for a week or so." Joe said he was surprised to find that the olive oil made the bats more springy. Unlike corking, it wasn't illegal, probably because baseball brass never learned of it.

Joe accepted what was offered to him in 1939, $25,000, and he dealt solely with Barrow. Ruppert, who took pleasure in humiliating DiMaggio the previous spring, died in January at age seventy-one. Left behind was a photo taken at Yankee Stadium after the great holdout. Ruppert, wearing a suit and vest, a bow tie, and a fedora, has his arm around a very young-looking DiMaggio. Both men are smiling. Joe autographed it for me with the legend, "The hand on my shoulder was not always that friendly, especially during contract negotiations."

For the first time in four seasons, DiMaggio was in the Yankees lineup on Opening Day, and he got off to a fast start. His luck ran out seven games into the season, however, when his spikes caught in the dirt as he chased a fly ball. He ripped a muscle in his right leg and was out for more than a month. But DiMaggio's injury was made insignificant by what happened the following day. Lou Gehrig took himself out of the Yankees lineup and ended his consecutive playing streak record at 2,130 games. The disease that would eventually take his life, amyotrophic lateral sclerosis (ALS), had advanced to the point where he could no longer fight it. DiMaggio lined up with his teammates on July 4 when Gehrig made his famous "luckiest man on the face of the earth" speech.

Nothing on a baseball field ever affected DiMaggio more than that speech, and it stayed with him for the rest of his life. At his own farewell appearance at Yankee Stadium on September 27, 1998, DiMaggio patterned his speech after Gehrig's. To DiMaggio, Gehrig was the greatest Yankee. "Look at his RBIs, Morris. That's the key," he said. Gehrig never drove in less than 112 runs in each of his thirteen full seasons in the majors. Joe credited a lot of his own success to the fact that he batted third, just ahead of Gehrig. "They didn't want to walk me with him coming up next, so I got balls that were pretty close to the plate."

Before the 1939 All-Star Game, which was played at Yankee Stadium, DiMaggio had promised Dorothy that he would hit a home run for her. He did, and the American League won, 3–1. That propelled him into a great second half of the season. He drove in runs and hit homers at a merry clip and was batting .400 late in the season. Then, he woke up one morning with an infection in his left eye. The eye was swollen and hurt, but he said nothing to McCarthy. Again, the macho Italian Stallion was going to tough it out. Even so, he thought that McCarthy would take him out of the lineup, but it never happened. The manager told him, "If I take you out of the lineup so you can hit .400, you will always be considered a cream puff." Joe told me, "It wouldn't have been so bad if it was the right eye, but it was the front eye as I stood at the plate, so I couldn't see the ball until it was past me." He finished the season with a .381 average, still good enough for the American League batting title, and chipped in 126 RBIs and 30 homers. He also won the first of his three Most Valuable Player awards, and the Yankees won their fourth straight championship, sweeping the Cincinnati Reds in the World Series.

"It was a wonderful year, but hitting .400 would have been nice," DiMaggio said. He never really forgave McCarthy for not taking him out of the lineup when he had the eye infection. Even five decades later, DiMaggio was still complaining about his former manager's decision. "I couldn't see, but McCarthy wanted to get the record for most victories in a season, so he kept me in there, and my batting average dropped. I was hitting over .400 when that happened." McCarthy and the Yankees fell short of the record for wins in a season, but they did win 106 games.

After the Series, Joe took Dorothy to San Francisco to meet his family, and on November 19 they were married in the biggest wedding North Beach had ever seen.

His marriage had nothing to do with it, but Joe told the Yankees he wanted $40,000 in 1940. The batting championship and MVP award were his main arguments. Barrow was impressed enough to give him a hefty raise to $35,000, which DiMaggio accepted.

That spring, the newlywed admitted he had not thrown a ball or lifted a bat since the World Series, and he and his bride motored to training camp at a leisurely pace. When they got there, they stayed at an out-of-the-way place, about 10 miles from the field.

Joe's euphoria ended suddenly during a preseason exhibition game at Ebbets Field in Brooklyn. He slid into second base on a double and injured a knee. It was characteristic of DiMaggio that he would hurt himself while sliding in an exhibition game, because he went all out in every game, regardless of whether it counted in the standings, or whether the Yankees were ahead by a lot of runs or far behind. His oft-repeated credo was, "There may be a kid out there who will see me only this one time. I owe it to him." So, for the fourth time in five years, DiMaggio missed the Yankees' opener.

A month later, he had a different kind of problem and was summoned to the office of Commissioner Kenesaw Mountain Landis. The Yankees were disturbed by persistent reports that Joe Gould was acting as DiMaggio's agent, and that he was getting a percentage of Joe's salary. Agents were strictly forbidden by baseball, as club owners did not want people "stirring up" their players and telling them to demand more pay. In Gould's case, the Yankees made sure that Landis also knew that this Broadway character not only was a boxing manager, but he also reportedly had connections to "unsavory people," including gamblers and bookies. The Yankee hierarchy figured that would get the commissioner's attention, since he had been brought on to clean up baseball after the notorious Black Sox scandal in the 1919 World Series. The Yankees said they were not concerned about any other deals Gould was arranging for Joe, such as lining up product endorsements, radio shows, or movie appearances, only his baseball contract. DiMaggio denied that Gould was involved in that, and Landis believed him. Joe got off the hook.

Gould, a smooth talker with a rapid-fire speech delivery, got into much more serious difficulty during World War II. He was an army captain stationed at the Brooklyn Navy Yard with the job of procuring equipment. In 1944, he was found guilty in a court-martial of conspiring to defraud the government of more than $1 million in contracts and was sentenced to three years of hard labor. Gould got out after nearly a year and then was bounced from the army. Joe heard about it from boxing announcer Sam Taub, who shook his head and clucked, "He shouldn't have done it during war time."

DiMaggio missed 22 games in 1940 because of his bad knee, and when he came back he was slowed for a while longer, both in the field and on the bases. At the end of the season, he had 31 homers and a .352 average, and a second straight batting championship. But for the first time in his five years as a big leaguer, when the season ended he had no place to go but home. The Yankees did not get to the World Series.

By then, Joe was being heralded as the greatest player the major leagues had ever known. "No such thing as the greatest," Joe always insisted. He also would get upset when sportswriters and fans marveled that he played so effortlessly he made playing look easy. It was his instinct and natural ability that made him so great, they explained. "Bull," he would say when I quoted some of the things written about him. "I came to the park an hour and a half early. I took fungo practice every day. I lost six pounds a game wearing that woolen uniform. I kept drinking coffee one after the other to get fluid back in my system."

About the instinct attributed to him, he said, "With every pitch, I would get in position, ready to go, like the first basemen do, like the shortstops do. From out in center field, I watched every pitch. When it was a curve ball, I knew where it would be hit, and I took off. I gambled a lot, but I was ninety percent right."

Joe Cronin, who managed the Boston Red Sox during DiMaggio's early years with the Yankees, had no doubt why New York was so successful in that time. "There were four American League clubs that could have won the pennant: the Yankees, Red Sox, Indians, and Tigers. Whichever one of those teams had DiMaggio was going to win. That's the kind of a difference he made."

2

THE STREAK AND BEYOND

DiMAGGIO OFTEN FELL BACK on the ballplayers' cliché when he was asked if his 56-game hitting streak in 1941 would ever be bettered. "All streaks are meant to be broken." When DiMaggio died nearly fifty-eight years after his amazing accomplishment, the record was intact. As the 1900s ended and a new century and new millennium began, no one had even come close to DiMaggio's name atop that page in the record books.

The anniversary of his feat was celebrated long into his retirement at events in New York, San Francisco, south Florida, and Chicago, and Joe was expected to speak at all of them. In January 1991, he noted in his diary that he had already been invited to six dinners in connection with the fiftieth anniversary of the streak, including a pre-game ceremony in his honor at Yankee Stadium. He wrote, "If I knew this would be taking place due to the streak, I would have stopped hitting at 40 games."

That was his public stance. It was good for a laugh in after-dinner speeches, but privately, he was very proud of the mark that towered over all hitting records, the way Mount Everest dominates all other peaks in the Himalayas. During Mark McGwire's record run at 70 homers in 1998, Joe and I watched a telecast of the game in which the Cardinals slugger hit numbers 67 and 68. Roger Maris' thirty-seven-year-old record had already been shattered. "McGwire's record will be broken, too," Joe predicted, and Barry

Bonds proved him right, just two years later. He said there was less pressure trying to break something like a home run record than a hitting streak. "You can hit ten homers in a week, take a couple of days off, and then hit some more home runs. In a hitting streak there's no room for error. You don't get a hit in one game, and it's all over." He said the same was true for Lou Gehrig's record for playing in consecutive games. "I never thought anyone would break that, but Ripken did. If Gehrig's record was broken, mine could be, too." DiMaggio said the pressure from the media and the fans during his streak was greater than the pressure of getting a hit in a game. He believed that pressure might protect his record.

As proud as he was of that streak, however, he did not consider it his greatest accomplishment. That, he said, was being on teams that won ten pennants and nine World Series in his thirteen years. The true team player that he was, DiMaggio insisted that his hitting streak would not have meant as much to him if the Yankees had not won the pennant and Series that year.

◆ ◆ ◆

As spring turned to summer in that fateful year of 1941, America was caught up in the excitement of DiMaggio's legendary streak. The story moved from the sports pages to the front page, where it shared space with Nazi Germany's blitzkrieg through Europe and its invasion of the Soviet Union. Radio stations covered the streak's progress in their hourly news broadcasts, and when he got a hit, some stations interrupted programs to broadcast a bulletin. Those brought sighs of relief, not only because DiMaggio got a hit, but because the bulletin was not about another success of Hitler's army.

Joe DiMaggio was the topic of conversation among friends and strangers alike, from all corners of society. "What did he do today?" was a popular question during the summer of 1941. A song was written about "baseball's famous streak that's got us all aglow," and a recording of it by Les Brown and his Band of Renown had the country singing, "Joe, Joe DiMaggio, we want you on our side." The music was arranged by someone named Ben Homer.

The streak took on particular importance in Italian neighborhoods all over the New York metropolitan area. Around Arthur Avenue in the Bronx, radios were placed on the fire escapes of the apartment houses so people could walk down the street and hear the progress of a game without missing a pitch. In parts of New Jersey and Connecticut, radios were perched on windowsills, and upstate in Utica, New York, a loudspeaker was hooked up to a radio to keep the Italian-American populace informed of what Joe D. was doing.

The streak began on May 15 at Yankee Stadium with a single against Eddie Smith of the Chicago White Sox, but Joe said he didn't realize that he had something going until early June, when the streak approached 20 games and sportswriters began to ask him about it in interviews. Actually, he was happy to be just hitting again, because he had been in a slump and was troubled by a stiff neck. Besides, there were other things going on in his life. He was going to become a father. Dorothy was pregnant with a baby due after the World Series, and the couple had moved into a penthouse apartment on West End Avenue in Manhattan, a couple of blocks from his buddy Lefty Gomez and his showgirl wife, June O'Dea.

During the Yankee Stadium commemoration of the streak in 1991, DiMaggio paid tribute to his teammates for the roles they played in helping him. Tommy Henrich was singled out for the action that took place in a game in the Bronx on June 26 against the St. Louis Browns. Eldon Auker, who whipped the ball toward the plate underhand, had stopped DiMaggio in his first three at-bats. The Yankees were leading 3–1 in the bottom of the eighth, and DiMaggio was the fourth man due up, so someone would have to get on base in order for him to bat again. If Auker got the Yankees out in order, the streak would end at 38 games. The crowd cheered loudly when Red Rolfe was walked, because that meant Joe would get to bat again, unless the next batter hit into a double play. Henrich was the next batter, and he was worried that he might do just that and end the inning. So, Tommy got McCarthy's permission to bunt, and he pushed Rolfe to second base.

Auker was surprised to read the next day that Henrich was afraid he would hit into a double play. "I couldn't get him out in a hundred years. He hit me like he owned me," a ninety-year-old Auker recalled from his home in Vero Beach, Florida.

Given that break, DiMaggio lined the first pitch from Auker into left field for a double. "The streak didn't mean much to me," Auker said. "All I was trying to do was get him out. I was just trying to win a ball game. If I wanted to stop the streak, all I had to do was hit him or walk him. I had no intention of doing that. I didn't want him on base."

Interest in the streak intensified a few days later when DiMaggio was in position to break George Sisler's American League record of 41 games. Joe reached that mark in the opener of a doubleheader in Washington. A hit in the next game, and Joe would have the new American League record, but he was more concerned about what happened while he was in the clubhouse between games. His favorite bat was stolen. "I treasured that bat," he told Henrich, whom Joe at first thought had taken it by mistake since their bats were next to each other in the rack by the dugout. Joe's had a special mark on the bottom of its handle. An usher told him someone had leaned over the railing, lifted the bat, and disappeared into the crowd of 31,000.

"He had loaned me another one of his bats a couple of weeks earlier," recalled Henrich, "and I had it on that road trip, so I gave it back to him." Joe used that bat to single in his fourth at-bat in the second game of the twin bill, and he had a new American League record.

Newspapers and radio stations relayed Joe's request that his favorite bat be returned—and it was. The fellow who took it was from Newark, New Jersey, and he displayed his trophy around town. Not very smart. DiMaggio had friends in Newark who were rather tough customers, and they were pleased to be able to do Joe a favor. The bat was brought to Yankee Stadium with the explanation that the young man who took it realized it was not the right thing to do.

A week before the lucky bat was returned, Joe tied Wee Willie Keeler's major league record at 44 games, setting off a delirious celebration by some 53,000 fans at Yankee Stadium. The record-matching hit was a single in the first inning of the second game of a doubleheader against the Red Sox. The record that had stood since 1897 fell the next day when DiMaggio homered in his third at-bat. As the streak grew, so did the Yankees' winning streak and their lead in the American League.

With the Yankees doing so well, McCarthy was willing to bend some traditional dos and don'ts to help the streak along. The most famous example was allowing Henrich to bunt against Auker, with the team holding a two-run lead in the eighth inning. Another instance came two days later in a game against Philadelphia. Johnny Babich walked DiMaggio on four pitches in his first two at-bats, and it was apparent that the pitcher's strategy for ending the streak was to walk the Big Guy. When the count went to 3–0 in Joe's third at-bat, McCarthy signaled permission to swing at anything he could reach. Swing he did, and he connected. The shot went straight for the mound, and Babich had to dive to the ground to get out of the way. The ball wound up in center field for a streak-extending hit. "When I got to first, Babich was still sitting on the mound, looking a little shaken," DiMaggio said. "I had all to do to keep from smiling."

Fast-forward to July 17, a date that would live in infamy among DiMaggio fans. By this time, the streak was at 56 games, and the frenzy surrounding it had infected the city of Cleveland, where the Yankees were for a series with the Indians. When DiMaggio and his roomie, Lefty Gomez, arrived at the stadium by taxi hours before the game, lines were already forming at the ticket booths. DiMaggio had garnered three hits the day before, and he was feeling good about that. Gomez, who was the starting pitcher that night, was chattering about everything but the streak. His strategy was to keep Joe from even thinking about it. The Cleveland cab driver had no such concerns, however. Recognizing DiMaggio, he wished him well, and said he hoped the streak went to 100 games. "But I have a feeling in my bones that you are going to get stopped." DiMaggio also recalled that the cabbie told him he would be stopped if he didn't get a hit in his first at-bat. Years later, Bill Kaval, a retired cab driver, called sportswriter Russell Schneider at the *Cleveland Plain Dealer* and claimed to be the one who drove DiMaggio and Gomez to the game that day. He said that after he told DiMaggio about his premonition that he wouldn't get a hit, Joe told him, "If I don't, I just don't," and he didn't seem annoyed or worried. Kaval said that Gomez was angry at him for the remark, but DiMaggio gave him a fifty-cent tip, which was big in those days. Schneider wrote that Kaval had two requests. "If you see DiMaggio, tell him I'm sorry that I put the evil eye on him . . . and would you ask Joe if he would autograph a ball for me?"

Norman Werksman, an auto parts salesman from Yonkers, New York, was in town on business, and he had a ticket to the game. How lucky can a guy get? Not only would he see the Yankees and DiMaggio, but he didn't have to stand in one of those ticket lines. The crowd of more than 67,000 was the largest ever to see a night game at Municipal Stadium, and about 27,000 bought their tickets that afternoon and evening. It was a night that Werksman never forgot. "You could feel the tension when DiMaggio came to bat in the first inning. He hit a shot down the third-base line. Ken Keltner, who was playing deep, made a backhanded stop and barely threw DiMaggio out," Werksman said. "The crowd went nuts. Everybody was standing and yelling."

"Everybody stood again when DiMaggio came up the next time. A lefty, Al Smith, was pitching for Cleveland, and he walked DiMaggio." Werksman recalled how he was one of maybe two or three people who took the seventh-inning stretch for the Yankees in his section. "Joe came up that inning and hit another shot at Keltner, and the guy made another fantastic backhanded stop and threw DiMaggio out. It was another close call. People were jumping up and down and screaming."

"A guy who had seen me standing for the Yankees patted me on the shoulder and said, 'Hey, don't worry. He'll get up again.'" DiMaggio did get another chance to bat, in the eighth inning with the bases loaded. Jim Bagby was brought in to face him. Werksman remembered the moment clearly. "DiMaggio hit a hard shot toward shortstop Lou Boudreau, who made a terrific stop on a bad hop, and turned it into a double play, and I figured that was it for the streak, unless the Indians tied the score." Cleveland almost did even the score, scoring two runs in the ninth inning, but the Yankees won it, 4–3. The hitting streak was over. "You never heard such noise," Werksman said. "The Indians lost, but their fans were cheering. It was crazy."

When Werksman finally got to the parking lot after the game, his car was nowhere to be seen. A police sergeant told him to wait until the crowd thinned, and he would have someone drive him to the police station to make an official stolen-car report. "While I was standing there, Keltner and his wife came by surrounded by four cops who escorted them to their car," Werksman said. "I guess they were afraid Kenny would be attacked by some Yankees fan." The salesman finally got into a police car for a ride to the station house, but he didn't need to go, after all. He spotted his car in the nearly empty lot. He had been so excited by the events that night, he had looked for the car in the wrong place.

Frank LaBono was the visiting team batboy for the Indians at the time, and he knew he was witness to history. "After the game, Joe went into the shower room, and none of the other guys went with him. I guess they figured he wanted to be alone. But he asked me to tell them it was OK to come in and get cleaned up because it's all over with."

LaBono said that if DiMaggio was upset that his streak was stopped, he didn't show it. He gave his interviews to the writers and posed for the photographers, managing to smile through it all. The teenager saw Joe take a sheet of paper from a shelf in his locker and throw it in the garbage. It was a letter from the H.J. Heinz Company in Pittsburgh, offering DiMaggio a $10,000 deal if he extended his streak to 57 games. Heinz's logo was, and still is, "57 Varieties," and the company envisioned a promotion tying into the hitting streak. "Who knows how long he had been carrying that letter around," said LaBono, who lives in suburban Cleveland. "I picked it up out of the trash basket, and I still have it."

One endorsement deal DiMaggio did get from the streak was with Wheaties. He appeared in newspaper ads extolling the "Breakfast of Champions," and his photo adorned the backs of cereal boxes. There may have been more than one deal with the cereal maker, but Joe told me about one for which he was paid $10,000. He was given the first installment in $100 bills, cash, before a game. He didn't want to leave the money in his locker, so he stuffed the bills into the pockets of his uniform. "After I ran for a ball, I would check the grass around me to make sure I hadn't lost any," Joe told me. "After chasing one fly ball, there was a whole trail of C-notes, which I quickly had to scoop up."

When DiMaggio was asked about the streak-ending game, he would often remark, "If it hadn't rained that afternoon, Keltner never would have been able to stop those balls, and I would have beaten his throws. The rain soaked the base paths and slowed them up." After Keltner died, his family sent DiMaggio the glove with which the third baseman had ended the streak. DiMaggio didn't want it, and he gave the glove to his granddaughter Paula. Had it not been for those two brilliant fielding plays, DiMaggio likely would have topped the 61-game streak from his minor-league days, because the next day he started what became a 16-game hitting streak.

Keltner relished his role in baseball history, and said he prayed before the game that DiMaggio would hit some balls his way. "Someone had to make those plays, and I'm glad he hit them at me. If I don't make those plays, they're base hits." He said DiMaggio was the greatest player he ever played against.

Joe said his brother Dom called him after every game to find out how he did, but that might have been an exaggeration because Dom had a unique way of keeping track of the streak when the Red Sox were home and playing at the same time as the Yankees. A Western Union ticker inside the scoreboard at Fenway Park provided scores and pitching changes of all games in progress, and it carried updates on the streak. The guy who posted the scores would yell updates through an opening in the board to left fielder Ted Williams, and Ted would tell Dom. Joe said when Dom called him, "by the tone of his voice, I could tell he wasn't that happy. It was as if he were saying, 'Why doesn't it come to an end already?'" True or not, that was the way Joe interpreted those calls from his brother.

In August of that year, DiMaggio's teammates surprised him with a silver cigarette-cigar humidor to commemorate the streak. It was a handsome piece that featured a likeness of Joe taking his famous swing and the numbers 56, to denote the number of games, and 91, the number of hits in the streak. On the front of the humidor an engraved message read, "Presented to Joe DiMaggio by his fellow players of the New York Yankees to express their admiration for his consecutive-game hitting record—1941." The names of the players, Manager Joe McCarthy, and the coaches were engraved inside the lid.

Joe sheepishly recalled how that presentation came about. "We were supposed to go to the movies that night, but Gomez, as usual, was late. I was angry, and I kept telling him to hurry up, and then he asked me to walk him to one of the other player's rooms, and that made me angrier. But when we opened the door, all the other guys were in there, holding up champagne glasses, and they sang, 'For He's a Jolly Good Fellow.'"

That was one of the fondest memories DiMaggio took away from his playing days. He kept the humidor in a vault at the Bowery Savings Bank, and gave it to Paula when she turned sixteen.

The year of the famous streak also saw DiMaggio win his second MVP award, even though Williams hit .406 that season. Joe batted .357 and reached the 30-homer mark for the fifth year in a row. Half of his homers came during the streak. Joe's performance also helped propel the Yankees to another American League pennant, their fifth in six years, and the Yankees beat the Dodgers in a five-game World Series.

After the Series ended, DiMaggio hung around New York to await the birth of his son. He didn't have to wait long. Joseph Paul DiMaggio Jr. was born on October 23, less than three weeks after the final game of the 1941 World Series.

Despite the euphoria of the birth of his first son and another championship with the Yankees, the 1941 off-season was not the happiest of DiMaggio's life. On December 7, the Japanese attack on Pearl Harbor brought the United States into World War II, and at the same time, the scene in the DiMaggio household was getting tense. Everyone in New York City wanted a piece of Joe. His fame had become enormous. Wherever he went, people wanted to shake his hand. Crowds surrounded him anytime he waited to cross the street. He walked into the Stork Club, and people applauded. The same thing at El Morocco and all the other places he and Solotaire went. All the while, Dorothy was home with the baby. Joe assured her that the demands on his time would let up once spring training started, and he promised that the two of them and the baby would spend more time together.

While America hailed DiMaggio, the Yankees took another view. Barrow asked Joe to take a salary cut of more than $2,000, with the explanation, "There's a war on." What did that have to do with DiMaggio's salary? "Well, American soldiers are being paid $21 a month," Barrow explained. None of them had hit in 56 straight games, nor had any of them helped the Yankees pull in big crowds and big dollars in the 1941 season. Joe was disappointed and angry at the club's offer. He figured out their strategy. Barrow knew that eventually he would have to give Joe a raise, but he would limit it by starting him off with a figure even lower than he had been paid the previous year. DiMaggio had planned to start by asking for $50,000 and let Barrow whittle away at that. Eventually, Joe wound up with a raise to $42,000, but he was left with a very bitter taste and the feeling that he was being taken advantage of. That resentment stayed with him for the rest of his life.

In the spring, Dorothy and Little Joe accompanied Joe to St. Petersburg for training camp, but before long, his wife and son were in Reno. She prepared to file for divorce.

When the 1942 season began, DiMaggio got off to a bad start. A year after he was baseball's number one hero, Joe heard boos. His reaction was typical DiMaggio: "I'd rather hear the cheers, of course, who wouldn't? I give the fans all I have. But, I'm out there playing for the club and myself. That's how I make my living." He finished the season batting .305, the lowest thus far in his seven-year career, and his string of 30 or more homers ended when he hit only 21. Nevertheless, the Yankees won 103 games and captured the pennant by nine games over the Red Sox. For a team player, it was a matter of mission accomplished.

◆ ◆ ◆

DiMaggio enlisted into the army early in 1943 and spent the next three seasons playing baseball in the service, as did many other big league stars. His relationship with Dorothy alternated between attempts at reconciliation and separation, and he developed an ulcer that put him in the hospital. When he was given a medical discharge from the army in September 1945, his weight had dropped to 187 pounds, about 14 pounds lighter than when he entered the service.

In 1946, the Yankees began spring training in Panama. That was a break for DiMaggio since his good friend Joe Nachio was well established in that country by then. Nachio and Joe had met in 1940 in Philadelphia when Nachio was getting a tryout with the Athletics. He struck up a conversation with Joe at the ballpark before a game, and he invited the Yankees star home for an Italian meal cooked by Nachio's dad. "There was shrimp ala marinara, eggplant in tomato sauce, spaghetti with sauce," Nachio recalled. "My father was a great cook." DiMaggio stayed until nearly midnight, talking with the Nachio family while eating fruit and cracking nuts. The friendship started that night endured until DiMaggio's death. The two Joes corresponded and talked by phone occasionally, and when the Yankees went to Panama, Nachio had a chance to show DiMaggio around the city he knew so well—the restaurants, the clubs, and the senoritas. "We had a pretty good nightlife in Panama City. It was a really hot town," Nachio said. "Joe McCarthy was sleeping at the U.S. military base, so he didn't know what the guys were doing." Nachio was very popular with women. He was single, looked like a movie star, and had an elegant way about him. DiMaggio was an instant hit with the ladies. By then, he and Dorothy were divorced, and what Panama had to offer was exactly what Joltin' Joe needed.

Unfortunately, after three seasons away, Joe did not come back to baseball with a bang. Even though his statistics would have made many other Hall of Famers proud, 1946 was one of the worst seasons of his career. He batted .290, the only time other than his final year when he failed to reach .300, and he drove in 95 runs. DiMaggio missed 22 games with injuries, including the start of what developed into major calcium deposits in his right heel. The team also underwent major changes. The Yankees had new owners, Larry MacPhail, Dan Topping, and Del Webb. McCarthy quit as manager in May and was replaced by Bill Dickey, a former catcher and teammate of DiMaggio's. McCarthy, known in the press as "Marse Joe," was the only manager DiMaggio had known in the majors. He was a disciplinarian, but DiMaggio didn't mind that, and he was the epitome of Yankee Pride, except when he was drinking. "He was worried about the way the team was playing, he was drinking too much and he wasn't eating right," Joe said. DiMaggio never forgot the pat on the back he got from McCarthy when he embarrassed himself in the 1936 All-Star Game. But DiMaggio wanted to forget that 1946 season. The Yankees finished third, their lowest finish in his entire career.

The following season began like another that would be best forgotten. Joe was in the hospital twice during the winter. In January, a bone spur was removed from his left heel, and because the wound did not heal properly, he was back in the hospital in March for a skin graft. Dr. Rock Positano, who became Joe's regular foot doctor many years later, said DiMaggio shuddered when he was told about the treatment he would receive at Johns Hopkins in Baltimore. "They sewed maggots into his heel to eat out the festering flesh, something doctors would do back in the Civil War days," Positano said. "They covered the maggots with a jar. Joe told me he would get sick to his stomach if he looked at what was going on." But the treatment worked. Still, DiMaggio didn't start swinging the bat until the first week in April. He missed yet another Opening Day, but when he returned, he did it in style, with a three-run homer against the Philadelphia A's in the opener of a doubleheader.

The 1947 Yankees had a new look. Bucky Harris was the new manager, Yogi Berra and Bobby Brown, both of whom came up briefly at the end of the previous season, were regulars, and pitcher Allie Reynolds had been acquired from the Indians. Joe took credit for Reynolds. "I had recommended that we get him," Joe said. "I wanted him on our team because I couldn't hit him when he was with Cleveland."

Berra's stall was two away from Joe's in the Yankees clubhouse. To him, DiMaggio was not the aloof, silent type that others saw. "He talked, but you had to start the conversation. If you said, 'hi,' and started a conversation, he would talk to you." Berra also disagreed with those on the team, including Henrich, who said Joe preferred to dine alone. "He liked to go to dinner with people he knew. He wanted company. He liked company." The first time they went to dinner, Joe picked up the check, which he would do when he ate with a rookie. He felt sorry for rookies because of how little they were being paid. DiMaggio was making $43,500 that year, the highest salary on the team.

One of Berra's first encounters with DiMaggio was in the outfield, by accident. Berra was the right fielder, and they collided while chasing a ball in Joe's first game back. "After that," Berra said, "he told me, 'Anything you can get, holler. If I don't hear you, I got it. Got it?' I told him, 'Yeah.' A couple of games later, a ball goes to right-center, and I didn't want another collision so I hollered that I had it. He stopped running because he didn't want to collide with me. But I couldn't get it, and the ball fell in. He didn't say anything," a still-grateful Yogi remembered more than fifty years later at the Yogi Berra Museum and Learning Center on the Montclair State campus in New Jersey. Berra, however, denied a story that Brown told me about DiMaggio bawling out Yogi after the rookie failed to run out an infield pop up that dropped in. "You're a Yankee now. You run out everything," DiMaggio reportedly said. "It never happened," Berra claimed. Yogi did incur the Big Guy's wrath when he begged off catching the second game of a doubleheader on a sweltering day in Washington. Berra got the message DiMaggio delivered and bore no resentment for the lecture. It was part of learning to play in the major leagues.

Aside from Berra's rather rough introduction to his outfield mate, another memorable encounter occurred in the Yankee Stadium expanses. Joe Nachio remembered the moment vividly: "It was an afternoon game in July 1948, and there were about 56,000 people in the park. Suddenly, there was a strange hush. A little kid about six years old was on the field with a pad in his hands, and he ran straight to DiMaggio. There was not a sound, as if the people held their breaths, waiting to see Joe's reaction. What would he do? Joe got down on one knee, took the kid's pad and signed it. He patted the boy on the butt and sent him on his way back to the stands. The applause was thunderous. After the game, a reporter asked him, 'Do you think that was the right thing to do, sign an autograph in the middle of a game?' Joe told him, 'You know what the right thing to do is? Improve security so nobody runs on the field.'"

The biggest news in baseball in 1947 did come out of New York, but it wasn't in the Bronx nor did it involve anyone in Yankee pinstripes. Jackie Robinson was about to break the color barrier with the Brooklyn Dodgers. Integration of the American pastime received some opposition in both leagues. Nachio was with Joe when reporters pressed him for his opinion. "He never answered any question without thinking first," Nachio said. "He kept his mouth closed, stared at the ground, and then he said, 'You know what my opinion is? Can he do the job? That's what counts, not his color. Can he do the job? If he's good enough to play, then he deserves to be in the big leagues.' DiMaggio was one of the game's major stars, and I think his support carried a lot of weight with some who might have been on the fence."

That was typical of Joe. I never heard him say or do anything that could be interpreted as prejudiced. On the contrary, he was sympathetic to minorities. After all, he was one, and had heard remarks and witnessed slights directed at Italians.

DiMaggio won his third MVP award that year by a single point over Williams, as both stars demonstrated that they could come back after the war had interrupted their careers. Williams won the third of his four batting titles with a .343 average. DiMaggio batted .315 and led the Yankees to another pennant. Red Smith wrote, "The guy who came out of San Francisco as a shy lone wolf, suspicious of Easterners and Eastern writers, today is the top guy in any sports gathering in any town. The real champ."

The Yankees also won another World Series, beating the Dodgers in seven games. That was the Series in which Gionfriddo made his famous catch next to the 415-foot sign at the left-field bullpen railing in the Stadium, robbing DiMaggio of what would have been his third home run of the Series. When we talked about that moment many years later, Joe told me, "It was not a great catch. It was a good catch, but it came at an important time." Gionfriddo saved a three-run homer, allowing the Dodgers to win the game 8–6 and tie the Series at three victories apiece.

At the time, DiMaggio was sharing a three-room suite at the Madison Hotel with Solotaire, and George's seventeen-year-old son, who was staying with them, went to the game that day. "I had a seat in the upper left-field stands, and I had a great view of the ball coming out toward us. I was elated, it looked like a sure home run until Gionfriddo caught it," recalled Robert Solotaire, years later. "We had dinner reservations at the Pierre Hotel, not too far from the hotel, but Joe was in no mood to go out. He sat around in his undershorts with an expression you usually see only at a wake. He said nothing, just stared out the window. My father said nothing. Finally, my father and I went to the Pierre; Joe called room service or ordered from Reubens, a restaurant across the street where he liked the roasted chicken." George Solotaire said it took DiMaggio a week to shake the depression, and even another World Series celebration couldn't do it.

DiMaggio liked the younger Solotaire, whom he called Bobby. He made Bobby the hero of Bronxville High in suburban New York when he came to speak to a school assembly. The relationship soured at George Solotaire's funeral, when Bobby neglected to get Joe a car in the funeral cortege to the cemetery. DiMaggio was unforgiving of the slight, and the younger Solotaire never saw him again.

◆ ◆ ◆

At the Yankees 1948 home opener, Joe was presented with his MVP trophy by Thomas Dewey, then governor of New York and the favorite to win the Republican nomination to run against President Harry Truman. The Yankees played the Red Sox that day, and Boston, led by new manager Joe McCarthy, won the game, 4–0.

New York finished third that season behind Cleveland and Boston, but DiMaggio, who played in all but one game, led the league with 155 RBIs and 39 home runs, while also batting .320 and striking out a mere 30 times. He may have been inspired by the contract negotiations the previous winter with owner Dan Topping and the new general manager, George Weiss. The result was a $70,000 salary, second highest in Yankee history, behind only Babe Ruth's $80,000 in 1930 and 1931. Joe liked Topping, and he enjoyed talking baseball with him over a cup of coffee in the owner's suite, but he despised Topping's partner, Larry MacPhail.

Among the games that year that DiMaggio remembered most fondly was one played in Cleveland in late May. He hit three home runs, two of them off Bob Feller. "It just didn't seem fair the way I hit that guy, because he was one of the toughest right-handers in baseball," DiMaggio said.

The Yankees were out of the pennant race going into the last weekend of the season, and DiMaggio was limping from the pain in his right heel. The Yankees closed the season in Boston, and his father was at the game. Giuseppe and Rosalie had come from San Francisco because Dom was to be married in about a week. The Red Sox were in a torrid battle for first place with the Indians, but Joe didn't want to show any favoritism. Just as he had clobbered the Indians and Feller, he wanted to do the same to the Red Sox, even if it meant keeping his brother from the World Series—or maybe it was *because* it would keep Dom from the Series. Joe got seven hits in the two games, including a home run, and when he left the field on the final day, he was applauded by Red Sox fans. When he limped to first after getting a single off the left-field wall—the Fenway feature he liked the best—he took himself out of the game. The Bostonians knew class when they saw it, and they showed some of their own with the ovation. The Red Sox and Indians finished the season in a dead heat, and the Indians won the pennant in a one-game playoff before going on to capture the World Series.

DiMaggio's first postseason appearance was at the 21 Club for the announcement that Casey Stengel was being named the new Yankees manager. Casey had been managing the Oakland Oaks of the Pacific Coast League, and he knew many of the same Bay Area people that Joe did. But DiMaggio was not there to play "do you know" with Stengel, who was busy enough with his circuitous marathon explanations that completely baffled members of the media. Joe had been asked by Topping and Weiss to show up at the announcement, and since he was about to ask them for a $100,000 salary, he thought it would be a good idea to accept the invitation. The restaurant was only a short walk from Toots Shor's, but for Joe, it was a painful one. His right heel still was hurting.

A few weeks later, DiMaggio was in an operating room at Johns Hopkins again to have a bone spur removed from the troublesome heel. The operation would have a monumental effect on his 1949 season, and eventually, on his career. He blamed it for his early retirement, five years earlier than he had planned. The surgery was botched, according to Positano.

"Joe had what is called a Griffiths procedure, where the spur was cut out, but the surgeon also removed the fatty pad that cushioned the bone," Positano said. "So, Joe had bone rubbing on bone, which gave him pain when he walked and excruciating pain when he ran. They don't even do that procedure anymore." The surgery was done in November, and Joe recuperated in his new residence, a four-room suite at the Hotel Elysee. The hotel was on 54th Street and was popular with Broadway theater people. Ethel Merman said it was pronounced "easy-lay."

Nachio spent ten days with the recuperating DiMaggio, and he remembered the experience as pure hell. "He couldn't move anyplace. 'Pick up the goddamn phone, order some food, go out get some fruit, take a walk up to Reubens and get some sandwiches, or how about some hot dogs, baked beans, and potato salad?' That's what I had to endure."

It was not the first or the last time that Nachio put up with a demanding DiMaggio. During a previous siege, DiMaggio saw Nachio, suitcases in hand, heading for the hotel room door. "Where you going, Joe?" he asked. "Joe, I need a vacation," Nachio told him. "I couldn't take it anymore," Nachio recalled later. "The media would upset him, and he would get cranky and cantankerous. So, I moved to a different floor in the same hotel, the Madison. He found out where I was, and he came up, packed my clothes in my suitcase and brought it back to his suite."

DiMaggio asked him, "What's the matter, you can't put up with me?" Nachio replied, "Joe, after three days, it's very tough." From then on, after the two spent three days together, Joe would wonder, "Are you getting tired of me?" Nachio would explain, "I'm not tired of you, Joe. I'm tired of all the pressure you're subjected to. As you suffer, I suffer more for you."

Why did Nachio put up with it? "When you know the faults and shortcomings of a person and you remain his friend, you are a true friend," he said. That he was, until the very end, when Joe called him his "oldest and most loyal friend."

DiMaggio's pain in 1949 was eased somewhat when he became baseball's first $100,000 player. He was finally the highest paid Yankee of all time, surpassing the Babe, who had died a year earlier. His tender heel still troubled him at spring training. "That's to be expected," he was told. "Don't worry about it. Soon, you won't feel it anymore." The Yankees were on an exhibition-game swing in Texas when the pain got so bad that Joe thought he would pass out. "It felt like someone was sticking pins into my heel." He was flown to Baltimore and readmitted to Johns Hopkins, where he was treated for a serious infection; a "hot condition" is what the surgeon called it then.

Joe was on the all-too-familiar crutches again when he went back to New York to recuperate. It was a long recuperation. He missed 65 games and didn't play until June 27. But that was the least of the DiMaggio family's health problems that year. His father died in May, and his mother was diagnosed with cancer. The ache in Joe's right heel disappeared suddenly sometime in late June, and he was driven up to Yankee Stadium to take batting practice. When he felt no pain in the heel, he did it again the next day, and again had no pain. Because his hands had become so soft during the long layoff, however, severe blisters developed in his palms. The Yankees were on the road at the time, and when they came back, Joe played an exhibition game against the Giants on June 27 without any ill effects.

On June 28, the Yankees left without DiMaggio for a night game in Boston, and Joe made the familiar five-block walk from his hotel to Shor's for lunch. A surprised Toots greeted him, "You crumbbum, what are you doing here?" Joe said that was when he realized he might have made a mistake by not going with the team. He thought he would wait for the Yankees to return from Boston before rejoining them. "Jump on a plane," Toots advised him. That's what Joe did. He made his comeback with a single and a two-run homer to help the Yanks to victory. He hit three home runs in the next two days and drove in nine runs, as the Yankees completed a three-game sweep. "It's Great To Be Back," proclaimed the words under a full-page picture of Joe on the cover of *Life* magazine. The byline said Joe DiMaggio, but the ghostwriter was Emmett Hughes, who later became President Dwight Eisenhower's main speechwriter.

By the time Joe was playing again, seven-year-old Joe Jr.'s education was over for the year at the Walt Whitman private school on Manhattan's East Side. He was delivered to Yankee Stadium to spend time with his dad. Joe was sitting at his locker stall sipping coffee and smoking a cigarette, as he always did after a game, and he asked Bernie Kamber to take Joey outside and play catch with him. "The kid and I went through the runway from the clubhouse into the dugout, and there I was on the field throwing a ball at Yankee Stadium. No one was in the stands, the place was empty, but I felt like Red Ruffing," Kamber said.

During the late 1940s and in Joe's last two years with the Yankees, when the team was home for an afternoon game, Kamber would drive to the stadium from midtown and bring DiMaggio back to his hotel. Kamber was a top-level movie publicist, and celebrities were his business, yet he was thrilled just to be in

DiMaggio's company. "I worked with Rita Hayworth, Deborah Kerr, Burt Lancaster, Sir Lawrence Oliver, and many, many others, but DiMaggio was different. He was special. I was a baseball fan all my life, and he was the best." Joe would get him tickets sometimes and Bernie would go to a game, but mostly he was satisfied being Joe D.'s chauffeur. "I'm talking about it more than fifty years later, and I feel like a big idiot, but in those days, it was my pleasure. Just to sit with him in the clubhouse talking with Phil Rizzuto, Billy Martin, Gil McDougald." (Boy, did that sound familiar to me.)

Kamber and Solotaire were handy to have around in mid-September when Joe was slugged by a virus and had to be hospitalized just as the Yankees and Red Sox again were engaged in a frantic race for the pennant. "We got him back into the Elysee from the hospital, but he felt terrible and looked worse," Kamber said. "He had lost 12 to 15 pounds, he had been coughing, he was out of breath. He had been in bed for two weeks." But the Red Sox came to New York for the final two games of the season, leading by one game. If Boston won Saturday, it had the pennant. The Yankees had to win both games. The question was: Would DiMaggio be at Yankee Stadium?

"We took a cab to Saturday's game," Kamber said. "The fellows in the clubhouse looked surprised to see him. I don't know if it was because he was there or because of how pale and thin he looked. When Joe got up for batting practice, all the Red Sox were on the top step of the dugout watching to see what he would do. Crack, into the stands, crack, into the stands. He hit every ball into the seats. Rizzuto said that's when the Red Sox knew they were beaten."

Before the game there was an hour-long tribute to DiMaggio, beginning with Ethel Merman singing "Take Me Out to the Ball Game," which was Joe's favorite song. He would sing it to my daughters and grandson and to his own grandchildren and great-grandchildren. Merman had been one of Joe's favorites ever since he saw her in *Annie Get Your Gun*. He laughed when he recalled her performance at the Stadium. "She had such a powerful voice, she didn't need a mike." What he seemed to remember most from that day was that when his mother was brought onto the field by his brother Tom, she went to the front of the Red Sox dugout and kissed Dom first, and then Joe. Talk about sibling rivalry! His mother told the reporters she was rooting for the Red Sox because Joe "got all the presents and Dominic got nothing."

Joe was presented with a huge inventory of gifts from fan organizations and Italian-American groups throughout the metropolitan area, including two cars, one of which was for his mother. DiMaggio made a speech and had to struggle to keep from crying. "New York is the friendliest town in the world," he said. "I'd like to thank the Good Lord for making me a Yankee." Nearly 70,000 fans cheered for about five minutes, and the applause resumed whenever he came to bat in the game. He had a double and a single and helped the Yankees come back from a 4–0 deficit to win 5–4 on an eighth-inning home run by Johnny Lindell. That tied New York with Boston for first place, so the winner of Sunday's game would win the pennant. Typical of the long-standing rivalry between those two clubs, the Yankees won the pennant with a 5–3 victory that afternoon, but DiMaggio left those who were present with an indelible memory. His legs "felt tired" from about the sixth inning on, undoubtedly a side effect of his virus. He hit into a double play in the bottom of the eighth inning, and in the ninth, a fly ball by Bobby Doerr sailed over his head. He didn't have the strength to chase it, and Doerr made it to third with a triple. That's when DiMaggio took himself out of the game. When the fans realized that he was walking off the field, they saluted him with a standing ovation.

For the third time that decade, the Yankees faced their rivals from Brooklyn in the World Series, and for the third time they came out on top. After the five-game Series, DiMaggio went home to San Francisco to repair his body. It had not been one of his better years. Though he batted .346, he played in only 76 games and drove in a career-low 67 runs. Still, he displayed the heart of a champion by coming back from the heel injury and the virus to help his team to another championship.

◆ ◆ ◆

That off-season, Joe was determined to get his legs back in shape. He blamed some of those woes on his failure to fully heed Cobb's advice to do a lot of walking. So, that winter, he was again seen walking in boots through the Marina district and up and down the hills of San Francisco. He also played a lot of golf and ate a lot of his mother's cooking. His weight, which had dropped to 178 pounds by the end of the 1949 season, was back to about 205 when he showed up for spring training. For the second straight year, he was a $100,000 player.

Joe was in the Yankees' Opening Day lineup for only the fourth time in twelve years, and he had six hits in a three-game series in Boston. When he went into a slump early in the season, however, Casey Stengel became convinced that Joe, at age thirty-five and with a history of injuries, had slowed, and the manager began to contemplate changes. DiMaggio broke out of his slump in mid-May with a big series in Cleveland, but by then Casey had decided he wanted to put the younger Cliff Mapes in center field. He sent Mapes out to replace DiMaggio in the middle of a game. Maury Allen wrote that Joe told the young outfielder to go back to the dugout with the message, "I'll tell Casey when I want to come out." When the inning ended, DiMaggio trotted off the field and strode through the dugout and into the clubhouse without saying a word to Stengel. Casey told the press that he wanted to move DiMaggio to first base. "It will add years to his career," he explained. That was strange territory to Joe, and he was not happy about going there. His first reaction was to try for a laugh. "Just tell me where first base is, and I'm ready," he told Shirley Povich of the *Washington Post*. The move lasted one game. Hank Bauer was put in center field, but Bauer got hurt, and Joe went back to his old position. Stengel, however, was not finished toying with DiMaggio. He benched him for a couple of games and dropped him in the batting order for a few more games. Joe said he requested one of the benchings because his knees had stiffened.

DiMaggio did not think much of Stengel as a manager, even though the Casey-led Yankees won ten American League pennants and seven World Series championships in his twelve years. "He had the horses," was Joe's explanation for Casey's success.

Joe went on a home run rampage in September, hitting three in one game against the Senators, including a 400-foot drive that was the first ever to land in Griffith Stadium's left-field bleachers. Joe finished the 1950 season with 32 homers, 122 RBIs, and a .301 average. Not too shabby for an old man. DiMaggio had a way of rising to the occasion, performing whenever the pressure was on.

Just as DiMaggio seemed to be returning to his old form, the Yankees were undergoing some changes to the makeup of the team, with the old order beginning to give way to the new. Included in the new order were infielder Billy Martin and pitcher Whitey Ford. Martin was an Italian from the Bay Area, like DiMaggio, but the similarity ended there. Billy was brash and playful, in contrast to Joe's grace and class. Yet, Joe liked the kid, well enough to invite him to dinner and pick up the check. He let Martin kid him and even play jokes on him. He admired Billy's competitive spirit. "If there was a way to win," DiMaggio said, "Billy would find it."

Martin regarded Joe not so much as a legend but as an older brother. But Billy being Billy, it was inevitable that at some point he would go too far and cross DiMaggio's line. And he did, more than once. One such instance occurred in the 1980s during one of Martin's stints as Yankees manager. DiMaggio walked into a restaurant in New Jersey where Billy was drinking. Martin had a load on and was loudly boasting about his ability with his fists. That attitude had gotten him in fights before, and Joe may have foreseen another one in the works. At any rate, he walked up to Martin, put his hand on his shoulder, and told him, "You're acting like a horse's ass." Billy glared at him, and everyone tensed, expecting a fight, but Martin said, "You know, Joe, you're right," and he left.

Bernie Kamber was with DiMaggio when the Yankees went up against the "Whiz Kid" Philadelphia Phillies in the 1950 World Series. The two were resting in their room at the Warwick Hotel in Philadelphia when Martin knocked on the door. "Whatya doing?" Billy asked. "We were watching television," Kamber remembered, "Joe lying on one bed and me on the other. Billy flopped down on the floor and sat there watching TV with us." The rookie Martin had played only briefly that season, and he wasn't even on the Series roster, but he was along for the fun.

The Yankees won the first two games of the Series in Philadelphia. After Vic Raschi pitched a two-hitter in the first game, DiMaggio hit a home run off Robin Roberts in the tenth inning of game two to win it for New York.

Kamber said that returning to New York with DiMaggio was a great thrill. "When we came into Pennsylvania Station, there were what seemed to be millions of people waiting for Joe to get off the train. I walked with him and it was like I was the one who hit the home run. They cheered, and it was as if they were cheering for me. I will never forget it." The Yankees completed a World Series sweep by winning the next two games at Yankee Stadium.

◆ ◆ ◆

Joe had another busy off-season. He and Lefty O'Doul traveled to Korea and Japan. In Korea, they visited the troops and got close enough to the fighting that they could hear the sounds of battle.

"It was no police action," Joe said, referring to the term used by politicians at the time. "It looked like an all-out war to me." His most vivid memories were of the GIs in the hospitals he visited in Korea and Japan. In Japan, he and Lefty gave instructional clinics in six cities. After he retired, Joe went back to Japan several times, including on his honeymoon with Marilyn Monroe. He had a major influence on baseball's popularity there, and he is credited with planting the seeds that, at the beginning of the new century, were producing a bumper crop of Japanese and Korean players for the major leagues.

Hank Aaron said that by the time he went to Japan with DiMaggio to promote baseball in the 1990s, youngsters already were fixated on playing in the majors. "Joe had more to do with inspiring interest in baseball in Japan than I or anyone else who went there, because Joe went there many years earlier, and everyone who knew about baseball knew about Joe DiMaggio."

DiMaggio and Japan's home run king, Sadaharu Oh, were recruited to be the spark plugs for the World Children's Baseball Fair, which was to attract young players from countries around the world. The first fair was held in Los Angeles, and DiMaggio was there. He also went for five years in a row when the event was held in Japan. Aaron saw him in action twice there and was amazed at DiMaggio's active participation. "I thought he would sit in the stands and sign autographs, but no, he was out there on the field talking with the young people, telling them about hitting and fielding and how to throw from the outfield. And, he was in his eighties by then. And I'll tell you this, those kids were giving him their undivided attention."

◆ ◆ ◆

The Yankees trained in Phoenix in 1951, and when DiMaggio got there, he told three reporters that he would retire when the season ended. The story broke just as the writers were reporting the other big news in camp: the arrival of Mickey Mantle, a nineteen-year-old shortstop in the Yankees farm system. There was no way the young prospect was going to play shortstop with the Yankees, because Phil Rizzuto was entrenched there, so Stengel asked DiMaggio to tutor the kid from Commerce, Oklahoma, on how to play the outfield in the majors. Casey later sent DiMaggio on an off-season secret mission involving Mantle. He asked DiMaggio, on his way home to San Francisco, to stop off in Oklahoma and tell Mantle's father to lay off the kid. From the day Mickey was born, Mutt Mantle was determined that his son would be a major league shortstop. He named him after Mickey Cochrane, the Tigers Hall of Fame catcher who was Mutt's hero, and he never ceased putting pressure on his son. Joe made the trip, and not just for the good of the team. "The Yankees paid my fare home," DiMaggio said. That made him feel good.

Mantle opened the 1951 season in right field, but he was already being touted as DiMaggio's replacement. How's that for pressure? Mantle responded by striking out a lot—74 times in 96 games in his rookie outing. The youngster was in awe of DiMaggio, and he avoided eye contact with him, even when Joe talked to him about his fielding and hitting. Mick was sent back to the minors for a while to relieve the pressure.

Mantle conceded that he felt intimidated by the man to his right when he was in the outfield. "It was pretty nerve-wracking," he told a TV interviewer. "I was only nineteen." Mantle reached the World Series in his first year, which made him nervous enough, and there was the Great DiMaggio next to him in the outfield. Before the second game of the Series against the Giants, Stengel told the kid outfielder that DiMaggio's heel was bothering him, and he likely would not be able to cover as much ground as he usually did, so Mantle should be ready to take the balls coming to right-center. "Willie Mays hit a fly to right-center, and I ran as hard as I could to get there," said Mantle. "I got under it and I was just ready to make the catch when I heard 'I got it.' I looked over and Joe was standing under the ball. He had come farther than I did, and I could outrun him. But, he had an instinct. He was an instinctive ballplayer."

Mantle was seriously hurt on that play in the 1951 Series. When he pulled up to let DiMaggio catch the ball, the rookie's right foot caught in a sprinkler head in the outfield grass. He went down hard. Mantle told Houston sportswriter Mickey Herskowitz that as he lay there in pain with a bone protruding from his leg, DiMaggio advised, "Don't move. They're bringing a stretcher." Mantle wasn't sure what impressed him more, the terrible injury or seeing his outfield mate cover so much ground to make that catch.

DiMaggio himself played in pain all through the 1951 season. In April, he had pains in his neck and shoulder; in June, he pulled a leg muscle, and for the third time in his career, he took himself out of a game.

In addition to the physical injuries, DiMaggio was also mourning the loss of his mother to cancer in June. Joe and Dom made frantic flights home, hoping to say goodbye to her, but neither made it in time.

Joe DiMaggio played hurt throughout his career, but he had too much pride to play when he could not give his best. He didn't want to embarrass himself, and he didn't want to hurt the team's chances of winning. During a game in July, Stengel sent Jackie Jensen into center field as DiMaggio's replacement, which angered Joe, but that time, he said nothing. Stengel said he made the move because DiMaggio was hurting. The next day, he wrote Joe back in the starting lineup, but Joe told the manager he was still hurting.

"There's no snap in my swing," DiMaggio told Joe Reichler, the Associated Press' top baseball writer. "I know what's wrong, but there's nothing I can do about it." His batting average had fallen to .261, and Stengel dropped him from fourth to fifth in the batting order, moving Berra into the cleanup spot. "It's got me down in the dumps," he admitted to Reichler. Still, some of the old Joe D. was left in him. In a game against the Indians at Yankee Stadium, Berra was intentionally walked, with a runner on second and two out, to bring up DiMaggio to face Bob Feller. "How the mighty have fallen," a writer quipped in the press box. The writers leaning over their typewriters chuckled. Joe and the press were barely on speaking terms at the time. Those who had lavished him with praise in the good years were quick to pound away at his shortcomings now, some with glee. "I have a bad day, you guys want to fire me," he complained. But the writers had nothing but good things to say that day. DiMaggio belted a two-run triple. How about that!

DiMaggio's rapport with the press was generally good, especially with the New York writers. Before he left San Francisco for the first time, he had been warned to be wary of the New York press. Joe was a favorite of the photographers, who most of the time found him willing to go along with their requests for poses, no matter how contrived. "The best time to get him was during batting practice before the fans got there," said Harry Harris, an AP photographer who covered the Yankees for decades. "Once the fans got there, he shied away from posing. They would line up against the railing in the box seats and bug him. 'Bet you don't get a hit today,' stuff like that. They would get on Rizzuto, too. Phil would smile affably, but mutter under his breath, 'That sonofabitch, I'd like to jam this ball down his throat.'"

Joe played in only 117 games in 1951, batted .263, hit just 12 homers, and drove in 71 runs. It was his worst year by far in the majors, yet Topping urged him to come back for one more season at the same $100,000 salary. Topping was a real DiMaggio fan, and he was campaigning for Joe to come back for a farewell season late into the night before DiMaggio announced his retirement.

Joe's tenth and final World Series was against the Giants, who had ridden Bobby Thomson's famous "shot heard 'round the world" home run to a playoff victory over the Dodgers. DiMaggio was back in the fourth spot in the batting order, and he had six hits in the six games, including a two-run homer. In his last at-bat, in the Yankees' Series clincher, he doubled to right. "He was very proud of that," said Kamber. "He talked about that for weeks. 'My final major league hit was a two-bagger.'" Unfortunately, he was thrown out at third base on the next play, a bunt by Gil McDougald.

At my first meeting with DiMaggio, I told him how I would never forget the ovation he received when he walked across the diamond to the dugout for the last time at Yankee Stadium. "Mr. Engelberg," he said, "I did not walk across the diamond; I ran because I was embarrassed." I always thought he may have slowed down on that play so he could be thrown out, and that way get a chance to cut across the infield and give the fans an opportunity to say goodbye with that final ovation—the Yankees had a 4–1 eighth-inning lead at that point. Otherwise, he would not even have been noticed running in from the outfield after the ninth inning, and there would have been no farewell salute.

On December 11, 1951, the Yankees called a news conference at their Fifth Avenue office. The crowd of reporters, columnists, radio and TV people, and newsreel cameramen was so large that the media was divided into two rooms. The cameras rolled and Joe looked squarely into the lenses as he announced, "I've played my last game of ball."

"Old injuries caught up with me and brought on new ones. I found that it was a chore for me to straighten up after I had retrieved a ground ball. In short, I was not pleased with myself any longer and all the fun had gone out of playing the game."

But it was more than that for Joe. It was Yankee Pride. "I feel that I have reached the stage where I can no longer produce for my ball club, my manager, my teammates, and my fans the sort of baseball their loyalty to me deserves." Tom DiMaggio told Maury Allen that his brother quit because "he wasn't Joe DiMaggio anymore."

Winning was what baseball and life were all about to DiMaggio—not his 56-game hitting streak nor his three MVP awards. Those nine World Series championship rings were what he cherished most because they symbolized victories. It was that drive to win that carried him through his later years and made him a success in business. He lost only one battle, his final one, with cancer, but as he did with everything in his life, he gave it a hell of a fight.

3

LIVING LEGEND

IT IS AMAZING WHEN YOU THINK ABOUT IT. Joe DiMaggio spent thirteen years playing major league baseball, and then was celebrated for fifty years afterward. He played the role of an American sports legend and gave command performances all over the United States, in Latin America, the Far East, and Italy. He was the grand marshal of parades, from the Orange Bowl in Miami to Columbus Day celebrations in Chicago and New York. He was the featured speaker at dinners, the prime attraction at celebrity golf tournaments, and the most sought after "pitcher" for throwing out the ceremonial first ball at ballparks, from the Little Leagues to the majors. With all this, there were times he felt used. "I have a full load," he wrote in his diary in 1992. "I keep saying to myself after the coming months of appearances, I'm going to sit back and nix demands. No truer words were said than the quote, 'What have you done for me lately?'"

Even when he was in his eighties, silver-haired and bent with arthritis, he still was the heroic Yankee Clipper, one of the greatest of all time. People who had not yet been born when he retired stood and cheered when he was introduced.

That's why Joe was puzzled when he was in a store in northern California and heard Paul Simon and Art Garfunkel wondering over the store's sound system, "Where have you gone, Joe DiMaggio?" His reaction was, "Hey, what the hell are they talking about? I haven't gone anywhere. I'm still around. Don't they see me on television doing the Mr. Coffee commercial?" And, as a quick afterthought, he complained that the song's writers "never paid me for the use of my name." Simon later met Joe in Lattanzi, a restaurant in New York's theater district, and explained that "Mrs. Robinson" was a lament for an American era that was lost, a time of perfect heroes and innocence that DiMaggio represented. Joe felt pretty good about that.

That song may have touched a nerve because DiMaggio often fretted about his image of being aloof and a loner. "Don't say I'm a recluse or a hermit. It bothers me when people say that," DiMaggio told Marv Schneider during an interview for the Associated Press on Joe's eightieth birthday. "I do things. I get around." But, he conceded, "There are times when I like to have my privacy."

The same was true when he was playing. He was unapproachable to some. Tommy Henrich and DiMaggio were teammates for eleven years, yet Henrich said they never had dinner together. Gil McDougald and DiMaggio both came from San Francisco, but their conversation never got passed the "hi" stage. "He was not the one you would start a conversation with," said McDougald, who was an awed rookie in DiMaggio's final year. "Everyone treated him like an icon." Nevertheless, McDougald was left with a pleasant memory following an encounter on a New York sidewalk after both former Yankees were retired. DiMaggio offered his old teammate a chance to do a Bowery Savings Bank commercial with him, saying it might help Gil's office-maintenance business in New Jersey. "I said to myself, 'Wow. He's thinking about me and my business.' I thought that was pretty damn nice of him." Still, McDougald's lasting impression was that DiMaggio kept to himself. "I was sorry for him because the fun in baseball is the camaraderie," which Tommy felt DiMaggio missed.

DiMaggio did pal around with Lefty Gomez in the early days, and with Billy Martin at the end of his career. Both were blithe spirits who made Joe laugh. Then, there was Joe Page, a starter who became a brilliant relief pitcher. They were roomies on the road for a while, until DiMaggio locked Page out one night in Boston. It was an unusual pairing. Page was a two-fisted drinker, while DiMaggio was a one-beer-a-night guy when he drank, and that wasn't very often. DiMaggio went to bed early when the Yankees played day games, and he didn't like being awakened by Page stumbling in after curfew. As Joe told the story, he warned Page that he was locking the door at 10:00 P.M. and would not get out of bed to open it. "I put a chair up against the door so he couldn't get in," DiMaggio said. "I was awakened about three in the morning by someone rattling the door knob. I looked over at Joe's bed and it was empty. I rolled over and went back to sleep. When I got out of bed about seven in the morning, Page's bed still was empty. I took the chair away and opened the door, Page fell into the room, sound asleep. He had been sleeping with his back against the door." Joe thought it amazing that Page pitched a couple of brilliant innings that night.

Eddie Lopat, who pitched for the Yankees during DiMaggio's last four years with the club, saw Joe as a lonely man, who "led the league in room service." Jerry Coleman, another former teammate, said DiMaggio ate in his room to avoid the autograph seekers. "He couldn't walk into a restaurant or the hotel coffee shop without someone jumping on him for an autograph." When DiMaggio did dine with a teammate, Coleman said it was because, "he wanted one of us to be a buffer from the fans."

◆ ◆ ◆

Being the constant target for autograph seekers was part of the price DiMaggio paid for his fame. As Joe Nachio put it, "He was an idol, and an idol is idolized. That put him under tremendous pressure." The pressure remained for the rest of his life, and because of that, there were days he didn't want to be Joe DiMaggio. Those were the times that he refused requests for autographs. "I have no life," he would complain then. "I can't go anywhere. I have no privacy. It's no fun, Morris."

Joe sometimes deluded himself into thinking that if he sat in the back of a restaurant no one would see and recognize him. Once, while having lunch with Rita Sokoloff, my firm's office manager, he shushed her when she called him Mr. DiMaggio. "People will hear," he said. "Don't use my last name. Call me Joe." Rita could not bring herself to use his first name, so she settled on "Mr. D." in public. As funny as that sounds, it seemed to satisfy his desire to preserve a semblance of anonymity, even though his face really made that impossible.

Hank Aaron, another easily recognized baseball immortal, said DiMaggio was the victim of much more pressure from the public than he. "I went through something similar during the year of my home run chase, but Joe DiMaggio kept getting it long after he retired," said the man who hit more home runs than anyone else in baseball history. "He was pulled on and tugged on every which way you could pull a guy."

Aaron felt the heat of the media and public most when he closed in on and then surpassed Babe Ruth's home run record, and it got quite nasty with racist overtones and death threats. Still, Aaron believed DiMaggio had to endure pressure more constantly and longer because he played in New York and because of his marriage to Marilyn Monroe. "He was always in the limelight. They wouldn't let him breathe. They would not let him be himself. Joe DiMaggio, like everyone else, needed some air space. He would tell me that everybody wanted something from him, and he was right."

Joe didn't like being Joe DiMaggio in the early 1980s when I met him, because he wasn't making money. When Joe was doing quite well financially, however, in the 1990s, he didn't complain as much. Life was sweeter. Life was good. Of course, there always were perks to being Joe DiMaggio. He would get celebrity service. At restaurants, he never had to wait for a table. At airports, they would carry his luggage and rush him right past the lines. He was Joe DiMaggio, and he would make sure that he would be treated like Joe D. by giving the airport people autographs whenever they asked, and that was virtually always.

Joe felt he had an obligation to fans. His friend, restaurateur Mario Faustini, remembered an incident in the early 1990s when he was driving DiMaggio to LaGuardia Airport in New York. Joe had taken a Lasix pill, a diuretic, so they had to make a quick pit stop in upper Manhattan. Faustini double-parked, and Joe rushed into a restaurant. The people inside this off-the-beaten-path place must have been startled to see the Yankee Clipper suddenly appear. Meanwhile, Faustini sat in the car looking at his watch and worrying that Joe was going to miss his plane. Finally, Mario went to see what was causing the delay, and there was DiMaggio surrounded by people and signing autographs. Only the warning that he would miss his plane got Joe to stop. "I saw he was worried while we were heading for the airport, and I told him we had enough time," Faustini said. "But he wasn't worried about that. He told me, 'I hope those people I missed aren't upset with me.'"

Sometimes, being so accommodating backfired on him. "The airline hostesses were a pain in the ass," he wrote in his diary after a flight in the summer of 1993. "Signed many things, which I didn't mind, but to wake me up while in a sound sleep upset me. And, then, as always happens, when some lady gets an autograph, then a good part of the people on the plane get in line for one."

There was another incident aloft that got to him, a white-knuckle episode in a plane being shaken by severe turbulence. "I was holding on for dear life," he recalled. "The fellow in the seat in front of me turned and asked for my autograph. I said, 'Are you crazy? The plane is going to crash, we are going to die.' The man turned back in his seat. When we landed and we were walking up the aisle I asked the fellow why he would ask for an autograph at a time like that, when I was sure that we all were going to perish. 'That's why I asked you,' he said. 'I didn't think you would refuse my last request.'"

All celebrities have to deal with intrusive autograph seekers, but DiMaggio possibly more than others because he was so recognizable. In the 1980s, Joe visited Nachio in Panama, and they flew to Nicaragua in a private plane to go tarpon fishing. They landed at a small airport in Costa Rica and presented their passports at customs, and one of the clerks recognized DiMaggio. There was no escape, even in that remote part of the hemisphere. Word quickly got around to a nearby United Fruit banana plantation that Joe DiMaggio was at the airport. "We were back on the plane, ready to take off and fly to the place where we would go fishing. Suddenly, the plane was surrounded by field hands, some carrying the machetes they used to cut the bananas from the trees," Nachio said. "They were chanting 'Joe DiMaggio, Joe DiMaggio.' Two were wearing tattered and dirty pinstripe jerseys, one with the No. 5 on the front. Joe got out of the plane, and one of the field hands showed him a ball they had been using; it was made of rags tied with a string. Joe shook hands all around, amazed that he was known in a place so isolated. He promised that when he got back to New York he would see to it that fifty autographed baseballs were sent to the plantation, and he did."

Some years earlier, DiMaggio and Bob Feller were invited by Nicaraguan president Anastasio Somoza to throw out the ceremonial first pitches to open that country's baseball season. DiMaggio wanted Nachio to go with him. "You speak the language. I need an interpreter," was his excuse. Nachio saw the trip as a great opportunity to fish for freshwater sharks in Lake Nicaragua, so he went along, and accompanied by a presidential security officer, they flew to the lake in a small plane. They were nearly there when the plane's motor began to sputter, and the pilot put down in a meadow. Out of the jungle came a group of Indians, whom Nachio described as having "rings in their noses, feathers around their necks, and fierce looks on their faces." DiMaggio and Nachio were nervous, and Joe asked his buddy to speak with them. "You speak their language." Nachio corrected him. "No, I speak Spanish. These guys must speak some Indian dialect." DiMaggio, drawing on his movie-going experience, suggested, "Tell them we come in peace." Nachio held up one hand in a friendly gesture, and with the other, he pointed at Joe. "Joe DiMaggio," he declared, and then mimicked a baseball swing. The Indians nodded and smiled. "Joe DiMaggio, Joe DiMaggio," one of them repeated, and he, too, took a cut with an imaginary bat. The two Joes never were certain if the Indians really knew DiMaggio, or if they thought that Nachio's charade was a form of greeting.

Nachio had no such doubts about another DiMaggio sighting that took place off the Pearl Islands in the Pacific Ocean. The two went down there for a fishing trip, and one day DiMaggio was sunning himself on the deck of the boat, his prominent nose pointed skyward, when a cruise ship flying the Australian flag sailed close to them. "I looked up and there were about twenty people on the railing waving, and some were calling out to Joe," Nachio said. "That time, I was impressed. They were all Australians. How did they know Joe DiMaggio? I said, 'Your streak didn't make you famous. What made you famous was your schnozz,' and he said, 'Don't ever repeat that.'"

DiMaggio's recognition factor amazed Nachio. "I would walk down a street in New York with Stan Musial, Eddie Mathews, or Carl Yastrzemski when they came in for an Old Timers game. They were all famous, all were in the Hall of Fame, and yet nobody who passed us would turn around. Joe would be recognized in places like Panama, Venezuela, Nicaragua, and the Dominican Republic. In New York, he would stop traffic, like the time we were going to the Plaza Hotel for lunch. A cab came to a screeching halt, and the driver jumped out with a dollar bill in his hand. 'Sign this, Joe, please.' Joe stopped and signed it. Three more cabs stopped. Before you knew it, five cabs were blocking 59th Street. A cop came over to see what was going on. 'Joe DiMaggio, a one-man jam,' he said. 'You gotta move, Joe, but how about giving me an autograph for my kid?'" Joe knew he was at fault for the tie-up because he had violated one of his rules: "Never stop walking when you're signing, because they will come out of the woodwork. You have to keep walking."

Despite such scenes, or maybe because of them, New York was DiMaggio's favorite city, or at least on a par with San Francisco. He may have given New York a slight edge because of the restaurants, from Le Pavillion in the early days to Le Perigord and Bravo Gianni's in later years. He had dined well in most of Europe's great cities, but it wasn't like New York, and food didn't have to be elegant cuisine. He returned from a trip to Moscow in the early 1960s to report, "It was OK, but you can't get a corned beef sandwich there." No Stage Deli anywhere near Red Square.

DiMaggio continued to live in New York after he retired, and there were DiMaggio sightings all over town because he liked to walk. Gerald Stern, who was George Solotaire's nephew, spotted DiMaggio at the Luxor Baths. Stern's stepfather owned Molly Mog's Pub, where DiMaggio was always a welcome guest. That got the thirteen-year-old, wide-eyed kid an introduction to the Yankee Clipper. "He was standing there in the corridor getting hit by a high-pressure hose, which supposedly stimulates the muscles," Stern said. "He had a body like a Greek god, nothing but muscle, not an ounce of fat on him, and this was two years after he retired."

◆ ◆ ◆

Though DiMaggio could barely walk down the street without attracting attention from the public, he was disappointed that he was never offered a front-office job in the Yankees organization. Dan Topping said that Joe never told him he wanted a job. That was DiMaggio's way. He didn't ask for anything; he had to be asked. When Topping couldn't talk Joe out of retirement, he asked him to do commentary on fifteen-minute TV shows before and after home games, and DiMaggio accepted. He claimed he was intimidated by the microphone, and when he was a player, he was often nervous about being called on to make a speech at a dinner. He would rehearse in front of whatever friend was around, and Nachio was one of them. "He would sit me down in his hotel room and give his speech over and over, and then he would ask me, 'Did I say it right. Did I sound OK?'" Through the years, DiMaggio gained confidence, so by the end of his career, he was ready to face a microphone with the same positive attitude with which he met pitchers. He did a TV show for Buitoni pasta, where he talked baseball and answered questions ostensibly from youngsters in a studio. The show was seen in New York, Boston, New Haven, Philadelphia, and Miami. "He was marvelous with the kids, completely at ease, and he enjoyed it," said Leonard Lewin, a sportswriter who wrote both the questions and answers for the show.

Giovanni Buitoni was so delighted by DiMaggio's association with his pasta that he put him on the payroll the following spring as vice president of public relations for the West Coast, and made him one of the directors of Buitoni's operation in France and Italy. "He will coordinate everything," Buitoni said. That was *boni* with Joe, even though he was not quite sure what he was supposed to do.

The pre-game and post-game commentaries for the Yankees were done from a studio beneath the stadium. Joe would have former teammates and visiting players on as guests. Stengel appeared on the first show and presented Joe with a dictionary, but told him he was only lending it to him "because I haven't finished reading it yet."

After his television gig, DiMaggio received offers for various front-office jobs around baseball. He was offered a public relations position with the commissioner's office, but he turned it down when he found out that the pay was only about $20,000. Years later, when his friend Edward Bennett Williams owned the Baltimore Orioles, Joe was put on the club's board of directors. In 1967, DiMaggio accepted a job with the Athletics when owner Charlie Finley moved the team from Kansas City to Oakland. Joe was hired as a vice president, and then he became a coach during spring training. He felt strange being in an A's uniform instead of the familiar Yankee pinstripes, but he was proud that his presence helped the new team get much needed publicity in the Bay Area. He also had a more practical reason for taking the job. He wanted to extend his baseball employment to twenty years so he could get his pension to the top level.

That spring, the A's had a talented twenty-one-year-old rookie named Reggie Jackson on the squad. Jackson got a lot of one-on-one instruction from DiMaggio, as did Sal Bando and Joe Rudi. DiMaggio stayed on as a coach with the A's for three seasons, but he wasn't around when his instruction paid off. In 1971, the Oakland A's began a five-year run as the American League's West Division champs, during which time they became the only non-Yankee team in baseball history to win three consecutive World Series.

DiMaggio eventually did go to spring training as a batting instructor for the Yankees, but it was not until George Steinbrenner bought the club that DiMaggio was made to feel welcome at Yankee Stadium. He would grouse about the summons from the owner, because that's what DiMaggio did. "I have to go up there. He's honoring me for the twentieth time to sell tickets because they're playing Detroit, a last-place club." But Joe never said "no," and he looked forward to going to the Old Timers games and to the tributes he received. He also had a genuine affection for Steinbrenner.

DiMaggio's presence at those get-togethers of retired Yankees players always gave a big boost to ticket sales. Marty Appel, a former Yankees public relations director, said that was the reason DiMaggio's requests for tickets were always honored. In his book, *Now Pitching for the Yankees: Spinning the News for Mickey, Billy, and George*, Appel told of Joe's telephone calls one summer for freebies to be left at the "Will Call" window—two for a cab driver, two for the doorman at the Americana Hotel. Joe was always cordial and very polite, Appel said. "If it's a problem just say so," or "Marty, old buddy, if there is a problem, I will understand." This went on all week, and Appel was elated at the wonderful first-name relationship he and DiMaggio had established. He was eagerly anticipating a face-to-face meeting with the "legend of legends" one Saturday. When DiMaggio arrived, Appel thrust out his hand, and introduced himself. Joe never broke stride as he passed him.

At the Old Timers games, DiMaggio always took the first seat in the dugout. You would have thought he had a contagious disease, because no one wanted to sit next to him—not Rizzuto, who adored him; not Berra; not Henrich; and certainly not Mantle, who always seemed edgy in his presence. Maybe they were afraid to talk with him. I don't know, but I always hesitated to sit with Joe on those occasions because I felt awkward being on that bench when all those old Yankees stars were standing. But Joe would motion for me to take the spot next to him.

DiMaggio and Mantle played together for only one season, 1951, and they were never close. Years after both had retired, they were at the same card show in Atlantic City, and DiMaggio was in a suite doing private signings. Mantle approached the table and greeted Joe. DiMaggio finished the autograph he was signing, glanced up for a second, responded with a quick, "Hi, Mickey," and went back to what he was doing. At another show, Joe was bent over a table signing a ball when he was told, "Mickey is here." His response: "Mickey who?" DiMaggio was annoyed that Mantle did not conform to the role of being a retired Yankees great. He rolled his eyes when Mickey showed up in the Yankees skybox at an Old Timers Day wearing what Joe considered inappropriate attire, black jeans and a black golf jacket, and with his arm around a woman who was his agent and "lady friend." That was Joe's noble way of describing her. It was no secret that Mickey cheated on his wife, but Joe thought it was in bad taste for him to openly flaunt his behavior.

Mantle must have sensed Joe's feeling. When the two shook hands that particular afternoon, Mickey turned his head to avoid eye contact. Wherever DiMaggio sat or went in the skybox, Mantle's eyes followed him, and Mickey went out of his way to avoid getting close to him. Although Mantle was no admirer, he made it no secret that he was in awe of what DiMaggio had done as a player.

Longtime Yankees fans still debate who was the better center fielder, DiMaggio or Mantle. Mickey believed that DiMaggio was the best ever to play the position, for any team and at any time. He marveled at Joe's instinctive abilities when it came to chasing down a fly ball, his base-running skills, and maybe most of all, the fact that he struck out so few times. "He had only eight less homers than strikeouts," Mantle pointed out in discussing Joe's batting skills. He was right; Joe hit 361 home runs and struck out a mere 369 times in 13 seasons. Mickey confessed to his closest buddies after a few beers that his own speed in the outfield and on the bases was hampered by his leg injuries, and that he struck out "too many damn times." One of the friends he told that to was Whitey Ford, a teammate of both DiMaggio and Mantle. The pitcher was much closer to Mantle because they were drinking buddies, and Ford would always assure Mantle that he was the better of the two. "The truth is, Mickey was right. DiMaggio was better," the Hall of Fame left-hander later conceded, with the wisdom of a man in his seventies. DiMaggio would have chuckled at that. He usually referred to Whitey by his nickname, "Slick."

At the 1995 Old Timers Day, less than a month before Mantle died, I sat with Steinbrenner, watching the events on television. Steinbrenner told me that Mickey made a videotape from his Dallas hospital room that would be shown on the large video screen above the bleachers. I wondered, under the circumstances, if Mickey would replace DiMaggio for the honor of being the last one introduced, but Mantle's video was played before Joe was introduced. The ovation understandably was loud and long because everyone knew Mantle was dying. Then Joe was introduced, and the crowd's reaction was explosive and prolonged. "Joe always does that, no matter what," Steinbrenner said. I responded, "That's because he is the greatest and most loyal Yankee of all."

◆ ◆ ◆

Of all the special days for Joe at Yankee Stadium, the most memorable was the last one, on September 27, 1998, only weeks before his cancer surgery. The celebration in 1991, however, also stands out because it commemorated the fiftieth anniversary of DiMaggio's 56-game hitting streak. The Yankees planned to give him a Chrysler LeBaron convertible. That definitely was the wrong car for a seventy-seven-year-old grandfather, and that's what I conveyed to the Yankees. Joe didn't like convertibles; he thought they were dangerous. He had been driving a ten-year-old Toyota Camry around the San Francisco area, so what would be a fitting replacement? How about a 420 SEL Mercedes? George Steinbrenner did not even blink when he approved the purchase of the $75,000 car. It was a knockout model, white with a Yankee-blue pinstripe and a small "NY" logo on the driver's side of the rear fender. DiMaggio's former teammates lined up to watch the presentation. Mantle whispered out of the side of his mouth to Ford,

"I'm not so sure he'll take it. He's going to check to see if it has a full tank of gas."

Joe made himself available for a news conference before the ceremony, which surprised the press and me. He chided the younger reporters for some of their questions, saying they weren't even born when he retired, and he refused to answer other questions because they were repeats. But his mood turned brighter when he spotted Henrich, who had played so important a role in the hitting streak. "Where are my 1941 teammates? Come on up here." He described how each had been helpful during the streak.

After the presentation of the car, DiMaggio made a speech, but not the one he and I had collaborated on. He took note of his teammates' contributions during those memorable 56 games, as he had planned, but then he ignored the script and summoned Rizzuto, a teammate from the 1941 team. He put his arm around Phil, then a Yankees' broadcaster, and called him one of the greatest shortstops of all time. "I should know," Joe said. "I watched him from behind from 1941 through 1951." Then he announced, "Phil, you are my Hall of Famer." That quote was a headline the next day in a New York tabloid. Joe made that rare public endorsement to say thanks to a guy who had been a buddy for many years, but he also wanted to send a message to the Hall of Fame Veterans Committee, which had passed up Rizzuto year after year in its voting. Charlie Gehringer, a Hall of Fame second baseman, was a member of the committee, and DiMaggio blamed him for blocking Rizzuto as well as Tony Lazzeri. Joe was convinced that Gehringer didn't like Italians. Earlier that year, Lazzeri finally did receive enough votes from the Veterans Committee to gain entrance to the Hall, and Joe was determined that Rizzuto would follow. The repeated snubs made Rizzuto an underdog in DiMaggio's mind and, therefore, a cause to champion. Three years later, the committee finally voted Rizzuto into the shrine at Cooperstown, New York. DiMaggio's backing found a sympa-

This rare photo shows Lou Gehrig high-jumping over a bat held by DiMaggio in some training camp foolery in 1937. Gehrig won DiMaggio's admiration, mostly for his ability to drive in runs. *Courtesy Frank LaBono*

A young Joe poses with his father, Giuseppe, and younger brother Dom.
Author's Collection

Frank Crosetti, Tony Lazzeri, and Joe DiMaggio (left to right) were buddies
from the day the three of them drove from San Francisco to Joe's first spring
training in Florida in 1936. *Bettmann/Corbis*

Ty Cobb poses with his arms around DiMaggio brothers Joe (left) and Dom at Seals Stadium in San Francisco. Joe, who was already with the Yankees at this time, donned the uniform of his old minor league team for an exhibition game. At the far right is another former Seals standout, Lefty O'Doul. Cobb and O'Doul were important influences on Joe in his early years. *Author's Collection*

This autographed photo, signed for my fifty-second birthday, shows Joe sliding home in the tenth inning of the final game of the 1939 World Series against the Cincinnati Reds. Reds catcher Ernie Lombardi had been bowled over by Charlie Keller moments earlier and is taking what became known as the "Schnozz's Snooze." *Author's Collection*

In 1946, the Yankees started spring training in Panama. DiMaggio's friend Joe Nachio, in hat and glasses, lived in Panama and had a lot to do with bringing the Yankees there. Standing to the right of Nachio is Yankee pitcher Joe Page. Seated, from left to right, are two unidentified players, followed by outfielder Gene Woodling, catcher Bill Dickey, DiMaggio, manager Joe McCarthy, second baseman Joe Gordon, and shortstop Phil Rizzuto. *Courtesy Joe Nachio*

Two legendary Yankee center fielders pose together at an exhibition game before the 1951 season. It was Mickey Mantle and Joe DiMaggio's only year as teammates, as "the Mick" took over the center-field job the following season, after Joe's retirement. *AP/Wide World Photos*

DiMaggio thanks the Yankee Stadium crowd and the Yankees organization for the truckloads of gifts he received on Joe DiMaggio Day in 1949. Famed Yankee broadcaster Mel Allen is standing just to Joe's left. *AP/Wide World Photos*

Joe enjoys a nice plate of homemade spaghetti, courtesy of Mama Rosalie DiMaggio, in their San Francisco kitchen. *Author's Collection*

Joe is the center of adoration at a family gathering at the Beach Street house in San Francisco that Joe bought for his parents in 1936. Poppa Giuseppe and Mama Rosalie DiMaggio beam at their son and grandchildren. DiMaggio's siblings complete the picture. Brother Dom is second from the right, next to Rosalie. *Private Collection*

The DiMaggio family reunited for Christmas 1945, as Joe celebrates with his ex-wife, Dorothy Arnold, and their four-year-old son, Joe Jr. There was talk of a reconciliation, but it never happened. Arnold married stockbroker George Schubert several months later. *Courtesy Gerald Stern*

Although Joe Jr. said that he and his father were "from different planets," they did have some touching moments together. Here the two frolic in the sun and surf on vacation. *Courtesy Robert Solotaire*

The DiMaggios had been fishermen for generations, starting on the waters off Sicily. As a teenager, Joe complained that the smell of fish and the waves made him queasy, and he elected not to follow in the family tradition—much to his father's disappointment. Joe apparently overcame those problems enough to become an avid sports fisherman. *Author's Collection*

Joe takes some batting practice with his brothers behind the family restaurant on San Francisco's Fisherman's Wharf. Brothers Tom and Mike make up the well-dressed pitcher-catcher battery. An overturned ice bucket serves as home plate. *Author's Collection*

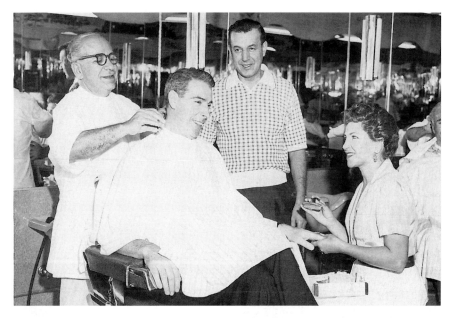

Joe Nachio once said of his close friend Joe DiMaggio, "There are three things I would not want to be: his tailor, his barber, or his driver." Here Joe appears to be thoroughly enjoying the pampering. *Author's Collection*

DiMaggio sits with his friend George Solotaire, Broadway's number one ticket broker (left), and famed Hearst columnist Walter Winchell (right) during a day at the races. *Courtesy Robert Solotaire*

Joe proudly escorts his movie-star wife Marilyn Monroe, at the New York premiere of *The Seven Year Itch* in June 1955. Joe puts on a grace and charm that hide his strong feelings of disapproval of that film's most famous scene, in which Marilyn's skirt billows up provocatively as she stands on a subway grate. *AP/Wide World Photos*

Joe strolls hand-in-hand with ex-wife Marilyn on a beach near Sarasota,
Florida. She had just left a New York hospital, where she was treated for drug
and alcohol addiction. DiMaggio had tipped off AP photographer Harry Harris
that Marilyn would be with him on that beach for this exclusive photo op.
AP/Wide World Photos

Joe DiMaggio and Frank Sinatra were honorees at a party at the Italian Embassy in 1958. These two celebrated Italian-Americans were close for a period, but had a falling out in the early 1960s as a result of Sinatra's romantic involvement with Marilyn Monroe. *Author's Collection*

thetic ear when Ted Williams was put on the committee, although Williams always had been a strong Rizzuto booster anyway. "We would have got into the Series more than we did if we had [had] Phil on our team," he said.

Rizzuto, who hit .307 as a rookie in 1941, had a 16-game hitting streak the same year as DiMaggio's 56-game run. "No one knew, though, except me and my mother," he said.

Phil also had a special role in the story of the streak-ending game. As usual, DiMaggio was among the last players left in the clubhouse that night. He asked Rizzuto to wait for him, and the rookie was delighted to have been asked. "We walked up the hill toward the Cleveland Hotel," Rizzuto recalled, "and he never moaned or second-guessed about those two plays Keltner had made." On the way to the hotel, the two passed a bar and grill. "Joe said he was going in, and when I made a move to join him, he said he wanted to be alone. Alone? The place was packed with Indians fans. I hadn't gone 20 feet when I heard him yell for me. He had forgotten to get his wallet from the trainer's trunk, where we locked our valuables before the games. He asked how much money I had. I had eighteen bucks, which was all I needed for a two-week road trip. He borrowed it and went into the bar. He never paid me back. When he heard I was telling that story, he offered me the $18, but I said, 'Forget it. You'll ruin a good story.'"

About the Mercedes he received at the fifty-year celebration, Joe didn't want to pay to have the car shipped to Florida, so it was driven there. Then he fretted about the income tax he would have to pay on the $75,000 list price, so an arrangement was made in which some Mercedes dealers got together to give him the car as a gift. Joe never had any of his cars washed or waxed, because "that was a waste of money," and he made no exception for the expensive white Mercedes. He would wait for a heavy south Florida downpour to do the job. His lack of attention to that beautiful car troubled me, so when he was out of town for an extended period, I would have it washed and waxed. He didn't know about it and never noticed the difference.

DiMaggio had the toughest time pumping gas into that car, and many times the attendants would take pity on him and do it for him. I suggested that he use the full-service section in the stations, but he balked. "I'm not going to give them that extra money just to hold that hose for me."

Incidentally, I hated the color white for a car, but after Joe got his, I, too, bought a white Mercedes. Soon after he died, I went back to a black one. I'm embarrassed to say that's how much I wanted to curry favor with him. He said black cars were dangerous to drive because "no one can see them at night."

◆ ◆ ◆

In addition to the Yankee Stadium celebration, another event marking the fiftieth anniversary of the hitting streak was the unveiling of a bronze statue of Joe DiMaggio at the National Italian-American Sports Hall of Fame, then located in Arlington Heights outside Chicago. Keltner was brought from a convalescent home in Wisconsin for the ceremony. "What the hell is he doing here?" DiMaggio asked when he spotted the man whose two great plays helped end the streak. Keltner hobbled over to Joe with the help of a cane, and they shook hands. "You know, Kenny, you were lucky it rained that morning," DiMaggio said. "You never would have stopped those balls."

Joe had been inducted into the Italian-American Sports Hall in September 1978. He was the pride of the organization, and a huge pain in the neck to its founder, George Randazzo. Among those inducted with Joe were his brother Dom, jockey Eddie Arcaro, football players Gino Marchetti and Charlie Trippi, and the late Vince Lombardi. Despite the impressive list of names, the success of the event hinged on Joe agreeing to be there. A friend who knew DiMaggio wrote to him that Randazzo would contact him at a Chicago housewares show, where Joe was to make an appearance for Mr. Coffee. When Randazzo got there, scores of people were lined up at the Mr. Coffee booth. Randazzo made his way through the line and introduced himself to the man who had been his boyhood hero. DiMaggio glared and snapped, "Nobody tells Joe DiMaggio where to go and when to be there." Randazzo had no idea what DiMaggio was talking about, and told him so. Later, when Joe saw Randazzo on the fringe of the crowd around the booth, he approached him and announced, "You have a fifty-fifty chance." Thus began what for Randazzo was a nerve-wracking relationship that lasted twenty years.

DiMaggio's induction was to take place at a sold-out dinner at a Holiday Inn in Chicago. Randazzo did not know for sure until after 1:00 A.M. that day that Joe would be there. DiMaggio was in New Orleans watching Muhammad Ali regain his heavyweight title from Leon Spinks, and Randazzo left airline tickets at the airport, praying that Joe would pick them up. Meanwhile, at the hotel, the prime suite was readied and personnel were alerted, including the food manager. At 1:30 A.M. the phone rang in Randazzo's room. Joe had arrived. Thank God! Randazzo rushed to the lobby and introduced himself. "I welcome you on behalf of the National Italian-American Sports Hall of Fame. . . ." DiMaggio's reply was succinct, "Don't give me none of your bullshit."

One of DiMaggio's closest friends in Chicago at the time was Don Ponte, the Pizza King, who owned the Midwest Cheese Company, supplier to all the pizzerias in Chicago. Ponte was the eager, generous, fun-loving host whenever DiMaggio came to town. He knew that Joe would be hungry after that late-night trip from New Orleans, so he had a monstrous seafood platter sent to Joe's suite, including huge shrimp, cold lobster, scungilli salad, and calamari. There was no way that DiMaggio, even with his huge appetite, could eat all that, so Ponte invited two women from the Gaslight Club to join them. Joe's voracious appetite was sated.

The next morning, Randazzo and some of his associates were in the hotel coffee shop when DiMaggio arrived and sat alone in a booth. A man quickly slid into the seat opposite Joe, and his conversation starter included the words "Marilyn Monroe." Nearby was Tony Derango, a 6-foot-4, 300-pound Chicago police officer. He knew that Marilyn was a subject DiMaggio would not deal with, and he pounced. With one huge hand on the guy's shirt collar and the other on the seat of his pants, Derango lifted the man from the booth and carried him to the door. He returned to introduce himself and assured Joe, "While you're here you don't have to worry about anyone bothering you."

DiMaggio usually showed up at the organization's annual dinner and mingled with the likes of Tony LaRussa, Alan Ameche, Lou Carnesseca, Willie Pep, Rocky Graziano, and Boom Boom Mancini, but Joe was ambivalent about his Italian heritage. "He wasn't a card-carrying Italian," said Rock Positano. "He told me, 'Beware of those guys who say, Hey, we're *paisans*. Those are the guys you want to avoid.'" Yet, from the time he drove across country with Frank Crosetti and Tony Lazzeri, he was more comfortable with the likes of Berra, Martin, and Rizzuto. Joe was wary of people he thought might be prejudiced against Italians, and he would describe himself as "just another Italian baseball player."

Joe held a special place in the Italian-American community, and he played a role that was uniquely Italian, according to Pellegrino D'Acierno. The professor of Italian culture described DiMaggio as "*La Bella Figura*," a fine or beautiful figure. He displayed that attribute in the way he carried himself and played, a studied nonchalance, being above the fray. He rarely, if ever, would argue an umpire's decision or get into a fight on the field. He would not use profane language in the presence of women. Not only would he not swear if women were in his company, but if someone else did, the offender would suffer the "Sicilian stare." DiMaggio dressed as a *bella figura* should. No matter how hot the weather, his suit was always neatly pressed, the jacket correctly buttoned, his tie carefully knotted, and his shoes perfectly self-shined. (In all the years I knew him, I never saw him pay for a shoeshine.)

His gestures regarding money reflected this special image. He declined the $100,000 offered by Dan Topping to play one more year with the Yankees in 1952 because he was no longer the Joe DiMaggio he had been. He rejected $2 million to cooperate on an autobiography because it would have meant sharing with the public his private thoughts about Marilyn Monroe. He picked up the tab at dinner with some rookie teammates because he was making a Joe DiMaggio salary, which was much more than they were getting. It was the right thing for a man of his stature to do. The same was true of tipping generously. While he was reluctant to pay to have his shoes shined or his car washed, he gave airport skycaps $5 or $10 to carry one bag. Image was everything.

Should someone of equal stature want to pick up the tab, however, that was all right with him. He regarded it as a tribute to *La Bella Figura*.

DiMaggio was regarded as *La Bella Figura* for as long as he lived, and that set him apart from other Italian sports heroes. Kathleen Salvo remembered the first time he appeared in her Italian pastry shop in Hackensack, New Jersey. "I was busy behind the counter and I heard this buzz from the customers. It was different from the usual chatter that goes on. I looked up and saw this old, gray-haired man, who was very well dressed. Like a count. A woman whispered to me, 'Joe DiMaggio.' I thought, 'Boy, he got old.' But he was so distinguished. He was standing there, waiting his turn, and all the people around him did everything but bow. 'I heard you have very good lemon ice,' he said. Everyone watched while he tasted it. 'Well, it is very good,' he said. He offered to pay, but how could I take money from Joe DiMaggio? He took a $5 bill from his wallet and put it in the cup for tips."

Whenever DiMaggio returned for Salvo's lemon ice, word quickly got around the Hudson Street neighborhood. People would rush in to see him, and soon Kathleen was ripping blank bills off the pad near the cash register so her friends and customers could get his autograph. He never refused anyone in the store.

Once we were just getting into a car in lower Manhattan when an Italian woman, dressed in black, as the widows did in those days, approached him as he sat down. She bent into the car, grabbed his hands and kissed them. She said, in accented English, that she would rather kiss his hands than the pope's. Rattled, DiMaggio didn't know what to say, so he asked her, "Would you like an autograph?"

There were times when Joe was not sought after for being the great ballplayer. He also was the husband and lover of Marilyn Monroe. It was in that role that he was invited to Argentina, but he didn't realize that until he got to Buenos Aires and found that all the questions had to do with Marilyn. He didn't care for that, of course. Nachio, who accompanied him on the trip, explained that soccer was numero uno, dos, and tres in that country. Baseball was nowhere. DiMaggio became cranky and his ulcer acted up. That was a problem when it came to dinner. Joe's ulcer wanted him to eat at 6:00 P.M., but in Buenos Aires, dinnertime is about 10:00 P.M., and that's when he was invited to dine. When he complained about that, Nachio told him, "When you are in Rome, you have to do as the Romans do." DiMaggio replied, "I'm never a Roman, I'm Sicilian, and I want to eat now." They were the guests that night of a businessman who owned a racetrack, and he had invited some other prominent people to meet DiMaggio. Nachio's plea about honoring Argentine tradition went unheeded, and the two of them left the party and walked to an Italian restaurant. About the only thing Joe liked about Buenos Aires was that there were places to get good southern Italian cuisine. "Mucha salsa tomate, por favor," he learned to say.

No matter what city he was in, Joe always seemed to be drawn to an Italian neighborhood. Sometimes, he found his way into somebody's dining room or kitchen for a home-cooked Italian meal. Frank LaBono, the visiting team batboy for the Indians in the 1940s, invited Joe to his parents' modest Cleveland apartment for a spaghetti dinner. DiMaggio accepted on the condition that there be no crowd. "He really enjoyed the dinner, and then when we came downstairs, there was a crowd of people asking him to sign pieces of paper. My father said he just told the guy who ran the gas station on the corner."

◆ ◆ ◆

Joe often wondered why all the fuss. "I'm just an Italian ballplayer," he would say. Of course, he was much more than that. He was a baseball deity, called on whenever something special was happening. When the Florida Marlins were brought into the majors in 1993, DiMaggio was invited to throw out the first ball at their inaugural home game. "I'll be an American Leaguer throwing out a National League ball, but I'll do it, because it's historic," he said.

Joe got a ride to the game in a Florida Highway Patrol car driven by officer Peter Cohen, who was born in Brooklyn, not too far from where I had grown up. He had driven Joe before and was DiMaggio's favorite Florida cop. Joe got another kick at the ballpark when he met Charlie Silvera, who had been a backup catcher when Joe played for the Yankees. The ball for the pitch was delivered to DiMaggio by FedEx, and he marched out to the mound dressed for the occasion in a dark suit and tie.

Benito Santiago, the Marlins catcher, caught the ceremonial ball and returned it to DiMaggio. Joe felt that ball had an historic importance, so he wanted to put a special message on it. We sat in the VIP box where he wrote and then rewrote something on a piece of paper until he had it just right. When he finally was satisfied, he wrote the message on the ball along with his signature. "This is very important," he told me. "It will be in the Hall of Fame."

He proudly handed the ball to the Marlins owner, Wayne Huizenga, who put it in his pocket without even glancing at it and walked away. Joe was stunned. "Fuck him. He's no baseball man. He doesn't even know what I just gave him." His rare use of profanity told me that Joe really was angry. He asked me for another ball, on which he wrote the same message: "This is the official first ball thrown out for the Miami Marlins franchise." No great prose, but he was satisfied. "This is the real one; the other is a fake," he declared. He didn't think much of Huizenga after that, and he said the Blockbuster Video owner was not fit to own a baseball team. Joe's assessment proved right on target when Huizenga decimated the Marlins after they won the World Series in 1997. He made a lot of money from the fire-sale deals, and then sold the club for $150 million. He had paid $95 million for the franchise.

On the other hand, DiMaggio thought that George W. Bush knew baseball when he was a part owner of the Texas Rangers. Joe was invited to the 1995 All-Star Game at The Ballpark in Arlington, Texas, which was built while Bush was one of the owners. By that time, George W. was governor of Texas, and he was at the game as an interested observer. We had front-row seats at the railing, which Joe warned me were in the danger zone for foul balls. "If a ball comes this way, duck underneath the railing. Don't move to the side, just duck, and fast." I wondered if we were being used as shields for Bush and Commissioner Bud Selig, who were seated behind us. I was seated between Joe and retired pitcher Nolan Ryan, the most famous Ranger of them all. I had met Ryan some time before that, and as we chatted during the game, he asked, "Is Joe mad at me? He hasn't said a word." I explained, "No, that's just the way he is." Joe was busy eating. A young lady was stationed at his side in the aisle for the sole purpose of providing him with ice cream, popcorn, peanuts, and pretzels.

Leaving a game with Joe was a chore because you had to get through all the autograph seekers and people who wanted to shake his hand. Joe rejected my suggestion that we leave early, because he wanted to see Jeff Conine hit. Conine, then with the Marlins, had been active in fundraising for the Joe DiMaggio Children's Hospital, and the two often had lunch together. Conine homered in the eighth inning and put the National League in front 3–2. Joe loved it, and so did the crowd, which gave Conine a rousing ovation, even though the homer would beat the American League that night. DiMaggio waited until Conine acknowledged the cheers before he left. He didn't want the stir that always accompanied his departure to detract from Conine's moment. Back at the hotel, like a proud uncle, DiMaggio switched from one TV channel to another to see Conine being interviewed. Meanwhile, I wrung sweat from the long-sleeve white shirt I had worn in temperatures that must have hit 100 degrees. DiMaggio had worn a suit and tie that night, which meant I did, too.

One trip I didn't make with Joe, to my great regret, was to Baltimore to see Cal Ripken break Lou Gehrig's record for consecutive games played. Ripken was DiMaggio's type of player, a throwback to the old days. It would be another blue-suit night, and Joe wanted to make a speech befitting the occasion. As we worked on it, he assured me he would read it rather than wing it, as he did most often. Read it he did, because of the event's importance. He felt he was representing his old teammate Gehrig that night. Ripken put icing on the cake by hitting a home run, which Joe saw as evidence of Cal's ability to rise to the occasion when the pressure was on. The Orioles infielder displayed that ability again in his final All-Star Game in 2001. In his first at-bat, after stepping out of the batter's box to acknowledge a standing ovation, he hit a home run.

Derek Jeter of the Yankees was another player DiMaggio admired for playing well under pressure. But his choice as the best all-around player at the turn of the century was Ken Griffey Jr. of the Reds. Joe admired Griffey's ability to hit and field. He complained that the quality of fielding had declined in the majors.

On the subject of fielding, Joe dissolved into laughter when he described Jose Canseco getting hit on the head by a fly ball when he was with the Texas Rangers. We got off the elevator on a visit to DiMaggio's urologist, Joel Martin, and Joe was telling me about a game he had seen on television the previous night. He ran down the hallway and almost crashed into a wall as he re-enacted the scene, which ended with the ball bouncing off Canseco's head and into the stands for a home run. I didn't think it was that funny, but DiMaggio couldn't stop laughing. He liked Canseco, because he played in the fundraiser games for the Joe DiMaggio Children's Hospital, and he admired the outfielder's power, especially on the golf course. Joe was in a golf course locker room after playing a round when the place was shaken by a clap of thunder. "Must be Canseco on the eighteenth tee," Joe said.

DiMaggio would never knock another player in public, but he was not shy about expressing his opinion in the privacy of our conversations. Mark McGwire did not make DiMaggio's All-Star team. "That's all he does, hit home runs," Joe said as we watched McGwire during the season he set the record with 70. "Look where the Cards will finish this year." They wound up fourth in their division, and the next two years, even with McGwire hitting homers, they were third and fourth again.

"Just look at those pitches," DiMaggio complained. "Right down the middle. It's like batting practice. If Bobby Feller were out there, or Allie Reynolds, he wouldn't be smacking those homers. They would dust him off, throw him inside, throw at his head. He wouldn't have been allowed to hit so many homers in my day."

Winning games was not about swinging for the seats all the time, Joe said. "Getting on base by a walk, even getting hit by a pitch, stretching that extra base, moving up a base runner, punching the ball to the opposite field, that's what wins games. How many times have you seen McGwire do that?"

DiMaggio was in Mama Mia's restaurant in Hollywood, Florida, watching television when McGwire hit number 62 to break Roger Maris' record. Everyone in the crowded place had been trying not to stare at Joe, but when that home run was hit, all restraint vanished and heads turned to see his reaction. He was worthy of his old Seals nickname, "Deadpan Joe."

◆ ◆ ◆

Among all of baseball's greats and near-greats, the player perhaps most closely associated with Joe DiMaggio was Ted Williams. They were paired as heroes of the same generation, legends who both left the game in their prime to serve their country during wartime. As a Yankee and a Red Sox, they were on opposite sides in one of the game's oldest rivalries, and they played on the same side in nine All-Star Games. In retirement, they were also brought together at many Old Timers games. Once they were driven onto the field in separate golf carts and circled the park in different directions until they met at home plate, to the delight of the crowd.

Williams marveled at DiMaggio's all-around ability as a hitter and outfielder. "I never saw him look bad," he said, "and he made it look so easy." Some fans, especially those in New England, were upset when DiMaggio won the MVP award in 1941 ahead of Williams. That was the year of Joe's 56-game hitting streak, but it was also the year Williams hit .406, making him the last major leaguer to hit over .400. Williams also led the league with 37 homers, while DiMaggio was tops in RBIs, with 125, and he led the

Yankees to another pennant. Williams had no argument with the baseball writers' selection of DiMaggio. "I didn't feel robbed or cheated," he told sportswriter Joe Durso in the biography, *DiMaggio: The Last American Knight.* "DiMaggio had that 56-game hitting streak, and he was a great player on a great team." It's also interesting to note that although Williams struck out only 27 times in 1941, DiMaggio struck out a mere 13 times.

With all the connections between them, DiMaggio's views on Ted Williams surprised me. DiMaggio said the two had little in common other than the number 9, which Joe wore on his jersey when he first joined the Yankees and which was Williams' number throughout his career. "Ted Williams' greatest fan is Ted Williams himself," Joe said. He felt Williams tooted his own horn to try to bolster the argument that he was the greatest hitter of all time. "He was a great hitter, but there's no such thing as the greatest in any sport," DiMaggio asserted. Through the years Joe was quoted as saying Williams was the greatest left-handed hitter or even the greatest hitter, but chances are he never said either. In Joe's opinion, Lou Gehrig, Babe Ruth, Rogers Hornsby, and Ty Cobb were better hitters than Williams. "Tell him to hold up his hands." That was DiMaggio's way of pointing out that the Red Sox never won a World Series in the Williams years. "Where are the rings?" he asked. DiMaggio's nine championship rings could fill both hands, minus a thumb. He measured his own success not by his individual statistics, but rather by the Yankees win-loss record in his thirteen years.

He thought Williams was a selfish player because he concentrated on one thing, his hitting, and neglected trying to improve his base running and fielding. Joe agreed when Williams said that if he didn't have Dom in center field, he would have been in big trouble.

Tommy Henrich, the Yankees right fielder from 1939 to 1951, told me that in a clutch situation—runners on base, two out in the ninth inning, and his team trailing by one run—he would pick DiMaggio over Williams as the hitter he wanted at the plate. Tommy really didn't answer my question, "How would you compare the two as hitters?" But he felt that when the game was on the line, DiMaggio saw it as his responsibility, and he came out swinging. Joe didn't care if the pitch was two feet off home plate or a foot off, he was swinging. Williams, by contrast, would settle for a walk. When he was playing, nobody on the Red Sox even came close to getting the number of walks that Williams did, and half a century after he retired, he still held the team record for bases on balls in a season. Henrich agreed with Joe that Williams was too concerned about his batting average.

Despite DiMaggio's feelings about Williams, and even though he was bitter that Ted never showed up for the Legends Game benefit for his hospital, Joe attended the opening of the Ted Williams Museum in Hernando, Florida. He believed the place was created purely as a commercial venture by a Boston realtor to draw people to that obscure, out-of-the-way area of Florida, but he went because he was concerned that his absence would generate speculation that he was jealous of Ted.

For Joe, a highlight of that trip to Hernando was the twenty-minute ride with Stan Musial from the hotel to the museum. Musial took out his harmonica and asked for requests. He said he could play fifty tunes. Joe wanted his favorite, "Take Me Out to the Ball Game." Musial played it and Joe sang it. What a Hall of Fame duet that was.

I noted that Musial was wearing a World Series ring that day. "The only reason he has it is because of me, because I had a poor World Series," DiMaggio said. The only World Series that the Yankees lost of the ten in which DiMaggio played was in 1942, when the Cardinals won in five games, taking the last four. DiMaggio had three hits in the opener, but just four in the last four games. "Well, at least he's got more rings than Ted,"

DiMaggio said. Musial laughed, knowing how much importance Joe placed on those World Series rings. In addition to his 1942 ring and the one from 1944, when the Cardinals beat the Browns, Musial earned a championship ring in 1946, when Stan's Cardinals topped Ted's Red Sox in seven games.

The dedication ceremony for the Ted Williams Museum was held in a tent set up for the occasion. Joe was asked to speak about Williams' prowess as a hitter. That was expected, but unexpected was DiMaggio's place in the procession preceding the speeches. Joe was asked to walk in with Ted. I thought that honor would have gone to Williams' son, John Henry, but DiMaggio had it all figured out. "Ted thought that if I walked in with you," he told me, "I might get a louder ovation than he would get if he was escorted by John Henry."

On the flight home, I asked Joe if Williams would make his all-time all-star team of nine players, not counting himself. He didn't answer, but at the 1997 World Series, he commented that if he had to include a current player in the outfield, Griffey Jr. would be his choice to join Babe Ruth and Ty Cobb.

Joe would have made Pete Rose an infielder on that team for his hitting, fielding, and attitude. Rose was brash and abrasive, much like Billy Martin. But Joe shook his head in despair when he talked about Rose's fondness for gambling, whether it was betting on sports or tossing piles of chips onto the casino tables in Atlantic City. Joe got to know Rose when they visited U.S. troops in Vietnam, along with Jerry Coleman, Tony Conigliaro of the Red Sox, and Yankees PR director Bob Fishel. Joe was as popular with the soldiers in Vietnam as he had been with those in Korea nearly twenty years earlier.

"It was embarrassing," Coleman said. "Joe had been retired for sixteen or seventeen years and all those kids were nineteen and twenty, but the only one they wanted to see was Joe DiMaggio. I said to Pete, 'Hey, what are we doing here?' That was before Pete Rose became *the* Pete Rose."

"Hey, the world's greatest player, let's get going," Rose would needle him, and Joe got a big kick out of it. Pete said the only reason he agreed to the trip was that he felt it would give him a chance to really get to know DiMaggio. He admitted that when they ventured to where the sound of gunfire could be heard, he was frightened. "But Joe wasn't, so I figured everything would be OK." DiMaggio was at ease strolling through the hospital wards, talking with the wounded, some sitting in chairs, others flat on their backs in bed and encased in bandages and casts.

◆ ◆ ◆

Joe was not a flag-waver, but he considered visiting the nation's troops to be his patriotic duty. I saw an example of his patriotism at my daughter Laurie's wedding. One of my daughter's friends, Lisa Stein, had flown combat missions with the Air Force during Desert Storm, and she was introduced at the reception. DiMaggio had been the main attraction up to that point, in his white yarmulke, seated at table number five. But suddenly Lisa was in the spotlight, and a feeling of patriotism swept over the gathering. My family and guests, including Joe, rose to their feet and sang "God Bless America." He was moved by the scene and told me, "She got a bigger ovation than I did, and she deserved it."

Joe chatted with the other guests and, as usual, was a big hit. He preferred person-to-person talks to formal after-dinner speeches because he was uneasy in front of large audiences, especially in the days before he retired. As he grew older, though, he became an accomplished speaker, and he enjoyed doing it. Joe traced his early reticence to his lack of education. He worried that he would use a wrong word or say something that would betray him as a high school dropout. After he retired as a player, he educated himself about current events and financial affairs by reading newspapers and books and by watching the all-news cable TV stations and C-SPAN.

Still, he never felt completely at ease when interacting with people who were highly educated. Money had nothing to do with it, since he accumulated more wealth than most of the intellectuals and professionals with whom he came in contact.

In D'Acierno's opinion, DiMaggio's silence was culturally based and had little, if anything, to do with any feelings of inferiority stemming from his lack of formal education. The professor reasoned that DiMaggio was acting from his Sicilian background and its practice of *omerta*, which the Mafia adapted into its code of silence. *Omerta* was the closed-lipped manner in which Sicilians dealt with outsiders: "What I am saying is nobody's business but mine and my family's." D'Acierno also noted that DiMaggio came from a home where language was a problem. His parents had difficulty with English, and Joe, typical of first-generation Italians born in the United States, had problems with the Sicilian dialect his mother and father spoke, so he solved it by saying little.

DiMaggio made a major leap in overcoming feelings of inadequacy about his education, whatever their origin, in 1995 when the Lotos Club, one of the country's most prestigious literary organizations, honored him with a state dinner. The Lotos Club was founded in 1870 "to promote social intercourse among journalists, literary men, artists, members of the musical and dramatic professions and such merchants and professional gentlemen of artistic tastes and inclinations." The list of those previously honored with state dinners included Mark Twain, Oliver Wendell Holmes, Ulysses S. Grant, Harry Truman, Dwight Eisenhower, Leonard Bernstein, Helen Hayes, and Arthur Miller. The Lotos Club wanted someone special to mark its 125th anniversary, and DiMaggio was the one selected, although he couldn't quite figure out why. "I'm just an Italian baseball player."

After being told he was the first athlete to be honored, he asked if any other Italian had been given a state dinner. He was told that Enrico Caruso had been so honored. Being teamed up with the great tenor was good enough for Joe, and he accepted the invitation.

Despite the bitterly cold night, the clubhouse just off Fifth Avenue was packed for the black-tie event. The ballroom was not large enough to accommodate the crowd, so the double doors were left open and tables were set up in the foyer where the speeches could be watched on closed-circuit television. The audience was made up mostly of men. Writer Kitty Kelley, one of the few women to grace the assemblage, explained, "Many wives gave up seats to sons and grandsons." Kelley surrendered her place to no one, and with her husband, she joined the reception line for a chance to shake hands with the man with the so-recognizable face and the "perfect silver hair." DiMaggio stood there for an hour until everyone had a chance to shake his hand and chat. Kelley said the man in front of her told Joe that his grandmother had prayed for him during the hitting streak.

Electricity was in the air as the event began with speeches by New York Mayor Rudolph Giuliani and former Yankees Phil Rizzuto and Bobby Brown. Rizzuto said DiMaggio was his security blanket on the field. "When I turned around and saw Joe in center field, looking tense and ready for the pitch, I knew we could win, even if we were losing by nine runs in the eighth inning."

When Phil came up to the Yankees in 1941 from the sidewalks of New York, DiMaggio was his idol, and being his teammate didn't change Rizzuto's perspective. "I would stand there in the clubhouse watching him shave. I'd watch him get dressed and knot that tie just so. My teammates must have thought I was kind of strange."

Rizzuto pointed to Brown, who had recently retired as American League president, and said that when the young infielder first came up to the majors in 1946 and 1947, he was a shortstop. "I was a little worried about my job . . . until I saw him field." Brown eventually made the team as a third baseman.

DiMaggio selected Brown to introduce him at the Lotos Club, not only because he was a former teammate, but because of his credentials as a cardiologist and an articulate intellectual. The good doctor did not let him down. He spoke about DiMaggio's attributes as a hitter, fielder, and team leader who led by example. Brown said that, through the years, the Red Sox were better than the Yankees man-for-man, and yet New York came out on top in their close pennant races. The same was true against the Dodgers in the World Series. The difference, according to Brown: "We had Joe."

When it came time for DiMaggio to speak, he singled out some members of the audience, among them "another player from San Francisco, and he had a lot of hits, too"—violinist Isaac Stern. Joe told two of his old reliable stories: his cross-country drive with Crosetti and Lazzeri to his first spring training camp, and Cobb's letter-writing intervention to get him a better contract. The audience was obviously delighted, and so was Joe.

The club's tradition was to have the honored speaker drink beer from a large stein. First, though, two Lotos officers sipped from it. When I saw that, I thought, "Oh, oh, that's going to be a problem." Joe had an obsession about avoiding colds, so much so that if someone shook his hand while he was seated in a restaurant, he would march to the men's room to wash his hands before resuming eating. He would avoid eye contact as he hurried back to the table so he would not be stopped with a handshake because that would have meant an about-face to the washroom sink. I saw that happen several times. But that night at the Lotos Club, he did not flinch from the stein that had been touched by other lips, and he gulped down the beer.

Usually, when a speech ended, Joe would hurry through the kitchen and scoot out the back door to avoid autograph seekers. Not at the Lotos Club. For more than an hour, he sat on a bench signing the menu and chatting with a collection of people from the publishing and art worlds, bankers, and businessmen. He thoroughly enjoyed himself. Even after the place cleared out, he didn't want the evening to end, so we went to Oscar's in the Waldorf Astoria for pancakes and a review of the evening. I could see how pleased he was to have made a hit with that distinguished audience.

Another boost for DiMaggio's ego was his friendship with Dr. Henry Kissinger. Both were patients of Dr. Rock Positano, and they were introduced to each other in his office. They would seem an odd couple, but Kissinger said they always found plenty to talk about, and not just baseball. "He had his opinions about domestic policy and foreign policy, and we talked about that." Asked about those views, Kissinger was blunt if not diplomatic. "I'm not going to tell you."

When Kissinger arrived in New York as a teenager from Germany in 1938, soccer was his sport, but the Giants and Yankees were the teams talked about in Washington Heights, a neighborhood of refugees near the George Washington Bridge in the upper reaches of Manhattan. DiMaggio was the supreme hero in New York, including Washington Heights, and soon Kissinger found his way to Yankee Stadium to see what the fuss was about. What did he know about baseball? Nothing. What did he know about Joe DiMaggio? Less. The teenager usually sat in the bleachers out of economic necessity, but when Bob Feller pitched against the Yankees, young Henry dug deeper into his pocket and sat behind home plate because, "Joe used to hit his pitching extremely well." Kissinger told that to DiMaggio when they met forty years later. He then did what everyone else did—he asked Joe to autograph some baseballs.

In 1998, the two sat together at *Time* magazine's seventy-fifth anniversary bash at Radio City Music Hall, and at the dinner honoring DiMaggio as an American Sportscasters Association's Sports Legend, Kissinger was called on to introduce him. Kissinger had been made an honorary ASA member the previous year, after confessing in a TV commercial that he always wanted to be a sportscaster but was rejected because of his "New York accent."

Incidentally, DiMaggio refused to take any money for that appearance. "Not only wouldn't he take an honorarium, he refused expense money," said Louis Schwartz, the organization's executive director. "He said, 'You've given me this very special honor. Why would you pay me on top of it?'" What Schwartz didn't know was that DiMaggio had learned the organization was having a rocky time because of negative publicity in two New York newspapers, and Joe wanted to help. His appearance packed the main ballroom at the Marriott Marquis.

At an impromptu news conference before the sportscasters' dinner, DiMaggio was asked about a story going around that the Yankees were thinking of leaving their stadium in the Bronx. He said he didn't want to get involved in such discussions, since he had just gotten into town and didn't know much about the details. He made it clear, though, that he had no sentimental attachment to a place where "you have to hit the ball halfway to Connecticut to get a home run." The vast spaces in left-center field at the Stadium were a major sore point with him, and he spoke about it again during his speech that night. He said when he first came up, the sign on the wall said 500 feet, which was a slight exaggeration. "Later, they brought it in three different times. They got it down to 457, then they brought it in to 399. Now, I think they are going to destroy the ballpark all together, so I won't have to suffer anymore looking out there at that fence." Of course, the park still sits proudly in the Bronx.

He once told his great-granddaughter, Vanassa Hamra, that if he had played in another stadium, he would have hit 700 homers. Another slight exaggeration, perhaps, since only Henry Aaron and Babe Ruth ever reached that number, and DiMaggio hit "only" 361 homers in his thirteen seasons. DiMaggio was asked about the extra-base hits he had prevented because he was so fast and had so much room to run at Yankee Stadium. His smile said, "So nice of you to bring that up."

Those who hadn't seen DiMaggio for a while were saddened to see how bent over his posture had become and how white his hair was. But, as usual, he delighted his audience. His story that night was about how pitcher Bobo Newsom convinced Philadelphia Athletics owner-manager Connie Mack to sign him just as the club was about to play the Yankees. Bobo was signed on and got the start in one of the games in the series. He got the first two Yankees he faced, but then DiMaggio hit a home run into Shibe Park's upper deck in left. When the inning ended, Mack asked the pitcher what he had thrown DiMaggio. "A good fastball, sir," was the answer. "I want you to curve him. Curve, curve, curve," Mack instructed.

When DiMaggio came to bat again, in the fourth inning, Newsom threw him a curve, and Joe hit it over the roof. "As I was rounding the bases, I saw Bobo standing between third and home. He cupped his hands and was shouting into the A's dugout, 'Mr. Mack, he hit yours farther than he hit mine.'"

That one was in Joe's repertoire of favorite stories, those he told over and over again. He enjoyed the response those yarns got from audiences all over America. Also, as a Yankee, he was guided by the principle that if you have a winning lineup, stick with it.

4

———•———

BIG DEALS

NOT LONG AFTER I FIRST MET Joe DiMaggio that morning in 1983, I realized that he rarely did anything without a specific purpose, and that was true of our first meeting. Through our mutual friend Cal Kovens, Joe had learned of my reputation as a lawyer and of my roster of clients, which included Mrs. John Paul Getty, the Revsons, Senator George Murphy of California, and Bert Parks, among others. He checked me out.

About three weeks after that first breakfast, DiMaggio called me. He was concerned about his future as a spokesman for the Bowery Savings Bank. He had become the centerpiece of its television and newspaper advertising campaign. He had been told the bank was having financial difficulties and was likely to be taken over by the FDIC or a group of investors. He learned that the new investors would either phase him out after fifteen years or seek to reduce his compensation. He told me that either possibility would be disastrous because he needed the money. Commercials for the Bowery and Mr. Coffee were his prime sources of income. I agreed to represent him in negotiations with Bowery Savings Bank, and told him there would be no fee. DiMaggio protested, saying he would not feel right unless he paid me something. I told him we would cross that bridge at another time.

I realized how unsophisticated DiMaggio was when it came to finances, and that he had been shortchanged, both as a player and as a celebrity businessman. In the latter case, it was because he had a low opinion of his value in that role.

When he ended his thirteen-year career as one of the greatest players of all time, DiMaggio had less than $50,000 to his name. He complained about how taxes drained his income and about how difficult it was for him to save money, even though he was an exceedingly careful spender. Dorothy Arnold had primed the siphon by going to the courts to press for more alimony and child support.

Now, approaching age seventy, he was worried about his income from the Bowery. We set out to address that concern, and we flew to New York separately. He stayed in what is now the Sheraton Hotel on Seventh Avenue, where he paced through the "Joe DiMaggio Suite" and sipped diet soda while I negotiated with the Bowery brass.

I concluded my presentation by telling the Bowery representatives that there were three things you must never do to Joe DiMaggio: "You don't embarrass him, you don't trade him, and you never cut his salary. He is a Yankee."

Joe liked that. He was proud of being a one-team man, because loyalty was a big part of his makeup. He told me that over the years he had rejected offers of more money from other financial institutions that wanted him as their spokesman. He considered himself a member of the Bowery team—just as he was a member of the Yankees team for his entire big league career.

When the talks ended, I called Joe and told him to meet me at the Stage Deli. "What happened?" he asked. I told him that the news was good, but he would have to wait until lunch to find out. Of course, he created a stir at the landmark Seventh Avenue restaurant, where New Yorkers usually strive to give the impression that they barely notice celebrities. Not so when DiMaggio walked in. Heads turned, the lunch-hour buzz was punctuated with loud whispers of "Joe D., Joe D. is here." Even the nonchalant waiters were excited. Being at DiMaggio's side amid the excitement made this Brooklyn boy feel like a big shot. Whenever I had eaten in the Stage, I invariably found myself looking at Joe's unsigned photo on the wall. Now, I was staring across the table at the real thing.

The news I had for DiMaggio was better than good. It was fantastic. The new contract with the Bowery was for three years, with a substantial payment if the bank chose not to renew for a fourth year. DiMaggio's income would be as much as three times higher than it had been. The deal would put him well on the road to becoming a millionaire, but more important, it was the biggest financial victory of his life. He gained confidence in himself and knew that I was his man from that day on. That was so important to me! I felt like a son pleasing his father.

Impressed by what I had accomplished, he stopped chomping on the pickles and coleslaw and asked how much I would charge for representing him that morning and in the future. I had told him in Florida that there would be no charge. Why did he ask again? Possibly, he wanted reassurance, or maybe he was embarrassed that I was even paying my own airfare and hotel expenses.

"No charge, Joe. It was my pleasure to represent you today, and to get you what you deserve," I said. "And there will never be a charge for representing you."

Still, DiMaggio took a checkbook from his inside jacket pocket and wrote me a check from Yankee Clipper Enterprises for $20,000. I gulped, looked him right in the eye, folded the check, and handed it back. And it wasn't because he had misspelled my last name.

How could I take money from a man I had idolized almost all my life, a man I once had wished was my father?

He chuckled and obviously was embarrassed. To ease his discomfort, I told him that he would have to pick up the tab for our corned beef sandwiches. But this once-gifted athlete, whose reflexes still were quite good, never did master the quick moves needed to pick up a check. I paid, which I did for the rest of his life, not only for what we ate in restaurants, but also for the food in Joe's refrigerator, repairs to his car, his dry cleaning, and his haircuts. I considered it a privilege, and in return, I got the pleasure of being with him and speaking with him daily.

Although I negotiated millions upon millions of dollars in deals for DiMaggio, I never took a nickel from him. No amount of money could have bought what I gained through my association with him. I was transported from the mundane life of a probate, estate, and tax lawyer to an exciting new world. I lived a Yankee fan's dream. I walked into Yankee Stadium through the players' entrance with the man regarded as the greatest living Yankee. I sat in George Steinbrenner's private box, talking baseball with the Yankees owner, Reggie Jackson, Phil Rizzuto, and the others who showed up at Old Timers games and other special occasions.

There were advantages for DiMaggio as well. From his trust in me, I was able to introduce him to the financial and moneymaking world on a level much different from anything he had ever been exposed to. In thirteen years with the Yankees, including ten in which he received a World Series share, his compensation barely reached a total of $500,000. Sometimes he would earn that much in a single day by signing memorabilia in my conference room.

In addition to a sizeable fee, he was paid airfare and hotel expenses, which by the mid-1990s reached $3,000 per trip. Sometimes, two or three promoters each paid him $3,000 for the same trip to New York. He really got a kick out of that. Payback time!

It wasn't only money, though. When he went to a fundraiser for a charity, he waived the honorarium and the expenses, and charged only for his airfare.

Because of our attorney-client relationship, I have resisted answering questions about the amount of money DiMaggio earned from memorabilia signings, personal appearances, and endorsements in the time I represented him. Joe Nachio said DiMaggio told him it was $80 million. I laughed and reminded Nachio what his old buddy would often say: "Yes, but what about the taxes?"

Turning DiMaggio into a moneymaking machine was not terribly difficult. His name and image were golden marketing tools. The Bowery and Mr. Coffee soon learned that. What astounded me was that Joe hadn't realized this. He felt inadequate when it came to the business world, and for many years, memorabilia dealers and card show promoters played on this inferiority complex to make a lot of money at his expense.

The most difficult aspect of representing DiMaggio was protecting his name and making sure he was sufficiently rewarded. This meant being tough and showing no mercy to the scoundrels who sought to take advantage of his image and name. I became the bad guy to a lot of people, but that was not my concern. My concern was making sure they did right by DiMaggio. Sure, I made enemies. They took pot shots at me throughout those sixteen years, telling Joe that I was cheating him, taking money from him and was not to be trusted. Joe knew better. The guys who no longer could use DiMaggio as their money machine also tried to discredit me with his grandchildren. Jim Hamra, his grandson, decided it was time to speak with Joe about it. "A lot of people are saying that you really need to look out for Morris. What do you think?" DiMaggio replied, "Morris is the only one in my entire life who never tried to screw me."

There was at least one instance when Joe ignored my cautions, ultimately to his chagrin. In 1997, he was given $48,000 to speak at New York's 21 Club at a birthday party for a big-time business executive. When Joe learned that the host had hidden a tape recorder under the table to record his speech, he was furious. He complained how I should not have let him go, forgetting that I had urged him not to. "You should have insisted," he said.

◆ ◆ ◆

Nowhere in baseball's multitude of record books is the historic milestone recorded. It should be, because never had there been such a happening. On August 16 and 17, 1993, Joe DiMaggio signed 1,941 bats for nearly $4 million. Dealers sold some of those for $3,995 each.

Even before that momentous occasion, the power of DiMaggio's signature as a moneymaker was spoken of in awe within the memorabilia industry. Everyone in the business wanted to hook into it. Not all of them did it successfully.

Paul Goldin, board chairman of Score Board, Inc., called me in the fall of 1991 and said he wanted DiMaggio to sign memorabilia for his publicly held corporation, which was in the business of selling such items. DiMaggio was willing to talk about it, so we invited Goldin and his son, Ken, to my law firm's office at the Yankee Clipper Center in Hollywood. Joe said this would give us home-field advantage. He wasn't kidding.

Starting with his well-marked reserved parking space out front, my office was a DiMaggio memorabilia museum. His uniform from the San Francisco Seals and a No. 5 Yankees jersey were preserved behind glass; autographed baseballs commemorating highlights of DiMaggio's career were in a showcase; signed bats were strategically displayed; and the walls were adorned with scores of photos of DiMaggio, some alone and some with other sports celebrities. The collection stunned people who walked into the office. Memorabilia collectors salivated at what they saw. It was not the value of the pieces that impressed them as much as the knowledge that no one else had these items. The bats especially made them take notice because DiMaggio did not give away bats, nor at that time would he even sign one. My collection of bats was built by my birthdays, since Joe gave me one each year. My mother, children, and grandchildren also got bats from Joe as gifts, which meant the recipient was very special to him. He placed such a high value on those autographed mementos.

The Goldins arrived for our meeting wearing slacks and shirts open at the collar. True, it was a Sunday morning, but Joe and I were in our full business uniform of blue suit, white shirt, red tie, and wingtip shoes. Image always proved a powerful negotiating tool. As DiMaggio said, it was everything.

Paul Goldin offered DiMaggio a multimillion-dollar, two-year contract requiring that he sign 1,000 baseballs and 1,000 photos a month. We followed our standard negotiating strategy, which was to have Joe present in the room during the initial discussions. He would then excuse himself, saying he was taking a break to go to the men's room or to run an errand. When he left, I went into my sales pitch, portraying Joe as the world's greatest sports figure and a legend without peer. My lavish praise was from the heart, because I truly believed what I said.

By the time DiMaggio returned later that morning, I had negotiated the contract up to $7.5 million. I laughed at Goldin's offer of $55 for each signed ball, and we got the figure up to $125 per ball and $150 for a photo.

After finalizing the agreement, we decided to go for breakfast at the Deli Den, a neighborhood place where the atmosphere and aromas revived my memories of kosher-style delicatessens in Brooklyn. The menu and showcases were filled with Jewish soul food: lox, whitefish, herring, pastrami, corned beef, pickles, bagels, and rye bread. It was said that you could put on weight and load up on cholesterol from the smells alone. The place was a favorite of Joe's and mine. We had spent hours there, eating and talking in a booth that had become our turf. Nobody ever bothered us. The waitresses just brought more coffee and rugalach, a fruit-filled miniature pastry. That's where I wanted to go to celebrate our deal with Score Board. Joe and I went in my car, as we always did after all negotiations so we could discuss the deal, and the Goldins followed in their car. Joe approached these deals with the same attitude he had during baseball games: they were the opposing team, and to ride in the same car would violate the commissioner's no fraternizing rule. He was ecstatic when I went over the financial figures during the three-minute drive. "Tell me again," he said. It made him feel good just to hear the numbers. The Goldins, I imagined, were congratulating themselves for having signed DiMaggio.

The check for breakfast came to about $35 and was put on the table between DiMaggio, who had just made $7.5 million plus extras, and the Goldins, who figured to make at least as much from selling the DiMaggio memorabilia. Guess who paid the tab? Me, who didn't make a dime on the deal. I knew there was no way Joe would reach for the tab, and I didn't want the Goldins to say they took DiMaggio and his lawyer to breakfast. Joe liked that; he felt it showed we were in control.

Score Board's announcement that it had signed Joe DiMaggio did wonders for the company's stock. Over a period of months, it went from $2 or $3 to $6 or $7 and eventually to $34 before the bottom fell out when the company went broke.

DiMaggio, as usual, was earnest about fulfilling his end of the deal. He came into my office twice a month and signed the memorabilia. He would sit in the conference room with me and Harry Bryant, a very knowledgeable representative of Score Board, and methodically put his autograph on baseballs and photos. As the year was coming to a close, Score Board requested that a December signing be put off until January. About $300,000 was involved, and the company wanted to present a rosier year-end statement. That was fine with us, but we decided that DiMaggio would sign the memorabilia in December, and we would hold it until January. That was sort of an insurance policy if Joe became too ill to sign or Score Board went bust. No matter what happened, DiMaggio would be protected. If DiMaggio died before the year ended, the money would go to his heirs. I was always concerned that if something went wrong, Joe would blame me. That never happened, but the tension was awful, and as I look back at those years, I realize it was miraculous that I managed to avoid a heart attack or an ulcer.

In return for agreeing to put off the December payment, DiMaggio received 20,000 stock options. By then, Score Board's stock was up to about $10. He eventually sold it at $33 or $34, bringing him an extra $500,000. Even though DiMaggio owned just one stock at the time, Washington National, the equity market fascinated him. The financial section was the first he read when he got the morning newspaper.

For the next year after the deal with Score Board, Joe talked about how "we" outsmarted them, and he boasted to his friends how, at seventy-six, he had made his biggest killing on Wall Street. It was also his first, but by no means his last.

DiMaggio continued his twice-a-month chore of signing baseballs and photos in my office, which he did enthusiastically and speedily. In fact, he was too fast for Score Board. The items were high-priced and didn't sell as quickly as DiMaggio was signing them. Before long, the company ran into cash flow problems.

Score Board's mistake was not that it agreed to pay DiMaggio so much money, but that it opted to pay him over two years rather than five. The Goldins wanted the shorter term because they were concerned about how long DiMaggio would be around to keep signing. He outlasted their company by several years.

The Goldins had made another costly mistake. While it did have an exclusive contract with DiMaggio, the exclusivity clause only prohibited DiMaggio from signing for other companies. Card shows were acceptable. I had negotiated for Joe to be allowed to continue to do three or four shows a year. So, for the first year of his deal with Score Board, fans and collectors could buy a photo autographed by DiMaggio at a card show for $150. A similar item bought through Score Board cost $499. No wonder the lines waiting to get to Joe at the shows were always the longest in the building.

It was around that time that DiMaggio stormed out of a card show in Orlando, vowing to never do another one, because he caught a dealer trying to pull a little swindle. That happened on a Sunday. On Monday, I called Score Board with an offer: DiMaggio would stay away from the memorabilia shows if the company would pay him what he would have received from the shows, about $500,000 a year. The Goldins agreed, and Joe took a year off from those card show signings. When he did go back, the crowds for him were larger than ever.

As Score Board's cash flow problem persisted, the company sought to slow the pace of the signings and payoffs. I told the Goldins that to do so would be a breach of contract and that we could put DiMaggio back on the memorabilia market. Score Board pretty much kept to the schedule, but eventually, it went bankrupt and had to dump its DiMaggio memorabilia on the market to pay its bills. By then, Joe had been paid in full. That deal gave him his first big payday. Joe also made more on the sale of his stock options than he had in all his thirteen years with the Yankees. In fact, in a two-day signing in my office, he made nearly as much as he did with the Yankees.

◆ ◆ ◆

Even though Score Board went belly-up, we knew there were many other opportunities out there, and I was eager to explore them. But I stuck to Joe's rule: don't go to them, let them come to us. The power of DiMaggio's signature being what it was, it was not long before another outfit was knocking on our door, Score, which signed him on to autograph baseball cards.

One of Score's investors was Barry Halper, who was one of the world's most active baseball memorabilia collectors and also a limited partner in the Yankees—very limited, about three percent. In the words of John McMullen, former owner of the New Jersey Devils, "There is nothing more limited than being a limited owner of the New York Yankees." Halper's home in Livingston, New Jersey, was a virtual memorabilia warehouse, filled with racks of uniforms and jerseys, cases of autographed baseballs, a multitude of bats, and a library of autographed scorecards valued at more than $30 million.

"Look at that collection," DiMaggio remarked on a visit to the home. "I made him a millionaire. He traded off my name." In addition to the uniform jerseys and other items he autographed for Halper, Joe had introduced Barry to several of his former teammates and other retired players, whom Halper pressed for autographed memorabilia. In the early 1990s, Halper was vice president of baseball operations for the Yankees, and he used his access to the Yankees locker room to stock his treasure trove.

He was a shrewd collector and knew how to get what he wanted. When he wanted a uniform jersey that Lou Gehrig had worn, he used his knowledge that Gehrig's widow liked scotch. He delivered a case to her apartment and went home with the prize he had sought, which was worth a lot more than the booze.

About one-fifth of Halper's collection was bought by the baseball commissioner's office for $7 million and then donated to the Hall of Fame in Cooperstown, which has a Barry Halper wing. About 2,500 other pieces were auctioned off by Sotheby's for more than double that amount.

Joe did what he did out of friendship, but he came to realize that Halper had used him to build a successful memorabilia business for himself. He had been a frequent dinner guest of the Halpers, and he even went to Paris with them for a week when Halper's wife took a gourmet cooking course. Eventually, however, Joe came to believe the friendship was a calculated ploy to keep him in position to be used as a source of autographs and memorabilia. Halper used DiMaggio more than anyone else.

Halper had a modus operandi. He would get Joe in a good mood by taking him to dinner, and then, almost casually, he would produce something for DiMaggio to autograph. Usually, Joe would do it as a favor. Not all the time, though. Once, after dinner, Halper opened the trunk of his car in the parking lot, and in there were several DiMaggio photos all neatly laid out. Halper took a pen from his pocket. That was too much for Joe. "Who the hell does he think he is?" Joe asked me rhetorically in telling the story. "He buys me off with a meal?" That was just one of the several times Joe broke off with Halper and stopped talking to him.

One of the biggest disputes occurred at Halper's home, where DiMaggio had been invited for a promotional contest in which Barry was involved. Halper assured me there would be no media there, and I, in turn, assured Joe. When Joe arrived, the first person he saw was a photographer. He wanted to leave immediately and go back to the city, but the driver that Halper had sent to get him was nowhere to be seen—deliberately, Joe was sure—and he was stuck. A story and photos of DiMaggio and Halper appeared the following day in USA Today, further fueling DiMaggio's anger.

Halper had an uncanny knack for angering Joe just when he thought he finally had made DiMaggio his best friend. After the dedication ceremony for the Joe DiMaggio Children's Hospital, Joe went with Barry to his nearby home in south Florida, where Barry put out a spread of Jewish deli food, chopped liver, baked salmon, whitefish, and salads. DiMaggio was feeling great. All was right with his world. And, for the time being, it was OK in Halper's world too. They were buddies, or so Barry thought. A screw-up soon followed, however, and that time, it was funny, at least to me as an observer. During a breakfast at the Deli Den, Halper stuck a fork into DiMaggio's plate and extracted a home-fried potato. The ever-proper DiMaggio recoiled and gave Halper a look that said, "We are not that close, buddy."

Halper, though, thought he was close enough to call late into the night for DiMaggio's advice. An entry in Joe's diary tells of such a call. Commissioner Fay Vincent had forced Steinbrenner to step down as managing general partner because of his dealings with self-described gambler Howard Spira, although their involvement had nothing to do with gambling. Joe Molloy, who was then married to Steinbrenner's daughter Jessica, ran the Yankees as managing general partner until Steinbrenner returned in March 1993. Halper, who was disappointed he didn't get the job, was assigned to work with general manager Gene Michael on player transactions, and he had to report to Molloy, who made the major decisions. Apparently, there was friction between Barry and the boss' son-in-law. Halper called Joe one July night in 1992 to complain that Molloy was having a conversation on a speakerphone earlier that day and had asked him to leave the room. "When Barry showed his displeasure, Molloy told him if he didn't like it, he could resign. Pretty harsh words," DiMaggio wrote. "Barry asked me what he should do. I told him he would have to evaluate his need for what he likes doing." In a postscript, DiMaggio conceded he had evaded the question, but added, "Frankly, I would have told Molloy to 'shove it.'"

Eventually, DiMaggio got fed up with those late-night phone calls, so he had caller ID installed. When he saw Halper's number show up on the display, he wouldn't answer.

Halper did not come off well in DiMaggio's diary. Joe groused that after a lunch in New York, Barry had asked him to sign a Yankees' uniform top. "He already has four uniforms that I signed for him several years ago. He has a lot of guts asking me to do that. With my signature on the uniform it would be worth over $100,000." In another entry, DiMaggio conceded, "I was a little cool to him."

What upset Joe in that instance was that he felt Halper had assumed the role of a booking agent for DiMaggio's personal appearances. "If I told him once, add another dozen times, that I don't want him to be a third party in any of my transactions, and that he should have them contact my lawyer in writing why they are trying to get in touch with me." (His lawyer at the time happened to be me.) He also wrote in that entry, "I don't want Barry to have the reputation that if you want to get in touch with Joe, 'call Barry.'"

Halper further incensed Joe in 1991 when he took it upon himself to communicate with officials of the Columbus Day parade in New York regarding their desire to have DiMaggio be the grand marshal. Joe was reluctant. "They have been trying for years to pay me the honor," he wrote, "but I just flat-out refuse them." This time, they were pressing the fifty years theme, the fiftieth anniversary of the 56-game hitting streak. Barry had complained publicly that New York had not given DiMaggio adequate recognition, and that unless the Columbus Day people were willing to right that "oversight," they could forget about DiMaggio. Joe was repelled by the idea of tradeoffs. "It is not my style." He noted that "I like New York, and I have the same feeling for them (the people) that they have for me." He also told his diary that he might just do the parade, "but only if I get their word that they will disregard what Barry said. No tradeoffs. Politics is not my style."

As it turned out, DiMaggio accepted the honor, and he enjoyed his participation in the parade immensely, from meeting Cardinal John O'Connor at 6:00 A.M. Mass at St. Patrick's Cathedral to getting a peck on the cheek from an old friend, actress Gina Lollobrigida. Joe obviously took his role as grand marshal seriously. "Had a difficult time with keeping people in the parade [staying in] their place," he wrote.

Despite the overall pleasant experience of participating in the parade, Joe did have a couple of public run-ins during a reception in the cardinal's residence on Madison Avenue, behind the cathedral. The first one involved Halper. Joe apparently still was upset with the memorabilia dealer for his role in setting up his participation in the parade, and DiMaggio's sense of propriety was further offended when Halper and his son showed up wearing sports shirts and no jacket. He told them, rather loudly, to leave. His greatest ire that day, however, was directed at Bill Fugazy, a wealthy travel agent and close friend of Steinbrenner's. DiMaggio was convinced that Fugazy, like Halper, was cashing in on their association to make lucrative deals. "Making money on my back," was the way he described such instances. He had told Fugazy how he felt about that, and he often banished the businessman from his good graces or took him "out of the phone book." The evening before the parade, DiMaggio had received a phone call in his hotel room from Fugazy's sister, who was a nun. She urged Joe to be nice to her brother. Joe was polite and respectful, of course—after all, this was a woman and a nun he was talking to—but, he could not let Fugazy get away with that. "Tell your brother to stop using you to do his dirty work, sister," he said. The next day, Joe seethed as he stood on the reception line with Cardinal O'Connor and saw Fugazy approach. Out came Fugazy's hand, extended toward Joe.

"No, sir," DiMaggio snapped. "That hand has been in my pocket too many times." Fugazy moved on to the cardinal, who wore a puzzled smile.

DiMaggio's dislike of Halper intensified when Joe became convinced that Barry had purchased the eight World Series rings that DiMaggio had reported stolen from his room at the Hotel Lexington. After DiMaggio died, Halper auctioned the ring from Joe's last Series, 1951, for more than $37,000. As the lawyer for the DiMaggio estate, I wrote to Halper and Sotheby's, warning that the ring could not be sold. That's when Halper came up with the cock-and-bull story that the rings were not stolen, but that DiMaggio had traded them for lodging. Knowing how DiMaggio cherished those World Series rings and regarded them as symbols of his career, who could ever believe that he would exchange them for a place to live? Besides, DiMaggio rarely paid for his hotel rooms, as there was usually some kind of a public relations deal working; Joe's presence often was payment enough. The theft of the rings prompted a written apology from the Hotel Lexington, along with an invitation to stay free at the same suite, 1806. "You may find it comforting that all rooms now have electronic safes," said general manager Sam Bhadha.

When DiMaggio learned that Halper had his missing World Series rings, he fumed, "I should turn the asshole in to the FBI for buying stolen property." I explained that, if he did that, he would be called on to give testimony, which meant he likely would be questioned about his relationship with Marilyn Monroe, something that pained him to talk about. There was a matter of a *Playboy* magazine cover featuring a nude photo of Marilyn. Halper told Ira Berkow of *The New York Times* that he got DiMaggio to autograph the cover by promising Joe that he would never show it while DiMaggio was alive. After Joe died, Halper sold the autographed *Playboy* cover at auction for $30,000. With that auction, Halper violated another pledge: he had assured Joe that he would only sell his memorabilia if his wife and children were desperately ill and he needed the money. Knowing Joe as I did, I find it hard to believe that he would have signed a nude photo of Marilyn for Halper or anyone else. He would have ripped that cover to shreds.

Halper got in a jam after DiMaggio's death over other memorabilia pieces that were allegedly stolen. The 1999 catalogue of the Barry Halper Collection of Baseball Memorabilia offered for sale some original contracts that DiMaggio, Mickey Mantle, Ted Williams, Hank Aaron, and Jackie Robinson, among others, had signed with the Hillerich & Bradsby Bat Company. The Louisville-based company was surprised to see those items listed in the catalogue—for thousands of dollars at that—because an employee had told H&B that those documents had been accidentally destroyed. Halper's lawyer claimed Barry had acquired the documents from a dealer twenty years earlier. H&B sued Halper in federal court for return of those contracts.

The suit never went to trial. Halper took the contracts off the market, and the documents were returned to Hillerich & Bradsby. "Among them was the DiMaggio contract," said Bill Williams, a company vice president.

DiMaggio's deal with Score, like the one with Score Board before it, eventually led to major financial problems for the company. Once again, the aura surrounding DiMaggio had dazzled otherwise-astute business people, and they overpaid him. In both cases, DiMaggio was protected, and he got his money up front. In less than two years, he signed a few thousand baseball cards for Score and received $125 for each. Score wanted to package thirty cards and put them in a tin box with Joe's picture on it. We told them that would be all right, but they had to pay DiMaggio $4 a box before the tins were produced.

He liked to tell his friends, "Morris bankrupted two companies." That was not true, of course. Their emotions bankrupted their thinking. Joe despised memorabilia dealers and he saw both Score and Score Board as nothing more than sophisticated dealers. He enjoyed "sending them to the showers" even more than the money he made from them.

DiMaggio's memorabilia deals didn't always end in somebody's bankruptcy, however. A deal we set up with Bradford plates made money for everyone. Artist Steven Gardner, using a photo as a model, had painted a picture of DiMaggio swinging a bat. Joe said it was the best painting of his swing he had ever seen. "Look

at that, the way he's got my heel, just the way I turn it! It's perfect!" he marveled.

In our initial discussion, the Bradford executives told me they
had paid Ruth and Gehrig advances of $6,000 each. I told them
that would cover DiMaggio's round-trip air fare. Joe received a six-
figure sum up front as an advanced royalty. We licensed 150,000
unsigned plates at $2 a plate, and these were sold all over the
country. As part of the deal, Yankee Clipper Enterprises, Inc.
received 5,000 free plates, which cost Bradford about $6 each to
produce. (Yankee Clipper Enterprises was established as a corporation in 1980, before I met Joe, to serve as DiMaggio's memorabilia business. It probably was created to limit his exposure to
being sued personally and to set up pension plan benefits for
him.) The Bradford plates were packed in Styrofoam, fifty to a
carton, and shipped to Joe's Deering Bay condominium, where he
would sign them.

Imagine what that looked like. The 100 boxes were piled up in
this splendidly furnished apartment, Styrofoam everywhere. We
set up an assembly-line system for Joe to sign the plates. The system involved Martha Lee, a paralegal from my office and a woman
adored by DiMaggio; Les Kushner, a junior law partner in the
firm at the time; and myself. Lee took a plate out of the carton and
unpacked it from the Styrofoam; Kushner wiped the oil off the
plate and gave it to Joe, who was seated at his dining room table.
DiMaggio signed it and handed it to me; I held it for twenty seconds while it dried, then I gave the plate to Martha who put it
back in the Styrofoam, sealed it with Scotch tape, and returned it
to the carton. Each carton was carried to another room to keep
the signing area clear for Joe.

Every now and then, his pen wouldn't write, so Joe shook it
to get ink into the tip. Before long, the apartment's $80-a-yard
gold carpet was speckled with ink. He didn't realize what was

happening to the carpet, and when I told him, he said, "You know, it looks better now."

It was August, and because of DiMaggio's aversion to air conditioning, it remained off and the windows were open. The apartment was like a steam bath, over 100 degrees. Kushner and I finally took off our suit jackets and undid our ties. On the second day of the six-day project, Martha rebelled and said we had to close the windows and turn on the air conditioning for the plates to dry. "What do you think, Morris?" Joe asked. Wanting to appease him, I said I didn't think it was necessary. How stupid that was. Thankfully, though, Joe was extremely protective of Martha, and taking pity on her, he gave the OK to turn on the air conditioning.

We sold the signed plates back to Bradford, which put them on the market to sell for $249 each. DiMaggio cleared about $1 million on that deal.

◆ ◆ ◆

Of all the memorabilia deals that Joe was involved in, nothing compared with the bat signing deal in 1993. In the sports memorabilia world, it was akin to Joe's 56-game hitting streak or Wilt Chamberlain's 100-point game. It was something really special. One reason was that Joe had gone through his entire career and well into retirement refusing all but a few requests to sign bats.

He did sign bats for me and members of my immediate family to mark special occasions. When I first asked him in the mid-1980s for a bat, I was unaware of his dislike for putting his signature on a piece of wood. I was not a memorabilia collector, but when some of the collectors learned I had an autographed bat, I was offered $9,000 for it. Starting in 1984, DiMaggio gave me a bat every year on my birthday. When I turned 56, he included the notation, "Keep the streak going," a reference to his hitting streak.

When my daughter, Laurie, joined my law firm, Joe gave her an autographed bat with the legend "Welcome to the Majors," and "You made the right choice." My grandsons Harrison and Monty Joe received bats with the messages, "Keep Your Swing Level" and "To a Future Center Fielder." All bore the rare "Best Wishes" before the DiMaggio signature.

There may have been isolated and obscure DiMaggio bat signings I didn't know about, but I am aware of only four others. He autographed a bat for the DiMaggio Children's Hospital; another for David Ruffner, a son of Miami tax attorney Charles L. Ruffner; one for Yankees outfielder Paul O'Neill; and the Christmas present he gave to Martha Lee. Ruffner had worked with me on an involved tax matter for DiMaggio. On a visit to my office, he brought along his teenage son, who arrived with a bat in hand. Joe and I exchanged glances, and I thought, "Uh-oh, here we go again. He's going to throw both father and son out of the office." But Joe took the bat and asked David, "How would you like me to sign it?" The boy said, "Any way you like, Mr. DiMaggio." And it was over, that easily. No explosion, not even a low grumble.

As for O'Neill, Joe admired the intense desire that Paul displayed on the field, but he turned down the outfielder at least twice when he was asked to add his name to other Hall of Fame signatures that O'Neill had collected on a bat. Finally, at what DiMaggio probably knew would be his last appearance at Yankee Stadium, on September 27, 1998, Joe asked O'Neill if he still wanted his autograph, and DiMaggio signed the bat.

Other than these few instances, DiMaggio refused just about every other request, and there were many. In April 1990, Halper interceded on behalf of a dealer who offered DiMaggio $1 million to sign 900 baseballs and 200 bats. "As soon as I heard bats, I shot it down," Joe said.

Never mind dealers; he wouldn't sign a bat for his own grandchildren, whom he adored, nor even for Joe Nachio, his friend for nearly sixty years. The most extreme example of his refusal to autograph bats came at the Joe DiMaggio Children's Hospital, for which he would do almost anything. A nurse who dressed like a clown and entertained the kids used a huge cotton bat in her act. That bat was signed by every celebrity who visited the hospital, from ballplayers to governors. Joe refused to add his name. It was only a toy, but he still wouldn't autograph it.

The Nachio bat story was a classic. A year or two before Joe's fatal illness, Nachio was visiting from his home in Panama, and he brought along a bat he had purchased in a local sporting goods store. "You want me to sign a bat!" Joe exclaimed. "Are you fucking crazy?!"

Nachio was very hurt and would not speak with DiMaggio for months. He missed Joe's friendship during that time, but kept his distance. Finally, they met in the steam room at the LaGorce Country Club and had dinner together as if nothing had happened. The subject of the bat autograph never came up. Months later, DiMaggio and I returned to my office from lunch and he was in an expansive mood. I thought the time was right. "Joe, let me give Nachio one of the autographed bats hanging on the wall," I said. "He loves you." His mood suddenly changed. "Morris, butt out," he retorted angrily.

After DiMaggio's funeral, Nachio and I flew back to Hollywood together. We went to my home, and the first thing I did was take two autographed bats from their brackets on the wall and give these to Nachio. He began to cry and said, "I hope Joe is not upset."

DiMaggio's aversion to signing bats was not completely arbitrary. It stemmed from his first deal as a pro, when he was eighteen and playing for the San Francisco Seals. On July 24, 1933, during his rookie year with the team, he signed a contract with the Hillerich & Bradsby Bat Company, which promoted itself as "sole manufacturer of the celebrated Louisville Slugger baseball bat." DiMaggio agreed to give H&B exclusive rights to his name and autograph when it came to "the manufacture and/or sale of baseball bats." The agreement tied up DiMaggio for twenty years. In return, he had his choice of a set of golf clubs or $100. Joe, who was playing for $225 a month, took the money.

Forever after, Joe felt that H&B had taken advantage of him, a teenager who had dropped out of high school and had no financial acumen. He was not allowed to have an agent or attorney to represent him. That transaction may have been in DiMaggio's mind for the rest of his life, whenever he made another deal. It most certainly was in his thoughts whenever he was asked to sign a bat. He always felt he was being shortchanged, and I kept that resentment in mind whenever I negotiated a deal for him.

"DiMaggio signed what in those days was our standard contract," said H&B executive Bill Williams, who noted that Babe Ruth signed a similar contract in 1917. "The reason for the $100 or a set of golf clubs was that we offered the deal to everyone who was signed to a minor league contract, and only one in fifty actually made it to the major leagues, so it was a big gamble." Only the bats signed by the big leaguers were sold in retail stores.

In 1993, sixty years after DiMaggio signed that contract, we received a proposition to sign bats for a record multimillion dollar amount. I thought this was a fantastic deal for him, but I proceeded cautiously, picking my spot. Starting in March, I discussed the idea only when he was having a good day, usually after dinner as we were reading newspapers and relaxing. He would barely look up and say, "Morris, I'm never going to sign bats."

One day in June, Joe was in my office conference room for hours signing memorabilia. When he finished, we took a long break for our usual lunch of tuna fish salad or egg white omelets and returned to the office at about four o'clock. We discussed the closing prices on the stock market, the interest rates, his grandchildren and great-grandchildren, and a few other topics. He was in a terrific mood, so I brought up the bat deal again. He promptly rejected it and headed for my private bathroom. Exasperated, I said, "Joe, it's nothing but a fucking damn piece of wood."

I surprised myself with the outburst. I had never cursed in front of Joe, and he rarely did in front of me. (We also never discussed sexual topics; ours was very much like a father-son relationship when it came to that.) Joe stopped in his tracks and turned to face me. He obviously was shocked to hear me curse. He looked me squarely in the eye and said, "Morris, this is not a piece of wood, it is a piece of my history." He resumed his walk to the bathroom.

DiMaggio stayed in the bathroom for almost fifteen minutes, while I sat and worried that I had made a major mistake by hounding him about the bats. I decided I would apologize as soon as he came out. I had learned when you make a mistake with DiMaggio, the best thing to do was to admit it right away, and don't try to cover it up or excuse it. Joe was straightforward and expected nothing less from those close to him.

When Joe returned, he said, "You want me to sign the bats, I'll sign the bats. But I'm doing it only for my grandchildren and great-grandchildren." I stood up and attempted an apology. "Joe, there's no need to sign the bats if you don't want to. I should never have pushed you on this. You don't need the money." He replied, "Morris, I keep telling you. It's never the need of money that people do things for; it's the want of money."

Our deal was with Chicago promoter Jerry Romolt and his Pro Sports Services outfit. He wanted DiMaggio to sign 1,750 bats. My immediate thought was, "What a nothing number! Who would remember that?" To give this special occasion the significance it deserved, I wanted 1,941 bats to be made, to mark the most famous year in DiMaggio's career. Romolt had already made a deal to sell 1,000 bats to the Home Shopping Network and 750 to the Madison Group. Yankee Clipper Enterprises would purchase the remaining 191.

DiMaggio wasn't happy whenever a middleman came into a deal, because it meant the guy would take his cut, which would add to the price for which the item would sell. If Joe signed something for $150, for example, the middleman would add his $60 and wholesale the item for $210. That meant the item would retail for $450 to $500. DiMaggio was all for the retailers making a profit, since they were the ones taking the biggest risk, but Joe felt the middlemen were making an easy buck at the expense of the fans.

The bat signing was to take place at the Hillerich & Bradsby plant in Jeffersonville, Indiana, near Louisville, Kentucky. I didn't plan to be there myself, for two reasons. I knew I had pushed DiMaggio into the deal and was worried how he would react when he sat down to sign his first bat, especially since a middleman was involved, and particularly because that middleman was Romolt. Romolt was among the top four on his hate list, along with Barry Halper and memorabilia dealers Steve Hisler and Bill Rodman. The second reason I didn't want to go was that, whenever I left Florida in the summer, my allergies and hay fever acted up.

When I told Romolt that I wouldn't be there, he panicked. Suppose DiMaggio wouldn't go without me and called the whole thing off? Romolt said he would pay my law firm $15,000 to get me to the signing. I told Joe about the offer, and he liked the idea that Romolt would have to shell out that extra money. DiMaggio also liked the fact that he was never charged a fee when I put together a venture like this for him. He knew that if he had to pay my law firm or me as an agent, the fee would be about ten percent, in this case several hundred thousand dollars.

Once, when we were handed a big check for another deal, he said, "Morris, how about a check for you?" He was talking about giving me a $10,000 gift, and it seemed he didn't quite know how to do it. "I don't need your money," I said. Looking back at it, I am not sure if he was serious or joking, or if he was testing me.

Since the $15,000 from Romolt was not coming out of DiMaggio's money, in Joe's mind that meant he was beating the promoter out of that money. Shed no tears for Romolt, though. He boasted he made $1 million by "flipping" or pre-selling the bats to the other two companies.

Romolt was a former Chicago cop, but as far as DiMaggio was concerned, he was an unsavory character. Joe, usually not one to gossip, noted that Romolt always had "a second cousin" in every city they visited. Mostly, these "cousins" were blondes and about twenty-five years younger than Romolt, who was in his fifties, and married. Joe called Romolt a "Candy Store Guy"—in DiMaggio's lexicon, the type that hangs around street corners bragging about their money and sexual conquests. Those were two subjects Joe never discussed, even though he had plenty to brag about in both cases. Romolt also liked to tell jokes, which never got a laugh from DiMaggio. "*Reader's Digest* stuff," Joe would say after Romolt attempted a joke. That Romolt was a buddy of Halper's only provided another reason to dislike him.

Joe described some of Romolt's vulgar behavior to me one day when we were on our way to Dodger Stadium for a game in July 1994. Joe and I were in Los Angeles for a dinner for the Cedars of Lebanon Hospital. Dodgers owner Peter O'Malley had invited us to the game. Romolt, also in town for the dinner, met us at the VIP gate outside the stadium, strode in with our party, and went to the owner's box with Joe and me. During the game, Romolt panned his binoculars around the stands looking at women, especially those in tank tops. He had choice comments for those he found special. "Look at the tits on that one." "Check out the big bosoms that one is carrying." Joe looked at me and arched his eyebrows as if to say, "What did I tell you?"

Regarding the H&B deal, we could not control the price the bats would be sold for, but Romolt told me when we first discussed the idea that he would add no more than $300 to the price so that each bat would sell for about $2,700. Somebody got greedy, however, and when the bats went on the market the price was $3,995.

Harry Bryant of Score Board, a memorabilia authority, said that the price would drastically limit the number of bats that would be sold. "Maybe 600 people in the whole country would pay that amount for a commemorative bat," Bryant said. He knew what he was talking about.

Joe and I showed up for the signing dressed in suits, shirts, and ties. It was a stifling August day, and about 100 degrees in the H&B factory. Although the bats that Joe was to sign were ready, the ovens were on in the factory to manufacture other bats. Rex Bradley, who had been with the bat company seemingly forever and had known DiMaggio for almost as long, handled the signing procedure. I had developed a great deal of respect for this short, wiry old timer. He was keen on detail.

When I first spoke with Bradley about the deal and gave him the approval to produce 1,941 bats, I was told that Joe and I would have to sign affidavits, because no bat could be released without DiMaggio's permission. After that initial call, Bradley called me back to verify that I was with a law firm. When he received the affidavits, he called again and told me, "That's not good enough." He wanted DiMaggio to personally tell him that it was all right to produce 1,941 bats, and Joe had to get on the phone. A Joe DiMaggio model bat, DL29, cost $800 to $1,000 unsigned, because Joe limited the number that could be made. The plate with Joe's name was kept in a vault.

The signing took place in a cage where Joe was seated in front of a special board on which Bradley placed the bats one at a time. After each bat was signed, Bradley removed it and placed it on a metal cart; when about 100 bats were loaded on, he wheeled the cart into another caged storage area. That meant he had to bend down 1,941 times to lift each bat and bend down another 1,941 times to put the bats on another cart. His shirt soon was drenched with sweat.

I always thought that Bradley deserved a tip from Romolt for his backbreaking work, but I don't believe he ever got so much as a thank-you. Bradley asked Joe to autograph a bat for him, and Joe put him off with his usual response, "Not now, later," which usually meant never. But before we left, DiMaggio personalized a signature on a bat for Bradley—which was nice, but it meant Bradley could never sell that bat.

The bat signings were witnessed by officials of the Home Shopping Network and the Madison Group, and some other people invited by Romolt, who was showing off his deal with Joe DiMaggio. The heat in that cage was too much even for Joe. He loosened his tie and took off his jacket. That was the signal the others had been waiting for, and they quickly followed his example. Everyone's shirt was soaked through.

The day was not without a crisis. We were getting the money from Romolt, and he was to get it from the Home Shopping Network and the Madison Group. Romolt gave us $2 million up front, before Joe sat down. The remaining $1.6 million was to come after the first 1,000 bats were signed. So, after Joe signed 1,000 bats, I asked Romolt, "Do you have the other check?" He told me, "It's here, don't worry." A couple of minutes later, I asked him again, and that time he said, "It's on its way." I knew something was wrong.

"Keep pestering him," Joe urged me. That's when I learned that the Home Shopping Network had come through with its money, but the Madison Group was late with its payment for 750 bats, so Romolt was unable to produce his second check at the designated time. He kept telling me, "It will be here, don't worry." I wasn't worried. He was the one who had to worry. He was in default under terms of the contract, and that meant we could keep the bats and the money he had already paid.

I took Joe away from the signing rack and to another room. "As your lawyer, I have to tell you the ground rules. The contract has been breached. That means you can keep the money and all the bats, and can screw Romolt."

"That's not right," said DiMaggio, even though he had the legal power to ruin this man he despised. When I approached Romolt he was white as a sheet and his hands were trembling. "This is what we are going to do," I told him. "We are going to sign the rest of the bats, but they are going to stay here for thirty days until you get the money from the Madison Group."

When the Madison Group finally came up with the money, Romolt penalized the company for its default. He kept 165 of its bats as the penalty. Not only did we waive our right to keep Romolt's down payment and all the bats, we didn't even take a penalty charge from him, yet he penalized his customer. DiMaggio was furious when he learned that. If the portion of defaulted bats went to anyone, it should have gone to Yankee Clipper Enterprises, because DiMaggio had lost thirty days' interest on the money due him.

After sweltering in that cage signing bats for seven hours, DiMaggio decided to make it a two-day trip, and he put off signing the last 150 bats until the following day. He got into a conversation with Pee Wee Reese, the Brooklyn Dodgers Hall of Fame shortstop who lived in Louisville and was working for H&B. In addition to their various matchups in the Yankee-Dodger World Series battles of the 1940s and early 1950s, the two had played against each other during World War II in a game in Honolulu. Joe was with an Army Seventh Air Force team and Reese was on a Navy team. They reminisced about a home run Joe had hit that was said to have been the longest ever hit in Hawaii.

Joe asked Bradley to make three brown DiMaggio model bats, and that was done in less than half an hour. Joe's name was carved in gold on the barrel. He gave me two of those bats and one to his granddaughter Paula. I donated one to Xavarian High School in Brooklyn, and it sold for $10,000 at a silent auction to benefit the school on January 24, 2001. Reese signed the other brown bat and it was given to one of my grandsons.

Joe relaxed after the signings ended for the day, and he looked forward to being taken out to dinner. I had been hoping we would get back to Florida that night because my allergies and hay fever were really bothering me.

DiMaggio and I were in a party of fifteen seated at a long table in a very pricey restaurant. Everyone but us was involved in a lively and noisy discussion. As he usually did in those circumstances, Joe listened rather than talked. As Pellegrino D'Acierno so aptly sized up DiMaggio, "He had the capacity to be alone in the presence of others." Most of the talk was about Joe, how great he was and how he would outshine all current players. "You are the greatest living former ballplayer," someone said. "I'm the same kid as I was when I played for the San Francisco Seals," Joe responded. He was having a terrible time. He also lost his appetite and passed up the enticing menu offerings for a salad and bowl of pasta. I did, too.

I felt that he was tolerating the lot of them at the table only because he was being paid so much money. DiMaggio believed that they would never sell enough bats to get back their investment, let alone make a profit, not at the prices they had in mind. They were talking $8 million. These weren't Picassos they were talking about, these were pieces of wood. DiMaggio had the knack for getting these types of wheelers and dealers to thank him for the privilege of giving him millions of dollars while making them feel guilty it wasn't more.

When Joe went back into the cage the next morning to finish the job, Reese told him that 500 extra Joe DiMaggio model bats had been made by mistake and would have to be shredded.

"What waste!" I proclaimed. "Sell them to us." Reese checked with someone in the company and said we could have the 500 bats for $50 each. "How can you charge Joe DiMaggio $25,000 after what this company did to him in 1933?" I said, reminding him that Joe had been given a choice between $100 and a set of golf clubs. "You used his name for twenty years and didn't give him an extra penny."

Joe took delight in hearing that. Reese was uncomfortable about H&B's treatment of DiMaggio, even though it was sixty years in the past. I told Pee Wee that I agreed that rather than shredding those bats, H&B was entitled to make some money, but that $25,000 was a bit much. When we finally agreed on a price, Joe took out the Yankee Clipper Enterprises checkbook he always carried and wrote a check for $16,000. Joe considered that as great a victory as the millions he made in seven hours. Once again, the Yankees beat the Dodgers.

Romolt drove us to the Louisville airport, and bragged about how much money he had made on the deal. On and on he went, driving under 30 miles per hour on a major highway. Joe grew more impatient with every slowly passing mile. Finally, he told Romolt to pull over. "Morris will flag down a cab or call us one on a cell phone," Joe said, and he was serious. Romolt knew he could never let that happen if he wanted to stay in DiMaggio's good graces, so he stepped on the gas. But it was too late, Joe dropped him from the book for years. "All that money has softened his brain," Joe whispered to me.

At the Louisville airport, I showed Joe the checks we were taking home and he was ecstatic. He had more than made up for the short shrift he got in his first bat deal. "Morris, take something for yourself out of that," he said as he indulged himself with a second look at the checks. I guess he was talking about a ten percent agent's cut, but I didn't take it. Joe must have liked that, too. It was a wonderful trip, even though I sneezed my way through it.

Those 500 extra model DL29 bats saved from the shredder were shipped to Joe's apartment at Deering Bay. When they arrived, we used dollies to roll them from the truck to Joe's first-floor apartment. Martha Lee, who was helping us, remarked, "I'm sure glad he doesn't live in the penthouse."

The bats were blanks, which meant each one had to be signed. "Joe, sign them 'Yankee Clipper,'" I requested. "I ain't signing 'Yankee Clipper,'" he replied, even though that would add to the signature's value. I told him the plan was not to sell the bats until after his death. They would be a legacy for his granddaughters and great-grandchildren. "Your grandchildren can sell them."

"I ain't signing Yankee Clipper."

"But, Joe, you can defer taxes on them until they are sold."

That did it. Using a marker, he deliberately signed "Yankee Clipper" on 500 bats.

Once again, we set up an assembly line to do it. Joe sat at the dining room table and each bat was placed in a signing rack that H&B had made for him. Each bat had to be taken out of its tube, signed, held for thirty seconds until the ink dried, put into a plastic bag, and then put back in its tube. There were a dozen tubes to a carton. The boxes holding those bats were kept in a locked closet until Joe moved out of Deering Bay, and then they were stored in the guesthouse on Joe's property in Harbor Islands. Those bats were special to him because they were like certificates of deposit for his heirs. Yankee Clipper Enterprises sold 485 of the bats to a television shopping outfit prior to Joe's death for $1.25 million. Joe thought that was a good idea. "Sell them, sell them," he said when he was told that Paula and Kathie had agreed the time was right, even though he was still alive. Looking ahead, we didn't want to flood the market with DiMaggio memorabilia after his death. This strategic decision paid off for his estate because the bats that were left when he died were sold as a separate product.

Of the 191 signed bats that were ours from the original 1,941, we sold 175 a year later to B&J Collectibles. Scott DiStefano negotiated the deal for B&J, because Joe would not have anything to do with Bill Rodman, whom he described as "that criminal." (Rodman was the true owner of the company, even though the stock was held in his wife's name.) B&J marketed the bats as part of a package with a ball and a photo of Joe.

The Home Shopping Network got Whitey Ford to go on television and hawk the bats that they had bought. Not many sold at $3,995, maybe 450 total. HSN wound up dumping its bats to Score Board before Score Board went broke, and the Goldins traded the bats to someone for photos. Everyone got stuck with those bats, except Joe and Romolt.

◆ ◆ ◆

Rodman and DiStefano were central figures in another controversial signing deal, one that came to be the subject of slanderous innuendo and falsehoods. For Joe DiMaggio Day at Yankee Stadium in 1998, which proved to be his farewell appearance at the Stadium, the Rawlings sporting goods company produced commemorative baseballs bearing a facsimile of Joe's signature and an artist's rendering of his famous swing. In Richard Ben Cramer's biography, *Joe DiMaggio: The Hero's Life*, he wrote that I "secretly" bought 2,000 of those commemorative baseballs and planned to "mix those in while Joe was signing . . . and make a cool four hundred grand," which, supposedly, I would share with DiStefano. The truth is, there was no secrecy about it at all. Joe DiMaggio told me to buy additional commemorative balls, but I was unable to accomplish the mission. I tried, but my offers were rejected, and I never bought those baseballs. Furthermore, there was absolutely no way anyone could get DiMaggio to sign 20 balls let alone 2,000 balls he didn't know about—he had a calculator in his brain.

The history of those baseballs went back to 1996, when Rawlings wanted to produce a commemorative ball for the Yankees and/or Major League Baseball to be used in a game during a special day at Yankee Stadium. DiMaggio said he would give his approval for the ball, but only if Rawlings gave him 30,000 of the special balls.

Apparently, that was too heavy a price, and no deal was made. DiMaggio changed his mind after commemorative balls were produced for Mickey Mantle, Jackie Robinson, and Cal Ripken. He told me to try to revive the deal. Under the new proposal, DiMaggio would get a maximum of 15,000 balls as compensation, but only 10,000 was guaranteed. The remainder, up to 5,000, would depend on the number of commemorative balls Rawlings sold to B&J Collectibles, more specifically, Bill Rodman. We were not privy to their deal, and DiMaggio didn't trust Rodman, so he was convinced he would never see that final installment of baseballs.

Joe told me to try and get those last 5,000 balls from Rawlings or from DiStefano. Mike Thomson of Rawlings said he couldn't sell them to Joe because his company had an exclusivity agreement with B&J. I kept trying, at Joe's behest, and asked Thomson to at least sell me 2,000 balls, but that didn't work, either.

Not only was DiMaggio aware that I followed his instructions and had asked Rawlings to sell me the commemorative baseballs, but he also said if I was successful, Yankee Clipper Enterprises would pay for them. Joe knew of all of my telephone conversations involving those baseballs, and he authorized me in writing to do whatever I could to acquire them. Also, Joe offered to sign 20 of the commemorative balls for Rawlings if the company would release the 2,000 balls to him. That, of course, would mean more revenue for Rawlings.

I asked DiStefano to try to get us 2,000 balls through his own business, Atlantic Coast Sports. DiMaggio liked Scott, and he wanted to help him start his own memorabilia business; he threw a lot of moneymaking deals Scott's way, and that gave DiStefano a major lift. Still, DiStefano said he could not sell Joe those base-balls while he still worked for Rodman, because Joe was suing B&J over some alleged forgeries. Since DiStefano wouldn't sell the baseballs to Joe, we decided that I would try to buy them from Scott, and Joe would sign them. Under that proposed deal, Scott would get twenty-five percent of the commission, I would get seventy-five percent, which I would then turn over to Yankee Clipper Enterprises. Joe liked that; he called it a "creative idea." He also told me to work with Scott on ways of marketing the allotment of commemorative balls he was assured of getting.

◆ ◆ ◆

The 1993 bat signing at H&B provided DiMaggio with his biggest payday ever, but his association with Mr. Coffee gained him his most fame. Many in the TV-addicted generation that grew up after DiMaggio's playing days knew him not as the Yankee Clipper, but as "Mr. Coffee." His television commercials gave him new national fame, and were responsible for the huge success of the coffee-making device. Vincent Marotta, Mr. Coffee's president, contacted DiMaggio in 1972. Someone from Cleveland who was friendly with Joe had given the Cleveland-based Marotta DiMaggio's phone number in San Francisco. When Marotta called, DiMaggio told him that Joe's sister, Marie, was using the coffee-brewing machine at that very moment to make breakfast coffee. "I won it at a golf outing last week," Joe said.

When Marotta asked Joe to do TV commercials, his reaction was typical. He said no. But he changed his mind the next day, and the relationship lasted for about fifteen years. Marotta, now in his late seventies, spends much of his time playing golf in a Jack Nicklaus gated community in Palm Beach Gardens, Florida, where he has a palatial home. He said DiMaggio was a pretty fair golfer. "He hit a long ball, but he didn't have the perfect form he had in baseball."

Joe did so many personal appearances for Marotta that many people believed he owned the company. DiMaggio was in a restaurant in San Mateo, California, when a woman complained to him that her Mr. Coffee machine did not keep her coffee hot. He politely explained that he was just a spokesman for the company and he suggested she write a letter to the factory.

Even though he extolled the virtues of the Mr. Coffee machines to millions of Americans, DiMaggio mostly drank Sanka, which he made from those small envelopes. His coffee maker was a kettle of boiling water. A videotaping was done in my office for some promotion, and they put about fifty Mr. Coffee machines around the place. Joe managed to wind up with all of them, plus the blazer he wore for the taping. He carefully selected who would get a machine, and he was so selective that when the process was completed, he still had forty or so left. What he did with them, I never learned.

By the end of his tenure as Mr. Coffee's spokesman, Joe was making more than $300,000 a year from the deal, but it ended abruptly when he discovered that something had been added to the contract at a renewal without his knowledge. DiMaggio was always on guard to be sure nobody was putting over anything on him, and he read every word of every contract he ever put his name to. A breach of his trust ended the deal with Mr. Coffee.

◆ ◆ ◆

Another potentially lucrative sponsorship deal ended before it began when DiMaggio got wind that shady business was afoot. Gary Esposito, a young businessman who operated some Famous Original Ray's Pizza places in New York, impressed DiMaggio with a tremendous proposition. This blond, blue-eyed smart dresser wanted to use Joe's name on an international chain of fast-food Italian restaurants, DiMaggio Cucina, and he was willing to pay big for it. He was talking about $2 million a year for twenty-two years, and Joe was to get $75,000 a month while negotiations were going on. DiMaggio Cucinas would be all over the United States and parts of Canada and overseas—even Italy! Joe flew up from Florida for a dinner meeting, but first Esposito invited him to a Famous Ray's in downtown Manhattan, near Chinatown. Joe, Martha Lee, and I were driven there in a limo. I told the driver to wait; it wasn't going to take long, Joe just wanted to sample a slice and we would be on our way. It took even less time than we thought. The visit was arranged for 4:00 P.M., during a lull between lunch and dinner. When we walked in, the place was packed with guys in suits and ties and some well-dressed women decked out in expensive jewelry.

Joe immediately realized it was show time, and he was the attraction. "It's a setup," he said. Things went from bad to worse. "Hey, Joe, how was Marilyn?" one of the wise guys inquired. Martha was asked by one of the ladies in attendance if she was Marilyn Monroe's daughter. Joe took Martha by the arm and hustled her into the kitchen, saying over his shoulder to me, "We're getting out of here." He led the way to the back exit when he suddenly backtracked and told one of the startled kitchen workers, "We're taking a pizza to go." We sat in the back of the limo eating the pie, and though he said nothing, I knew that Joe was furious. Still, Joe, Martha, and I went to dinner as planned with Esposito and a group that included Gary's wife and child, his lawyer Ray Mantle, and some others. DiMaggio, who sat next to me, said nothing during the entire meal. The way Marilyn's name had been tossed at him put him a funk, deep in thought. I sensed that the DiMaggio Cucina idea was in deep trouble.

A couple of days later, the deal was dead. According to federal authorities, pizza wasn't the only product being sold at the Famous Original Ray's on Third Avenue and 43rd Street. More than seventy people were charged as part of a drug operation. There were about thirty "Ray's Pizzas" in New York, some known as Famous Original Ray's, some as Original Ray's, and others as Famous Ray's. Although the federal prosecutor said that only one restaurant was selling drugs, once Joe learned of the drug bust, it made no difference to him if there was a connection or not with the place from which he had stormed. There would be no DiMaggio Cucinas. He never heard from Esposito again, but he did get the $225,000, for his indulgence during the three months the idea was alive and under negotiation.

Such events only heightened DiMaggio's highly suspicious instincts. In his mind, someone was always out to take advantage of him, to "make money off my back." He was particularly upset about what he considered shabby treatment from major league baseball, which he had promoted for so many years. In 1992, a friend named Norm Meier and his son Brad wanted Joe to help them to get Major League Baseball Properties to license stick-on pennants they had produced. The Florida Marlins had approved the use of their name, and the Meiers wanted to sell the product throughout the majors. The Meiers got Joe's attention by offering him three percent of the gross revenue if he secured the license and approval. Dolphins quarterback Dan Marino had about a twenty-five percent share of the company, called Universal Heights. DiMaggio set up a meeting with officials of Major League Baseball Properties so that the Meiers could make their presentation. DiMaggio was told there should be no problem, "but. . . ." The "but" had Joe worried. "Properties wanted something in exchange," he wrote in his diary. "They didn't tell me what."

DiMaggio found out at the meeting. Frank Simio, who was a vice president for licensing at MLB Properties, wanted him to participate in an endorsement pool. As DiMaggio understood the plan, each player would contribute whatever money he made into the kitty, and the receipts would be divided equally so that a player "down on his luck" could benefit. DiMaggio was all for helping the guys who needed it, but he bristled when Simio told him he had a duty to "give something back to baseball." DiMaggio snapped, "I would like to know who has done any more than I for baseball, and I was doing it long before you people were around." When he started to mention the charity appearances he had made for baseball, Simio interrupted to say, "This is not a charity."

DiMaggio was embarrassed that the scene was played out in front of the Meiers. "He should have confronted me alone," DiMaggio said. He wrote of Simio in his diary, "If he had any class, it was in his ass." "Blackmail" is how DiMaggio characterized MLB Properties' desire to tie its approval of the Meiers' project to his participation in the endorsement pool.

When Commissioner Fay Vincent learned about what had happened, he called DiMaggio. Joe told him he wanted a written apology from Properties. Vincent told Joe he was right, and said he thought "those young people" had mixed oranges and apples because DiMaggio's participation in the endorsement pool should not have been tied to the Meiers' pennants project. DiMaggio got his apology from the commissioner and MLB Properties, but he wrote that the apologies were weak. He was unhappy because, as he put it, "I had to defend my honor," and he added, "I think the commissioner's office stinks."

Ten years later, Simio, then a vice president for finance at Fordham University, had a different recollection of the meeting. He said because DiMaggio was a legend, he never would have told him he had to participate in the pool, but he did ask him to help out. "There is a difference," Simio said. "A favor for a favor. That's the way of the world." Of DiMaggio's complaint that he was being blackmailed, Simio said he told Joe that if he chose not to participate in the pool, Baseball Properties would look at the application on its own merits. Bottom line: Joe did not get involved in the endorsement pool, and Joe did not get approval for the license.

◆ ◆ ◆

DiMaggio was a target for both schemers and legitimate businessmen because he had a golden image that brought him golden opportunities. People and corporations paid handsomely just to have him nearby, hoping that his fame and reputation would rub off on them. That was the reason he was invited to live in a $650,000 apartment in Deering Bay and was paid six figures a year for doing it. His only obligation was to play golf three days a month on the condo's golf course. When I told him about the arrangement, DiMaggio wondered if he could play thirty-six days in a row to fulfill his obligation. I explained that the developer wanted people to see him on the property at least three days a month.

The developer was the Codina Group, founded by Miami businessman Armando M. Codina, whose partners included future Florida governor Jeb Bush. DiMaggio was regarded as the ideal spokesman for the age and income segment the Codina Group was seeking as customers. In addition to exquisite furniture and carpeting, Joe's apartment came complete with dishes and pots and pans. The developer even paid for his telephone and cable television. The Codina Group shelled out more than $200,000 for the furnishings, yet Joe could not even remember the color of the sofa six months after he was out of there.

DiMaggio was one of the first to move into the development, and when I visited, I found him vacuuming the apartment in his wing-tip shoes, black over-the-calf socks, a Yankees T-shirt, and a pair of underwear shorts. It was a breach of his "image is everything" philosophy. He complained, "This joint doesn't even have a broom." I went out and got him a broom and a dustpan. I had already bought him the vacuum cleaner. Then, it was, "Can you imagine a place like this without a treadmill or an exercise bike?" After hearing that two or three times I went out and got him both. I can't remember ever seeing him use either piece of equipment, except as a rack for hanging his suits and shirts.

The Deering Bay complex was located on water, near the ocean, and it was beautifully landscaped. Joe had a first-floor apartment, with high vaulted ceilings. The master suite was huge, and there were two more bedrooms at the other end of the apartment. DiMaggio believed that the company wanted to use him to attract the 2000 Olympics to Miami so that they could cash in on all the construction that would go on in the Olympic Village. Whether or not that was the case, the effect of his presence at Deering Bay was startling. The residents, sophisticated successful businessmen and their wives, would stop in their tracks when they saw him. He turned heads wherever he went. Joe enjoyed the role of being the neighborhood hero, but he always was on guard, as if he were waiting for someone to pounce and either grab his hand or ask for an autograph. When we walked into a restaurant in the community, he would imitate a fighter pilot sizing up potential attackers, and whisper to me, "Autograph at three o'clock, another one at six o'clock, handshake at nine o'clock, a guy with a baseball story at noon."

In the two years he lived there, DiMaggio used this lavish apartment as a warehouse for his bats, Bradford plates, baseballs, and whatever else came along. He also had boxes and boxes of T-shirts and golf balls stacked around the place. He got those whenever he was invited to a celebrity tournament, and he played in many of them. There were at least half a dozen fully loaded golf bags, which were gifts from tournament sponsors who were obliging when Joe would show up and say, "I forgot my clubs." Since Joe was the big star, the sponsors always made sure that he played with the best team, so that when a picture was taken of the winning foursome, Joe DiMaggio was in it. And he always took home the prizes. According to Joe Nachio, "Anything they gave away as prizes, he wanted." There were television sets with their cords still untied and electric razors cluttering the apartment.

It was the same thing at his home in San Francisco. Marie, who lived in the house, warned her brother not to bring anything more into the place, "because I'd have to put it on the roof, and the roof will cave in." She said every room and every closet was filled with things her brother had received for playing in a tournament or just for showing up some place. "There's no room in the house, the garage is filled up, and so is the spare bedroom," she said.

DiMaggio's dislike of air conditioning—he always complained of being cold and said air conditioning made his arthritis worse—created a problem in Deering Bay. Green mold formed on a lot of things, but he merely brushed it off and said, "Just like new."

Joe was never happy living in South Miami. He was a restaurant guy, and he missed the pasta and pizza places, the Chinese restaurants, and the Jewish-style delicatessens that he frequented in Broward County. He also groused about the one-hour trip from his apartment to my office, which he made at least three times a week. He did not like to drive. One of the most frightening experiences of his life was when he fell asleep on the way to lunch in Martinez, California, in the summer of 1991. His car jumped a divider curb, and that woke him. "It could have been a disaster," he said. "Put me in a car and I have my best sleep." The fear of nodding off was only one reason he was unhappy about that drive to my office. He let me know several times about the money he was spending on gas. I had a set of his car keys, and I would fill up his car's gas tank. He knew what I was doing, but he said nothing about it.

Around that time, a gated development called Harbor Islands was being built in Broward Country on the Intracoastal Waterway in Hollywood, where I had decided I would move my family. It was about a mile from the ocean, and I thought that would be perfect for Joe, who was raised on San Francisco Bay and enjoyed being near the water.

Ami Tennel, who was in charge of the project, had noticed my Dodge Caravan with the "DIMAG 5" license plate when I drove around looking at sites in the development. He also had seen me with DiMaggio in restaurants. Tennel asked if DiMaggio would be interested in becoming a spokesman for Harbor Islands. Joe still was under contract to Deering Bay, but I felt Codina would have no objection to releasing him, since most of the units had been sold and DiMaggio was getting a lot of money just to play golf three days a month. I called Joe from my car and told him he would be moving in about a year to a house right across a narrow street from mine. He was to be a total guest. He wouldn't even have to pay for electricity, and he didn't have to do anything for the development except be there, and that meant no golf obligations. He was overjoyed.

My hunch about Codina being agreeable to let Joe go proved to be correct. The only problem was that DiMaggio's unit at Harbor Islands was a year behind schedule. In the interim, the developer put DiMaggio in a one-bedroom suite at a new Holiday Inn in Hollywood, and he thought that was wonderful. Fresh towels every day, room service, and no responsibility other than to be sure not to lose his key. He was five minutes from my office, and he was there four or five times a week. He would watch television or talk with my staff and clients about politics, sports, or the stock market. The only taboo subject was Marilyn Monroe. My staff knew that, and some of my clients learned it the hard way when the mention of her name abruptly ended the conversation and sent DiMaggio out of the room.

DiMaggio eventually moved into a 3,500-square-foot, five-bedroom home in the community. In all the years I knew him, he was never happier. His grandchildren and great-grandchildren flew from the Bay Area to stay with him three times a year. He was near his friends and his favorite restaurants and the children's hospital he had become so interested in. Joe would explore the 200-acre development in a gas-powered golf cart I bought for him, greeting residents as he passed them. Two or three times a week, both of us would get into the cart, stop in a shady place, and talk for a couple of hours or read *The New York Times*.

Free of any obligation to be involved in the community, Joe got very much involved. That was his style, just as long as no one was requiring him to do something. There was a Land Rover demonstration and Joe was right in the middle of the action, holding a hot dog in one hand and shaking someone's hand with the other. He talked baseball with the kids, and told anyone who would listen what a great place it was. He even took a ride in one of the vehicles with the owner of the local dealership; he was disappointed that the dealer didn't offer him a free car. His presence at a New Year's Eve party was a major topic for months. DiMaggio lived at Harbor Islands for two years and died there.

While living at Harbor Islands, Joe made personal appearances all over the country, and the ones he enjoyed the most were golf tournaments. One such tournament he remembered not for what happened on the course but what occurred later. It was a benefit for the Boys Town of Italy and was played in Fort Lauderdale, Florida, in March 1990. There was a cocktail party afterward, and Joe wanted to shower and shave before going. (He was skipping the dinner that followed, because he was coming to my surprise 50th birthday party.) DiMaggio was given a key to a priest's room at the clubhouse and was told he could use it to take a shower. He had just finished shaving and was about to get into the shower when there was a knock on the door. A woman's voice demanded, "What are you doing in my room?"

Joe was stark naked, and he explained through the closed door that there might have been an error since he was told that a priest had been assigned the room. Joe said to the woman that since he was already undressed, he would shower and be out in ten minutes. He also told her that if it made her feel better, she could call security. The woman did indeed bring back someone from security, who recognized Joe. "Lady, that's Joe DiMaggio who was in your shower." The woman recovered from her scare in time to ask for several autographs. Joe was happy to oblige, but before leaving he asked the security man to get a statement from the woman confirming that nothing was missing. "It was scary—I was afraid she would come in with a golf club," he said.

The following day, Joe was in another tournament, this one on Williams Island, where he was paired with O. J. Simpson as celebrity partners in a charity event to benefit AIDS research. Two men had successfully bid in an auction the previous night for the honor of playing with Joe and O. J. in a foursome. The men failed to show and two others joined DiMaggio and Simpson to play nine holes. "I kept my commitment," DiMaggio wrote in his diary, "but I was annoyed at the people who got me involved."

Simpson later was high on DiMaggio's list of people he didn't like. Joe had seen the famous Los Angeles freeway chase on television, and he watched the trial as if he were a member of the jury—the way things turned out, he watched the proceedings probably more carefully than the jurors. Joe was a CNN and C-SPAN freak anyway, but the Simpson trial became an obsession with him. We were in New York one day when the trial was being televised, and he sat in front of the set for seven hours, watching even the reruns of the highlights and all the analysis. Joe was flabbergasted when the jury cleared Simpson of murder. "The greatest miscarriage of justice I ever saw," he said.

"If I was innocent of something they charged me with, they would need two or three guys to hold me down to put on the handcuffs," DiMaggio said. "But Simpson made no fuss when they put the cuffs on him. That told me something."

Simpson was all over the front pages in Los Angeles when we were there for the Cedars of Lebanon dinner a couple of weeks after the arrest. There was a cocktail party for the sports celebrities before the dinner, and NFL running back Marcus Allen asked the athletes to pray for Simpson. DiMaggio was having none of it. "I'm going to throw up," he said. Robert Shapiro, one of Simpson's lawyers, was at the dinner with his young son, and he had a shopping bag full of baseballs. He asked DiMaggio to sign them. Joe had autographed two when I realized what was going on. "Joe, the card show is over," I told him. "No more autographs." I couldn't get over Shapiro's balls, a whole shopping bag full of them. "He probably wanted to give them to the judges," Joe said.

DiMaggio later met Simpson's lead lawyer, Johnnie Cochran. Joe was having lunch with Rock Positano in Bravo Gianni's on the east side of Manhattan, when Cochran walked in with Al Sharpton. Neither was on DiMaggio's list of favorite people. The two went to the back of the restaurant. "Doc, do you think they want to come over and say hello?" DiMaggio asked. Positano told him that since there were only five people in the restaurant, it wasn't likely that Sharpton and Cochran would miss him. They came to the table, and the three of them had a very cordial conversation, most of it about Muhammad Ali, whom Joe admired. When they left, DiMaggio had a twinkle in his eyes, meaning he enjoyed meeting both of them.

◆ ◆ ◆

Clearly, not every occasion or group that hoped to gain something by association with Joe DiMaggio was out to take advantage. In 1997, Joe agreed to participate in a fundraiser for Xaverian High School in Brooklyn by accepting an award from the school at a dinner. Much of the money raised at the dinner would go to a fund for students at the school who suffered from learning disability. Joe thought that was great, and when he visited the school, located in an Italian neighborhood in Brooklyn, he felt even better. "We are in Joe DiMaggio country," said Salvatore Ferrera, the school president. "The kids knew that their parents and grandparents worshiped him, because they heard about Joe D. when they were growing up, that he was the greatest ballplayer who ever lived." DiMaggio was happy with the project. After Joe died, I wanted his memory to be a continuing inspiration to the kids in the neighborhood, so I donated to the school forty pieces of signed memorabilia that Joe had given to me and members of my family over the years. The pieces were worth about $150,000 all together. Some of the items were displayed in the school lobby and some were auctioned in fundraisers. Joe would have said the donation was "the right thing to do," and that's why I did it. In addition to the Joe DiMaggio scholarship fund, there is now a Morris Engelberg scholarship fund at Xaverian, a Catholic school. Not bad for a Jewish kid who went to an Orthodox parochial school only a few miles away.

Academia was an area where DiMaggio often found favor. For a guy who dropped out of high school for lack of interest, he did quite well in accumulating college honors. He received honorary degrees from Columbia University and New York University and proudly marched in with cap and gown to receive them. He received a standing ovation at Columbia with graduates, their parents, and probably some faculty members shouting their affection for him.

Nothing, though, compared with his reception at a Florida International University commencement on May 5, 1993. Cal Kovens, who had introduced me to Joe, was a major benefactor to the school, which reached out to an inner-city community. It was Kovens who suggested to the school that it honor DiMaggio. Joe's first reaction, as usual, was to reject the idea. I explained that his presence would give a boost to FIU and its students. Most of them were the first in their families to graduate from college, and many had overcome enormous obstacles to do that.

He thought over what I said, and apparently his allegiance to the underdog took over, and he agreed to go. He received a long standing ovation when he walked into the ceremony, which was held at the Arena in Miami. After congratulating the graduates, he went into his repertoire of baseball stories. He told one about his old roommate, Lefty Gomez. "We were playing a game in Detroit. The Yankees were leading 2–1 in the bottom of the ninth, and the Tigers had a man on first with two out. The batter hit the ball to Gomez on one hop, and all he had to do was throw it to Lou Gehrig at first base and the game was over. Instead, for some reason—we called him Goofy, remember—he turned and was ready to throw to second base, but neither our shortstop Frankie Crosetti nor second baseman Tony Lazzeri was there. So, he threw to Lazzeri between first and second. All hands were safe. Lazzeri just didn't throw the ball back to Gomez; he walked with it to the mound and demanded an explanation. Gomez told him he had seen a headline in a newspaper the day before that read, 'Lazzeri: Smartest Man in Majors.' Gomez told Tony that's what flashed through his mind when he didn't know what to do with the ball. 'That's why I threw it to you. I wanted to see what you would do with it.'"

DiMaggio concluded by saying, "That was baseball—a game—and in a game you usually get at least a second chance and maybe more. But you are going out into real life. Use your new education to make the right decisions. You may not get a second chance. God bless you all, and good luck."

The crowd rose to its feet, applauding, and the graduates threw their caps into the air. They weren't supposed to do that until the ceremony ended, but DiMaggio had inspired them; it was their salute to him. He was touched by the experience, and said so in his diary.

Four years later, he also showed up at the university's twenty-fifth anniversary party. John Kozyak of Miami was also there, and he was surprised to see DiMaggio. Just a few miles away the Marlins were playing in the sixth game of the 1997 World Series. "When I told Mr. DiMaggio I was impressed and surprised to see him, he put his hand on my arm and said, 'Young man, I committed to attend this event six months ago, and I keep my word.'"

That indeed was Joe DiMaggio. I never knew him to break a promise.

5

KING OF THE CARD SHOWS

Joe disagreed when I told him there was no one else alive who got more money for his signature. "You're wrong, Morris," he said. "The queen of England is the highest paid signature in the world, because she signs only royal documents, so it's impossible to get her signature on anything else."

Joe spoke from experience. When Prince Charles came to Palm Beach, Florida, Joe saw an opportunity to add a queen's signature to his collection of baseballs with presidential autographs. He put his name on a ball for the prince and asked his friend Loy Anderson to present it, along with a ball for Queen Elizabeth to sign. But Charles explained that his mother signed only royal court papers. When the queen visited Baltimore, Joe asked Larry Lucchino, then an Orioles executive, to try for the signature, but again he was rebuffed.

DiMaggio was more cooperative. He autographed baseballs for Dwight Eisenhower, Ronald Reagan, both George Bushes, Mikhail Gorbachev, Fidel Castro, and thousands upon thousands of others who stood in line for hours and paid as much as $175 for his signature.

DiMaggio was the king of the memorabilia business.

My brother Lester once said to him, "It's not Alan Greenspan who controls the economy, it's you." Joe was puzzled. "You can change a $1 bill into $400 by just signing it," Lester explained. DiMaggio's signature on anything from a restaurant menu to a bat could bring from $150 to $2,000, and that was wholesale.

He was the number one draw for card shows, where celebrity athletes were paid to autograph baseballs and other memorabilia. At first, the shows were a setting for selling primarily baseball cards, but they grew into a big business. I was not involved in that aspect of Joe's business for the first few years. From 1984 through 1988, he did three or four shows a year and made relatively little money. He was averaging probably $10 to $20 for signing a ball and was paid a flat fee for a three- to four-hour show, usually $7,500. The promoters were getting $50 to $75 for each of his autographs.

Joe had no idea of how much his name and image were worth, and his failure to realize this impeded his success. He negotiated on his own, which was a drawback, because he lacked confidence in his ability to get more money from the promoters. He thought small. He was more excited about receiving $750 to $800 for airfare and expenses than the $7,500 to $10,000 fees he was getting for being at the show itself. He felt that he was beating the promoters out of a few bucks on the expenses—but in reality they were beating him out of a lot more money where it really counted.

In the fall of 1988, DiMaggio invited me to a card show at a hotel in New Jersey's Meadowlands, virtually in the shadow of Giants Stadium. The place was jammed. Joe had agreed to stay three hours. The show lasted four and a half hours.

"Joe, this is crazy. It has to end," I told him. "You are finished being paid by the hour. You're not a plumber, an electrician, a lawyer, or an accountant. They get paid by the hour. You are Joe DiMaggio. No more $7,500 for three and four hours." I told him we would raise his minimum for a card show to $25,000, then to $50,000, and then to $75,000. "At the right time," I said, "you will be paid by the piece and not by the hour."

Joe looked at me as if I were crazy. Maybe I was, but I was also right.

I got the same look from Steve Hisler, the show's promoter, when I told him that Joe's fee for a three-hour appearance was being raised from $7,500 to $25,000. I also explained that his travel expenses no longer will be $750 or $800. "He has to fly in from San Francisco and stay at a hotel. Expenses will be $2,500."

I had one more bit of news. "From now on, I will be at every card show with Joe, sitting next to him."

Some promoters, or dealers as they were known in the industry, would sneak in items for Joe to sign and sell them later for a lot more money than DiMaggio was getting. I intended to stop that.

It was a twenty-minute ride back to Manhattan, and I knew that the news of our new pay scale was traveling much faster than that to others in the world of memorabilia. There are no secrets in that business.

When I told Joe what I had just done, he said, "They'll never pay it. I'm just an Italian baseball player." Once again, DiMaggio's feeling of inferiority was coming out. That called for a locker-room pep talk, and I was ready. The setting, though, was more elegant, Hunan Park on Columbus Avenue and 70th Street, his favorite Chinese restaurant in New York.

"Joe, you are much more than an Italian baseball player. You are America's only hero, and probably will be the only sports hero for years to come. While the others are tarnishing their images with drugs and booze and getting into trouble with the law, you, Joe DiMaggio, are above all that. There is only one America and only one Joe DiMaggio, and there will never be another." He looked at me, stunned, and responded as he often did when something sounded right to him. "That has a nice ring to it."

Soon, he went to his first $25,000 card show. We did a few more at that figure. The dealers passed on at least some of the increase to their customers, but the lines for DiMaggio's autographs still were three hours long. In 1990, the fee went up to $50,000 per show. The card show promoters hated me. I was their common enemy. They complained to each other that I was ruining their business and DiMaggio's reputation with those high demands. Joe laughed and said the promoters were mad because I was making them share their profits with him and his family.

"Let me be the bad guy," I told him. "Don't get involved in the negotiations and don't listen when they rap me. The bottom line is that you are finally getting what you deserve for the card shows."

We were back in the Meadowlands in 1990 for a show on a Sunday in November, when the Giants were playing less than a mile away. Again the turnout was tremendous. Joe and I were in the car waiting to be driven back to Manhattan when Hisler knocked on the window. "You were right, Morris, you were right. Joe deserves $50,000 for doing this."

"That's the old rate, Steve," I said. "The new rate is $75,000, and the travel expenses are now $3,000." I knew that by the time Joe and I had gone through the Lincoln Tunnel into Manhattan, the new fee would be known from coast to coast.

In previous years, Joe would sign a ball or a photo for $20. Dealers often would buy the tickets that were required to get something autographed and have their friends or relatives— "beards," as they called them—stand in line for the signature. The dealers would then sell the item for $100 to $125.

Joe was furious when he became aware of what was going on. At a show in Orlando, he actually got up from the table and stormed out the building. I had left his side for about fifteen minutes, and when I returned, he was gone. That had never happened before. Typically, once he sat down, he stayed until we took a break to visit the men's room. I was frantic. Where had he gone? I found him in the parking lot leaning against my van, seething, his face red with anger, sweat pouring down his face in the humid, 85-degree weather.

He told me he had seen the show's promoter give a boy some money, probably $10, to get on line with ten or twelve pieces. Joe would not have been suspicious if the kid had come to him with three or four pieces, and he rarely said no to a youngster. But when this boy came through the line two or three different times, Joe figured out what was going on. He kept his eye on the kid, and sure enough, he saw another man, probably another dealer, give the boy money and another item to be signed.

As the scene was described to me, Joe threw his pen in the air, left the table, and headed for the exit. He still had forty-five minutes left to complete his three-hour commitment. It was a two-day deal with the promoter, former lawyer Dick Gordon. The first show was on Saturday in Oklahoma, and they flew together to Orlando for the second show the following day. We received half the money in advance and a certified check for the balance that morning.

I knew there was no way Joe was going back into the hall, not as angry as he was. "This is my last card show," he fumed. "These guys are all creeps." I drove around trying to calm him down. We sat in a park in Lake Buena Vista for a couple of hours looking at the ducks and talking.

"Joe, you're right. You don't have to do card shows anymore," I told him. "You can sit in an office signing this stuff, and there will be no aggravation. Your health is more important. And, besides, you've got enough money to give up these shows." After those assuring words and some pizza, he felt better.

By the time I got back home to Hollywood, I had been up for more than twenty-four hours, because my wife and I had attended an engagement party before I set out for Orlando at 3:00 A.M. After a good night's sleep, Joe flew back to Hollywood, and I met him for breakfast, just for the satisfaction of being with him. I was exhausted from lack of sleep—as I look back at it now, I realize I must have been off my rocker.

◆ ◆ ◆

Of course, that show in Orlando was not DiMaggio's last. After a two-year break, for which he was paid by Score Board, he went back to the signings. It wasn't simply the money that brought him back. Joe liked meeting his public too much to give up the shows.

The rules changed, however. The minimum guarantee for three hours went to $125,000. Eventually, it was increased to $150,000. The dealers were also limited to making $25 for each item he signed. If the ball or photo sold for $150, the promoter got $25 and Yankee Clipper Enterprises received $125. In addition, we restricted the number of items dealers could buy, so the fans who waited in line would have a chance at more items and at better prices. Dealers with more than five pieces had to wait until after the show to have those items signed, and when Joe did finally sign for the dealers, he would ignore them. Even after that treatment, the dealers would profusely thank him.

DiMaggio never ceased to be amazed that people would stand in line for his autograph, sometimes for as long as five hours. He made it a point to look directly at the person who was getting the autograph and shake hands. He always gave permission for a photo to be taken with him. That's why dens and living rooms all over this country feature photographs of DiMaggio in a suit, shirt, and tie posing with a proud family member.

Joe didn't need any encouragement to pose for photos, but he was even happier to do it when I suggested that people in line be invited to take pictures so that they would return at a future date for him to autograph the photo, for which he charged $175. Since I sat next to him at the shows, I was in many of the photos. Some people would even ask me to autograph the picture, but I declined. I remembered the Old Timers Day when DiMaggio spotted Barry Halper signing autographs. "Those people don't even know who he is," Joe said. "What an egotistical jerk!"

At a show in Atlantic City, a heavyset fellow in his seventies moved up the line and finally was in front of DiMaggio. With him were two youngsters who were about ten or twelve. "That's Joe DiMaggio!" he said to the kids. "Oh, my God, it's Joe DiMaggio!

Joe, these are my grandchildren. Could I take a snapshot?" DiMaggio beckoned for the youngsters to get next to him, and they posed together. But granddad was shaking so, he couldn't hold the camera steady, and he was sweating.

"Calm down, calm down," DiMaggio urged. "I don't want you to have a heart attack at my show."

The grandchildren stood there, holding up the ball and smiling as their grandfather continued to struggle with the camera. He was pushing the wrong button or something. Finally, to the relief of everyone, the flash went off.

"Take another one in case it didn't come out," Joe said, and he got up and put his arm around the man. Talk about a Kodak moment. I'm positive that grandpa never forgot his close encounter with Joltin' Joe.

That was an example of the feeling DiMaggio had for his fans. I've seen other baseball celebrities, including Mickey Mantle and Ted Williams, who never even looked up when they signed something. With them, it was strictly business. It was more than that to Joe. He really enjoyed his fans, especially the kids. He was like Santa in a department store before Christmas, except no beard and no red costume. The little girls would climb on his lap and kiss him while their parents snapped away with their cameras. He always had a "thank you" for the fans, and they replied with, "Thank you, Mr. DiMaggio," "God bless you, Mr. DiMaggio," "Stay healthy, Mr. DiMaggio." He would say to me, "I feel strange that they are thanking me because they are paying me." DiMaggio had the ability to charm women of all ages at the shows, even when he was in his eighties. They would run around the table where he was sitting and hug him. "I just love you, love you, love you," they would gush.

The cynics will say, "Oh, sure, DiMaggio enjoyed the fans. It wasn't the fans, but their money." No question, he liked the money he made, but he felt guilty that people were paying $150 for an autographed photo. He rationalized this by saying, "Well, if I don't charge it, the dealer is going to charge them $499."

There were two kinds of people at those shows, the fans and the investors. Some wanted his signature as a keepsake, to pass down as a family heirloom. Others saw it as an investment. "I'm going to put these six balls in a vault," a blue-collar guy in his thirties once told Joe, "and by the time my kid is ready for college, these will pay his tuition." DiMaggio smiled, but after the man walked away, he told to me, "I should have told him to get a good mutual fund."

◆ ◆ ◆

Joe went into the card shows with the same spirit he took to the ballpark during his career. He saw them as challenges. A wonderful example was a 1996 show at Hofstra University in Hempstead, New York, on a frigid Sunday morning. The gym was freezing. He began signing at 9:30 A.M., and by the time the session ended around 6:30 P.M., he had signed more than 2,000 baseballs, photos, and various other memorabilia. The promoter could not remember anyone doing more in a single day. The average for a sports celebrity, such as Mantle or Williams, was 700 to 800 autographs. DiMaggio's endurance was quite a feat considering he was eighty-two years old and working in a freezer-like environment. Of course, he did make more than $300,000 that day.

Joe's granddaughter Paula was with us, which delighted Joe because it meant she was there to see him set a record for the number of items signed. He was proud of that, especially since the fans were paying $150 for a signed baseball and $175 for a photo. Several times he asked me to guess the size of the crowd, and he wondered how close we were to reaching 2,000 signed items.

DiMaggio's competitive nature often came through on the memorabilia circuit. At one signing in 1989, DiMaggio asked

Gerald Stern, George Solotaire's nephew and a major collector, what Mantle was charging for an autographed ball. Stern told him $35, which was the same as what DiMaggio was charging. A week later, Joe's price was $40. He had to be number one. At the end, a ball with his autograph was selling for $175, of which DiMaggio received $150 and the promoter got $25. By then a Mantle-signed ball was selling for $85. One reason DiMaggio's autograph on a ball was worth so much was because he limited the number he signed. At the start, he would sign as few as 50 balls at a card show, and after I set new ground rules in 1993, he signed 1,000 for each show. He did only about five shows a year, so he signed about 30,000 baseballs in his last six years. (By comparison, Pete Rose or Ted Williams probably signed more than 100,000 baseballs over the same period.) There are many more than 30,000 baseballs out there with DiMaggio's signature, but most of those are forgeries. When word got out in 1998 that Joe had cancer, some 9,000 baseballs with his signature showed up on the market within weeks, but none was actually signed by him.

At least one of the big memorabilia dealers employed a forger so expert at duplicating signatures that even the fellow whose signature was copied had a tough time telling the difference. The FBI asked for Joe's help in 1990 with some baseballs that bore his signature. DiMaggio wrote in his diary how he and two agents sat in a room in the Cathedral Hotel in San Francisco and for more than an hour studied balls that the FBI had sent from Ann Arbor, Michigan. DiMaggio said there was no doubt that it was his signature, but there was a lot of doubt about whether he had put it on those baseballs. "I have not signed that many baseballs for anybody," he told the agents. "I sign balls for individuals, which I like doing, but only 50 to 100 at card show appearances, one per person."

DiMaggio told the FBI that forged autographs were common. "Especially mine and Mantle's," he said. He also told me that signatures of lesser-known players were actually erased from balls and replaced by forged signatures that were worth more. One specific example he cited involved Cecil Fielder's autograph being removed and replaced by forged autographs of Mantle and Ted Williams. "The last time Mantle signed baseballs was when Bobby Brown was president of the American League, and Ted didn't sign many after the new guy [Gene Budig] took over, so they had to get older balls to counterfeit the signatures. This crook had a whole batch with Fielder's signature." Even though Fielder hit 51 homers for the Tigers in 1990, his signature on a ball was selling for only $15 to $20. By 1996, Williams had been slowed by a couple of strokes and wasn't signing many baseballs, so the price of a Williams ball went up as high as $200.

While DiMaggio used the law of supply and demand to his advantage, other Hall of Famers were not particular about the number they signed. A memorabilia industry joke: What's more valuable than a ball autographed by Bob Feller? Answer: A ball not signed by Bob Feller. The great Indians pitcher put his signature on baseballs for more than sixty years, and never bothered counting. Nolan Ryan signed 100,000 balls in one year. Harry Bryant of Score Board made a road trip with Ryan, and was awed as the pitcher sat in a chair watching television signing ball after ball while carrying on conversations with several people.

Joe signed quickly, but he worked at it as if he were taking an exam in school. He really got into it. At the signing at Hofstra in 1996, for example, I realized at about 2:00 P.M. that DiMaggio had not taken a break all day, not even to go the men's room. As a matter of fact, neither had I, so I suggested the time had arrived. The line waiting for him in the gym was about three to four hours long. His response: "We can't let these fans wait for nothing. We have to finish everything today. There's no show on Monday, and a lot of them will be shut out." He was genuinely concerned about not disappointing those who had shown up.

Getting DiMaggio to a restroom at a public event like this was a job in itself. We often planned the route in advance, and sometimes, getting there quickly with the fewest interruptions meant leaving the building and walking outside to another entrance. When fans saw that Joe was taking a break, they would rush to the restroom to meet him when he got there. People would applaud him and shout, "Joe, we love you." There were pats on the back and camera flashes going off. Joe acknowledged the fans with waves, but we knew that stopping would delay his return to his task and create problems that could prolong an already long day.

On these organized trips to the men's room, everyone in our party would form a circle around Joe as he walked. One of us or a security guard would clear the men's room, and the rest of us would stand guard outside the door. Among Joe's worst fears was that a photo of him at a urinal would wind up in a tabloid or one of those other supermarket rags. He had a close call at that Hofstra show. The men's room was cleared, and Joe and I were the only ones in there. He was in an ebullient mood because of the success he was having that day, and we had a long, jovial conversation as we washed our hands. I walked out first and faced a mob waiting to see DiMaggio make his exit. Cameras were at the ready. I turned to hold the door for him and was stopped cold by what I saw. His genitalia were outside his fly. He had been so engrossed in conversation that not only had he neglected to zip up, he also forgot to tuck in. "Look down, Joe," I warned. He did and quickly backed himself into the men's room, and was bent over in laughter. I don't remember ever seeing him laugh so hard. "Joe, that definitely would have been front page on every supermarket rack in the country, and probably on *Entertainment Tonight*, too." Joe laughed about it for the rest of the day, but I knew that he wouldn't have been so giddy had I not saved the day with that warning. I would have been out of the book for weeks, if not months.

◆ ◆ ◆

After so many years of attending these functions, we had the mechanics of the signings down to a routine. Somebody would check to see that those waiting on line had purchased the same number of tickets as the number of items to be signed. Some had as many as eight items, especially around Christmas when they would give the memorabilia as gifts. The baseballs might still be in their boxes or the photos in envelopes, and to keep the line moving, someone had to make sure everything was out and ready to be signed.

That wasn't always easy. People would jockey for position, and there were arguments about who was trying to crash the line. Collectors would offer me gifts to move them up. But the only ones we expedited were the elderly, especially those with walkers or in a wheelchair.

I sat next to Joe and prepared the items for signing. If someone had five baseballs and three photos, I would put all the balls together and then the photos. That was to keep DiMaggio from having to change pens. He had about fifteen pens in front of him. He used ballpoint pens to sign the baseballs, and thick felt Sharpies to sign photos and other memorabilia. He would pick up two balls at the same time and sign them together. He could sign five in ten seconds. He was very fast and accurate. "I have to give the paying customers my best signature," he would say.

Joe educated me about pens and memorabilia, and I passed on the information to the people who came up for autographs. Don't use a Sharpie to sign a baseball. The signature fades or turns green on a ball in six months. A lot of balls signed by Lou Gehrig and Babe Ruth became worthless because the signatures faded. Don't use black ink to sign a ball because collectors want a signature in blue ink, and that's what they pay the most for. Joe wanted the fans to be educated about this because he didn't want them to waste their money.

There were times when an entire family came to the table—grandmother, grandfather, parents, kids, cousins, sons-in-law—and each had a ball or a photo, which created confusion about what belonged to whom. We had one of our crew stand there to sort it all out. People would get so excited they would snap pictures, shake hands, and walk away without their signed memorabilia. "Hey, don't you want these baseballs?" Joe would say.

There were strict rules about what could be signed and how they could be signed. For example, until shortly before his death, Joe would not sign caps, jerseys, or bats at the shows. His explanation was, "If you give it all away, there is no more mystique. You have to hold back something."

DiMaggio signed fewer than seventy-five caps at shows during his lifetime, at $375 each. He would also sign batting helmets, which the promoters sold for $375. Joe received $350 for each signed helmet. After Joe died, Neiman Marcus was charging $750 each for several hundred caps advertised as signed by DiMaggio—but they weren't genuine. Like about ninety percent of the items on the market said to have been signed by DiMaggio, these were forgeries. When we notified Neiman Marcus, the store withdrew the caps.

Some of the dealers who sold items with forged DiMaggio autographs were so unscrupulous that even a certificate of authenticity was worthless. Such a certificate usually doubles the price of the item. A perfect example was a batch of baseballs on which DiMaggio had added "HOF 55" to his signature, signifying the year of his induction into the Hall of Fame. Those were signed in my office in the presence of only Rita Sokoloff, Scott DiStefano, and myself. No more than 1,000 balls were signed that day. Yet, many thousands more were out on the market with a certificate of authenticity pledging that the person who signed the certificate was present for the autograph session. If he was, he had made himself invisible.

At the shows, people brought in pieces of wooden seats from Yankee Stadium, Ebbets Field, or the Polo Grounds, where the

Dodgers and Giants played before moving to California. They asked for his signature on their artwork. These were all considered flats, and were the same price as a photo. Although the contracts gave Joe the right to refuse to sign those unusual items, he seldom did. He would tease some of those autograph seekers, just to see their reaction, but then he came through for them. He enjoyed the byplay.

Any book about DiMaggio was a no-no because none was an authorized biography, and he refused to give them authenticity by signing them. He would autograph other sports books, especially those about the Yankees. He sought out a page on which there was a story or photo relating to him. When people asked him to sign the cover, he would say, "You don't want that. It's not my book."

People brought up photos of him with Gehrig, Henrich, or Lazzeri, and he would recall for me when the picture was taken and a story about it. Joe was careful where he signed the photo, and would never sign across someone's face, for example. He picked a spot that would not mar the picture. Nor did he like to write anything on a ball but his name. Sometimes he came close to losing his temper when he was asked to add something personal with his signature. Usually, he ignored the request, so anyone who has an autographed ball bearing a special note from DiMaggio owns a relatively rare souvenir.

Now and then, someone would try to slip a nude picture of Marilyn Monroe under a scorecard or baseball picture, hoping that Joe would not see it and would sign it. Commercial dealers were the most devious. They would present a large photo of Joe swinging a bat, and underneath was a cutout space for his signature. Pasted under the photo was a nude picture of Marilyn. DiMaggio's signature on something like that would be worth a lot of money. Some may have slipped through, especially in the final years. When we caught someone using this trick, Joe urged me to contact the FBI, but I felt that type of publicity would actually increase the price of those items.

Joe always refused to sign any Marilyn Monroe memorabilia. Someone might hold up a photo of Marilyn and say, "Hey, Joe, sign this for me." That would sometimes rattle him, but he quickly regained his composure. He would not even give the satisfaction of looking at his tormenter, while someone in our group would move the guy out of the line and out of the place. That task often fell to my son-in-law, Herb Milgrim, a Florida attorney who once was a tough, streetwise athlete from New Jersey. Joe admired the way Milgrim handled such problems.

◆ ◆ ◆

In addition to me, my son-in-law, and DiMaggio's granddaughter Paula, the contingent that worked the shows at times included my daughter, Laurie; Jerry Cantor, then one of my partners; Rita Sokoloff; Martha Lee; and Joe's other granddaughter, Kathie Stein. With the exception of Paula and Kathie, who were employed by Yankee Clipper Enterprises, we were unpaid volunteers. As material was being gathered for this book, Rita told an interviewer, "It was hard work, and when I got tired during a long day, Mr. Engelberg would say, 'You don't know what a legend you are working with. People would pay to be here and do what you are doing.'"

Joe regarded the group as "his people," and he insisted we dress the part. He set the standard, always wearing a suit, white shirt, and tie. Milgrim once showed up without a tie. He was wearing slacks, a blue blazer, and an open-collar shirt. "Herb, get a tie and put it on," DiMaggio commanded.

Joe usually was very moody before a signing, which put me under a lot of stress because it became my job to calm him and get his mind off the event. If he wasn't at ease, once the session began, anything could set him off, especially if someone shouted something like, "Hey, Joe, what about Marilyn?" I could count on a tension headache as a byproduct of those sessions, and I always had Tylenol at the ready. For Joe, I had handy a supply of his favorites: M&Ms, cough drops, and Diet Coke. When things got really bad, he took a "hot dog break," for his favorite fast food, with beans.

Sometimes, when he appeared to be sullen, he was actually suffering in silence from the arthritic pain that would stiffen his upper back and neck when he leaned over a table autographing for hours. He refused to take any painkillers, even Tylenol. He preferred the "Italian Stallion" role, macho to the core. One time, in the fall of 1996, he was in the office doing a signing with the artist Robert Stephen Simon for a painting Simon had done of Joe. Simon had put his signature on only a few pieces when he complained that he couldn't do any more because he had a sore finger. Sokoloff, who was there during the signing, recalled that Joe was very unhappy about that. "Mr. D. let the artist know that he had played when his neck hurt and his foot ached, and now this fellow wanted to quit because his finger bothered him," Rita said. "He had no tolerance for anyone who complained about a little pain."

The tension of working with DiMaggio at shows was enormous, and it usually took me a couple of hours to recover. Before one event at the Marriott Glenpointe in Teaneck, New Jersey, in January 1997, we were sitting in a small room next to the hall where the show would be held. Joe was signing mail orders or mail-ins from people who could not be at the show and had sent their items to be signed to the promoter, along with a check. The balls, photos, and other pieces were lined up on the table, about 400 of them. Joe was signing them. It was a nervous time because he always worried that promoters didn't give him an accurate count and were slipping in items that they would later sell. We counted and recounted and decided there was a discrepancy of nineteen items. That could have meant some items were being hidden inside others.

I started to shake the various pieces, and out fell two *Life* magazine covers featuring a photo of DiMaggio. Suddenly, everything stopped, a frozen moment. "Hold on," said Joe. "I want an exact count on the number of items you got in the mail or I'm not picking up the pen." The dealer insisted he knew nothing about those two cover photos. "It must have been my guys," he said. Joe accused the dealer of knowing what was going on. He believed the dealer was allowing his employees to slip in items they could sell, and that would be their compensation for the day. DiMaggio was ever alert and suspicious. As Nachio said, he would have made a great director of Scotland Yard.

There was a knock on the door, and by this point Joe was really on edge. He said to me, "Nobody comes in here. Nobody. No exceptions." This being New Jersey, the knock at the door could have been Rizzuto rushing in to ask Joe to sign something, or Berra, who had a museum about thirty minutes away, or Reggie Jackson. Joe was in no mood to talk with anyone.

I opened the door a crack and there was Joe Torre, who less than three months earlier had managed the Yankees to a World Series championship. I didn't recognize him. He was wearing a leather jacket, not his Yankees uniform or the sweatshirt he wears in the clubhouse. He looked smaller out of uniform. "Could I speak to Joe?" he asked. "Joe is not seeing anyone until after the show," I replied.

Fortunately, someone who did recognize Torre got word to DiMaggio that the Yankees manager had asked to see him. When DiMaggio stopped for a coffee and doughnut break, he met with Torre briefly.

Despite the tension, Joe was feeling great, having made more than $200,000 that afternoon. When it was all over, he put on his coat and headed back across the George Washington Bridge with Paula to have a dinner at Alex and Henry's Roman Garden in Eastchester. He had talked about the meal with great anticipation all afternoon, telling us about the shrimp, steak, and rigatoni with fresh tomato sauce that he would have. Before leaving the Marriott Glenpointe, he checked the box of doughnuts that he had been noshing from all afternoon, without offering any to the rest of us. Two were still in there. He picked up the box, put it under his arm and left, also taking with him the gifts he had received that afternoon. I stayed behind, too exhausted to go anywhere.

◆ ◆ ◆

Martha Lee was a regular fixture at Joe's signings during this time, and she and Joe became very close ever since she started working for me. Because of their age difference, it was more of a father-daughter type of relationship than anything romantic. He was in his seventies and she, a divorced mother of two daughters, was in her thirties. He surely harbored thoughts about what might have been if he were younger; he once confided in her that "the old equipment isn't what it used to be." He also told me that Martha reminded him of Marilyn Monroe. Like Marilyn, she was an attractive blonde with a stunning figure, although Martha was thinner.

Because Joe would spend a great deal of time with Martha when he was in the office, I began to wonder if something romantic was brewing. My concern grew in Dick Burke's New York apartment when I passed DiMaggio's bedroom and saw Joe and Martha sitting on Joe's bed. The door was open, and it was a very innocent episode. Joe was shining his shoes and wanted someone to talk with. Still, I decided that if something was happening, it was time to head it off. It is never wise to have a staff member of a law firm, or most any type of firm for that matter, to be romantically involved with a client. So, I transferred Martha to the firm's office on Worth Avenue in Palm Beach. That move was aimed at reducing the contact between the two, and it did.

Martha was a bright lady, and she knew why I did what I did. "It could have developed into a deeper relationship," she said. "Both of us probably were thinking in those terms. It was leading to something. We were getting too close." Martha said the transfer upset her emotionally, and she turned to food for solace. Her scale showed it. The move also bothered Joe, who missed their frequent meetings in the office, and he called her at home in the evenings more than he ever had before.

Those calls were mostly, as Martha put it, "to shoot the breeze." "He would ask me about my daughters, and things like that, because he didn't see me anymore. Then, he asked me to drive down so we could go to dinner. He didn't like to drive, especially long distances. So, I would drive to his place—he would say, 'let me pay for your gas'—and we would go out to dinner and chat. I totally enjoyed his company. He was a gentleman."

One call from DiMaggio was a cry for help. His television set was acting up and he couldn't figure it out. Martha drove an hour and a half each way to fix it. "He relied so much on television for entertainment and I knew he would be miserable without it," Martha said. "It was at times like that I realized I was needed."

Being needed by him was the main reason their relationship developed. When DiMaggio moved into Deering Bay, a luxurious development near Coral Gables, Florida, she proved to be of tremendous help. Living in hotels as he did, DiMaggio was in the habit of tossing the shirts and underwear he had worn on a chair or couch and leaving it for the maid. The same for towels. There were no maids in his Deering Bay apartment, and by the end of the first week, the place was a disaster area. Martha Lee and Rita Sokoloff took turns driving from Hollywood to try and make some order out of chaos. Martha did his laundry, mending, cleaning, and grocery shopping. He never asked her to do any of those chores, but she did them because she had a deep affection for him and because, as the only daughter in a family that included four brothers, she was accustomed to doing such duties for her father and grandfathers. "I knew it was appreciated, and it was my way of showing affection." There was another reason Martha did the household chores. The apartment was loaded with memorabilia, and DiMaggio was worried that a cleaning woman may have lifted a piece or two. Martha, who oversaw the cleaning, decided, "It was just easier if I did it."

Joe showed his appreciation by giving her autographed baseballs on her birthday. He gave her thirty-five when she turned thirty-five, and thirty-six on her thirty-sixth birthday. He also gave her a bat as a Christmas present, which was extremely rare for him to do. It showed how much he cared for her. Joe also tried to give her a $10,000 check, but my firm's policy barred all personnel from accepting cash gifts from clients.

Martha's father, a retired opera singer, had long been a DiMaggio admirer. He was thrilled that his daughter had met his favorite ballplayer. She and DiMaggio posed for a photograph specifically for her dad, who was ailing. Unfortunately, he died a couple of days later and never got a chance to see it.

In addition to their meals together in Florida, Martha was DiMaggio's frequent dinner date at restaurants in New York, and she learned there was no privacy when dining with him. "People would approach him for an autograph just as he was putting a fork to his mouth," she said. "I became protective of him, and put up my hand or waived them off. People must have wondered who I was."

This protectiveness was a two-way street. Soon after Martha was hired in 1985, Joe saw that she had been bruised. He learned that she had been lifted up and thrown by her husband. When she was hit a second time, DiMaggio told her, "If you hang around any longer, it will be like a ball game. Three strikes and you're out.

Don't give him a chance to do it again." Martha took the advice and left her husband the very next weekend. "Mr. D. inspired me," she said.

◆ ◆ ◆

If I had a list of all the card shows I had arranged and attended with Joe, there would be an asterisk next to the one in Atlantic City in June 1998, the last one he ever did. For the first time, DiMaggio was to add "Yankee Clipper" to his signature for the public, something he had resisted for years. That's why the memorabilia people remembered the show at Bally Park Place Casino. I had a different reason. For the only time in our sixteen years, Joe and I had a public disagreement, and I walked away from him. It could have been a total break, as it had been with others in his life, had he not backed off when he realized he needed me for more than making money. I was the guy who tended to his everyday needs, provided emotional support, and turned him on to a different way of life in which family relationships were important.

By then, we were operating under a well-organized system, quite different from the days when Joe would show up protected only by a handshake and without safeguards to prevent him from being cheated by the sleazy characters in the memorabilia business. Now, for each appearance, he was armed with a ten- to fifteen-page contract that was so detailed it specifically listed each item that could be signed and those that couldn't. The agreement specified that before he sat down, he would be paid by certified check or a bank check made out to Yankee Clipper Enterprises. Half his fee was paid thirty days in advance, so if the dealer canceled, Joe at least would get some remuneration for having taken himself off the market on that date.

Another protection for Joe I learned about from being an IRS agent. I warned him never to take cash from the dealers at those shows. Those promoters would walk around with bags of bills to pay the athletes, and some well-known former baseball stars got in big trouble by taking fistfuls from those bags with assurances that nothing would be reported to the IRS. Those players were courting trouble because the dealers would report those payouts as business expenditures.

As memorabilia collecting became more popular, so did the subtleties of signing autographs. An additional word or special phrase along with the autograph was a big deal. At private signings, but never at card shows, Joe would sign some things, "HOF 55," the year he was inducted into the Hall of Fame. This made the ball or photo more valuable. The same was true for adding MVP 39, 41, 47 to his autograph, his uniform number 5, or 361, his career homers. He told Sokoloff his favorite number was 56. He gave her a signed poster commemorating his 56-game hitting streak, and he gave her an autographed baseball for her fifty-sixth birthday on which he wrote, "Happy 56 to Rita." Joe asked her not to sell any of the memorabilia unless she needed the money, and not while he was alive. Sokoloff, a no-nonsense, all-business woman, said she would never sell the one with the number 56 on it nor the one he gave her on her fiftieth birthday. That one was special to him, too, because it was the fiftieth anniversary of his hitting streak.

On the subject of specially signed balls, Jerry Romolt once offered him $1,000 a ball for every one he signed "Joseph P. DiMaggio," and he refused. He probably could have made $1 million doing that, but he said, "That's not my name. My name is Joe DiMaggio." Yet, Joseph P. DiMaggio was the signature he had to use on all legal documents. His determination not to use it on baseballs and other memorabilia was another example of his desire to hold something back.

DiMaggio knew that adding "Yankee Clipper" to his signature would significantly increase the autograph's value, and he had been waiting for the right time to do it. To him, the longer he could put it off, the better. This was another example of his desire to keep some of his assets in reserve, and he regarded that phrase as an asset. Over the years DiMaggio had signed items for me, members of my family, and certain people on my office staff with "Yankee Clipper," but never for the public. I advised him that the memorabilia show in Atlantic City was the right time to finally make public the Yankee Clipper tag. I also wanted to test the market, because Joe had 500 bats signed "Yankee Clipper" in storage from the H&B signing. A dealer having no connection with the Atlantic City show was prepared to pay him a lot of money for signing 200 posters. The amount would increase substantially if Joe added his famous nickname—and such an apt nickname at that. The fastest of the old sailing ships were called Yankee Clippers, but Joe had given the name new meaning with the way he glided after a fly ball.

DiMaggio begrudgingly agreed to add "Yankee Clipper" to his autograph, as if he was doing me some big favor. The poster signing was scheduled for Friday, the day before the two-day card show. Although he wasn't particularly happy about making this concession, DiMaggio wanted Paula and her oldest daughter, Vanassa, to be there for the historic occasion and to help out during the signings.

A key figure in this notable signing was Scott DiStefano, who was involved in a memorabilia operation based in Atlantic City. DiStefano was DiMaggio's man in Atlantic City. Joe would look for him at the airport as soon as he landed. Scott kept his life smooth and uncomplicated in the city's hotels and restaurants, where the crush of people sometimes can make things hectic. Scott was born in the city, and his late father, Joe, had played the drums with bands in local clubs. The younger DiStefano had worked in the casinos, both as a dealer and in management as a pit boss, and that was where he met his future wife, Laura, who also was in casino and hotel management. When Laura became pregnant, she quit work, and he supplemented his income by selling baseball cards. He bought the cards from B&J Collectibles and sold them to fellow employees. That went so well, he expanded his market.

"I wasn't a big baseball fan, but I was a collector," Scott said, "and that's what got me started."

DiStefano's connection with B&J got him his first meeting with DiMaggio. In 1995, Joe was in Atlantic City for a card show at the Taj Mahal, and Joe was doing private signings for dealers in a suite beforehand. DiStefano and a friend brought 200 baseballs and some photos for DiMaggio to sign. Sitting and anxiously waiting for their turn, they heard DiMaggio grumble, "Let's get this goddamned thing started." That made them even more apprehensive.

DiStefano had it all figured out. He told his friend to sit next to DiMaggio, and he would be at the other side of the table, arranging the items, and hand them to his buddy for Joe to sign. "I'm not going to sit next to him," said the friend, who was both awed and intimidated. So, the job fell to Scott, and that turned out to be best thing that ever happened to him.

DiMaggio got into a conversation with DiStefano, and found it interesting that Scott was born in Atlantic City and that his father had been a musician in a club owned by Joe's buddy, Skinny D'Amato. He asked Scott about his young family, about his plans for a future. Whatever the reason, DiMaggio was impressed with the thirty-eight-year-old, even if he did violate Joe's dress code by wearing khaki jeans and a short-sleeved sport shirt. DiMaggio asked for his business card and said, "Let me know if there's anything I can do for you." In the memorabilia world, that was like getting a key to a gold mine.

DiMaggio determined that DiStefano seemed genuine and trustworthy, unlike other dealers, and Joe wanted to help him, especially since Scott seemed to be struggling with a growing family. Joe asked me to call DiStefano and invite him to do business with us. That was the opening DiStefano needed. B&J made a deal with Yankee Clipper Enterprises. DiStefano flew down every month to my office, where Joe would autograph 1,000 baseballs and photos, and Scott's employer would sell them.

A friendship developed between the two, and they would go to lunch and sometimes dinner together on the signing days. Joe would ask his advice about memorabilia and about certain dealers. Since Scott was about the same age as Paula, DiMaggio also sought his opinion about a car he wanted to buy for his granddaughter.

Later in their relationship, when Scott was trying to go out on his own, Joe gave him a chance to dip into the pot of gold attached to DiMaggio memorabilia. One deal enabled DiStefano to sell "stat balls." Joe did only 160 of those balls, and they were special because he wrote, in his own handwriting, the key numbers of his career—his lifetime batting average (.325), his career homers (361), the year he was voted into the Hall of Fame (55), the length (56) and year (41) of his hitting streak, and of course, his uniform number (5). "He made a lot of mistakes putting all those numbers on the balls," DiStefano remembered. "It took him three days to complete the job. Finally, we put a piece of paper with the numbers in front of him, and he copied them." After all, he was in his eighties.

Sometimes when Scott came down to Florida for the signings, he would bring his young daughter, Rachel, and drop her off to visit his mother in West Palm Beach while he went on to my office. One time, however, their plane was delayed; if he took Rachel to her grandmother's apartment, he would be late for his appointment with DiMaggio. So he brought her to the meeting. The four-year-old Rachel sat quietly and patiently coloring while Joe and her father took care of their business. Scott excused himself at one point, and when he came back, his daughter was twirling DiMaggio around in a swivel chair. "Rachel," an embarrassed DiStefano said, "you must not bother Mr. DiMaggio." DiMaggio was laughing, "Bother me? We're having a great time."

Joe then took Rachel by the hand and walked her around my office, pointing out the scores of photographs of him covering the walls, something he never would have done with an adult for fear of being regarded as polishing his ego. "That's me, honey, when I was a ballplayer," he explained. "No, it's not," Rachel responded. "You're too old." DiMaggio burst into laughter.

Two and a half months before the show in Atlantic City, a hole developed in the macula of my right eye's retina, and I was in danger of losing the vision in that eye unless I had surgery. As part of the healing process, I had to keep my face down, toward the floor, twenty-four hours a day for two to three weeks. I would either sit in a chair with my face down or lie on my stomach with my nose in the mattress. Try that for about fifteen minutes and you will get an idea of how uncomfortable it was. Joe came to my house to see a telecast of a fight between Evander Holyfield and Mike Tyson. I was lying there with my head down, watching a TV set placed on the floor. "This is barbaric," DiMaggio said when he saw what I had to do. He said he could never do it. Meanwhile, he was watching the fight on a big-screen TV and devouring a full-course dinner I had ordered from Mama Mia's. "Joe, when it comes to saving your eyesight, you will do anything," I told him.

When my doctors told me I couldn't fly for four months, Joe suggested we cancel the Atlantic City trip. Was he being overprotective of me, was he jumping at the chance to get out of the special signing, or was he reluctant to go into that Atlantic City turmoil without me?

There was no way I was going to put off that historic poster signing and the money Joe would make. We'd find a way to get there. We considered hiring a chauffeur to drive both of us from southern Florida to Atlantic City and back. That meant sitting in the back seat of a limousine for about thirty hours each way with Joe DiMaggio and listening to him complain about the Yankee Clipper signing. Joe was willing to go by limo, but I decided to take a train to Philadelphia and then be driven to Atlantic City. Joe offered to go by train with me, but I felt that would be too arduous for him, so he flew.

What should have been a twenty-eight-hour train ride turned into a thirty-four-hour ordeal because of a derailment in front of us in Jacksonville. DiStefano met me in Philadelphia and drove me the rest of the way. It was a steamy afternoon and I hadn't had a shower in more than a day, so I rushed up to my room, took a quick shave and shower, changed into a fresh shirt, put on a tie, a blue blazer and gray slacks, and went to the lobby. DiMaggio was waiting for me. "Morris, you are ten minutes late!" Until this day, I don't know if he was serious. But I do know you should never be late when meeting DiMaggio because he was never late, and to him there was no excuse for being late, short of death. In fact, he was chronically early.

A number of people were gathered in the room to see DiMaggio put that new signature on the posters. The moody side of Joe was evident that day, as he ignored my attempts to talk with him at the signing. I couldn't get a laugh or a word out of him, which was very unusual. He put on his somber face and had conversations with memorabilia industry people, whom he despised. By doing that and freezing me out, the way a child would do, he was trying to punish me. I was annoyed and angry. I had made the tedious trip by train to be with him, as usual without compensation, and had to be away from my business for almost a whole week. So, I felt I had good reason to resent being snubbed.

The signing ended at about 6:00 P.M. and DiMaggio, for the first time that I could remember, turned down my invitation to go to dinner, nor did he invite me. Instead he went with Paula and DiStefano. Actually, I was relieved that I wasn't invited, because it would not have been much of an evening, not with the mood DiMaggio was in. I tried to figure out the reason for his surliness. Was it his aching back? Was it because I had been ten minutes late after traveling thirty-four hours to get there? It never even occurred to me that he was upset with me for having him sign "Yankee Clipper." We had planned for months on testing the market to determine the value of that signature. The dealer had sold the posters even before DiMaggio signed them, and Joe got $120,000 for about an hour of pushing a pen.

But that was it; it was the Yankee Clipper thing that was bugging him. He angrily told that to DiStefano at dinner. Adding those two words to his signature meant he was giving up something else he had been holding on to, another piece of his mystique had chipped away. Nevertheless, as I had anticipated, using those words added substantially to the price of balls, photos, lithographs, and anything else he signed that way. From that day on, he added "Yankee Clipper" to his signatures on thousands of items that were later sold by his estate for millions of dollars.

The card show on Saturday began about 10:00 A.M., and when Joe did not say good morning, I knew it was not going to be a good day. He was still miffed. We had not gotten together for our ritual pre-show breakfast. Never in all our previous shows had he ever criticized my selection of pens to be used for the signings. He did this time. And he also complained about items I selected or rejected for him to sign. He was especially rude to Paula, but he was charming to the dealers and others in the memorabilia business he had little use for. Again, like a child, he was rubbing it in, trying to get under my skin. I figured I was about to get dumped, dropped by the wayside like all the others in his past. His buddies in New York and Atlantic City had been trying to undermine me for years. "He's got too much control," they would tell him. "Get rid of him." Now, I expected he would do it, and the way I felt at the time, it would have been fine with me.

If I hadn't been so upset, I would have found his sudden coziness with the memorabilia gang amusing. Many times when we were heading for a show or some signing deal, DiMaggio would say, "Morris, beware. In their business there are only four types of people: felons, forgers, phonies, and liars." Some of them, he told me, were notorious for cheating on their wives with girlfriends they had in cities around the country. That offended DiMaggio's sensibilities because he knew their wives, and he felt awkward because he also knew their girlfriends. Not nice people, he would say—and yet there he was being chummy with them.

I was going about the monotonous task of putting the correct pen in his hand and tilting the photos in the right position for him to sign, when it happened. I handed him a blue Sharpie pen to sign a 16-by-20 photo. He slapped my hand and said, "You are moving too slow." I looked at him, dropped the pen, and said I had to go to the men's room. I never returned to the table. Instead, I went up to my room and stewed. About 150 to 200 items remained to be signed, but I wanted nothing more to do with those things or that ungrateful rat. The Joe DiMaggio I first met on February 1, 1983, was gone, flushed down the toilet. "Who needs this aggravation," I thought. "He needs me more than I need him."

That evening, I was supposed to join DiMaggio, Paula, and some others for dinner at Peregrines at the Hilton, one of the classiest restaurants in town. DiStefano had booked our party weeks earlier, and Joe had been long anticipating it. He had talked about how he would order the most expensive steak on the menu. The house was picking up the tab—just as the DiMaggio party was comped the night before at the Sands, where they dined exquisitely and expensively at Medici. The hotels and casinos in Atlantic City were delighted to have Joe DiMaggio in their restaurants. The tourists and gamblers were sure to go home and say,

"So, there was Joe DiMaggio sitting about 20 feet away from me, eating a steak. Can you believe it?"

When DiStefano called to say he would pick me up at seven o'clock for dinner, I told him that I wasn't going because of what had happened earlier at the signing. There was no way I would sit at a dinner table with DiMaggio. I explained to DiStefano that not only did that slap on the hand hurt my feelings, it may have damaged my credibility to pursue other ventures for DiMaggio. The incident had been witnessed by people with whom we did business, and many of those creeps were just waiting for the chance to get at Joe without me, his protector and negotiator.

Scott pleaded with me to change my mind. Paula had backed out of the dinner, too, after a disagreement with her grandfather over what she would wear. (He frequently tried to influence how she dressed.) DiStefano said he could not handle DiMaggio alone, especially with the attitude Joe was displaying. My job after any show was to brighten Joe's spirits by telling him how much money he had made, how well he did in providing for his family, and how he had delighted his fans. I had no desire to charm DiMaggio this time, but DiStefano was close to desperation. He implored me to put my feelings aside and help him out.

Memorabilia people were always worried that DiMaggio would decide to quit the card show circuit, which would be a major blow to the industry because he had become its linchpin. His departure would mean a substantial loss of money. The dealers figured that his appearance at a show was good for 2,000 admissions, usually at $6 a piece. Many people who bought tickets weren't even interested in getting Joe's autograph. They just wanted to get a look at him, bask in the glow of his fame or snap pictures of him.

In addition, about 200 vendors would rent space at the shows and set up tables to sell baseball cards, books, and memorabilia signed by other sports figures. DiMaggio's presence virtually guaranteed a big crowd, meaning more income for the vendors and more for the promoters, who could charge $200 to $300 for each table.

All of them would suffer if DiMaggio packed it in, so they had a financial interest in keeping him happy. That's why it was so important to Scott that Joe be content that weekend. Maybe it's an exaggeration, but in a sense, DiStefano was the point man for the whole business that night. If that was the case, he was perfect for the role. First of all, DiMaggio liked him, even though he was a memorabilia dealer. If there was a list of dealers that Joe liked, Scott might have been on it alone.

I agreed with DiMaggio's assessment that Scott was a good guy, and I didn't like to see him in a tight spot that night in Atlantic City. So I agreed to go to dinner with him and Joe. I walked alone to the restaurant along the boardwalk and tried to calm myself. It had been a traumatizing experience, being treated as I had by the man I regarded as my friend and for whom I had done so much.

The mood at dinner was lightened somewhat by the presence of Vanassa and Rachel in their little-girl finery at that posh restaurant, Peregrines, but there was precious little conversation between DiMaggio and me during dinner. Joe fulfilled his promise to order the biggest, most expensive steak on the menu, and he also ordered one for his great-granddaughter.

DiMaggio knew I was angry. Usually he didn't care how his moods affected other people, and I do not remember him ever coming close to an apology. He knew that if someone who worked with him or was close to him walked away, there was always someone else eager to take his place. But this time there was more at stake. Perhaps he thought of all those deals I had done and those still to be done, but he also leaned on me for many other things in his personal life. What about the grocery shopping? He couldn't go shopping, even with someone to accompany him, because he would be mobbed before getting past the produce department. I took care of servicing his car, made sure he got to his barber and paid for his haircuts, the same with his dry cleaning and laundry. Most importantly, he trusted me for everything from his money to making sure he got to the doctors on time. He had become part of my family. My den became his den, my backyard his backyard, my refrigerator his refrigerator.

"You know, Morris," he said between bites of his steak, "sometimes I get upset during these card shows, but it's nothing personal." I looked him in the eye and said, "If you were a client I would let you know how I feel. But you are not a client, you are my best friend."

He patted my leg. That was his way of saying that everything was OK, like a third-base coach congratulating a player who just hit a home run. When we walked out of the restaurant, Joe put his arm around my shoulders. I had never seen him do that to anyone but his granddaughters. Still, I wasn't convinced of the sincerity of what he meant to be his apology, and I am not sure, even today, about his motive. Did he like me, or did he need me to make money for him and do those things that made his life run smoothly, or was it a combination of the two?

I walked back to my hotel alone after dinner. I was still angry and wanted nothing to do with him. I thought about what I would do. That was the only time in our years together that DiMaggio had acted so obnoxiously to me, and he tried to explain it by saying he was under tension. He was well aware that I did everything for him and had no ulterior motive. True, he regularly gave me several signed baseballs, photos, and those very special bats, but were those pieces of wood enough to put up with his surly behavior? I could have purchased everything he gave me for less than $10,000 a year. By contrast, each year he received more than a half-million dollars in services from me and my firm, plus all my personal time and friendship. Joe Nachio's wife, Isabelle, was right. "He's spoiled," she said. "And we are the ones who spoiled him."

Despite all my doubts, I knew, and hoped DiMaggio did as well, that of all the people in his life, he could count only two when the chips were down, Joe Nachio and Morris Engelberg. A few days later, when we were back in Florida, I told him, "There are three things you have in life: your health, family, and pride." He got the message, and the subject was never again mentioned. He died as my best friend.

6

JOE JR.

JOE DIMAGGIO'S HEART WAS BROKEN TWICE, once by Marilyn Monroe's death and then by his son. The stoic that he was, Joe felt the least said about either, the better. "My boy is a bum," he told me whenever I tried to talk with him about a reconciliation. "But he is a good boy," he would add minutes later as an afterthought. The last time DiMaggio told me that, his son was in his mid-fifties and a grandfather, but he was still "a boy." For some reason, the father could not bring himself to call his only child "my son," at least not in the time that I knew him.

Joseph Paul DiMaggio Jr. was born in October 1941, about a month after his father had concluded one of the most celebrated seasons in baseball history, the year of the 56-game hitting streak. Joe had been scheduled to make an appearance at a fire department benefit in Union County, New Jersey, but Little Joe's arrival changed that. The new father called Phil Rizzuto and asked him to take his place at the dinner. Phil, delighted at the chance to pinch-hit for his idol, drove from his home in Queens and made one of the most fateful trips of his life. After Rizzuto delighted his audience with stories about his rookie year, the fire chief invited him home for coffee. "And I met the chief's daughter, Cora," Rizzuto recalled. "I was sitting downstairs talking with her father, and I saw this wonderful-looking girl coming down the stairs. She was beautiful, the loveliest girl I had ever seen, and she was the woman I married."

The hitting streak had made DiMaggio a world-renowned celebrity. He was talked about, sung about, and read about—not just by sports fans, but also by people who knew he did something wonderful in baseball, even if they weren't sure quite what it was.

So, Joe Jr. became a celebrity by birth. Newsreels and newspaper photos showed the proud father and beautiful mother with the chubby-cheeked baby. "Joe and the Bambino" was the introduction to a newsreel film clip of father and son, with a chuckling announcer intoning, "No, not Babe Ruth, but baby Joe DiMaggio. And who knows? Maybe a future baseball star, like his famous father."

That thought stayed with people when they saw photos of the youngster at Yankee Stadium, when he was five or six years old, bat in hand, his dad's arm around him as if he were sharing batting tips. Joe Jr. and his dad were on the cover of *Look* magazine. For the very first issue of *Sport* magazine in September 1946, father and son were shown smiling happily on the front cover, dad in pinstripes and Joey sitting next to him, his little hand in a baseball glove.

Joe Jr. was the product of Joe's first marriage, to Dorothy Arnold. DiMaggio and Arnold had met on the set of *Manhattan Merry-Go-Round,* a movie made in New York in 1937. Joe not only had a speaking part, he crooned, "Have you ever been in heaven? I have, last night. . . ." The film was a musical revue typical of the Great Depression era, upbeat and designed to keep the audience laughing and tapping its feet. Cab Calloway was in the movie, as were Louis Prima and Ted Lewis, who brought along his clarinet and top hat. Henry Armetta, a character actor invariably cast as the strongly accented Italian restaurant owner, asks Joe, "Are you a tenor? A baritone? What are you, a basso?" Joe responds, "No, I'm a center fielder." Armetta then recognizes him and exclaims, "Joe DiMaggio! Joe DiMaggio!"

Legend has it that Arnold did not recognize DiMaggio at first, either. She was a twenty-year-old from Duluth, Minnesota, and *Manhattan Merry-Go-Round* was her first movie. Born Dorothy Arnoldine Olson, she had been in show business for five years by the time of her film debut. She and a teenage girlfriend sang and danced their way through the Midwest and parts of the Northwest in the Bandbox Revue. Her assignment in *Manhattan Merry-Go-Round* was to pose prettily here and there, dance with the other chorus girls, and flutter her eyelashes, all of which she did very well. Joe couldn't help but notice. "She was a real looker," he told me many years later. "She was a blonde, and a natural one," sounding very much like he was boasting. She was 5-foot-5, with a sexy body and shapely legs that turned heads.

After the filming, Joe apparently said nothing about Dorothy to his teammates, most of whom never even knew he was making the movie. One thing led to another, and before the week was out, Dorothy called home and exclaimed, "Guess who I met!"

Of course, she knew he was a famous baseball player, according to her sister, Joyce Hadley. Hadley said that the Olson family knew Dorothy was on to something big when Walter Winchell called long distance. America's most famous gossip columnist wanted to know how the folks felt about Joe and Dorothy being an item.

The couple dated for about two years, and the relationship was heading toward the next level by April 1939. At Yankee Stadium, a reporter asked DiMaggio, "Hey, Joe, what's this about you getting married this summer? It's on the AP wire." The wire service had reported that Arnold told a studio-arranged press conference in Hollywood that she and the Yankee Clipper were to be married that summer. "Well, that's the first I've heard about that," Joe said. DiMaggio insisted there would be no wedding that summer, because, for one thing, he was playing baseball. "Maybe in the fall," he conceded, "or maybe the following fall."

Dorothy went home to Duluth in July 1939, and on her hand was a huge diamond engagement ring. She excitedly told her family that Joe had not only pledged to marry her, but he had promised to hit a home run for her in the All-Star Game, which was being played at Yankee Stadium. The Olsons gathered around their radio and learned that a promise made by Joe D. is a promise kept. He hit a home run in the fifth inning as the American League won 3–1.

After the World Series, DiMaggio took his fiancée to San Francisco to meet Mama and the family. Dorothy began the process of converting to Catholicism.

The wedding took place in San Francisco on November 19, 1939, ten days before her twenty-second birthday and six days before his twenty-fifth. The setting was the church of Saints Peter and Paul in North Beach. Old timers still remember the event as one of the greatest happenings the old Italian neighborhood had ever seen. Not only was the church filled beyond its capacity of 2,000, but the surrounding streets were so clogged with people that traffic came to a standstill. Police estimated some 30,000 gathered in the streets. Dorothy, her bridal party, and her father, Arnold, had to walk the last couple of blocks to get through the crowd, and they made it only with the help of a police escort that cleared a path. Joe and his family also had a police escort, and they needed it to get through all the well-wishers who wanted to shake his hand or pat him on the back. Vince, one of his older brothers, showed up too late for the escort, but when his friends and neighbors recognized him as one of the DiMaggio brothers, they got him to the church on time. Actually, it wasn't really on time. The start of the ceremony was delayed thirty minutes until 2:00 P.M. because of the crush. The priest pleaded for decorum so he could begin: "This is the house of the Lord. I ask you in His name to be silent."

Getting out of the Saints Peter and Paul was every bit as tough as it was getting in. Again, the San Francisco police did the job, under the personal supervision of the police chief and the watchful eyes of Mayor Angelo Rossi. The wedding caravan, horns honking and sirens wailing, headed to Fisherman's Wharf for an Italian wedding feast at Joe DiMaggio's Grotto. Not only was there no tab, but the restaurant got national publicity from that dinner.

Wedded bliss lasted about two years, if that long. Joe discussed neither the bliss nor what followed with me, except for one shocking lapse from his usual closed-mouthed approach to private matters. He curtly explained, "I caught her in bed with a guy in a hotel three times." Where? When? With the same guy or different guys? His tone and his body language made it clear he would take no more questions on the subject. Nearly ten years after that conversation, and some fifty years after the divorce, Joe Jr. told me, "My mother was a tramp." He shared an obviously still-painful memory of a time when she did handstands in front of him and some of his friends. She wasn't wearing any panties! A drink or two could make her loud and seductive, Joe Jr. said.

During the baseball season, Joe was on the road half the time. The people around DiMaggio in those days said that during home stands, he spent at least part of most evenings with the guys at Toots Shor's. That glorified saloon was only a $1 cab ride from their penthouse apartment on West End Avenue, but he had other places to go and other women to meet. He confessed to a friend more than forty years later that the temptation was too great to resist. Nachio said the opportunities were always there. "Models, actresses, those who wanted to be actresses, and women who happened to see him in a restaurant or a hotel lobby. He was Joe DiMaggio and they wanted to get him in bed."

It was more than just his fame that attracted women, in Nachio's view. "In his own stark, quiet way, he was very charming. His silence and his nonchalance made him mysterious to women. You know why he was so silent? He was at a loss for words. But he must have been pretty good because a lot of those women came back for repeat performances."

Nachio remembered one attractive woman who told Joe that she was about to be married and intended to be faithful to her husband. "But I always wanted to meet you and have an affair with you, and now that we have met, I don't want this opportunity to go by. I want you to be my last fling," she said. Nachio surmised, "So, I guess they flung." Most of those flings were before and after his marriage—but not all of them.

Dorothy had never been a stay-at-home girl, longtime Broadway publicist Eddie Jaffe remembered. She enjoyed the nightclub scene before she met Joe and continued to do that with him during their courtship and early years of marriage. Sometimes, they double-dated with Yankees pitcher Lefty Gomez and his wife, June O'Dea. The Gomezes also lived on West End Avenue, about a half mile north of the DiMaggios.

Her new role as a stay-at-home mom was not the glamorous life Dorothy had envisioned when she came to New York. She had a very fashionable wardrobe, which included large-brim chapeaus that she wore slanted over one side of her face, but no place to show it off. Dorothy was not very happy, and she let Joe know about it.

"He left her home, and he always wanted her there," her sister said years later, looking back at what went wrong for an interview with the *Minneapolis Star Tribune*. "A wife had to be at his beck and call. That went over like a lead balloon for Dorothy."

Less than a year after Joe Jr. was born, in late spring of 1942, Dorothy Arnold and the baby were in Reno, Nevada—where divorce courts were a main industry. Joe began to mope about that, and some sportswriters covering the Yankees reported that General Manager Ed Barrow called Dorothy to tell her how much her husband loved her and missed her. It wasn't that the no-nonsense front-office boss was offering advice to the lovelorn couple; he was concerned about Joe's poor performance at the plate. Mrs. DiMaggio took the 20*th Century Limited* back to New York without filing for divorce. The squabbling continued, though, and it was just a matter of time before mother and infant son were back in Reno to live, when the baseball season ended. Then, with DiMaggio about to go into the army, there was another reconciliation, this one announced at a news conference in Reno. There were Joe and Dorothy posing with a smiling cherubic Joe Jr., and vowing that they were in love and back together. Not for long, though. The DiMaggios set up home near Los Angeles because Joe was stationed nearby, playing ball in the Army Air Force, and Dorothy was determined to again try for a career in the movies. They insisted they wanted to be together. But she went to court in Los Angeles and tearfully charged Joe with being cruel and indifferent, of not acting like a husband, of ordering her out of the house at times, and of not talking to her for days at other times. DiMaggio was not in court to hear the judge grant her an interlocutory decree, which meant they would remain married for a year, but he would have to pay her $14,000, plus $500 a month alimony and another $150 for child support.

There was talk of another reconciliation, but it never happened, although they did see each other from time to time, usually when Joe visited their son. Dorothy remarried in 1946, to George Schubert, a New York stockbroker, and their divorce four years later ignited new rumors that Joe and Dorothy would get back together. In fact, the two were together for Christmas that year—four days with Little Joe in a Nevada winter wonderland— but they then went their separate ways.

In 1951, nine years after she first filed for divorce, both were saying "maybe" when asked if they were thinking of remarrying. "Maybe" was Joe's favorite word when he was too polite to say "no" or wanted to buy time. Gossip columnist Louella Parsons quoted Joe as saying, "There is a strong possibility that there may be a reconciliation." He talked of a planned visit she and Junior were to make to New York to see him during the summer, and said it was possible they might remarry then. Hedda Hopper, another syndicated yenta, quoted Dorothy as saying she and Joe were thinking of reuniting.

DiMaggio confided to a longtime friend that he was concerned about the effect that Dorothy's two marriages and divorces were having on their son. "He must wonder how many fathers he has," DiMaggio remarked.

Nachio said Joey was not really close with either of his parents as a child. "He had no one to talk with on a son-to-parent relationship. At one time, his mother was living in the Waldorf Astoria and his father was in the Elysee Hotel, about a half-mile away. Someone would drop him off at the Elysee and he would stay there for a while, mostly watching TV, and then I would walk him back to the Waldorf Astoria to his mother. It was sad."

◆ ◆ ◆

There was no reconciliation in 1951, nor ever again. In 1952, Joe found Marilyn Monroe. That didn't remove Dorothy entirely from Joe's life, however, not as long as they had a son. By then, Dorothy had left New York and again was living in Los Angeles, doing an occasional club date as a singer and hoping to get a film breakthrough in Hollywood. Junior was enrolled at the nearby Black Fox Military Institute. Big Joe had retired as a player by then, and when he was in the area, he would take his son for the weekend or a weekend day. On one such day, Junior joined his dad and Marilyn at the Bel Air Hotel swimming pool, and a photographer took their picture. Dorothy was appalled at the sight of her eleven-year-old son posing with a swimsuit-clad Marilyn. What upset her, she said, was that the boy was being taken by his father to places where there was "drinking and jive talk." So, she went to court to try to reduce Joe's visitation rights, while increasing his child support payments. "No way," said Judge Elmer Doyle, "petition denied." What's more, he told Dorothy that she had made a big mistake by divorcing Joe DiMaggio in the first place. It was a resounding victory, one that Joe took as much delight in as he did in winning on the field or making a business deal.

Marilyn made Little Joe a big guy at school when she visited him. Celebrities were taken in stride at Black Fox, where the student body included the children of several Hollywood people— but Marilyn Monroe was something special. She and Joey hit it off from the start and formed a friendship that lasted until her death. They spoke regularly by phone, and one of the last calls Marilyn received the night she died was from Junior.

At times, she acted as a warm, soft buffer between him and his father, something a mother would do. A typical example was a day the three of them were heading for a stroll in Central Park and passed Rumplemayer's, an ice cream parlor in the lobby of the Hotel St. Moritz. Rumplemayer's was not your typical neighborhood ice cream parlor, unless the neighborhood happens to be fashionable Central Park South across the street from the park, with a lineup of very upper-class apartment houses and hotels that included the Plaza, St. Moritz, the Hampshire House, and Essex House. Joey, about twelve at the time, wanted an ice cream soda. "Do you know what they charge for an ice cream soda in there?" his father asked. "Let's go back to the apartment. I've got ice cream, chocolate syrup, and seltzer and I'll make you a soda."

Marilyn slipped Joey a $20 bill and nudged Joe into the St. Moritz lobby. She said she wanted to look at something in the boutique shop. Joey disappeared and enjoyed his very expensive soda. When Big Joe learned what happened, he was furious. He grabbed Marilyn under an arm and hurried her along Central Park South, loudly bawling her out. He didn't talk with her or his son for the rest of the afternoon, but that incident bonded Joey and Marilyn forever.

"I can never be your mother because you already have one," Marilyn told Joey, "but I want to be your friend."

Dorothy Arnold DiMaggio married again in the 1960s and ran a bar-restaurant in Palm Springs with her new husband. The couple eventually retired to Palm Desert, California, where she died of cancer in 1984 at age 66. Her movie career never reached the heights she had imagined, although she did land a fairly good role in the 1957 movie *Lizzie*, which shows up occasionally on those TV channels that show "old, old oldies."

◆ ◆ ◆

Junior headed East to go to prep school at Lawrenceville Academy in New Jersey. He had played some baseball as a kid while at Black Fox, lifted weights and showed some talent at golf. He went out for baseball at Lawrenceville, but when your name is Joe DiMaggio, you had to be better than just good. He wound up on the football team as a placekicker. The boy was intelligent, but he didn't like the discipline of going to class, and school officials informed Joe that his son had cut some classes. DiMaggio Sr. took the train from New York to talk to him about it, and he went to Junior's dorm room. The kid wasn't there. Joe waited and waited, into the night, but he never showed. It was a portent of things to come.

Junior was bright enough to get into Yale University, though having the name Joe DiMaggio didn't hurt. It was a double-edged sword. "Sometimes I cursed the name Joe DiMaggio Jr.," he said. Almost from the beginning, it was clear he was going to be in trouble. He did not like to study. He liked to drink beer and, according to his father, smoked marijuana. Not having lived at home very much since his preteen years, Joe Jr. wasn't quite sure where his home was at times, and he didn't have to answer to mom and dad. He had been pretty much on his own. Dad paid the tab at those expensive private schools and at Yale, and Junior always seemed to have spending money. Big Joe may not have been known as a big spender, but he certainly did not stint when it came to his son's education. He even offered Junior a trip to Europe if he improved his grades at Lawrenceville. Joey buckled down, got a good report card, and opted for a cruise as his reward.

A high school dropout, DiMaggio was proud that his boy was at Yale, then dismayed at what happened. "He got in with the wrong crowd," DiMaggio told Dr. Rock Positano. "He was a bright boy, and the dean would have done anything to keep him there. But, I told the dean I didn't want my boy judged by a double standard. He had to have the grades."

Joe admired what Positano had accomplished. The doctor had come out of a brawling Brooklyn neighborhood and excelled at Yale, where his thesis was approved with honors. DiMaggio opened his heart to the doctor. "I love him," he said of Joe Jr. "I tried to reach out to him, but I was rejected. He was a pothead."

It was out of Yale and into the marines for Junior, a seemingly unlikely switch for someone who did not take to discipline. On the other hand, the Marine Corps offered the same type of structured existence Little Joe had lived in since boarding school. He was stationed in San Diego, and he was proud of what he accomplished. He told me he was at the top of his class, and he did especially well in weaponry. When he completed the training, there was a ceremony, to which parents were invited. Joe said he didn't intend to go. That made Marilyn angry. "If you don't go, I will," she said. "You have let that boy down too many times. This time, either you go or I will." She may have shamed him into going.

While Joey was in the marines, he was married and divorced within a year. When his enlistment ended, Junior needed a job, and his uncle Dom came through for him. Dom and a local businessman, Bill Rubenstein, were partners in a polyurethane factory in Lawrence, Massachusetts, and Joe Jr. went to work for them. Uncle Dom opened his house to him, but Junior chose to sleep in the factory on a cot. Dom was impressed with his nephew, realized that he was bright, and he decided to put Joey in charge of a plant the company was building in Baltimore. The factory was destroyed by fire before it opened, but while he was in Baltimore, Junior was introduced to Sue, a widow with two preschool-aged daughters, Kathie and Paula.

"He was very intelligent and witty and I fell in love with him," said Sue. In short order, the two were married, and they packed the girls and their belongings into the company station wagon and headed for Lawrence, where Junior went to work in the factory. The newly formed family lived in North Andover. Junior adopted the two girls and they became Kathie and Paula DiMaggio, which was the first step to their becoming the main beneficiaries of their grandfather's substantial estate.

Big Joe was not thrilled with his son's choice of a wife. "I guess I was never on his 'best list,'" Sue acknowledged. But, whenever he was in Boston to see Dom, Joe Sr. visited his son and family in their apartment on the second floor of a two-family house. Joe immediately took to the girls. Kids always delighted DiMaggio—he felt relaxed around them—and little girls were his favorites. Through his son's adoption, he suddenly had two granddaughters.

Nachio joined DiMaggio on a visit to North Andover. "We took the girls out to get something to eat, just Joe and I, and he really got a kick out of being a grandpa to those kids. He was laughing and kidding them." So, Junior, who rarely could please his father, succeeded this time. Just how happy Joe was became apparent when he devised a plan to bring Junior's family to the Bay Area so that they could be closer. DiMaggio, who was living in the family home on Beach Street, put Joe Jr. into the polyurethane business with him and two other men, a veterinarian and Steve Alexakos, who had been an offensive lineman at San Jose State and had played a season for the New York Giants football team. So, after about two years working for Uncle Dominic, Joe Jr. moved his family to northern California.

Big Joe even suggested locations that he thought would be suitable for his grandchildren, not in San Francisco, but close enough where he could visit them. They settled in Lafayette, right next to Walnut Creek. Grandpa would come out for dinner about three times a week, and Sue tried to please him. "I cooked pasta gravy on Sundays, and I made enough so I would use it during the week on other dishes," she said. "But he wasn't coming for the pasta. He was coming to see the girls." Knowing Joe, I would say it was fifty-fifty. He liked his "eats," always thinking about his next meal, even while he was eating.

Sue worked in the office of the factory, which was in Oakland, and said "life was good." But then Joe Jr. got friendly with some people in San Francisco, and that led to major trouble because they were into drugs. According to Sue, Junior occasionally had used drugs back East, but he really got into them big time in the Bay Area. "Speed. He loved speed," she said. Once in a while, he did cocaine, and one evening he came home with some mescaline for them to use together. The drugs were the big lure in San Francisco. His trips there became more frequent, and sometimes he would stay all night.

Junior soon ran into problems at the factory. He and Alexakos squabbled, and Alexakos bought out the two DiMaggios. Sue complained that Big Joe didn't back up his son, but Junior felt he had let his father down again. Sue bore the brunt of her husband's frustration. He beat her. The girls saw it, and even as adults they were reluctant to talk about it—but their mother wasn't.

"It was very embarrassing, and I didn't want anyone to know," Sue said. "I thought it was my fault." She said the abuse began in the East when "he broke three of my ribs and had my face swollen out to here."

Junior, personable and intelligent, got a job running a trucking company in Oakland, and he liked it. Still, he continued to use a variety of drugs and batter his wife. "He was a crazy man behind the wheel," Sue said. "A cop stopped him and gave him a ticket. He came home and took it out on me." Finally, Sue left him, went to her mother's home in Carmel, and filed for divorce. "He came down and talked me into coming back. I told him, 'One more time and it's over.' And I stuck by that."

After they separated, Joey flaunted his charm, wit, and drug connections to attract new female friends. He was 5-foot-8, handsome, with light brown hair and the muscular look of someone who stayed in shape by lifting weights. He and Sue were not yet divorced, and he would call her now and then just to let her know he was still around. Occasionally, he would show up in person. About two years into their separation, in 1976, he sweet-talked Sue into letting him borrow her Ford station wagon, and he wrecked it in a terrible accident. Junior came close to dying.

"The doctors had to drill into his brain to get at a blood clot," Sue said. "They told me three things could happen—and none of them good. He could die, he could be paralyzed with limited brain function, or he could have a major personality change. Well, he lived and he wasn't paralyzed, but bingo, he sure did have a major personality change. He was never ever the same again."

When he was thirty-five, Junior hooked up with group of motorcyclists, and he became a familiar figure around Martinez, his father's birthplace. Joey had some second and third cousins in the area, and he hung out with them. The local police got to know him, too, not only for the company he kept, but for his occasional strange behavior.

"He called me once from jail," his ex-wife remembered. "He had been in a fight, and he wanted me to bail him out. I hadn't seen him in three years, but I went and got him out. He was so angry that he kicked in the door. I said to myself, 'Why did I do this?'" Sue, who remarried and became a real estate broker in the Bay Area, said, "I absolutely loved the man. But I could not battle the drugs he was into." The last time she saw him was at his father's funeral, and she was shocked. "I couldn't believe what he looked like. He looked awful."

Junior had a similar view about his ex-wife. "She put on a lot of weight," he observed, and commented that she looked much older than he remembered. He made a motion with his hand to his mouth, as if to simulate someone drinking.

◆ ◆ ◆

There were many times that Big Joe and Little Joe lost contact with each other. The father was spending most of his time in south Florida, and it was during this time that I met him. He didn't talk much about his son, but I could never forget how I envied that lucky kid I saw on TV on the field with his father that day in 1949 when Joe was honored with all those gifts at Yankee Stadium. I knew that father and son were not close, that his son was divorced and living alone in the San Francisco area, and I suggested that it might be a good idea to bring Joey to Florida. I offered to fly to San Francisco and speak with his son. "I'm a pretty good salesman," I said.

"You don't know my boy," DiMaggio responded. "You're barking up the wrong tree. You would be wasting your time. It would be a mistake." Again, it was "my boy," never "my son." I dropped the idea.

Joe was speaking from bitter experience. He had tried to help his son—not emotionally, to be sure, because Joe didn't know how to establish a warm relationship with Little Joe—but he had tried to get his son on the right path. He funded him in that polyurethane factory in Oakland, and that didn't work. Then, after Junior lost his job with the Oakland trucking outfit, he asked his father to finance his venture in a trucking business. Joe came through with $75,000 for a Peterbilt tractor-trailer. Again, Big Joe was in for a disappointment, because Joey wrecked the truck and another business venture ended.

Joey disappeared for a while into what he called his hobo life, sharing cheap wine and beer with his biking buddies. At times, he would knock off a whole case of beer in one day. Some of his money came from welfare, some from his father. There were occasions when Big Joe couldn't find his son or even call him because Joey had no permanent home at that time, let alone a telephone. So, DiMaggio would leave money with his nephew, also Joe DiMaggio, who was distinguished by his middle initial, T. Joe T. DiMaggio was the son of Mike, the second oldest of the DiMaggio brothers, and Joe Jr.'s first cousin.

Joe T. and his wife, Marina, had a restaurant in Orinda in the early 1980s. When Joey would stop in for a meal, the DiMaggios would give him the money his father had left for him, but they didn't tell him where it was from for fear he would want more. "My uncle would tell me, 'I want to give him some money, but I don't want to give it to him all at once. So, piece it out,'" Joe T. said. Big Joe was worried that if he gave his son large sums of money "he would move in with some floozy and they would spend it on beer and wine."

Joe T. said that he and Marina also gave Junior some of their own money. "I would find out that Marina gave him money, and I'd get mad at her, but then I would take care of him, too." His cousins also would find odd jobs for him so he could have some walking around capital.

When the elder DiMaggio wanted to locate his son, he would get his buddy Sam Spear, who was the announcer on telecasts of thoroughbred races from Bay Meadows and Golden Gate Fields and also had a weekly radio show, to help him in the search. "Joe and I would take rides into the Napa wine country, and we would go through Martinez so Joe could look for his son," said Spear. Once, they spotted Joey walking in the gutter with his head down. He was very thin, dressed in jeans and a white T-shirt. His hair was a salt-and-pepper gray, but he hadn't started to wear the ponytail yet.

"Pull over, pull over. There's Joey," his father exclaimed. Spear parked and DiMaggio told him to stay in the car. Joe got out and shouted, "Joey, Joey, Joey." His son shouted back, "You don't know me. You don't know who I am. Leave me alone." He never stopped walking. "It was a poignant moment, and in a way, Joey was telling the truth," Spear said. "I feel they didn't know each other. Joe got back in the car. He was hurt and embarrassed. He said nothing, and I neither did I. I didn't want to invade his privacy. We just went on."

It was in Martinez at another time that DiMaggio tried to give his son a lesson about what it meant to battle the odds and come up a winner. He took Joey to the street where he was born. "My father came from Sicily, broke, without a penny, and he went down to that bay fishing every day to feed his family. He and my mother worked hard, and look at what the family accomplished." DiMaggio clearly was proud of his family's success story. Did his talk make an impression? Spear said he didn't know.

There was at least one other time when Sam saw father and son together, and getting along well. Big Joe was taking his son to a dentist friend to get some badly needed dental work done, and they stopped at Golden Gate Fields. "Joey was decently dressed, and he came across as a friendly, articulate fellow," Spear remembered. "Joe introduced him to several people, and he certainly wasn't embarrassed."

Joey's adopted daughter Paula and her husband, Jim Hamra, were there when DiMaggio and son showed up at a family function in Martinez with Big Joe's sister, Marie. "He wanted to be there, and yet he didn't," Jim said of Junior. "Everyone tried to make him feel welcome, like trying to get him involved in conversations, but he looked uncomfortable." His father, of course, was the main attraction.

Maybe Joey gave up because of all the failures in his life—his failure to go beyond one year at Yale, his business failures, his failed marriages, and his inability to establish a close relationship with his father or his mother. He didn't see Dorothy for about a dozen years, and when he finally did go out to southern California to try for a reunion, that didn't work.

◆ ◆ ◆

As he drifted into his fifties, Joey was a toothless, homeless character around Martinez and north into Pittsburg and Brentwood in Contra Costa County. He would be seen riding his bicycle through Martinez. For a while, he slept in the cab of a truck he later wrecked, and then he set up a makeshift home in an old refrigerated milk truck that had been abandoned in a field near Martinez. He broke his hip when he wrecked his bike, slamming full speed into a van. Junior was cited for drunken driving on a bicycle, a mishap that was played big in the local newspapers and caused further embarrassment to his father. Joe contacted Dr. Positano in New York about getting help for his son's broken hip, but apparently Junior wasn't interested in doing anything about it. His father was also concerned about the drunk driving charge, and he hired a lawyer to defend his son. Before long, Junior was hurt again when fell into a ditch and shattered an ankle.

After both of those accidents, he recuperated in his cousin Joe's home in Antioch, benefiting from Marina's gentle, loving care and renowned cooking. "He stayed a week or two and then took off," his cousin said. By then, Junior must have been off drugs. "He didn't have any drugs or alcohol while he stayed with us, and if he was addicted, he could not have gone two or three weeks without them."

"He was a troublemaker, but I miss him," Marina said. "He was a con artist," added Joe T. "He could con you out of anything."

After his ankle and hip injuries, Joey couldn't bike through the towns and instead had to walk, but he didn't seem to mind, even though he had a noticeable limp. He had walked a lot even before the accidents. Jim Hamra saw him on foot, going through Concord, the town next to Martinez. "I asked him if he needed a ride, and he said no. He came off as someone who still had his pride. 'No, I don't need a ride. I'm fine. Thank you very much.' He looked like a street person, but he didn't sound like one."

Nachio agreed. "His choice of words was above the ordinary person's. He was sensible and logical, and he talked with a great deal of reason," said Nachio, a graduate of Penn State and an intelligent, perceptive man.

In the mid-1990s, Junior lived and did odd jobs outside of Pittsburg, in scruffy Bay Point. He worked in one of two junkyards owned by Mike Fernandez, a man in his late thirties whose grandmother was a DiMaggio. Initially, Joey lived in a trailer in the junkyard, and then Mike fixed up a bungalow for him. "My guesthouse," Fernandez explained. By then, Joey was troubled by asthma and kept an inhaler in his pocket along with his dentures. He didn't like those teeth his father had bought for him, and he often lost them. According to Sue, when he got angry at someone, he threw those false teeth at them.

When his father was dying, Joey was targeted for interviews, most of which he declined. The checkbook journalists came out in force, and when *Inside Edition* offered him $15,000 he took it and did a masterful job of conning that TV tabloid show. He knew what to tell them and what not to. He carefully avoided revealing anything that would have delved into his father's personal life, which is what the producer really wanted. Joey turned down a much bigger sum to cooperate in a tell-all book about Big Joe, sort of a "Daddy Dearest." His father never had any fear about that happening. "My boy is loyal," Big Joe said. "He wouldn't talk, even for a million dollars." "He had no interest in money," said Fernandez. Joey later told me he took the $15,000 from *Inside Edition* to get better-fitting dentures.

When the inquiring reporters got too intrusive, Joey moved to Brentwood and into a house near Fernandez's other junkyard, in Contra Costa County. This was not too far from where Nachio and I found him to tell him his father had died. After the funeral, I convinced Junior to try south Florida. He showed up at the airport wearing faded jeans, a T-shirt, and sandals. In his hand was a small carry-on bag that contained all his life's assets. Again, he had no teeth, which he had either lost or thrown away, and his matted gray hair was tied in a ponytail. "He looked like the last of the San Francisco hippies," remarked Rita Sokoloff, my office manager. Joey, though, had a taste for the better things. He insisted on flying first class, which was hardly the transportation for the hobo lifestyle he said he craved.

In rapid order, we got him a simple Florida-style wardrobe, a complete physical examination by his father's doctor, Earl Barron, and an attractive apartment facing the beach in Hollywood. He was fussy about the apartments he looked at. "I don't like those windows, they're not big enough. I don't like that wall, the closet is out of place." You would think he was a decorator, not someone who only weeks earlier had lived in the back of a truck and in a junkyard. The top floor of the apartment house had a gym surrounded by plexiglass where he would pedal a stationary bike and watch the ocean. "It's important to keep in shape," he said.

It was actually his father who paid for the apartment and the clothes, since the funds came from the trust DiMaggio set up for his son. Junior was very interested in seeing the house in Harbor Islands where his father died.

I really got to know Joe's son in the three months or so that he stayed in Florida. I found him to be a warm, gentle person, and as everyone said, articulate and bright. He would hug me and other people he liked, which was quite different from his father. I never saw Joe DiMaggio Sr. hug anyone. Junior definitely had a thirst for beer. The evidence was empty cans and cartons that were cleaned out of the apartment every morning. He kept himself clean, except for the bottoms of his feet, which appeared to be permanently black.

Joe Jr. was an expert on sports trivia, and he was forever trying to test my knowledge. He liked pro basketball and knew the game, as I found out when we went to a Miami Heat game together. We ate in some of the same Florida restaurants his father liked. He showed up one day by himself at Mama Mia's, his father's favorite Italian restaurant in Hollywood. Joe Franco, the owner, a personable guy from Brooklyn, was not even thirty years old then. Franco said when Junior came in, "He had no teeth and was wearing thongs and a ponytail. I didn't know what to make of him. He introduced himself and told me, 'I know why my father liked this place, and liked you. You remind me of myself when I was your age.'" Joe Jr. ordered dinner, but barely touched his knife and fork. He had a couple of beers and took the food home. He was embarrassed to eat in public because his teeth did not "work well."

His asthma also gave him problems. He once called me at 3:00 A.M. and was barely able to get out the words that he was having a terrible attack. I jumped out of bed and sped to his apartment. On the way, I called Rita on my cell phone and told her to alert Memorial Regional Hospital, where the Joe DiMaggio Children's Hospital is located, that we would be there soon. The emergency room doctor and a gurney were outside waiting when we pulled up. Another time, Joey called about 5:00 A.M. to tell me he was having another attack. Since I was home alone with one of my grandsons, I called a cab to pick him up and alerted the hospital that he was on his way. Both times, his life was saved with oxygen and medication at the hospital named for his father.

Joey was lonely in Florida. His friends were in the Bay Area, and he longed to hang out with them and tinker with cars. Once he flew there for a visit, and another time Fernandez came to stay with him for a while in Florida. That was not enough for Joey, however, and he decided to make another visit to California. He apparently was in no hurry, though, because he took a train.

Less than a month later, and five months after the death of his father, Joe DiMaggio Jr. died at age fifty-seven, on August 6, 1999. He had a couple of severe asthma attacks while living in Fernandez's place in Bay Point. "Twice I didn't think I had time to get him to the hospital in Antioch, so I drove to a firehouse nearby and they gave him oxygen and took him to the hospital," Fernandez said. "Once, he told me, 'Don't bother, Mike, I'm going up to the house to die.'" He was taken to Sutter Delta Medical Center, about 11 miles away, but he had no heartbeat and was not breathing when he got there. Junior could not be resuscitated.

In his biography of DiMaggio, Richard Ben Cramer wrote, "six [sic] months after his father's death, Joey was dead, too, from an overdose of crank, heroin mixed with crack cocaine." That was news to the coroner of Contra Costa County. "That's definitely not true," said a clerk who read the death certificate. The death certificate listed the standard cardiac arrest as the immediate cause, due to hypoxia (lack of oxygen) as one of the contributing causes, along with chronic pulmonary disease—his asthma. Listed as "other significant conditions contributing to death" were "alcoholism, and severe gastroesophageal reflux." There was no mention of drugs.

Joey's remains were cremated and his ashes scattered 500 yards off the Pittsburg shoreline.

7

---•---

THE FAMILY

FISH. JOE DIMAGGIO HATED THE SMELL. Whenever we were near a dock in Florida where fishermen were unloading their catch, he would crinkle up that famous schnozz. His dislike of the fishy odor was one reason that as a teenager he resisted his father's efforts to get him to join the family enterprise, fishing. Another reason was that the rolling waves of San Francisco Bay made him queasy. So, by the time he was a teenager, it was clear to him and his family that he would not fulfill his father's plans for him.

Giuseppe DiMaggio was a fisherman, and so was his father and his grandfather and his grandfather's father, as he reminded Joe regularly. Giuseppe wanted his sons to continue the tradition.

The old-country DiMaggios fished the Gulf of Carini in Sicily, and they lived on Isola Della Femmine, a bleak place of rocks and water near Palermo. Many DiMaggios still are on that little island, although most are not directly related to Joe. Those who claim a kinship, especially the old timers, are amused when American tourists with their cameras come seeking family links with the famous Joe DiMaggio. By now, it's become oral history, passed down from father to son, about the local fisherman who, many years before, went to the United States, where his son became a famous baseball player. The story has grown with age. "That Giuseppe DiMaggio had five sons who were all very big stars in America," one woman behind the counter in a pastry shop told a visitor from New York. Only three made the major leagues, but, so what? The local tie was strong enough that Joe's death was reported in the Palermo newspaper—about 100 years after Giuseppe left the island.

Joe's mother, Rosalie Mercurio, also was from Isola Della Femmine. Her father made it to the San Francisco Bay Area before her husband, and he had sent word back to Sicily that the fishing was very good, which encouraged Giuseppe to make the trip. Rosalie followed about four years later, and they settled in Martinez, in the East Bay. DiMaggio built a little boat, which he named for his wife, and went to work fishing and crabbing in the bay. Rosalie cooked and bore nine children. The girls were Nellie, Mamie (Joe called her Mae), Frances, and Marie. The boys were Thomas, Michael, Vincent, Joseph, and Dominic. All the boys shared their father's middle name, Paolo or Paul. Joe was born November 25, 1914, the last of the DiMaggios to be born in Martinez. When he was an infant, the family moved across the bay to San Francisco's North Beach, where Dom was born more than two years later.

The four-room apartment on Taylor Street was larger than the one in Martinez, but with nine children, ranging from eighteen-year-old Nellie to infant Dom, quarters were cramped. Joe shared a bed with two other future major league outfielders, Vince and Dom.

Perceptions differ about those early days in North Beach. Vince and Joe remembered them as rough times, although Vince would emphasize that though "we were poor, we never were without food and clothing." Dom, the last surviving sibling, doesn't see it that way. "We were not that bad off," he said. "We lived comfortably. We weren't wealthy by any means, but that's why America is so wonderful. You can move up in life if you want to work at it, and that's what we did."

As Joe told it, there wasn't much money, especially when he was a teenager and the country was in an economic depression.

He recalled that a dinner staple was a stew consisting of crabs and fish, some his father caught, others Giuseppe got bartering with the other fisherman. A much improved variation of that *zuppa di pesce* was to become a feature years later on the menu at Joe DiMaggio's Grotto on Fisherman's Wharf. Joe also remembered from the old days a soup made of chicken bones and gizzards, but not too fondly. "My mother knew how to get the most from a chicken," he said. "Nothing went to waste." That philosophy stayed with Joe his entire life. Even when he had plenty of money, he rarely, if ever, left a restaurant without a doggie bag.

Clothes were passed from sister to sister and brother to brother. "By the time I got them from my brothers," he said, "patches were sewn into the pants and sweaters, and cardboard was pasted into the soles of the shoes." Perhaps this sheds some light on why he dressed so fastidiously later in life, and walked in only the best shoes. (He wore Allen-Edmonds shoes, the same brand I always bought, even before I met him.)

Before the Great Depression took hold, there was a time when things were looking up for the DiMaggios. Tom and Mike were putting in full days pulling fish and crabs out of the Bay, and Giuseppe had accumulated enough money to buy another boat. Tom used that boat mostly to do his crabbing. The older boys would get up with their father at 4:00 A.M. Vince was the next to do it, but halfheartedly because he would rather play baseball.

One of Joe's fondest memories of his father was him serenading them with Italian songs, especially "Santa Lucia," as they bobbed on the water and hauled in the nets. Poppa told his sons that all the fishermen back in Sicily, at least those on the Gulf of Carini, would sing "Santa Lucia" several times a day. Joe thought maybe it brought good luck.

Joe and Dom were recruited to help their father after school with his fishing nets, and they also sold newspapers on opposite street corners in San Francisco's business district. That's when their sibling rivalry first came to the fore. "He always got the best corner," Joe complained sixty years later. "He would stand there in his short pants and wire-rim glasses, playing on the people's sympathy, and he would sell more papers. He also was short and I was tall, so the customers felt sorry for him." Dom would rag his brother for trying to get out of fishing with their father, and he showed no pity for Joe's tendency to be sickened by the smell of the fish and the swells in the bay. Their mother was sympathetic to Joe, and Dom would tease his brother about that.

From what Joe told me, and from the way he talked about his mother, I believe that Rosalie had a significant role in forming Joe's attitude toward women. He was very protective of females, young and old, and he treated the older ones with a courtly reverence. He had no problem rejecting an autograph request from a man, yet he rarely turned down a woman. The same was true when he was asked to pose for a photograph.

Joe's attitude toward women, specifically older women, was evident in the way he treated my mother, which touched me deeply. Pauline Engelberg was about the same age as Joe, and she was active and alert into her eighties. An attractive, well-groomed grandmother, she prided herself on her independence, having lived alone, a widow, for more than fifty years. When she had to go to an adult residential community, she was terrified about losing her identity, and she worried about being able to make new friends. Despite her independence, she was shy and was concerned that she would be isolated in the dining room, where everyone already knew each other. She would be a stranger among strangers.

DiMaggio had a solution. "Morris, let's go over there and have breakfast with your mother." I asked the people who ran the retirement community to set up a private table where Joe DiMaggio and I could have breakfast with my mother. Not only did they arrange for the table, but a couple of the facility's executives joined us. My mother called them *machas*, big shots. There were 200 people in the dining room that morning, and all eyes were on the famous baseball player who was a hero of their generation. One frail elderly man pushed his walker to the table and thrust out his hand. "You were the greatest, Joe," he said. "I saw that catch you made on Hank Greenberg by the monuments at Yankee Stadium, and I'll never forget it." Seeing DiMaggio smiling and shaking the man's hand gave others courage and they, too, came to our table to recall moments that were special to them. DiMaggio was cordial and gave the appearance, at least, of enjoying himself. He probably did; who wouldn't enjoy adoration? The administrators went all out for this special guest, serving us the largest strawberries and most delicious melon the dining room had likely ever seen. My mother became an instant celebrity. After breakfast, Joe put his arm around her as we walked to the door.

"Pauline, your son Morris is a very special person in my life," he told her. My mother replied, "Don't I have two wonderful sons?" She was not going to let my brother, Lester, be slighted. "You sure do, you sure do," he said.

My mother was no baseball fan. She didn't know the Yankees from the Mets or the Dodgers, yet she had cherished and displayed in her apartment the signed bats and baseballs Joe gave her at her birthdays and every time he visited. A series of strokes put in her in the intensive care unit of the Memorial Hospital in Hollywood, in the same building as the Joe DiMaggio Children's Hospital. When I went to visit her one day she was wearing a T-shirt with the hospital's name on it. Her memory and brain function were failing. Seeing her like that made me cry, and I struggled for something to say. "Mom, do you know whose name is on that T-shirt?" I asked. "Of course I do, it's Joe DiMaggio." Joe treated my mother with the same respect and kindness that he showed his mama.

◆ ◆ ◆

Pellegrino D'Acierno agreed with my conclusion about Rosalie's influence on her son, but the professor also credited the father. "That's the Italian family. Most of those old timers, especially from southern Italy, did not trust the school system, and they did the job of educating their children about how to behave in the world. They were obsessed with that, even those who were poverty stricken. That's where Joe's behavior came from. It's a matter of being *educato* versus being crude."

Italian, or more accurately, the Sicilian dialect, was the language spoken by DiMaggio's parents. At the urging of their children, however, they made diligent attempts to speak English, sometimes with humorous results. The kids would try to hide their snickers. One story their father told had to do with the 1906 earthquake, when the family still lived in Martinez. He said he was preparing to leave for a day's fishing when he felt the earth shake and the water in the bay began sloshing about. In about an hour, the sun came up and he could see the smoke from the fires in San Francisco. That part of the account he told in Italian, and he finished in English to say that he thought Mount Etna, the volcano in Sicily, had "Come to America. I say, 'Come esta, Monte? You speaka Ingleesh?'"

Joe was uncomfortable speaking Italian. When I wondered how he communicated with his parents, he said he understood what they were saying, but had trouble talking with them. D'Acierno said that was typical of people in DiMaggio's generation of Italian-Americans; they usually were ill at ease with the language because their parents were. "For one thing, his parents didn't speak standard Italian; they spoke a Sicilian dialect. When they came to America, they had new problems learning another language, so they spoke a broken English and were caricatured because of it." Joe wanted no part of that.

He also was not very comfortable in school, and he dropped out of Galileo High after a year. He took a succession of jobs, including a stint in an orange juice–bottling factory. He also worked in a fish cannery, but the smell must have driven him out. As a lasting reminder of that job, he always insisted on solid white-meat tuna in his salads, and he doused it in lemon juice. Briefly, he worked on the docks, but lost interest in that, too. What DiMaggio enjoyed doing was playing baseball, especially the hitting part.

Vince, who was two years older, paved the road Joe took to becoming a ballplayer. Joe, Vince, and Tom were built alike, tall and thin. Mike and Dom, more like their father, were shorter and chunky. Mike had powerful arms, and Joe said that of all the brothers, Mike was the best ballplayer, even better than the three who made the majors. Mike and Joe played on some of the same semipro teams, although Mike was six years older. "He hit a long ball," Joe recalled. Mike was committed to fishing because he had a family to support, and he would play ball only on Sundays for a couple of dollars. He met a tragic death when he fell from the boat and drowned. "Joe told me he was terribly broken up about that," Nachio recalled. "He loved Mike, and his brother's death was the first tragedy in his life. He really felt his loss."

Joe was fishing off Mexico when Mike drowned, and Dom and Marie made frantic phone calls to some of his friends who might know how he could be contacted. Finally, George Solotaire was able to locate him. "I told him as best I could," Solotaire recalled to his son, Robert. "He gulped and there was a long wait" as Joe tried to regain his composure. DiMaggio had a premonition years earlier that something bad would befall Mike, who had some sort of a heart problem. At that time, Joe had received an emergency phone message to call home. "It must be about Mike," DiMaggio said. "I hope he only needs money."

To Poppa DiMaggio, baseball was a game, and not something you did when you were supposed to be working or at school. Giuseppe wanted all his sons, Joe included, to be fishermen, but his opposition to Joe bumming around the ball fields was not only because he wanted the boy in the boats with him. He also felt his son should have stayed in high school at least for another year or two. The hard-working father of nine was convinced that education was the key to making it in America.

Vince was much more serious about baseball than Mike. He went out of town to play, up near Oregon. He hit the big time, for a local kid, when he signed with the Seals. The Triple A club first shipped him to its affiliate in Tucson. When Vince eventually joined the Seals, he walked into the Taylor Street apartment and plunked down on the kitchen table $1,500, which included his pay and the signing bonus. "My father wanted to know where he stole it," Joe said. Giuseppe was impressed when Vince assured him it was all from playing baseball. Joe was delighted, because that money on the table helped his case to push baseball over fishing. Later, as Joe became more famous and wealthier, his father enjoyed sharing in his son's fame, and he allowed himself to be interviewed by sportswriters. He even ventured predictions about the number of homers Joe would hit, and he posed for newsreel cameras pumping his son's right arm and encouraging him to "make a home run."

Tom, the oldest brother, also played ball locally, but not well enough to give up his crabbing. He was an officer in a crab fisherman's association and developed the reputation for being the brains in the family. He negotiated Joe's contracts with the Seals and later ran the family restaurant, Joe DiMaggio's Grotto, which Joe had funded. The Italian restaurant quickly became a tourist attraction. In addition to the DiMaggio name on the building and on the arch over the entrance to the parking lot, there was a big neon sign of Joe swinging a bat. Joe even helped with the cooking on occasion, mostly for his own satisfaction, and he prided himself on baking sourdough bread.

◆ ◆ ◆

That DiMaggio family Italian restaurant came to be a source of rancor in Joe's relationship with his younger brother Dom. That ill feeling deteriorated into another sad chapter in Joe's life.

"We were close. We were all very close," Dom said of his family. At one time, the two brothers indeed were close. They worked out together during the off-season when both were in San Francisco, and they visited each other when they were rival center fielders for the Yankees and Red Sox. "He came to dinner at my apartment after a game in which he made two great catches, right up against the fence on balls that I had hit," Joe said of his kid brother. "I had invited him before the game. I said nothing about those catches when he arrived, and neither did he. I was fixing him a scotch and soda when he said, 'You know, Joe, I couldn't have gone back another inch on either of those balls.' I thought that was adding insult to injury."

Baseball had a strictly enforced rule against fraternization in those days, and it barred Joe from even waving to his brother on the field, not only during a game, but also before or after. He took the regulation very seriously and didn't like the idea that opposing players in this era would chat on the field before and after games and go to dinner together. He and Dom sometimes bent the rules outside the stadium. Dom occasionally would come to Joe's place in New York after a game, and Joe would go to Dom's when the Yankees were in Boston.

After both DiMaggio boys retired from baseball, Joe regularly traveled to the Boston area to see his brother. Dom helped Joe Jr. when Junior left the Marines and needed a job. But something happened to sour the relationship between the two brothers, and they didn't talk for about five years prior to Joe's death. A jarring example of their estrangement took place in 1995 at the dedication of the Ted Williams Museum in Florida. Dom and Ted were friends since they played alongside each other in the Red Sox out-field. The two DiMaggios came face to face in a Holiday Inn when an elevator door opened. Joe was getting off and Dom was getting on to go to the lobby. They looked at each other, but not a word was spoken. "Wasn't that your brother?" I asked Joe as we walked down the corridor to our rooms. "So what?" he replied.

The highlight of an annual fundraising weekend for the Joe DiMaggio Children's Hospital was the Legends Game, which featured retired major leaguers and celebrities. Dom was among those invited, and he called my office to say that he would attend if his brother personally asked him. A member of my staff took the message, and I showed it to Joe. "Screw him!" he exclaimed. "Why does he need a personal invitation? Why shouldn't I call the other forty-five players?" I didn't know what to say; after all, he was talking about his own brother. Dom blamed me, telling people that I didn't have Joe extend him an invitation. I guess it was his way of covering up the truth.

What had caused this rift between the two brothers? I believe Joe never got over having to sell Dom his share of the restaurant on Fisherman's Wharf. Joe needed to pay Dorothy Arnold $14,000 when they were divorced, and he didn't have the money. Joe felt his brother should have lent him the sum rather than forcing him to give up his share of the restaurant. Joe regarded the restaurant as his because he paid for virtually the entire business, and brought his brothers in. Years later, Joe had another reason for being angry with his brother. When Dom's biography, *Real Grass, Real Heroes,* was published in 1990, it had a picture on its cover of Joe swinging the bat. "He never asked me permission to use my picture because he knew if he asked me I would say no," Joe said. Then, there was the matter of their sister Mamie's estate. Dom was the executor, and he took the statutory fee for his role. Joe was furious that his brother charged the estate a commission because, by doing that, Dom had diminished Joe's share by $12,000. Dom would have received the same amount of money had he not taken the commission, since commission is taxable and a bequest is not.

Dom's wife, Emily, tried to get Joe to end the silent treatment of his brother, or at least to answer Dom's phone calls. Soon after Dom's book came out, all of us were at a dinner in Miami Beach honoring Cal Kovens as that city's Man of the Year. Kovens, who had set up my first meeting with Joe, walked me to the table where Dom and Emily were sitting, introduced us, and wandered away. I had never met Emily before, and the first thing she said was, "Do you know why Joe is angry at his brother? Because Dom finally got some recognition on his book and he can't stand it." It was an awkward moment. I didn't know what to say. I walked back to the table. Joe never went to Dom's table to greet him, and Dom made no attempt to approach his brother.

A year before Joe was stricken with his fatal illness, Joe received a five-page handwritten letter from Emily, asking for a reconciliation. He put the letter in his jacket pocket, and I never heard anything about it.

Joe was not fond of his sister-in-law. He called her "the Barracuda" and complained that she was snobbish and put on airs. When he moved into his luxurious apartment in Deering Bay, and surveyed the opulence, unlike any setting he had ever before lived in, he said, "Well, Morris, what do you think Emily would say about this?" Of his brother he said, "He always has to have the upper hand."

I felt bad about the ill feelings between the two brothers because I know how important my relationship with my brother, Lester, is to me. So I tried to bring the two DiMaggios back together. Ironically, Dom told people that I was responsible for the estrangement, when the opposite was true.

What troubled me more, though, was the way Joe treated his last surviving sister, Marie DiMaggio Kron, at the end. She was eight years older than her brother and a widow when she died in

1997. She lived in the Beach Street home Joe bought for his parents in 1936, and when he was in town, he would stay there with her. "There's never anything in the refrigerator," he complained, and that was of serious concern to Joe, who was a major league snacker and a league leader in opening the refrigerator door. "All she does is sit at the kitchen table drinking coffee and smoking cigarettes with her girlfriends. She never goes shopping." I pointed out that by then his sister was in her eighties. "It's not that far to the supermarket," he said.

He gave Marie plenty of money to run the house, and he trusted her enough to give her the authority to write checks for Yankee Clipper Enterprises. (It was almost impossible to tell their signatures apart; Joe, Dom, and Marie all had almost identical handwriting.) She answered his phone calls and read his mail for him. Those who wanted to get in touch with Joe anywhere in the world would call Marie, and if she knew you and knew that her brother would speak with you, she would tell you. If you didn't have those credentials, she would politely say that she hadn't heard from him in a couple of days, but invited you to leave a phone number. It was her nice way of giving you a brush-off. She made Marilyn Monroe feel at home when Joe brought his bride back to Beach Street after their honeymoon. Marie was a sweet lady.

She and Joe would go together to family functions in the Bay Area, especially Thanksgiving and Christmas dinners at the home of their nephew Joe T. In October 1989, when San Francisco, and especially the Marina District, was rocked by an earthquake, Joe rushed back to Beach Street because he feared for her safety; Marie was alone in the house. He eventually found her, staying with friends. The house was badly damaged, and Joe pushed contractors to get the work done as quickly as possible so that Marie would have a safe, comfortable place to live. A year later, DiMaggio put in a security system, and because he was worried about her health, he got her a pendant that would bring her immediate medical help with the push of a button. Marie's health had been failing by then, and she required blood transfusions on a regular basis.

In January 1992, while Joe was playing in a celebrity golf tournament in Aventura, Florida, he received a phone call that his sister had died. He made arrangements to fly back to San Francisco. As he was packing, he was told that it wasn't Marie who had died, but their older sister, Mae, who was eighty-eight. "I lived with that it was Marie for half an hour," DiMaggio wrote in his diary. He and Marie went together to their sister's funeral. "We kept it pretty private," he wrote. "She looked pretty good lying there." After the Mass and burial, Joe visited the graves of his brothers Mike and Tom, and his parents' crypt. "That leaves Marie, Dom, and me," Joe wrote, and he added his concern for Marie's health. "She continues to see doctors, two more yesterday. She is losing blood, but the doctors can't figure out why. She has a couple of pints a month and she only weighs 85 pounds. But she is tough."

Poor Marie was ignored in Mae's will, and the estate went to Joe and Dom. Joe, however, had taken care of Marie, who needed the money. Starting in the 1990s, he gave her a check every Christmas. But, he also got angry with her. He thought she might be selling some of the memorabilia that she often complained cluttered the house. Then, he said she took three bottles of Scotch from his locked cabinet and gave them to her daughter for a party. Marie received no more Christmas checks after that. He had bequeathed her the house plus an amount of money to live on, but he deleted her from his will after the falling out. That was so typical of DiMaggio; cheat him once and you were through, no matter who you were.

As it turned out, it didn't matter that she was removed from the will, because she beat him to the grave by almost two years. "How's your sister?" I asked him one day, knowing that she had been ill.

"Oh," he said, "Marie died a couple of weeks ago." She was ninety. That shocked me because I had communicated with Marie on a regular basis, and Joe knew that, yet he never told me she had died, in 1997. When Mae died, I heard about it the next day.

◆ ◆ ◆

The story of DiMaggio rushing back to the North Beach house following the 1989 San Francisco earthquake not only illustrates the affection he had for his sister, but it also reveals some inaccuracies relating to DiMaggio himself, as conveyed by others. Joe's friend Sam Spear had driven him to Candlestick Park for the third game of the World Series, just as he had taken him to the first two games in Oakland. "Joe did not make arrangements with the Giants to park in the lot where the players and the press parked, so we had to park in the Hunter's Point Shipyard dirt lot," Spear said. "We pulled in and the guy couldn't believe Joe DiMaggio would be parking way out there. He wouldn't take any money from us. As it turned out, that was the best place to park when the quake hit."

Spear said his first indication of the tremor was when he felt what he described as a pounding. "I thought it was the Giants fans trying to get something started. Their club was down by two games. Then, I saw the light towers swaying. Joe had been talking with league president Bobby Brown, who told him that the game was off. Joe said, 'They're going to call off this game. Let's get out of here.' We were among the first to walk out of the stadium. It would have been impossible to get out of the press lot, but we were able to leave that other lot right away and we headed back downtown. We were listening to KCBS, the all-news station. There was a report that the Bay Bridge had fallen into the bay and that there were fires in the Marina, where Joe and his sister lived. There was a lot of panic. Joe was cracking his knuckles and worrying about

Marie, alone in the house. We got up on one of the hills, and we could see fires in the Marina."

Spear managed to get into the Marina, and when he found that Beach Street was blocked off, he parked nearby, by the Presidio. "By now, it was dark, and we were looking for Marie in the streets around there. When we got to the tape blocking off Joe's street, nobody was being allowed in, but when one of the cops recognized DiMaggio, he let us through and took us to the house. Joe went in, but Marie was not there."

Richard Ben Cramer, in his book *Joe DiMaggio: The Hero's Life*, wrote about Joe leaving the ballpark: "So Sam Spear walked DiMag out to the Giants players' parking lot, where the limo waited. And Joe was on his way home. . . ." Spear himself corrected the inaccuracy: "We didn't park in the players' lot, and Joe didn't leave in a limo. He left in my Buick." Cramer also described DiMaggio coming out of the house with a garbage bag "which held $600,000, cash." Knowing DiMaggio and being so intimately involved in his financial affairs, I knew that couldn't be true. Joe didn't have anywhere near that amount of cash, and even if he did, he certainly wouldn't keep it in the house. He was very conscious of interest offered by the banks, and that money was important to him. Many times, when a check arrived, he would send it by FedEx in order to get the extra day's interest. The daily interest might be $6, and it would cost us $20 to express mail it to the bank. Spear, as far as I know the only eyewitness to the scene, confirmed my suspicions. "He did not have any bag in his hands. Absolutely not. He was in there only for a few minutes. He was wearing a sport jacket, and if he had any cash, there is just so much room in a pocket."

Spear also was aware, from many conversations with Joe, of DiMaggio's intense feeling that his money should be making money by accumulating interest in a bank, rather than stashed in the house. "He had three banks that he used for that purpose."

DiMaggio could not stay at Beach Street, so Spear invited him to stay at his home. Easier said than done. "I had to find my way out of the city. All the freeway entrances were closed. I drove around a pitch-black city trying to find a ramp to get on the freeway. By now, it was close to midnight. No street lights were working. We were going around in circles until finally I found an on ramp to get us home. He spent the night at my house." (Cramer wrote, incorrectly, that DiMaggio stayed at the Presidio Club.)

The following day, Spear brought DiMaggio back to the Marina and a schoolyard where officials were trying to bring order out of chaos. Everyone had to get in a long line, which eventually led to tables where officials sat with green cards, red cards, and yellow cards, each indicating the amount of damage to the buildings: "condemned," "partially condemned" or "not condemned." Joe was a celebrated fixture in that neighborhood, and people recognized him even though he was dressed rather casually, at least for him. He wore a knit shirt, open at the neck, under the same sport jacket he had worn to the game the day before. "People kept asking him if he wanted to go to the front of the line, but he declined with, 'Thank you, I appreciate it,' but he would not move up," Spear recalled.

Hearing that reminded me of times when we arrived at a restaurant where a table was being saved for us, and people were waiting in line. I would walk in alone and sit at the table. Only when I was seated, Joe would come in and sit with me. He didn't want people to say he crashed a line.

◆ ◆ ◆

Long before his last two sisters and his son had died, Joe had the start of a new family with the sudden acquisition of two granddaughters, Paula and Kathie, through Joe Jr.'s adoption of the girls. At first, DiMaggio was not happy about becoming an instant grandfather. He was not particularly pleased to have Sue, their mother, as his daughter-in-law, and there was the matter of his Italian ancestry. Had the girls been Junior's biological daughters, at least some Sicilian blood would have flowed through their veins, and that would have been fine in DiMaggio's mind. But they had not a drop, and that bothered him. I thought that was strange because Joe outwardly never made a major issue of his Italian heritage, and he had married two women who were not Italian. Yet when it came to passing on his bloodline, obviously it was important to him.

His disappointment evaporated when he saw the girls for the first time on a visit to Massachusetts, where Junior was living and working for Dom. Paula instantly became his favorite. "The first time I saw her, she was asleep in her carriage, and I felt so sorry for her. She brought tears to my eyes, she looked so cute, and I fell in love with her," Joe replied when I asked why he favored Paula.

Their father, who had been a helicopter pilot in Vietnam, had abandoned the girls, and they were being raised by their single mother. Joe, ever sympathetic to the underdog, saw that beautiful baby girl as someone in need of a knight in shining armor.

There was another reason Paula was his favorite. His parents regarded St. Paul as their patron saint. Their parish church was Saints Peter and Paul. All their sons were given Paul as a middle name, and Joe named his son Joseph Paul Jr. Now, there was Paula. She wasn't Italian, but she had the right name, and in Joe's words, she was "as cute as a button."

When DiMaggio brought Junior and his young family to the Bay Area to be closer to him, he would visit and take the girls for fast-food lunches and ice cream about three times a week. He thoroughly enjoyed being a grandpa. His son's divorce from Sue six years later did not change his relationship with the girls. Even when he spent more and more time in south Florida, he continued to be involved in their lives, and, especially in Paula's case, tried to control their lives.

"He wrote me letters," Paula said. "He always had an interest in what was going on with us, our grades, and what we were doing." It was unusual behavior for a man who approached personal relationships cautiously and was reluctant to show emotion. He didn't completely abandon his need for a private existence, however. He lived in well-furnished apartments at the beachfront Seacoast Towers in Miami Beach and at Deering Bay, but he always found excuses when I suggested that he invite his granddaughters to visit him. It was either, "They've got school," or "It's too dangerous for them to fly." He was a family man when he wanted to be, at his prerogative.

Whenever Joe was back in San Francisco, he spent a lot of time with his granddaughters, until they grew into their teens and had other interests and friends. However, a phone call from Joe was enough for Paula to call off dates with girlfriends so that she could be with him. If she or Kathie needed money for clothes or something for school, Big Joe came through. He often complained about what it was costing him, but he never rejected their requests, and he was more than generous.

Kathie was a good high school athlete, and the proud grandfather was often in the stands to watch her compete. He paid for her tuition, housing, and books at UCLA and at Cal-Berkeley, but with his usual caution and penchant for details, he went over the bills with her, item by item. When Kathie received her degree, he was at the ceremony. He also was at Paula's high school graduation in Walnut Creek. "I wasn't sure if he had made it to the ceremony, but everybody told me, 'your grandfather's here,' and I saw him later in the parking lot," Paula said.

DiMaggio was a celebrity, but people in the area grew accustomed to seeing him in his role as a grandfather. "He was always my grandfather," Kathie said. "He came to functions, and he watched me play sports. He was around enough that people no longer got excited."

When Paula went to beauty school, she lived in an apartment that Joe had bought and paid the maintenance on. He was very particular about the boys his granddaughters dated, and if some of Paula's dates didn't meet his expectations, he let her know about it. He also shared his opinions about what was appropriate dress for young ladies, and that caused some heated exchanges. Any argument with Paula left him miserable for the rest of the day, and they argued a lot. It wasn't only her boyfriends or clothes that bothered him; they squabbled about really silly, insignificant things in her life. He was a perfectionist about everything, and he wouldn't listen to suggestions that he was being overprotective and too controlling.

A monumental tiff occurred once on a golf course, after which Joe didn't talk with Paula for four months. He was playing golf with some San Francisco big shot and Paula was with them. She exhibited frustration with her play, and when he admonished her, she snapped back in a tone he didn't appreciate. Paula had committed the unforgivable sin, she had embarrassed him in front of someone else, and he took a long time getting over that.

Still, Joe found ways to try and make her happy without getting too demonstrative. In the 1990s, when he was doing well on the card show circuit, he put Paula on the payroll of Yankee Clipper Enterprises. She would get a handsome check for helping out at his signing table. In her typical unselfish fashion, Paula would always ask, "What about Kathie?"

Whenever the DiMaggio granddaughters were serious about a guy, the fellow found himself face to face with Big Joe across a table in a back booth at Liverpool Lil's, a casual, dimly lit restaurant near the Presidio. DiMaggio felt comfortable in that place, which was not too far from his house, and he went there regularly to talk about days long gone with some of his old buddies. Some of the guys would get on him for things that happened fifty years earlier, but it was all in good humor, and he enjoyed the banter.

There was big picture of DiMaggio in the men's room, swinging a bat. Roger Stein, who knew Kathie since high school and had been dating her since college, was invited to join her and her grandfather at Liverpool Lil's for dinner.

"I was pretty nervous," Stein said. "After all, in addition to being her grandfather, he was Joe DiMaggio. But he was really good about it. He made me feel very comfortable." Roger had played baseball since he was a kid, and he pitched at Cal-Davis. "I tried to talk about baseball, but he didn't want to at that point. We talked baseball often, but this time, he was more interested in catching up with Kathie's life at UCLA. People were sneaking looks at him, but he was just a grandfather talking with his granddaughter."

Eventually, Joe got around to learning what he wanted about Stein, where he went to school, what he wanted to do in life, and a little about his family. In the weeks and months that followed, when the two watched baseball games on TV, Joe would talk about the difference between the players of his day and the modern day, and the stock market. "The first thing he would look at in the newspaper, was not the sports pages, but the stock market tables," Stein recalled.

Joe also took his granddaughters and their dates to the California State Fair in Sacramento and had lunch at the racetrack lounge. When Kathie excused herself to go to the ladies' room, Joe gave Roger a nudge and told him, "Get up and go with her." Roger was puzzled, "To the ladies' room? Why?" Joe explained, "Because you have to watch out for her and take care of her."

When Kathie and Roger were married, DiMaggio walked her down the aisle. There were 200 people at the wedding, and when the ceremony was over, Kathie asked her grandfather if he would join them in the reception line. "What's that?" he wanted to know. "We all stand there and greet the guests, shake their hands, and welcome them," Kathie explained. "He said, 'OK,' and he stood there and greeted every one of the guests."

DiMaggio later circulated among those at the reception, meeting Stein's family, most of who were big baseball fans. "I told them not to bug him, and to treat him like everyone else. For the most part they did," Stein said. "He was terrific with my old Jewish relatives. We worried about how the two families would get along, the older Jewish side and the older Italian side, but it was great, and he was fantastic."

DiMaggio paid for the wedding, and Kathie said he went over the bill with the caterer, item by item. Sure enough, he found some mistakes, which resulted in a more accurate final bill that, of course, was to Joe's benefit. DiMaggio had an advantage in any disagreement because the other guy usually was ready to ask him for an autograph.

Paula had a guy she was really interested in, Jim Hamra, but in this case the suitor and the grandfather did not have a smooth introduction. "Joe and I got off to a bad start," Hamra recalled. Joe called Paula at her apartment every night, and one night, when it was exceptionally late, Jim answered. "I told him never to answer the phone that late at night," Paula said. "Well, he did, and what did he say? 'You have the wrong number,' and he hung up."

Eventually, Hamra got an invitation for lunch at Liverpool Lil's. Jim said when he and Joe met, the vibes weren't right. Earlier, DiMaggio had asked Paula what Hamra did for a living, and she said, "He does pools." "You don't want to be around someone like that," Joe replied. He thought Hamra made his money playing billiards in pool halls, but what he did was manage a company that cleaned swimming pools.

When Paula and Jim decided to get married, they knew the toughest moment would be telling Big Joe. They were right. "He wasn't too happy," Hamra said. "God wouldn't have been good enough for Paula, and he thought we hadn't waited long enough." But Joe walked Paula down the aisle and gave her away, just as he did for Kathie. He also offered to pay for the wedding, just as he did for her sister. But Paula and Jim opted for a smaller wedding and used the rest of the money to go into their own pool-cleaning business.

Joe Jr. was not at either wedding, and that was all right with Big Joe, who did not want him back in their lives. Whenever Paula and Kathie asked about their adoptive father, Joe told them, "Don't worry about him, he's fine. I'm looking out for him." Maybe he thought Junior had become too eccentric or unsavory for them, or possibly there was another reason. The women had come to regard Big Joe as their father, and he relished that role, maybe to the point where he didn't want any competition from Junior. I don't believe either Kathie or Paula would have married their husbands without DiMaggio's approval.

When the Hamras went into their pool-servicing business, Jim worked six days a week at it, and Paula was there with him until she was eight months pregnant. They worked hard, and the business grew to the point where Jim had ten men working for him. He rewarded himself by leasing a red BMW convertible. Joe spotted it in the garage, and that set him off. He let them know that he had never bought such an expensive car. (For years, he drove an old Toyota Camry, which he had gotten as a gift until the Yankees gave him a Mercedes.) It was not a good idea to make a public display of wealth, he said, and it would have been a much better idea to put the money aside for the children's education. Joe did what he always did when was angry. He gave Jim the silent treatment, but everyone else, including DiMaggio's friends in California and Florida, heard more than they wanted to know about that red convertible. After about a year, Jim got rid of it. He didn't want Joe angry at him, so he walked away from his lease on the car and paid the penalty.

That convertible was in keeping with the lifestyle that Hamra wanted to live. He liked to buy the best, whether it was clothes, food, or fine wine. DiMaggio would grumble about that. Joe always seemed to be putting a lot of pressure on Jim, but Hamra rolled with the punches, and he developed a deep affection for Joe. He was disturbed by the stormy relationship between Paula and her grandfather. The first time we spoke was when Jim called me at home and asked me to mediate a peace between his wife and Joe. The two hadn't spoken for about three months. I suggested that Paula and Joe had the same type of personality, and Hamra agreed, saying that Paula at times could be difficult. Joe's eyebrows rose when I told him of the conversation. "He backed me up?" From then on, Hamra and DiMaggio were buddies, watching sports on TV or playing golf.

Joe may have mellowed around his family, but his obstinate nature did not disappear all together. At a birthday party for Vanassa, the Hamras' oldest daughter, Joe suggested that a mat be put down near the pool to prevent someone from slipping. Paula disagreed, and they argued. DiMaggio sat in a car for two hours reading a newspaper and rejecting Jim's invitation to rejoin the party.

In those terrible days when Joe was suffering through his fatal illness, Hamra spent hours at his bedside. This 6-foot-plus strapping guy, wearing a backpack, became a familiar figure at the hospital where he arrived at about 7:00 A.M. I was delighted to see him because it meant I could leave and go to my office. Jim sat with DiMaggio even when Joe was asleep. When Joe was awake, Jim would hold his hand and read poetry to him. No one was more distraught than Jim Hamra when DiMaggio died.

Joe would squawk about Paula spending $5 for a melon, but then give her a new luxury car. When he took the Hamras for pizza when they were in Palm Springs for the Dinah Shore golf tournament, he got angry because Jim stayed behind at the hotel and ordered an expensive steak from room service. Yet, he gave Hamra a big check for Christmas. In fact, he gave each of his granddaughters and their husbands money for Christmas. I had explained that since the IRS permitted tax-free gifts each year, it was a good way to dispose of his estate without penalizing his beneficiaries. I added that when someone gives such a gift during his lifetime, it's like gold, but when it's given after death, it's like copper. Joe thought that was profound and asked where I had read it. I told him I hadn't read it, but I had heard it from my rabbi during a fundraising appeal. The first time DiMaggio sat down to write one of those gift checks, it took him an hour of hesitant penmanship and a little head shaking. But when he realized it was a good way to make his family happy, he actually enjoyed doing it. He would walk into my office and announce, "It's check-writing time." When Kathie and Paula had children, the kids went on the gift list. At the end, DiMaggio wrote eight of those family gift checks each year. When he became concerned about his mortality, he started giving out the checks at the start of the year, in case he didn't make it to Christmas. So, that year he wrote eight checks at Christmas, and eight more less than two weeks later.

The happiness that DiMaggio drew from his granddaughters was duplicated, and more so, with their children. Paula and Jim had two daughters, Vanassa and Valerie, while Kathie and Roger had a son, Mitchell, and a daughter, Kendahl. Vanassa became her great-grandfather's favorite, just as her mother had been. "Paula got her comeuppance," said her mother, Sue. "Just like Big Joe favored Paula over her sister, he favored Vanassa over her mother." Paula knew it. After a card show in San Francisco, about ten of us went to a Chinese restaurant for dinner and we sat at this huge table. I sat next to Joe, as I usually did, and Joe motioned for Paula to sit on the other side of him. He wanted to talk to the two of us about the card show. We were his audience while the others chatted about other things, not interested in what happened at the signing table. But Paula passed up the invitation to sit next to her grandfather. "Vanassa, you sit here," she said. "You're number one now, I'm number two."

Everyone ordered something, led by Jim, who picked two or three items, and a ton of food was brought out, twice what was needed. Bottles of wine and beer were jammed between the two dozen or so plates. Vanassa, who was about seven then and cute as a pixie, wearing a funny hat on her head, surveyed the table and declared, "Boy, this sure is a lot of food. Who is going to pay this bill?" DiMaggio broke up, laughing so hard he had to wipe the tears from his eyes with a handkerchief. (Incidentally, he knew who was going to pick up the $350 tab. Morris. Who else?)

DiMaggio taught his great-grandchildren how to play poker, and he delighted in playing tricks on them during the game. Once he sent them out of the room on a pretense and then set up the deck so everyone would get a wonderful hand, but he would have the best. He enjoyed seeing their startled expressions when he won. Vanassa and Valerie had two cats, and Joe made a big deal of walking with the girls to a store to buy sliced turkey to feed to their pets. Joe thought enough of that ritual to write about it in his diary. "Vanassa, who loves turkey, talked me into going to the store so she could have some, not only for her but she loves to feed it to the cats, who love it just as much." For years, I shopped for DiMaggio because he wouldn't go into a supermarket for fear of being recognized, but he had no qualms about going into stores with his great-granddaughters. The difference was he liked to see how proud they were at the attention their great-grandfather attracted when people stopped to ask for his autograph.

To them, he was just grandpa, "Big Joe," but they were astonished at his celebrity. After a shopping trip to FAO Schwarz in San Francisco, Joe and his family walked into a restaurant for lunch, and he was greeted with applause. Vanassa beamed and looked up at him with adoration. When all four of his great-grandchildren were in Florida, the whole bunch flew from Fort Lauderdale to

Disney World in a private Lear jet he had arranged for. When they got there, they were escorted past the long lines of people at the rides and attractions. People chased after him for autographs. Joe enjoyed telling that story, and he told it often, using eight-year-old Vanassa's words for the punch line: "You know, grandpa, you must be famous."

Joe took his role as the family elder very seriously. When he bought Vanassa a computer, he researched the market and sought opinions as if he were taking over a public company. "It's important to get the right computer because it is part of your education, and education is the most important thing in life." He wanted Vanassa and Valerie to go to a good private school, and it cost him a lot of money in tuition. When he was advised that this did not count against the annual gift he gave to reduce the amount of his estate, he liked the tuition idea even better. If Kathie's kids wanted to go to private schools, he would have paid for them, too, but Mitchell and Kendahl went to public schools.

When Vanassa was nine years old, she played on a softball team, and Joe was a frequent spectator, wearing his usual ineffective disguise of a hat and sunglasses. Jim was one of the coaches, but when he couldn't make it to one game, Joe volunteered to fill in as the first-base coach. One of the parents asked the third-base coach, "Who's that old guy coaching at first?" He was told, "That's Vanassa's great-grandfather." The concerned parent wondered, "Do you think he'll be OK? Does he know what he's doing?"

DiMaggio loved all his great-grandchildren, but he and Vanassa had a special relationship. When she was a little tyke, she would crawl up on his lap and sit there. She always tried to sit next to him in restaurants, and they would go for walks on the beach whenever they were at the seashore. He described taking Vanassa on a shopping trip. "Sometimes she selects something that her mom and pop don't like for her to get. She has that coy look and looks me straight in the eyes with that contagious smile, and I give her a 'yes' nod of the head. She can make you melt. And besides, I'm her great-grandfather." She once gave him a little seashell, which he carried in his pocket and cherished as if it were made of gold. It was with him as a good luck charm when he went into the hospital for his cancer surgery.

Joe got more than that seashell from his new family, of course. He got unqualified love and affection. The kids made his birthday a special occasion. When his great-grandchildren were little, they would put a party hat on him and tie balloons on his chair. He thoroughly enjoyed it.

"He had something to live for, and something he never had before. He had a new lease on life," said Joe Nachio. "He had a son who was a lost cause, he didn't get along with anybody else, and he found consolation, he discovered joy with his newfound family."

DiMaggio reflected on that joy several times in his writings. Something as simple as getting a Halloween card from Paula was worth a mention. When he spent Father's Day in New York so he could present Phil Rizzuto and his wife, Cora, with a watch at Yankee Stadium, he wrote, "My granddaughter started the day off by calling me and wishing me a Happy Father's Day." He noted that she was up at 7:30 A.M. to make the call and that he also spoke with Vanassa. "It made my day," he said. Looking back on the year gone by, he wrote on December 31, 1992, about some physical woes. "These are some of the things on the minus side. But I had some pluses—so I got no squawk coming. The highlights are Paula and the kids, and I do see Kathie and her kids as well."

I don't remember seeing him happier than he was five years later, when he brought his family to Harbor Islands for Christmas and New Year's Eve. He had a wonderful time seeing the joy on the kids' faces when they opened their presents. "Is that all you got?" he asked, no matter how many gifts each child had. Then he went into his pocket and peeled off a $50 bill for each of them. He and Jim made breakfast for everyone, and he took the kids fishing off the dock in his backyard. The residents of the development chipped in for a big New Year's Eve party, and there were mountains of food and a band. Vanassa, who was ten years old, asked me to dance, and Joe watched us with glee. As graceful an athlete as he was, Joe didn't dance. Those who knew him as a young man in San Francisco said he didn't dance even then, and he was rather shy around girls. After the party, as I drove them all to the Miami airport in the predawn darkness, he suddenly broke the silence. "You know, Morris, you cut a mean rug."

◆ ◆ ◆

At times DiMaggio reminded his grandchildren and their kids of their common bond, explaining his largesse by telling them, "You are my family." He backed up his declaration in his will. Virtually his entire estate went to his granddaughters and great-grandchildren. As a tax and probate specialist, I advised him, and he very reluctantly agreed, to bequeath forty-five percent of his estate to Joe Jr. He wanted to leave everything to Paula and Kathie and his great-grandchildren, but I explained that if he skipped a generation in distributing his wealth, his estate would lose an extra $1 million in a penalty tax. He began by saying he would give Junior $6,000 a year, since Joe was certain that whatever his son got would be spent on beer. I managed to get the amount up to about $20,000 a year. Because Junior died just five months after his father, his share was divided into Paula's and Kathie's trusts, and not evenly, either. It is a matter of public record that Paula got seventy percent of her grandfather's estate and Kathie received thirty percent. "I am trying to be true to my feelings, and keep haggling to a minimum," DiMaggio wrote about the will in his diary.

The $20,000 a year he bequeathed his son really didn't mean much because his will gave me liberal powers to invade as much of the principal as Junior needed. I had the power to give Joey the funds to buy whatever he wanted, something his father couldn't bring himself to do. In the brief time Junior lived after Joe's death, he bought what he wanted with his father's money, with one exception—I stopped at his request for first-class airfare.

I had all sorts of strategies worked out that could have saved DiMaggio millions of dollars in inheritances taxes, all perfectly legal and used by the nation's wealthiest families. It was my duty to inform him and his heirs of his options, family partnerships and the like, but he would not do it. "I like to put my hand in my back pocket and know my wealth is there," he would say. I told him that his way was taking millions away from his grandchildren and giving that money to the government, but he stubbornly refused to accept my recommendation. "Too much money will ruin their marriages," he would say, and too much would ruin his great-grandchildren's ambition and dampen their desire for education.

While their adoptive but estranged father was alive, Paula and Kathie were extremely generous with Joe Jr. About my power to invade the principal of Junior's trust, Paula said, "give him whatever he wants," even though it would diminish her share. Paula and Kathie loved Junior, but as he had put it, he was from a different planet.

Vanassa and Valerie each was left a sizable trust, while Mitchell and Kendahl each received half as much. Kathie did not resent that she and her children were given half of what Big Joe left Paula and her daughters. "My sister and I have always had a great relationship and we still do," Kathie said. "Paula took very good care of my grandfather, more than I did. I wasn't with him as much. I went out of town to college, and I didn't spend as much time with him."

It was a fairy-tale ending to an incredible story. Joe DiMaggio, despite his celebrity and wealth as an American legend, was a sorely unhappy man until the later years of his life. His happiness finally came through the two girls adopted by his son, with whom he had little to do. And for most of their lives, the two sisters, Joe Jr.'s adoptive daughters, had little to do with the man their mother married. Because of this quirk of fate, however, both women and their families became wealthier than they could have imagined— and were blessed with a paternal figure they all loved.

"I get so frustrated when I read that he was a lonely man," Paula said of her grandfather. "He very much had a family that loved him and that he loved."

8

MARILYN

Joe DiMaggio was in love with Marilyn Monroe until the moment he died. He took his last breath fully expecting to meet her in that other world, which he was certain existed. "I'll finally get to see Marilyn," were his last words.

It was a glamorous love story, sounding more like fiction than truth: the great sports legend and the sex goddess, two world-renowned celebrities, becoming part of each other's lives. It was true, all right. Marilyn was the Great DiMaggio's only love, the one who reached deep into his soul, where he kept his emotions under double lock. For the last thirty-seven years of his life, he ached at the thought of how close they had come to remarrying, only to be thwarted by her death. The date of their second marriage was set: August 8, 1962. But the kiss he gave her that day was far different from the one he had hoped for. That was the date Marilyn Monroe was buried. Joe leaned over her casket, sobbed that he loved her, and kissed her cold forehead.

The story of Joe and Marilyn was fascinating enough by itself, with their fame and their respective hang-ups. But add to the mix such other players as President John F. Kennedy, his brother Bobby Kennedy, Frank Sinatra, and mobster Sam Giancana, and the story took on a dimension almost beyond imagination. Given the people involved, it was perhaps inevitable that fiction and hype would be intertwined with the truth.

Even something as basic as the first meeting of Joe and Marilyn in the spring of 1952 has been recounted in several variations. Norman Brokaw, board chairman of the William Morris Agency, which represented Marilyn, claimed he introduced the couple. Brokaw's uncle, Johnny Hyde, was the William Morris vice president who signed Marilyn when she was still known as Norma Jean Baker. He set out to make her a star. "He also was madly in love with her," according to Brokaw. It was the young nephew's job to get Marilyn some attention in newspapers and magazines. Inadvertently, he brought her to the attention of Joe DiMaggio. In Brokaw's version of the first meeting, he took Marilyn to the Los Angeles television show *Lights, Camera, Action*, and then to lunch at the Brown Derby, where the crowd invariably included anyone in Hollywood who was famous and hungry. Bill Frawley, a Brokaw client and the actor who played Fred Mertz on *I Love Lucy*, was having lunch with DiMaggio. He came to the table and said Joe D. had noticed Brokaw's very noticeable dining companion, but was too shy to approach her. "He would like to meet the young lady," Frawley said. Brokaw told him they would stop by before leaving.

"Who's Joe D.?" Marilyn wanted to know when Brokaw told her who wanted to meet her. She may have been the only one in the Brown Derby, Hollywood, or even California who did not know about DiMaggio. He was in the first year of his retirement. "I explained that he was a famous baseball player, right up there with Babe Ruth and Lou Gehrig," Brokaw said. "But Marilyn knew nothing about baseball, other than that it involved a ball and a stick. I told her that he had been married to actress Dorothy Arnold and that he probably would ask for her telephone number."

Joe was very charming when Marilyn and Brokaw stopped at his table. He said something complimentary and added, "I've known Norman a long time, and he's a good friend. You are in very good hands." Brokaw said that the next day Joe called her for a date. Brokaw was among the first to know, since at the time

Marilyn lived at his grandmother's house, 718 North Palm Drive, and so did Johnny Hyde.

Version No. 2 of the first meeting is the one that appears in most Monroe and DiMaggio biographies because it is the one that was offered by Marilyn's public relations people, and she went along with it. In that telling, agent David March arranged a date at the Villa Nova restaurant in Los Angeles after DiMaggio had seen a publicity photograph of Marilyn and American League slugger Gus Zernial swinging a bat together. At least four of the biographers had the same story—that Marilyn was late for the 6:30 P.M. date, and March summoned her by phone. Either that was what they were told by Marilyn's public relations woman, or they copied from each other. "I guarantee you it's not true," Brokaw said. I agree with Brokaw. If it were true, Marilyn would have been history, because being late to meet the Great DiMaggio was an unpardonable sin.

Version No. 3 is the one that DiMaggio told me, Joe Nachio, and his own son, at different times. It's the one I have regarded as the true one, because I never knew DiMaggio to lie to me in all our years together. Joe said he was at Roosevelt Raceway, a harness-racing track on Long Island, with Edward Bennett Williams, the Washington attorney and his close friend. Joe must have been out only for an evening of dinner and conversation, because he never bet on a harness race. (He was the most suspicious man I ever knew and harness racing was constantly under suspicion.) Not interested in the trotters and pacers pulling men in sulkies, DiMaggio scanned the crowd in the dining room and his gaze stopped at, in his words, "this beautiful blonde with big eyes and big bosoms." He wondered who she was, and Williams told him. DiMaggio remembered seeing her in the photo with Zernial, and she looked even better in person. Williams introduced them, at DiMaggio's request, and he invited Marilyn to join him and Joe for dinner at Toots Shor's the following evening. The setting, where Joe felt most at home, was important, as was Williams' presence, because DiMaggio was often ill at ease in a one-on-one dinner conversation with someone he did not know—even at that stage of his life, as a mature, retired baseball star.

The first date obviously went well, because there were others, in New York and Los Angeles. Joe was taken with Marilyn, and she with him. "I met this marvelous man," she gushed to a friend. Apparently, neither she nor Joe took much time with the niceties of getting to know each other, because she soon extolled his sexual prowess in a conversation with Amy Greene, the wife of photographer Milton Greene. Marilyn apparently observed that DiMaggio's "biggest bat is not the one he had on the field." Joe indeed had a reputation for being a stud, the original Italian Stallion, and he undoubtedly found her as sexually appealing in the flesh as did most men viewing her films and photos. (I have no personal report of their intimacies because he never discussed his sexual adventures with me or in my presence.)

◆ ◆ ◆

It was more than sex that helped Joe fall in love with Marilyn, however. He was very moved when he learned of her sad childhood, and he felt that people in Hollywood were taking advantage of her desire to succeed as an actress. She had been born in the charity ward of a hospital to Gladys Monroe Baker, who worked as a film cutter for a Hollywood studio. Marilyn, at various times, would say she was an illegitimate baby, born between her mother's marriages to Jack Baker and Martin Mortensen, or she would say Mortensen was her father. In truth, she probably didn't know, and neither did her mother. More important, she never got to know her father, whoever he was. Shortly after Marilyn was born, her mother's mental illness reached the stage where she had to enter a sanitarium, and Marilyn entered the first of a series of foster homes, this one operated for profit by Albert and Ida Bolender. Infant Marilyn was less than two weeks old at the time, and she stayed with the Bolenders until she was eight years old. She had a succession of roommates and playmates in the house, because the Bolenders boarded other foster children.

Marilyn's grandmother, Della, lived nearby, but there was little contact between the two. Della had her own mental problems. Ida Bolender said that grandma showed up at her doorstep one day stark naked and tried to kick in the door. "I'm told she died violently in a straightjacket," Bolender was quoted as saying in Roger Kahn's *Joe & Marilyn: A Memory of Love.* Ida was into the "Wrath of God" sort of religion, and Marilyn heard a great deal about the wages of sin from her. She also learned about the wrath of Albert Bolender. Kahn reported that Bolender would punish the little girl for whatever sins she may have committed by pulling down her bloomers and whacking her bare bottom with a leather strap. When she was nine, Marilyn was put into an orphan home, or as Marilyn remembered it, "I had to be dragged in. I kept telling them I was no orphan." By then, her mother's emotional state had badly deteriorated. Marilyn left the orphanage when she was eleven, was shuttled from one foster home to another, and was sexually abused and given booze by some of the people charged with caring for her. "Nobody ever called me their daughter," she said of her life in those homes.

While Marilyn was at Van Nuys High, she met James Dougherty, who lived near the home where she was staying at the time. At the age of 16, she married him. He was 21. Marilyn later said she was pushed into the marriage by Grace Goddard, her foster mother that year. Her only other option was to go back to the orphanage, and she certainly did not want to do that.

By then, America was at war. Dougherty worked in an aircraft factory and Marilyn got a job in another defense plant. They had enough money to rent a studio apartment, but about a year later,

Dougherty said goodbye and went to sea with the merchant marine. What happens to an attractive, shapely young lady trying to make her way on her own in Hollywood? She was exploited by those who offered to help her career as a model or an actress. Marilyn had the body, the face, and the moves to do both, and also, the instincts required.

DiMaggio never revealed how much of her sad tale she told him, but she did talk with him about it and she found a sympathetic ear. Did he wonder that she may have allowed herself to be exploited and possibly may have enjoyed the role of the naive victim? Again, he never said. But she was the classic underdog, the type with whom he sided throughout his life. Joe wanted to become Marilyn's protector, and he attempted to do that during their marriage and for the eight years between their divorce and her funeral.

◆ ◆ ◆

Joe began a new life during the 1952 season. For the first time since he was a kid, he was talking about baseball rather than playing it. The Yankees' pre-game and post-game television shows kept him involved with the game, but he had a lot more free time, which he shared with Marilyn. They were seen at Joe's favorite restaurants and nightclubs, and his ticket-broker friend George Solotaire made sure they had choice seats to the biggest hits on Broadway. Marilyn visited DiMaggio's workplace, Yankee Stadium, and she added a rare beauty to the press lounge where the media freeloaded before and after games. Because Joe had to do the TV shows from the studio underneath the stands, there were times during a game when he couldn't be at her side, so he recruited friends to sit with her. Lenny Lewin, who collaborated with Joe on the Buitoni TV show for kids, once had the honor. "But don't ask me what we talked about," Lewin said. "All I remember is how pretty and how charming she was, and how everyone in the stadium seemed to be looking at us."

Joe and Marilyn's relationship received lots of attention in the gossip columns of New York's eight newspapers. Marilyn was about to start filming *Niagara* in upstate New York, and the studio press agents made sure that was no secret. What was a secret, though, was what happened when Marilyn arrived on location. She was lonely and made a phone call. Not to Joe, but to Bob Slatzer, a friend she had known for six years. They had met in the reception area at 20th Century Fox, where she was waiting for an interview, and he was trolling for stories as a summertime stringer for the Scripps Howard newspaper chain. Slatzer was back living in his home state of Ohio selling advertising for the *Columbus Dispatch* at the time that Marilyn called him. He was about to embark on a business trip east, and Marilyn invited him to stop by. She was staying in the General Brock Hotel on the Canadian side of Niagara Falls and a connecting room was available. DiMaggio was a great sexual partner, according to Marilyn, but he didn't drink. Slatzer, then 25, was accomplished at both. "When Marilyn died," he said, "I lost my best drinking buddy."

When Slatzer arrived at the General Brock, Marilyn was lounging in her room completely nude with a Jack Daniels on the rocks in her hand. There was a half-empty, or half-full, bottle on a table. Neither the nudity nor the booze surprised Slatzer. Getting naked was a favorite thing for her to do, whether she was alone or someone else was in the room. Drinking was another. "We sipped wine when we were starting out and poor," Slatzer said. "After the Jack Daniels stage, in 1961 and 1962, she drank champagne spiked with a couple of shots of vodka." A lot of drinking went on that weekend, and at one point, Marilyn decided it would be a wonderful place to get married because, as she put it, "we wouldn't have to go to Niagara Falls. We are already here." That thought had left her mind by morning, but Slatzer still stayed longer than he should have, and he lost his job.

Slatzer met DiMaggio twice. As a youngster in Marion, Ohio, he went to Cleveland to see the Yankees play the Indians. After the game, Slatzer went to the New York Central rail yards to watch the players returning to their Pullman cars. "DiMaggio was wearing a raincoat and carrying a bag. I asked him for his autograph and he said, 'Get out of my way, kid.' He kept walking." If that's the way it happened, it made Slatzer unique because DiMaggio rarely turned down an autograph request from a kid. George Steinbrenner, whose father owned a shipyard in Cleveland, also was among the youngsters who would wait at the railroad yard for DiMaggio, and he did not recall ever being snubbed.

Slatzer's next meeting with DiMaggio was no more pleasant. It came in late 1952 or early 1953 at a house Marilyn was leasing in Hollywood. "We had a date, and when I got there she wasn't home yet," Slatzer said. "Then, DiMaggio pulled up. He nodded at me, then went up to the door and rang the bell. When he rang it again, I told him that I didn't think she was home because her car wasn't out front. He lit a cigarette and ignored me." A few minutes later, Marilyn drove up, and pulled in behind DiMaggio's car. Her car hit his, but not enough to do any damage. "Aw, shit!" she said. That comment could have been about bumping DiMaggio's car or the awkward situation of two suitors being there at the same time. Each eager visitor reminded Marilyn that she had a date with him, and she invited both into the house.

Marilyn asked Slatzer to go into the living room, where there was a bar, and he poured drinks for himself and Marilyn. Joe declined. "I heard DiMaggio asking her why I knew where the bar was. It developed into a showdown over who would take her out that night, me or DiMaggio," Slatzer said. "She told us both to leave and to call her later. I wasn't about to tangle with him. I was about 5-foot-11 at the time and had played football and boxed, but he was Joe DiMaggio. I wasn't going to fight him."

Marilyn dated both men for the next couple of months, going out with Joe in New York and Slatzer in Los Angeles. Marilyn called from New York, where she had gone on a promotional trip, and told Slatzer that DiMaggio wanted to marry her. Not only wasn't she sure she wanted to get married again, after her unhappy experience with her first husband, Jim Dougherty, but she was concerned about Joe as a potential mate. She said he was very jealous, he wasn't much on conversation, and he knew as much about the movies as she did about baseball, which was zilch. She wondered out loud to Slatzer over the phone if she and Joe had much in common outside the bedroom. When Marilyn returned to Los Angeles in September, she told Slatzer she had no plans to marry Joe.

Marilyn's romance with Slatzer became a five-page cover story in *Confidential*, a scandal magazine, five years later. By then, she was married to Arthur Miller and Slatzer was married to his second wife. The thrust of the story was that while Joe was back east working on TV in 1952, Marilyn was frolicking with this young writer. Even though she and DiMaggio had been divorced for three years when the story was printed, Marilyn got an angry phone call from Joe, who thought she had planted the story as a publicity stunt. Slatzer, though flattered by being publicly described as one of Marilyn Monroe's lovers, was nervous about what his wife's reaction would be. Marilyn advised him, "Do what I'm doing. Keep quiet, and it will pass."

Slatzer claimed he and Marilyn were married in Tijuana October 4, 1952. "On the way back to Los Angeles, we heard DiMaggio on the radio, doing a post-game commentary about a Yankees-Dodgers World Series game," Slatzer said. "When we were back at Marilyn's house, he called and she told him she heard him on the radio, but she never mentioned that it was on the trip home from getting married."

Two days later, Marilyn and Slatzer agreed they had made a mistake, and he drove back across the border to see the municipal clerk who had married them. The marriage had yet to be registered with the Federal District, and for $50, the marriage certificate was retrieved from the office file, and the lawyer Slatzer had hired burned it. Slatzer described the event in his book *The Life and Curious Death of Marilyn Monroe,* and he confirmed the story during several interviews for this book.

◆ ◆ ◆

After the 1952 World Series ended, Joe flew to California and began courting Marilyn in earnest. Joe Jr., who was attending the Black Fox Academy near Los Angeles, joined them on some weekends, and Joe took Marilyn with him when he visited his son at school. Joe Jr. told dad he thought his girlfriend was great, and a lot of fun to be with. Joe Sr. thought so, too. In the idiom of the day, he was "head over heels" about her, he told Joe Nachio.

"He was consumed by his love for her," said Nachio. "He put her on a pedestal. It had to be the only time that Joe loved someone more than that person loved him, and she told me she loved him a lot. It was his obsession." Former teammate Jerry Coleman said, "He loved her to a degree that few women are loved."

Joe was impressed with what he perceived as Marilyn's intellectual side. More than thirty years later, he spoke about her love for the classics, both in literature and music. She quoted Chekhov, Dostoyevsky, and Balzac and played the music of Debussy, Tchaikovsky, and Beethoven. Joe was puzzled, "You're not the dumb blonde they want you to play in the movies. Why do you let them do that to you?" He also confided to me, as if he were letting me in on a big secret, that she was not even a real blonde. "They made her into one," he said, "and they made her a slut in the movies." The lovers occasionally read poetry together, which Joe said he enjoyed. She may have shared poetry readings with her next husband, but Miller was a playwright, while Joe DiMaggio was a ballplayer with one year of a high school education.

I thought it was interesting, maybe even humorous, that DiMaggio courted and married the sexiest woman of her time, yet in the rare instances that he talked about her, he usually mentioned some example of her intellectual attributes. He never discussed sexual matters with me, but he surprised me when he very earnestly described her as being on the chunky side, with "a big rear end," and "she had hair on her arms." The good stuff, I guess, he kept to himself.

During their courtship, when Marilyn was asked if marriage was in their plans, she told a friend, "he's thoughtful and fun to be with, but maybe we should leave things the way they are." This may have been the time she was living at 882 Doheny Drive, and Joe stopped short when he called on her for the first time there. The name above the doorbell read Marjorie Stengel. A puzzled DiMaggio wondered if, somehow, he had wound up at the apartment of one of Casey's relatives, but Marilyn was using an alias she borrowed from a woman she knew.

Bernie Kamber, DiMaggio's friend from New York, saw a couple in love when he met Marilyn in Los Angeles in 1953. Kamber was at the Beverly Hills Hotel on a business trip, when Joe called and told him that Marilyn was staying there, too. They arranged a meeting in the Polo Lounge and talked for about half an hour. DiMaggio knew that Kamber's office always rented a TV set for him when he was in Los Angeles. That was the only way to get television in a hotel room then, and Joe had a favor to ask. "Could Marilyn and I use your room while you're out?" Joe was a big fan of Westerns, and when Kamber returned from dinner at about 11:00 P.M., Joe and Marilyn were watching a cowboy movie. "Anything he wanted she went along with," Kamber said. The same thing happened the next night. "I thought it was pretty ridiculous. I was letting the most famous couple in the world use my hotel room, and they were watching TV."

Not too long afterward, Kamber found himself in the middle of a lovers' quarrel. They invited him to Thanksgiving dinner at the Brown Derby. Joe had arranged to get a table where they wouldn't be disturbed, and he already was there when Bernie arrived. But Marilyn was late, an hour late, as a matter of fact, and as each minute passed, Joe grew angrier. When she finally arrived, he was fuming, and he let her know it. She got angry at him for being angry at her, and they didn't talk to each other. "He talked to me, but she had very little to say, and it was mostly a silent dinner, but with all the fixings," Kamber recalled.

"Joe couldn't stand her tardiness; it drove him crazy," said Nachio. "He was the most punctual guy in the world, never late, and he couldn't understand why anyone would ever be late for an appointment. But Marilyn would turn on her charm. She had a great smile and knew how to use it. And with those big beautiful eyes, she would stare into his eyes and he would absolutely melt."

Nachio was a perfect listener for the two lovers at dinner one night at the Palm in New York, attentive but silent. When DiMaggio excused himself to go to the men's room, Marilyn complained to his longtime friend that Joe didn't like her Hollywood lifestyle of parties and socializing with friends, and he would rather stay home and watch television. He was "Too taciturn. Sometimes, he doesn't say anything, he just sits there," she said. When Joe returned to the table, Marilyn went to the ladies' room and it was Joe's turn to complain. His went on about her complete disregard of time. "We went to an awards ceremony in her honor, and she was an hour late," DiMaggio said. "We had to walk down the aisle for the presentation, and I was embarrassed. Everyone was looking at me, thinking I was the one who made her late. I told her that she tried to please everyone, but what she should do is please me."

Nachio saw Marilyn attempt to please Joe just a couple of hours later. The three were watching television when Marilyn began to snuggle with her Joe, and Nachio wondered if it was time for him to excuse himself. When Marilyn removed one of

DiMaggio's socks and began sucking on his big toe, Nachio said his good nights.

DiMaggio's dislike of the Hollywood crowd came into play when Marilyn asked him to accompany her to the studio Christmas party. He said he would be out of town, so she went without him. When she returned to her room at the Beverly Hills Hotel, a double surprise was waiting for her: a miniature Christmas tree with a handwritten "Merry Christmas" note, and the note's author, a smiling Joe DiMaggio. "It was the first time in my life anyone gave me a Christmas tree. I was so happy, I cried," Marilyn told columnist Sidney Skolsky.

◆ ◆ ◆

Marilyn's career was rolling in high gear in 1953 with the release of *Niagara, Gentlemen Prefer Blondes,* and *How to Marry a Millionaire.* But her work remained an abrasive issue in their relationship, as he continually complained about her roles as "sluts and prostitutes," and what he saw as her exploitation by the studio. "She went all over the country promoting the films, and she didn't get paid for it," he said, shaking his head in wonder.

Still, when Monroe asked DiMaggio to visit her during the filming of *River of No Return,* in the Canadian Rockies, Joe agreed. His decision no doubt was influenced by the wonderful time he and Marilyn were having in Los Angeles when she extended her invitation. It was July 1953, and they really were enjoying each other's company. There were dinners at Romanoffs, La Rue, and Chasens, and visits to the racetrack with other Hollywood people such as Desi Arnaz, Lucille Ball, Pat O'Brien, and Jimmy Durante. At evening's end, which usually was early, he and Marilyn retired to her home on Doheny Drive.

The couple had been brought closer by a tragedy in Joe's life, his brother Mike's drowning on Memorial Day. DiMaggio was devastated by that loss, and Marilyn helped him get through his despair by being sympathetic and comforting. Marie DiMaggio said Marilyn's compassion meant a great deal to her brother.

When Marilyn headed north for the Canadian woods, Joe was not far behind, and Solotaire went with him. What a sight that must have been. Solotaire was so much a New Yorker that whenever he made an expedition across the Hudson River to the nightclubs in Englewood and Englewood Cliffs, New Jersey, all of thirty-five minutes, he said he was going "overseas." DiMaggio was no less a city guy, and they found themselves in a strange environment in Jasper, Alberta, where they had flown from Calgary in a private plane. When they landed in a grass field, Marilyn Monroe was there to greet them. "She looked great and she was thrilled to see Joe," Solotaire said.

DiMaggio and Solotaire were put up in a log cabin. "Roughing it would be great," the two agreed. "Joe and I just made friends with a deer," George wrote to his son. "We won her over with some lump sugar, and she's lying right outside our log cabin." In describing the scenery, Mr. Broadway noted, "I've always been a sucker for a babbling brook or a waterfall. Well, I got off the nut here. A beautiful stream, rambling over rocks . . . a huge splashing waterfall that rapidly rushes through the deep canyon. . . ." The guys back at Toots Shor's would have been charmed, I'm sure.

DiMaggio wandered out to feed marshmallows to his new friend, the doe, when he encountered a small black bear. The animal waddled to the garbage can outside the cabin, pulled out a piece of toast and ate it. Joe was mesmerized. The bear looked at DiMaggio; he obviously didn't recognize him as the famed Yankee Clipper, because he finished his toast and returned to the woods. The two city slickers were told that if they ignored the black bears, the bears wouldn't bother them, but they were cautioned to beware of grizzlies because those were the dangerous ones. In fact, Joe and George were told that some grizzlies had to be shot recently because they got too mean. The next day, the two men were sunning themselves outside the cabin, and George dozed off when he heard DiMaggio scream. A small grizzly bear was sniffing Joe's bare toes, and when he opened his eyes and saw the curious cub, he yelled, "A grizzly, George, a grizzly." The bear took off.

While DiMaggio and Solotaire were keeping their eyes out for bears, the locals and summer vacationers were keeping their sights on Marilyn and Joe. That part of Canada, with its spectacular scenery, had become a popular location for filming Hollywood movies, but no one else had created anything like the fuss the two celebrity lovers did.

The woods were not so idyllic for Marilyn, however. She complained that director Otto Preminger was a tyrant and a bully, an opinion shared by many other actors. Then, while doing a scene at the river, she fractured an ankle. She hobbled around on crutches and had to be carried each time the shooting location was changed. "It hurts like hell," she told a sympathetic DiMaggio, who knew a great deal about the pain from foot injuries. DiMaggio decided that he would take a more protective role and, as much as he disliked watching moviemaking, he went to the riverbank to see Marilyn being filmed for an action scene on a raft. With Joe watching, Preminger became less demanding of his leading lady.

DiMaggio and Solotaire were involved in a very real action scene one morning as they were driven with Marilyn to a filming location about an hour from Jasper. A gasoline tanker truck caught fire on the road ahead of them and all traffic was stopped. An explosion rocked the truck and bright red flames shot toward the sky. The truck's driver disappeared, leaving behind a seared hat, jacket, and gloves. The theory was that he had been smoking, caught fire, and ran to the river. DiMaggio volunteered to look for the unfortunate fellow and, with a group of motorists, trudged through the thick woods to the river, but the driver was never found. A bulldozer pushed the smoldering truck off the road, and Joe, Marilyn, and George continued on to a spectacular waterfall where Marilyn did two scenes.

The travelers then headed for Banff, and the luxurious Banff Springs Hotel. Roughing it wasn't that bad after all, DiMaggio and Solotaire agreed. In reality, their biggest deprivation had been not having a telephone. But, after ten days in a log cabin where they had to make their own breakfast, the hotel suite in the Banff Springs Hotel was more in keeping with their standard of living. Joe and Marilyn dined a lot in her suite. Solotaire was invited the night they had buffalo steak. His critique to his son: "Not bad for a buffalo."

When filming was completed on *River of No Return*, Marilyn returned to her place in Los Angeles, and Joe headed for New York to play in an Old Timers game at Yankee Stadium. That game had special meaning to him because it was to honor the late Lou Gehrig, the teammate he most admired. Gehrig's mother and widow were to be there, and Joe was determined not to miss that day. The trip was not an easy one. He and Solotaire boarded a plane in Calgary at 3:30 A.M., but just before takeoff, the plane taxied back to the terminal for repairs. Dawn was breaking when they finally took off, and after stops in Winnipeg and Toronto, they made it to their suite at the Madison Hotel in the early hours Saturday. Less than ten hours later, Joe was introduced to a standing ovation at the stadium. He had been retired for less than two seasons by then, and he still was the very popular Yankee Clipper.

The Old Timers game matched a team of former players who were native New Yorkers, including Hank Greenberg, against a squad of retired Yankees. DiMaggio got an RBI double in his only at-bat, and when sixty-three-year-old Wally Schang hit a drive to right, DiMaggio brought the crowd to its feet by racing home in that familiar long-legged stride of his. He also made a fine running catch, which had fans saying he had lost none of the talent he had shown so many times in that park. His old roommate, Lefty Gomez, also got a hit in the game, and he kept Joe laughing with his post-game antics in the clubhouse. Among the others Joe talked with was Moe Berg, who had been a catcher with the Red Sox and a roommate of Dom's. He had the reputation of being the smartest guy ever to play the game and spoke seven or eight languages, including Japanese. DiMaggio called Berg "The Spy," because that's what he did for the United States before and during World War II. Years earlier, Gomez told Joe that before the war began, Berg had asked him for photos Lefty had taken on a trip to Japan in the mid-1930s. Berg, like DiMaggio, had given baseball clinics in Japan, and the two talked about their experiences. "They learn fast," Joe said. Berg agreed. Gomez wondered: "Did he ask you for any pictures?"

DiMaggio thoroughly enjoyed himself at that Old Timers Day, but he told Solotaire he wished Marilyn had been with him. He missed her.

Joe called Marilyn in Los Angeles on Saturday night and asked her to meet him in San Francisco. He flew out the next day, and the couple was together again at his home on Beach Street, where Marie fussed over them, cooked Joe's favorite Italian dinners, and made Marilyn feel like part of the family. "A sweet lady," Marilyn said. "But she's so thin. She's lucky. She can eat that linguine and not get fat."

Just when their relationship seemed to be sailing on calm waters, the first issue of *Playboy* magazine with nude photos of Marilyn was published late in the year. She had posed for a calendar in 1948, when she was hustling for a buck, and now that she was a famous star, someone else was making a buck from those pictures. Joe was angry, and he knew what people were thinking and saying, especially his Italian buddies, whom he envisioned clucking about this being a matter of honor. Having your girlfriend showing off her naked body to every guy with the price of a magazine was not unlike being a cuckold. But he wouldn't allow anyone the satisfaction of seeing his reaction, so he maintained his deadpan expression and silence. Joe had complained about the revealing costumes Marilyn wore in her films, and now she was seen wearing absolutely nothing. It was embarrassing! Nevertheless, about a month later, he asked her to marry him. That's how much he loved her.

She may not have been in love with him as much as he loved her, but something else happened that made it an opportune time for her to get away. Marilyn was lined up for a role in *The Girl in Pink Tights*. When Joe learned that Frank Sinatra was the costar, he asked her to get out of the film. He knew Sinatra and of his reputation for romancing his leading ladies. She wasn't too thrilled with the script anyway, and she did his bidding. Darryl Zanuck made a big flap over her withdrawal, and the studio suspended her. She now had free time.

Judge Charles Peery married the couple in his chambers on January 14, 1954. DiMaggio wanted a scaled-down ceremony, hoping to avoid the tumultuous scene that marked his church wedding to Dorothy Arnold. Lefty O'Doul and his wife, Jean, were there since they were to leave with Joe and Marilyn on a baseball-related trip to Japan that would also serve as the newlyweds' honeymoon. Reno Barsochinni, Joe's childhood buddy, was the best man. Marilyn's publicity people were not about to let so momentous an event go unnoticed, so they tipped off the press and a mob of reporters was waiting for the couple in the hallway. "It was a madhouse, but not as bad as the first one," Joe said. Though the press corps was much larger, the crowd outside was nowhere near the 30,000 who clogged the streets for blocks around Saints Peter and Paul Church for the 1939 wedding. Still, about 500 San Franciscans were there to see America's most famous husband and wife drive off, not in a limo this time, but in DiMaggio's car.

The DiMaggios headed south for their honeymoon, first to Paso Robles, where DiMaggio was widely reported to have asked for a room that had a TV set, and then to a friend's home in the mountains near Palm Springs. Unfortunately, a double dose of bad news went with them. Joe failed for the second straight year to be voted into baseball's Hall of Fame (there was no five-year waiting period for eligibility at the time). Also, a spokesman for the San Francisco Archdiocese said DiMaggio had been automatically excommunicated because not only was he divorced, but also because he had remarried in a civil ceremony. DiMaggio got grief from Bishop Fulton Sheen, best known for his deep-set eyes and television series, *Life Is Worth Living*. "You know who he was, don't you, Doc?" Joe asked Rock Positano. "He was one powerful son of a buck. He said he wanted to meet with me, and he started to lecture me that I shouldn't have married Marilyn in the first place. Can you imagine the balls on that guy! I told him. 'You have no right to tell me who I should and should not love. As far as I'm concerned, this meeting is over.'" Joe strode out of Bishop Sheen's office. DiMaggio continued to go to Mass, and, in fact, years later was greeted with an ovation at St. Patrick's Cathedral. Before he died, Joe received the last rites of the church.

Joe and Marilyn were astonished and a bit unnerved by the reception they received in Tokyo. Thousands of Japanese fans jammed the airport, and thousands more were in the Tokyo streets as their limousine and police escort headed for the Imperial Hotel, shouting "Banzai Joe DiMaggio! Banzai Marilyn Monroe!" A packed news conference awaited them. Marilyn drew most of the questions, but, Joe explained, "I wasn't as beautiful, and I had been to Japan before."

DiMaggio and O'Doul gave baseball clinics and Joe even played in an exhibition game. Marilyn was a pretty accessory at some of those appearances and at the receptions in their honor. She was asked at one of the functions if she would make a short hop to entertain U.S. troops in Korea, where the war had recently ended. Marilyn jumped at the chance and precipitated the couple's first argument as man and wife. Japanese TV showed clips of Marilyn's shows, sexy songs, sexy moves, and sexy wardrobe. Marilyn went all out, so much so that she was told by a high-ranking command officer to tone down her act. Television and newsreel images showed leering GIs and marines enjoying themselves immensely. Joe was not happy. "It's not much of a honeymoon," he told an interviewer. "I haven't seen very much of Marilyn."

Her return from that trip was the occasion when the widely misquoted exchange between the two took place. According to DiMaggio it went this way: She said "You should have heard it, 60,000 people shouting and cheering," and he said, "I have, many times." But apparently there was more to their conversation. Slatzer claimed that a maid in the Imperial Hotel heard the couple shouting at each other, and he quoted the maid as saying she saw Joe slam his bride against a wall. None of Monroe's other biographers who discussed the Tokyo trip mentioned that incident, although some wrote that she left Japan with a finger in a splint.

There had been reports from time to time that DiMaggio struck Monroe. Finally, I had to ask him point-blank if he ever did. A TV show's producer called in the late 1990s to tell me they were going to air an interview with an author whose newly published book quoted Marilyn as saying that Joe struck her on more than one occasion. The producer wanted Joe's comment. I dreaded asking him, and before I did, I tensely grabbed the side of my chair. He spotted that and realized something tough was coming. I don't ever remember seeing him react so angrily to a question. He jumped to his feet and began talking and pacing the room gesturing with his arms. "Hit her? Hit her? Never! Morris, once, years after we were divorced, I walked in on her and she was conked out. It was either drugs or booze, but whatever it was, she was really out of it. I opened the window and walked her around the room, slapping her face, trying to snap her out of it." He moved his right hand in a swatting motion as he told me this, to show me what he had done to Marilyn. He insisted that was the only time he had struck her.

Martha Lee told me that when DiMaggio learned that she was abused by her ex-husband, he put his arms around her and said, "No man has a right to put a hand on a woman." Lee said, "I can't believe he would have hit Marilyn."

When the Japanese honeymoon was over, the couple returned to the DiMaggios' Beach Street home. Marie offered to give Marilyn an advanced cooking course in Sicilian cuisine, which didn't excite the bride. She abhorred the smell of garlic, especially on Joe's breath, yet she enjoyed foods that were spiced with garlic, like Caesar salad. There was little else for her to do but read and watch television, because Joe wasn't around as much as she would have liked. He spent his days on the golf course and evenings playing cards with his buddies, often in a bar run by Barsochinni. Marilyn strolled into the bar one evening wearing a mink coat Joe had given her for Christmas just before they were married. She had been drinking. "When are you coming home, honey?" she wanted to know. Joe continued to play his hand. "I have a very nice surprise for you at home." He barely looked up and muttered, "Later." But she wanted him right then. "Look, Giuseppe, isn't this worth coming home for?" She opened her coat and there was nothing underneath it but Marilyn.

They also were seen frequently at the family restaurant on Fisherman's Wharf, much too frequently to suit Marilyn. She told Slatzer she and Joe always sat near the entrance where everyone could see them. "I felt like a freak in a sideshow," she complained.

She looked like anything but a sideshow attraction when Robert Solotaire met her for the first time that year. "I went to visit my father at the Madison Hotel and when I walked into the living room, she was sitting on a couch with Joe. They were back-lit by a large window. She was in shorts and a T-shirt and she was smiling that bright smile of hers." It was a sight that Solotaire never forgot. He was a student at Bard College at the time, and beginning his career as an artist. Marilyn inquired about the type of painting he was doing, and Solotaire remembered that "she spoke rather intelligently about art and artists that she liked."

Marilyn and George Solotaire got along very well. Both were in orphanages for a while as children, and when they talked about it, they found they had similar recollections of that sad time in their lives. "She alludes to her orphanage life a lot and, naturally, I keep her faded (the crapshooter's term that George used as a synonym for matched) with my experiences because a lot of incidents she brings up are reminiscent of my own," Solotaire wrote to his son. Solotaire, who gave the impression of being the epitome of a Broadway-wise man about town, had a soft spot for this woman, whose reputation in Hollywood was less than pure. "She is very naive, innocent, and exceptionally moral," he informed his son, who was twenty-three at the time, and had not asked about Marilyn's character.

Marilyn confided in George about her problems with Joe, that he was difficult at times and that he complained constantly about her involvement with people in Hollywood. Solotaire always defended Joe when other Broadway types would rap him, but he was understanding when Marilyn complained. "He's a moody guy, I know that," Solotaire said. "He's not the easiest guy to get along with, but he loves you, he always tells me that, so you have to try to make allowances for his moods."

◆ ◆ ◆

Marilyn was eager to get back to work, with the dispute over *Pink Tights* resolved. Despite Joe's misgivings, they moved to Beverly

Hills, where they rented a house on North Palm Drive. The peace accord between Marilyn and 20th Century Fox was announced at a news conference, along with the disclosure of a tentative agreement for her to star in *There's No Business Like Show Business*. Marilyn cooed to the press that marriage to Joe was wonderful, and they hoped to "have a lot of little DiMaggios." Shortly afterward, Marilyn became pregnant, though it was never announced, and she had a miscarriage. Monroe suffered from endometriosis and also miscarried when she was married to Miller. At one point, Joe and Marilyn talked about adopting a baby. They agreed the child would be blonde and blue-eyed. "You know, in Northern Italy the Italians are blonde and blue-eyed," he told her. Even long after Marilyn died, he was convinced their lives would have been different if she hadn't miscarried and they had a child together. "She probably would have quit Hollywood," he said, still in a dream world when it came to Marilyn.

Her next film was *The Seven Year Itch*, which meant she had to fly to New York for some scenes. Joe followed in a few days, because he had been hired by a news syndicate to report on the 1954 World Series between the Giants and Indians. That involved giving some of his insights on the games to a sportswriter who would "journalize" them under DiMaggio's byline. Joe had something special to report in the very first game, when Willie Mays made a spectacular running catch of a drive by Vic Wertz near the bleachers. Mays made his catch just yards from the spot in the Polo Grounds where DiMaggio had caught the fly ball to end the second game of the 1936 World Series, a feat for which he was saluted by Franklin D. Roosevelt.

Joe joined Marilyn in their suite at the St. Regis off Fifth Avenue. She had a midnight filming the night before the Series opener, so George Solotaire came to the hotel to keep DiMaggio company at the King Cole bar. That was where Walter Winchell found them, as he knew he would, shortly before midnight.

Hearst's star gossip columnist said he was headed for *The Seven Year Itch* filming, about five blocks away on Lexington Avenue and 53rd Street, and he invited DiMaggio and Solotaire to join him. Joe had blown up on the set of an earlier movie, when he saw the scanty costume Marilyn was wearing, and Winchell was hoping for a repeat performance that could get him a front-page byline in the *Daily Mirror*, his Hearst outlet in New York.

Joe declined the invitation with the explanation that watching Marilyn working made him nervous and it usually unnerved his wife, as well. Winchell, a persistent cuss, finally succeeded in getting the two men to accompany him. Joe and Marilyn both were to regret that short midnight stroll. The scene being shot that night became one of Marilyn Monroe's most famous photos. She was standing on a subway grate and her white skirt was being blown up by huge fans under the grating, revealing her thighs and flimsy panties.

The filming had been well publicized and several hundred people pressed up against police barricades to watch. Klieg lights turned the midnight darkness into daylight. The crowd, immediately noting DiMaggio's presence, greeted him with applause and shouted his name. Winchell used his connections with the film's publicity corps to make sure DiMaggio had an unobstructed view, which really wasn't necessary because the cops were only too happy to make a spot for Joe.

The scene was shot over and over again, and each time Marilyn's skirt went up despite her futile attempts to hold it down as the script demanded, the crowd roared and the kibitzers had something obscene or vulgar to say about her thighs and panties. DiMaggio was a picture of anger and humiliation. Solotaire tried to get him out of there and back to the King Cole bar, but the crowd had them penned in, and escape was impossible. "What the hell is going on here?" Joe wanted to know. It was a matter of honor, as it had been when Marilyn's nude photos appeared in

Playboy, but this time it was his wife, not his girlfriend, who had dishonored him.

Newspaper and magazine photographers captured the scene for the ages. A five-story billboard of that cinematic moment was put up in Times Square to promote the movie, and the pose became famous the world over, from Paris to Tokyo. Nearly fifty years later, strollers along the main street in the town of Burgos, Spain, could ogle a life-sized white statue of Marilyn and her panties, so famous did it become. Ironically, none of the dozen takes satisfied director Billy Wilder, and the scene had to be filmed again in a Hollywood studio.

On the night of the filming in New York, dressing-room facilities were set up in the basement of a small movie theater at the location where the scene was shot. DiMaggio and Solotaire went there to meet Marilyn, with Winchell tagging along, still hoping to catch Joe's eruption. Again DiMaggio kept his emotions under control, however; he was a model of restraint. Marilyn, exhausted by the ordeal and reclining in a chair, greeted Joe with her favorite name for him, "Hi, Giuseppe." He sat next to her, still showing no sign of his anger. They even posed for a photo together. Still, no blowup for Winchell to report.

About an hour later, the columnist tried again, showing up at the Stork Club, where Monroe, DiMaggio, and Solotaire had gone for a 2:00 A.M. supper. Solotaire was entertaining the couple with his ample wit. Unlike most Broadway characters, he did not deride people to get a laugh, and much of his humor was at his own expense. Making light of his short, stubby build, he quipped, "I want to hear two things before I die, 'Who's your tailor?' and 'Stay away from my girl.' I'm still waiting."

When Winchell came upon the trio, Marilyn was digging into a garlic-laced Caesar salad. Walter made some remark about Joe's Italian tastes rubbing off on Marilyn, and DiMaggio said he was no fan of garlic, which he wasn't. Then, he added, "But she eats it before going to bed." That was the best Winchell could get, and he used the quote in a column.

Joe and Marilyn walked to the St. Regis, and once they got behind closed doors, his restraint vanished. DiMaggio told her, "Whatever class you may have had, you now lost it," and there was a heated exchange between the two. Some of Marilyn's friends have said that night was the second time Joe struck her. The third supposedly took place less than three weeks later, the night before Marilyn and attorney Jerry Giesler held a news conference in front of her home to announce she was filing for divorce. Slatzer said Allan "Whitey" Snyder, Marilyn's longtime makeup man, received a call from her at about 5:00 A.M. and was asked to come to her home. She told him she had two black eyes and needed his cosmetic magic to cover them in time for the news conference. Snyder said when he arrived, Joe was sitting in the living room reading a newspaper. He motioned with his head that Marilyn was upstairs, which is where Snyder said he worked on camouflaging the shiners. Newsreel footage showed a distraught, tired-looking Marilyn standing next to Giesler outside her home as he announced the impending divorce, but no sign of black eyes.

Joe insisted that the argument over *The Seven Year Itch* did not trigger the divorce, but there is no question it affected the couple's relationship. While still in New York for the Series, he showed up at Toots Shor's, and Shor told author Maury Allen that Joe was still very upset when he joined the proprietor at the bar. Toots, who was well into a bottle of his own booze by then, listened to Joe's laconic account of the filming, and responded with a philosophical, "What do you expect from a slut?" Joe had no response. He left his drink on the bar and departed the premises without as much as a goodnight.

◆ ◆ ◆

Very soon after Marilyn filed for divorce, DiMaggio showed up in Panama. "The phone rang about four in the morning, and it was Joe," Nachio said. "He was at the airport and he asked me to pick him up. I brought him home and sat with him for three hours and he didn't say a word. He looked awful, devastated. I had known him fourteen or fifteen years by then, and I had never seen him like that. He just sat there staring into space. At seven o'clock, I said I was going back to sleep and I left him there." DiMaggio stayed with the Nachios for three weeks. "He said two words to my wife, Isabelle, 'hello' and 'goodbye.' He was traumatized." Nachio realized that his friend had come to Panama to escape the press' questions about Marilyn, so he asked no questions. He waited for Joe to tell him what he wanted to tell him, when he wanted to tell him. There was one light note. A little after dawn one morning, Nachio and his wife heard DiMaggio screaming. Nachio rushed into his bedroom where a frightened Yankee Clipper was standing on his bed staring at the floor where stood a lizard, its tongue whipping in and out its mouth. The Nachios' seven-year-old daughter picked up the reptile, held it by the tail and said, "Don't be frightened, Uncle Joe."

When Joe was ready to leave the house after about a week, he and Nachio strolled the beach and went to a nearby island to fish. Still, Joe said nothing about Marilyn until, while waiting for a fish to bite, he declared, "You always hurt the ones you love." Later, he uttered another sentence. "I tried to submit to her desires, and see if I could go along, but I just couldn't do it." He always was a man of few words. He returned to the United States, but six months later was back in Panama looking much better. He actually was cheery.

In the interim, he had received a phone call from Marilyn. She said being divorced didn't mean they had to end their relationship, he told Frank Scott, who lined up endorsements for DiMaggio, Mantle, and Martin. "Anytime you want to see me, all you have to do is call." It wasn't like Joe to share such things, but he may have just talked with Marilyn and was so happy he couldn't keep it to himself. The invitation may also have erased any doubt he had about his ability to sexually satisfy Marilyn. When he first learned of the divorce, his first question was, "Is there another guy?"

Everyone had an opinion of what went wrong, and they expressed it in newspaper gossip columns and magazine articles. On one side were those who said it was his fault because he demanded that she be a submissive wife who dressed and behaved modestly, and was not so much a part of the Hollywood way of life that he detested. Others held that she was to blame because she insisted on being Marilyn Monroe the actress and sex symbol, and that she was not a one-man woman. Nachio, who was an eyewitness to the brief but tumultuous marriage, saw it this way: "They lived in a fish bowl. They couldn't do anything without somebody picking up a story about it. That's what ruined their marriage, they were so famous. If it had been just Joe, a famous ballplayer married to an ordinary person, it would have been different. But they were two legendary figures married to each other. The media exploited that."

Monroe was granted an interlocutory decree on October 27, 1954, only nine months after their wedding. Early the following month, DiMaggio took her to Cedars of Lebanon Hospital, where she had a gynecological operation, and he stayed at her bedside after the surgery. Joe and Marilyn were together a great deal for a divorced couple. In fact, he was with her at the premiere of *The Seven Year Itch*.

He was also there for her when she and Arthur Miller were breaking up, and he was a frequent visitor at her Manhattan apartment, in a very fashionable building on 57th Street near the East River. Marilyn's maid, Lena Pepitone, was called at home on the last morning of 1960 and asked to come in on her day off to prepare a New Year's dinner for two that evening. The guest was

DiMaggio, Pepitone told William Stadiem, who wrote *Marilyn Monroe Confidential: An Intimate Personal Account*. When Joe arrived, he kissed Marilyn and Lena and made himself comfortable while Pepitone prepared spaghetti and sausage Neapolitan style. The next morning, Lena set out a big breakfast on the dining room table. Marilyn dined in a white terry-cloth robe; Joe wore suit trousers, a white shirt, and tie. Caught up in the romantic moment, Lena wondered aloud, "Hey, why don't you marry her again?" According to Pepitone, DiMaggio's response was, "Just too many differences for a marriage." Joe also assured Lena that he did indeed love Marilyn. The maid already knew how Marilyn felt. "I never loved anyone more than Joe," she had confided. "But when it comes to women, nobody is crazier than Italian men." It was like a Puccini opera.

As far as Lena was concerned, the new year, 1961, was off to a great start. She had received a $200 tip and a kiss from Joe DiMaggio.

Monroe's apartment, incidentally, was so spectacular that Marty Lederhandler, a retired AP photographer, vividly recalled it more than forty years later. "It was dazzling white. A white rug, a white piano, a white sofa, and white drapes." Lederhandler was assigned to take a photo of Marilyn, and he was forever a witness to her propensity for being late. "She was still married to Arthur Miller. He opened the door and told the reporter and me that Marilyn was fixing her hair and would be out in a minute. We sat on that sofa and Miller put a bottle of Scotch on the table with a couple of glasses and some ice." One hour later, when much of the Scotch had disappeared, Marilyn finally appeared. "She looked absolutely gorgeous," Lederhandler remembered. "She was wearing a black shift dress with a big white bow, and her hairdo was perfect."

Although he was no longer married to her, Joe still was upset about Marilyn's movie roles. He was working at the time for the

Monette Company, an outfit that supplied army PXs, and his job took him all over the world. After flying back from a business trip to Paris, he went from the airport to talk with Norman Brokaw of the William Morris Agency about his concerns. He found no sympathy. Brokaw said that it was Marilyn's career and there was nothing he could do about it. "If an actress has a chance to work with Clark Gable in *The Misfits*, it's a big thing for her career. She can't pass it up."

When DiMaggio did not seem impressed, Brokaw put it in a way that hit home. "Joe, suppose after you hit in 55 straight games, Marilyn asked you not to go to the ballpark the next day, for the 56th game. What would you do?" It was if a light had been turned on in Joe's brain. He smiled and nodded his understanding.

Shortly afterward, a serious problem that had been developing in Marilyn's life erupted, and it caused delays in the filming of *The Misfits*. Marilyn was addicted to barbiturates. She said she needed them to help her sleep. When she did fall asleep, she had terrible dreams, some of them about her troubled years as a teenager. "I did some bad things that made me hate myself," she told Pepitone. At her psychiatrist's suggestion, she entered the Payne Whitney Psychiatric Unit at the Cornell Medical Center in Manhattan. The facility was renowned for its treatment of drug and alcohol addiction, and it even had a floor for patients who would be locked in after working all day and stay until after breakfast.

When Marilyn entered the hospital, Joe was working as a batting instructor for the Yankees 1961 spring training in Florida. She called him there, and he asked what she was doing in a psychiatric hospital. "You're not crazy," he told her. Marilyn wanted to hear that. She always feared she would wind up like her mother and grandmother, "in a crazy house." Marilyn pleaded with Joe to rescue her again, and he did. He flew to New York and rushed to the hospital. "I raised hell," he said. "I told them I would take the place apart." After Marilyn was released in his custody, he wrote her a check for $5,000 to pay the bill, quite a handsome sum in those days, and he took her to another hospital, Columbia Presbyterian in upper Manhattan.

Joe worried about that check for the rest of his life. It cleared the bank, but he never got it back. "Do you realize how much that check could sell for? It's got my signature and Marilyn's endorsement." He never got the money back from Marilyn either. She was having financial trouble, despite the money she made doing *The Misfits*, and she never really shook her dependency on barbiturates. Also, her marriage to Miller was all but over. Miller had written *The Misfits* for her, and her problems during the filming were a major source of friction.

Marilyn flew to Florida to join Joe after she left Columbia Presbyterian Hospital. When the media learned that she was heading there, the Yankees camp became a magnet for writers and photographers from all over the state. DiMaggio knew that would happen, and he phoned Marilyn to tell her to stay at their motel. Joe approached Harry Harris, an Associated Press photographer, in the locker room. "Would you like to take a picture of Miss Monroe and me?" he asked. Harris said he would be delighted. Joe told him to be at a secluded part of the beach near Sarasota the following morning. When Harris and his wife, Teddi, drove to the spot, Marilyn and Joe were walking on the beach. He was carrying a fishing pole and she had her left arm tucked around his right arm. "She was wearing sunglasses, looking like she had a bad time the night before, and she had a kerchief around her head," Harris said. "She was pleasant enough, but when I asked her to take off the sunglasses, she said no. She asked me who was the girl in the car, and I said that was no girl, it was my wife. Teddi joined us, and she agreed that Marilyn shouldn't remove her glasses. 'You see,' Marilyn told me. She also refused to remove her kerchief."

Harris made a couple of shots, including one with the two of them holding a horseshoe crab that washed up on the beach. But the photo that was seen the most all over the world, and still is from time to time, was the one of the world's most famous couple walking arm and arm along the beach, both smiling happily, like two people in love.

"You know that song, 'Love is Better the Second Time Around'? It's true," DiMaggio said. Actually, it was still the first time for him because he never fell out of love with her. "He suffered from the want of her," Nachio said. "He couldn't find peace without her. He told me no one could ever take her place." As for Marilyn, she once told Slatzer, "Joe is OK to take in small doses," but now she wanted as much of him as she could get.

In June, she needed him again, because she went to New York Polyclinic for emergency surgery to remove impacted gallstones. George Solotaire was with Joe as Marilyn was wheeled into the hospital. "She was the worst I had ever seen her," Solotaire recalled. "She didn't seem to know where she was." The surgeon, John Hammett, told Joe that Marilyn was heading for trouble, because she was fooling with a dangerous mix of alcohol and barbiturates.

Joe had to go on another business trip to Europe. Marilyn returned to Los Angeles, where she added Sinatra to her barbiturates and booze.

◆ ◆ ◆

DiMaggio either could not admit to himself that Marilyn was promiscuous, or he wanted her so desperately he didn't care. Enough people told him about her reputation. He once told a friend that he doubted Marilyn and Sinatra had a sexual relationship, even though she made no secret of it, except to him. "Joe and Frank have more in common than just being Italian. Both are really something else in bed," she said. Marilyn was not bashful about discussing their sexual equipment with women friends. "Huge" was the word she used for both men, though she said DiMaggio had the more muscular body.

Marilyn moved in with Frank in August 1961. A visitor to Sinatra's house, who was shocked to see Marilyn walking around nude, called Joe in Europe. Going naked was just Marilyn being Marilyn, but Frank also told Joe's caller that Marilyn was drinking heavily and popping pills.

"Get your fat ass out of here," an embarrassed Sinatra told her when she walked in on a card game without a stitch of clothes, according to J. Randy Taraborelli in *Sinatra: Behind the Legend*. The book was among several that alluded to a sexual relationship between JFK and Marilyn. Marilyn told Slatzer she began a relationship with the president shortly after meeting him at the home of Kennedy's sister, Pat, and her husband, actor Peter Lawford, one of Sinatra's Rat Pack.

Sinatra and DiMaggio knew each other for years, but were not close enough to be called friends. (In Bernie Kamber's words, "Joe didn't have many 'friends.'") Joe was a year older than Frank, both had Sicilian backgrounds, and both were big boxing fans, so they saw each other occasionally at major bouts. But their personalities were very different. Joe was quiet and tried to avoid the spotlight. Frank could be boisterous and wanted everyone to know he was in the place when he showed up. He swung at some guys and threatened others. Joe never did either, at least, there is no record that he ever did and he never said anything about that to me. Both were heavy hitters when it came to sex, but only Frank's affairs made the newspapers. Joe was always discreet. And, when it came to work, both set standards for how their jobs should be done.

There were times when Joe, Frank, and Marilyn showed up at a restaurant or some gathering as a threesome, which created a monumental stir. Sinatra and Monroe seemed to enjoy the excitement and gossip they engendered much more than DiMaggio did. At one point, she thought that Sinatra would marry her, and

Frank seriously entertained that thought. Marilyn discussed with a friend which of the two men she would likely marry, much as high school girls would do. "At least Frankie wouldn't expect me to be a housewife," Marilyn said. "Maybe we were destined for each other," she mused. "He told me he was born on Monroe Street in Hoboken, but I told him Monroe wasn't my real name."

Joe and Frank were involved in a madcap caper in the fall of 1954, soon after Marilyn filed for divorce from DiMaggio. Joe was trying to get some evidence that he hoped to use to dissuade her from going through with the action. One of Sinatra's entourage, a private detective, spotted Marilyn's car in front of an apartment complex, and the three of them, DiMaggio, Sinatra, and the detective, burst into an apartment. It was not the one where Marilyn was having dinner with a female friend, but the apartment of Florence Kotz, who was asleep when her front door was broken open. At a State Senate committee hearing that followed, Sinatra swore he was waiting in the car when the intrusion took place. He told the panel he paid the detective $800, but he said DiMaggio paid him back, which was not true. Kotz sued, and the matter was settled out of court for $7,500, all of which was paid by Sinatra.

Sinatra and DiMaggio continued to get together at various times after that, and it was Frank who introduced Joe to Sam Giancana. The big-time Chicago crime figure was comfortable with Joe and so delighted to be in his company that he had to show off. He displayed the contents of a handkerchief he had in his jacket pocket: a ring, earrings, and a bracelet. Giancana said he wanted to give a gift to his girlfriend, Phyllis McGuire, one of the singing McGuire Sisters. "Which one should I give her?" Giancana asked. "They're all very nice," DiMaggio assured him. "OK, then I'll give her all of them."

Some thirty years later, DiMaggio was staying in a Hasbrouck Heights, New Jersey, hotel co-owned by his friend Cal Kovens. He was in his suite when he was alerted that McGuire had just checked in and had asked if he was there. "Get rid of her," Joe exclaimed. "Look, I'm seventy-two and she wants to spend the whole afternoon in bed. I can't do that anymore. She'll kill me." The singer was told Joe was not in the hotel and no one knew when he would be back. She left the next morning for Atlantic City and Joe came out of hiding.

Sinatra and Giancana both became DiMaggio's enemies early in the 1960s. Joe called Sinatra a "pimp" for the Kennedy brothers. "He used Marilyn's body to get close with the Kennedys, and get favors from them," DiMaggio said. Lawford, a Kennedy brother-in-law, agreed. "I was Frank's pimp and Frank was Jack's," he said.

The feud between Sinatra and DiMaggio lasted for the rest of their lives, although in Sinatra's view there was a truce in May 1979. Sinatra threw a big fundraising event at Caesars Palace in Las Vegas for destitute and ailing former heavyweight champion Joe Louis on his sixty-fifth birthday, and DiMaggio was among the scores of celebrities invited. The seating on the stage was in tiers, and Joe D. was in the prime row. His granddaughter Paula explained Joe's presence: "My grandfather loved Joe Louis more than he hated Sinatra." DiMaggio and Louis burst on the New York scene together in 1936, and each had a mutual respect for the other's talent. DiMaggio arranged for a baseball team sponsored by Louis to get old Yankees uniforms.

I am not sure if DiMaggio was aware of Marilyn's involvement with JFK when he returned from overseas for Christmas 1961. Whether or not he was, Joe talked about marrying her again, and she seemed agreeable enough for him to shop for a ring. She still had the ring he gave her when they married, and the fact that she kept it meant a great deal to Joe, because he knew she could have used the money its sale would have brought. It was a platinum band set with thirty-five baguette-cut diamonds. (The ring sold at a Christie's auction in October 1999 for $772,000, even though one of the diamonds was missing.) Joe wanted her to have a new ring to symbolize a new start, so he went to a longtime friend in Newark, New Jersey, mob guy Richie Boiardo, who may also have provided DiMaggio with that first wedding ring. "They called him Boots because he always made calls from telephone booths and his guys would say 'he's in a boot,'" Joe explained to me with a laugh. The new ring was valued at $6,500, but when Joe attempted to write a check, Boiardo said, "Forget about it." Joe's reaction: "I figured, why fight it."

That seemed to be DiMaggio's attitude about associating with "the wise guys," as he called them. If they got their kicks from taking him to dinner, that was all right with him. Being with DiMaggio gave the Italian mobsters a feeling of pride, and Jewish gangsters in Newark, Chicago, and Cleveland also basked in his company. Joe never had to reach for his wallet when he was with members of either group. He saw their efforts to treat him as their guest as a gesture of respect to someone who had made his mark in the legitimate world. Again, *La Bella Figura*.

Marilyn bought a new house in Brentwood and needed help with a down payment. Joe came through twice for about $10,000, in the form of loans that were repaid by her estate. Then she told him she was going to do one more picture, *Something's Got to Give*. DiMaggio was not happy about that, especially when he heard that her costar would be Dean Martin, another of Frank's Rat Pack. Not that he had anything against Martin; in fact, Joe liked him, but he was wary of Sinatra. Still, he was determined to "try and go along with her desires" so their relationship would go smoothly. The filming was anything but smooth. Some days Marilyn showed on the set, on other days she didn't. She interrupted production to fly to New York, slither into a dazzling gown, and sing "Happy Birthday" to JFK at Madison Square Garden. Her departure caused an uproar at 20th Century Fox, but the president's brother, Robert Kennedy, told Fox executive Milton Gould that the president wanted Marilyn to be there, and that was that. As usual, Marilyn was tardy, and that time she kept a packed arena waiting, leading to Lawford's prophetic introduction, "the late Marilyn Monroe." In less than three months, she would indeed be dead.

Marilyn never finished that movie, although she did a nude swimming pool scene that became legend in the industry. According to the documentary, *Marilyn Monroe: The Final Days*, the idea of swimming nude was Marilyn's, but it was director George Cukor, not Marilyn, who ordered everyone but the cameramen off the set. In that rather erotic scene, she tore off the flesh-colored body suit to swim naked and then posed with a large towel. But she had too many problems with booze, pills, and her emotional state to complete the film, and the production was shut down. Efforts were made to find a replacement for her, but Martin insisted the role had to be played by Marilyn and no one else. Earlier, Dino had griped about the delays she was causing, and Hollywood wondered if his turnabout was inspired by Sinatra or whether Martin felt pity for her. They were no strangers. Marilyn had socialized with Dean and his wife several times at the Lawfords' home.

Reeling from this latest emotional and physical distress, Marilyn once again asked for Joe's help, and he flew to Beverly Hills to be her protector and lover. When DiMaggio returned to New York in July, he really didn't need American Airlines. He was feeling so good he could have gotten there by flapping his arms. He called Nachio and asked him to be in California early in August. "He never actually told me he was getting married, but he said I should make every effort to be there," Nachio said. "And, he sounded great." DiMaggio didn't know that after he left California, Marilyn made a trip to Sinatra's Cal-Neva Lodge in Lake Tahoe, on Frank's jet. Taraborelli and Donald Wolfe, author of

The Last Days of Marilyn Monroe, both wrote about Marilyn being spaced out on drugs, and they alluded to Giancana having sex with her.

Taraborelli quoted a former FBI agent as saying the mobster was heard on a wiretap saying that by being intimate with Marilyn, he put one over on the Kennedys. Giancana's friends insisted that Sam would never have done something like that because it would have been an act of disrespect to Sinatra. Both authors reported that sexually explicit photographs were taken of Marilyn that weekend. Hollywood photographer William Woodfield said he actually saw the photos and negatives. Wolfe said DiMaggio flew to the lodge after being told what was going on, but, on Sinatra's orders, he was blocked from registering. If that adventure did happen as reported by those two authors, Marilyn was recovered enough by August 1 to sign a new contract with 20th Century Fox. She was ready to go back to work on *Something's Got to Give*.

On Friday, August 3, 1962, Monroe called Slatzer and was extremely agitated. She said that Bobby Kennedy had promised he would see her that weekend, and she had just heard on the radio that he was in San Francisco with his wife and children. Marilyn complained she was unable to contact him on his private number, and the Justice Department, which he headed, refused to put through her calls, as had been done before. "She said unless she heard from him over the weekend, she was going to call a press conference Monday and blow the lid off the 'whole damn thing,'" Slatzer said. He had a pretty good idea what that was about. Marilyn told her former lover and drinking buddy that Bobby had been sent on a White House mission earlier in the year to explain that the president was forced to end their relationship. Marilyn was shaken by the news, and the attorney general was sympathetic and consoling. Before Bobby left the room, he and Marilyn had started a relationship of their own.

Henry Weinstein, producer of the ill-fated *Something's Got to Give*, remembered that Marilyn was rather nervous when she told him she had a date with the attorney general, and wondered what questions she could ask him. "How about civil rights?" was among Weinstein's suggestions. "When she told me she had a second date, I asked her how things were going, and she said, 'I don't need any more questions.'"

Ethel Kennedy, RFK's wife and mother of his nine children, was not unaware that something was going on between her husband and Marilyn. Taraborelli tells of a remark she made in the presence of someone else that reddened her husband's face, and drew a warning from him never to mention Marilyn's name.

Slatzer gathered from his conversations with Marilyn that sex was a catharsis for RFK. Bobby would bask in the afterglow and talk about government investigations of Jimmy Hoffa and the Mafia, about Cuba, and whatever else he was working on at the time. Marilyn had trouble remembering all the details, and she didn't want to seem stupid or uninterested if he referred to them in their subsequent liaisons. Bobby had once called her a dumb blonde, which brought her to tears. "I'm not so damn dumb," she told Slatzer, "or I wouldn't be where I am today." Slatzer advised her to keep a diary, which she did, in a book with a red cover. Among the notations in there was Bobby's account of a CIA attempt to poison Fidel Castro with the help of Giancana. Bobby also complained about Sinatra's association with Giancana, and he warned JFK to cut his ties with Frank because of that.

On the Saturday night she died, Marilyn was so busy on the phone that Joe Jr. was twice thwarted from reaching her because of busy signals. He got through on the third try. "She didn't sound like a person who was unhappy, certainly not like someone who was about to kill herself with pills," Junior told me in Florida. "She was very pleasant and happy about getting married to my dad again. She told me that her wedding dress was ready and she would pick it up on Monday." She also expressed her delight when Joe Jr. told her that he had broken off with a woman Marilyn did not particularly like.

A few hours later, Marilyn's body was found by her housekeeper, Eunice Murray. She notified Marilyn's psychiatrist, Dr. Ralph Greenson, and when he got to the house, he called Marilyn's physician, Dr. Hyman Engelberg. (Although we have the same last name, and both are from New York, we were not related, at least not that either of us knew.)

There are many conflicting versions of what happened that night. Dr. Engelberg arrived at the house between 12:30 and 1:00 A.M. "She committed suicide," he said in his call to the Los Angeles Police Department to report her death. Looking back at it nearly forty years later, he hadn't changed his mind, and he described her as a manic depressive. "Today, they call it a bipolar personality, but manic depressive better describes her condition," Dr. Engelberg said. Closing in on his ninetieth birthday, he was still very active and had a clear recollection of that Saturday night in 1962. "I talked with her early that evening, and she was happy, in a manic phase," recalled Dr. Engelberg, who had been treating Marilyn for a sinus infection. The doctor said that she apparently went into a depressed state later that evening. "Some TV commentator said she received a phone call from one of the Kennedys, and that depressed her," Dr. Engelberg said, adding that he really didn't know what put her in that state of mind. "When a manic depressive gets depressed, it doesn't cause a suicidal impulse because there isn't much space for them to drop much further. But, if they are in a manic phase, and something happens to depress them, then they fall with a thud, and they grab anything they can grab."

Dr. Engelberg's thought was that Marilyn went for some chloral hydrate pills—also called "knockout drops"—which she probably picked up in Mexico, along with some Nembutal tablets he had prescribed to help her sleep. "Her liver was loaded with chloral hydrate," said Dr. Engelberg. "That probably was the main cause of death. The barbiturates I gave her contributed maybe a little, but it was not the main thing. At any rate, she just grabbed whatever she could grab at her bedside."

Jeanne Carmen, a longtime friend of Marilyn's and a former neighbor, didn't agree with the suicide theory. "Good Lord, no! Not a chance." Carmen spoke with Marilyn at 9:00 P.M., about two hours before she died, and like Joe Jr., she found her friend to be in a good state of mind. The two women confirmed an earlier date for Sunday morning when Carmen was to give Marilyn a golf lesson, and in Carmen's mind, that ruled out suicide.

Giving Marilyn Monroe a golf lesson was an adventure Carmen was not especially eager to repeat, but Marilyn had presented her with some golf clubs for her birthday a couple of days earlier, and she wanted to try them out. Carmen, who gave trick-shot exhibitions, once offered a joint lesson to Marilyn and Jayne Mansfield. "They were so bad," she said. "They showed up in high heels and I had them drop those in the golf cart. Jayne took out her powder puff and used it to clean the ball. They were resting the clubs in their crotch and having a fun time. I was a little more serious about golf. I decided this was not going to work out."

Marilyn and Jeanne often drank together and spoke frankly to each other of triumphs and disappointments. Monroe told her that she gave birth to a baby girl when she was 20, but had no idea what became of her daughter. Both women had a relationship with Sinatra, and he was a frequent topic of discussion. Marilyn also apparently held back very little when she talked about her ties to the Kennedy brothers. "She really cared about Bobby, and she really believed he cared for her," Carmen said. "But things were getting hot. She wanted to get married, and she started to get a little pushy. I said, 'Are you crazy? Think with your head, not your ass. These are ambitious people, ambitious men. Imagine you and your sexiness in Washington. No one would have it.'" Marilyn was not convinced, and her response was, "I'm Marilyn Monroe, and I know he loves me. I know I would make a great first lady."

Carmen said that during their final conversation, Marilyn asked her to bring a couple of sleeping pills; Marilyn wanted to be sure to get to sleep that night and be well rested. Carmen never did make the fifteen- to twenty-minute trip because she had been drinking earlier that evening and she went to bed early. She heard the phone ringing about 10:00 P.M. and assumed it was Marilyn, but she didn't pick up because she was half-asleep.

If Marilyn didn't commit suicide, that left either accidental overdose or murder as the cause of death. Carmen was in the latter camp, though she wasn't quite sure who was responsible. She said she had warned Marilyn to beware of her "gangster friends," especially Johnny Rosselli, a mobster with ties to the movie industry and a friend of Giancana's. Slatzer insisted there was no question that Marilyn was murdered, and that Bobby Kennedy was somehow involved. People who lived nearby told Slatzer that they saw the attorney general in the vicinity of Marilyn's home at 12305 Fifth Helena Drive the afternoon before she died. A handyman in the home, Norman Jefferies, was quoted by Donald Wolfe as saying RFK and two men actually were in the house that night.

The autopsy report by Thomas Noguchi, a deputy medical examiner at the time, attributed the death to "acute barbiturate poisoning," but he said the five-hour autopsy found no traces of the substance in Monroe's stomach or esophagus. Also, there was no coroner's inquest, nor was a blood sample taken from the corpse. Two or three days after the funeral, coroner Theodore

Curphey called the death a "probable suicide" and said Marilyn had taken forty-seven to forty-nine Nembutal capsules. Noguchi, who was left swinging in the wind, said his original report had been misplaced and he had reconstructed it from memory. Ironically, it was Noguchi who did the autopsy when Robert Kennedy was shot to death in the kitchen of a Los Angeles hotel.

◆ ◆ ◆

DiMaggio learned of Monroe's death in San Francisco. He was there to play in an Old Timers game, and he flew down to Los Angeles when he heard the news. After speaking with Marilyn's half sister, Berniece Miracle, Joe called the Westwood Mortuary to handle the funeral and the Westwood Memorial Park to arrange for a crypt. Soon, a grief-stricken Joe Jr. arrived from his marine base in San Diego. Big Joe took charge and issued orders. Barred from the funeral were Frank Sinatra, Sammy Davis Jr., Pat and Peter Lawford, Walter Winchell, Bob Slatzer, and as DiMaggio put it, "anyone else who put her where she is today." Sinatra showed up, but he was turned away. He left without making a scene, but later said, "That sonofabitch deprived me of paying my last respects. I loved her, too."

Among the twenty or so people DiMaggio did clear for the funeral service were Solotaire, Snyder, Dr. Engelberg, her psychiatrist Ralph Greenson, drama coach Lee Strasberg, and attorney Mickey Rudin, who had also been Sinatra's lawyer. Joe was the last one to leave the chapel after the brief service. Junior, who was in tears but standing tall in his marine blues, turned when he reached the door and saw his father bend over the coffin and kiss Marilyn goodbye. Joe Jr. felt very close to Big Joe at that moment, as they shared their grief over a woman both had loved.

"The Kennedys killed her," Joe declared to his son, and he later repeated the accusation to some friends. DiMaggio told me that he had given his son a manila envelope containing a statement concerning Monroe's death, to be opened after he died. "Something the world should know about is in there," DiMaggio told his son. When Junior came to Florida after his father's funeral, I asked him about that envelope. He had given me an opening by volunteering that he had talked with Marilyn the night she died—he said "murdered." He claimed he hadn't opened the envelope because he already knew the message his father had left behind. When I pressed him about it, he said, "Morris, I love you, but you are not Sicilian and I can't tell you." After several more beers, though, he was willing to disclose what Marilyn had told him about Bobby Kennedy. She said she spoke with RFK three or four times a week, and he told her about the work he was doing, and had mentioned which mobsters the Justice Department was going after. Marilyn would pass on some of those tidbits to Sinatra, according to Joe Jr. When I asked him if he agreed with his father that the Kennedys were responsible for her death, he said it was probably true. "She didn't die of natural causes, and she wasn't going to kill herself, not when she was about to remarry my father."

Big Joe knew about Marilyn's red-cover diary, and among the first things he did when he arrived at her home was to frantically look for it. He didn't find it. Slatzer said he learned the book was taken from the house with other items in the room, including pill bottles, as evidence. Nothing has been heard about that diary since.

Joe Jr. said his father had discussed with him the possibility that JFK or Bobby or both had been victims of mob-orchestrated killings. I broached the subject to him because that's what DiMaggio had told me, and I wondered if he had shared that preposterous theory with anyone else. "When you mess with the big boys . . . ," Joe had said to me, without finishing the sentence. According to Junior, his father declared that the Kennedy brothers got what they deserved. Those who knew how Joe felt about the Kennedys wondered what would happen when DiMaggio and Bobby met at Yankee Stadium during a tribute for Mickey Mantle on September 18, 1965. Kennedy was among those on the field when DiMaggio was introduced. Joe strode from the dugout, shook hands with the others on the field, and walked past Bobby as if he weren't there. It was a snub witnessed by a huge audience, both at the Stadium and on television.

In the 1990s, DiMaggio was invited to appear at a charity event at the Kennedy Center in Washington, and he agreed to go only after being assured that no Kennedy would be there. When I asked why he would bar family members who had never harmed him, he responded, "It's in their blood, and what they did to me will never be forgotten. They murdered the one person I loved."

DiMaggio was once eating lunch with Dr. Positano at Coco Pazzo in New York when JFK's children, Caroline and John Jr., arrived and were seated nearby. Joe's body stiffened in anger. He complained that the young Kennedys had been deliberately seated close to him by the maitre d', who thought he was doing him a favor. When Positano said he knew Caroline and John and "they were good people," DiMaggio replied, "I have nothing against the kids, but I can never forget what their father and uncle did to Marilyn, especially their uncle."

◆ ◆ ◆

Joe never forgot Marilyn, either. She intruded into his thoughts forever after her death, causing him great sadness. We would be relaxing in the office or in an airport lounge, sometimes in the midst of a conversation, when suddenly his head would droop. When I asked what was the matter, he picked up his head, looked right at me and said, "Don't you know, Morris, don't you know?" This often happened at exhilarating moments, like after he had signed a major deal or after he received a special honor. It was as if the joy he was feeling was dissipated because she wasn't there to share it.

Nachio said it wasn't only at those times that Joe felt that way. "No matter how many years went by, whenever he thought about her, he would go into a trance, I mean literally, a trance like he was in another world. We would be on a fishing boat in Panama, drinking a beer, and that look would come on his face, and I knew he wasn't even aware he was in a boat with me. His thoughts were with Marilyn."

Some people have written that DiMaggio never could bring himself to visit Marilyn's grave. That was not true, though it may have been true that no one ever saw him there.

Arthur Richman, a front-office official for the Mets and later the Yankees, accompanied DiMaggio on one of his visits. After a sports dinner in Los Angeles, Joe asked Richman to drive him to the Westwood Cemetery, even though it was nearly midnight. The cemetery, not much larger than a football field, was located right in the village, a couple of yards off Wilshire Boulevard behind some commercial buildings. Joe knew exactly where the crypt was, and the two men stood in front of it for a few minutes before leaving. That visit was under cover of darkness.

A few years before Joe died, he and Positano were in Los Angeles for the Jim Thorpe Awards dinner, and he asked the doctor to drive him to the Cemetery. This time, it was daylight. Joe said he would stay in the car, but he wanted Positano to go in and look at the crypt. "He gave me very explicit directions, and said he would ask me to describe what I saw," Positano said. "I got a bit lost in the cemetery, but when I asked where Marilyn Monroe's tomb was, someone pointed the way." Positano found that her coffin was sealed in a wall, with others above it, under it, and alongside of it. "Italians call it a *forno*, like an oven," he said. "I memorized what I saw, including a stone vase on the wall next to the plaque that read simply 'Marilyn Monroe,' and nearby was a granite bench. I went back to the car and told Joe. He said, 'That's all I wanted to know.' He told me he had that bench put there so visitors could sit." The plaque on the bench was inscribed, "In loving memory of Marilyn Monroe," and there was a notation of the dedication date, August 5, 1992, the thirtieth anniversary of her death. At the bottom of the plaque were the inscriptions, "All About Marilyn" and "Marilyn Remembered." Positano asked Joe why, after coming all the way out there, he hadn't gone in to see for himself. "Rock, a guy has been waiting for thirty years to get a picture of me visiting her. It's worth $10 million. Let him wait." Positano saw no one anywhere near the wall into which Marilyn's coffin had been entombed.

The stone vase was the one that held the roses Joe sent regularly. Marilyn had asked him to do that early in their relationship when he visited her in a hospital during one of her surgeries. "If I die, Joe," she had said, "promise me you will put roses on my grave." Neither Positano nor Richman saw roses there. After thirty years of fulfilling his promise, Joe stopped sending the flowers, oddly, after Dorothy Arnold died in 1984. He never said why. In going over Joe's bills, I never saw a bill from a florist. Occasionally some flowers do appear in the vase, as there were during a visit by a friend in March 2002. Obviously, Marilyn still has a secret admirer.

Some fifty yards from Marilyn's place in the wall is Dean Martin's tomb. His nameplate has the inscription, "Everybody Loves Somebody Sometimes." Jack Lemmon, who costarred with Monroe in *Some Like It Hot*, is buried across the lawn from her, not too far from Walter Matthau's final resting place. Mel Tormé is buried closer to Marilyn's tomb. Armand Hammer's remains are locked in a handsome mausoleum on the grounds. A lot of celebrities for so small a cemetery.

Aside from the visit to the cemetery, Positano had another reason for remembering that 1996 trip to Los Angeles: it was a close encounter between DiMaggio and Sinatra. Positano planned to go with Joe and some friends to Matteo's in Westwood. Joe thought that was a great idea. He hadn't been there in many years but remembered the restaurant's highly regarded escarole and beans. He said they were the best he had ever eaten. Because it was a Sunday night, and Matteo's was always packed that night, Positano called for a reservation. "Matty got really excited when he heard Joe D. was coming, and he got on the phone. He called Steve and Edie, he called Burt Lancaster, he called Jack Carter, he called Gregory Peck, and soon word was all over Beverly Hills that the Yankee Clipper is coming back to Matteo's." DiMaggio and Positano were heading for the restaurant with a friend, Howard Starks, when Starks' son called to the car phone from the restaurant's bar and said he had heard Matty call Sinatra to tell him DiMaggio would be there. Matty and Sinatra were buddies. Both were from Hoboken, and Matty knew Sinatra's parents. He said Frank wanted to come that night and make up with Joe.

"I knew if we walked in there and Joe saw Frank, I would be in big trouble, out of the book for months," Positano said. "He would have thought I planned it. So, we had a quick change in plans and we wound up at the Palm. When we got out of the car, Joe saw we weren't at Matteo's. I explained that Frank had found out where we were going, and he would be there to make amends. Joe took my hand and patted it. He said, 'Doc, you did the right thing.'"

◆ ◆ ◆

When DiMaggio would stay at the Sheraton Heights Hotel in Hasbrouck Heights as a public relations guest, the head of security there, retired cop Rocky Russo, looked out for him and chauffeured him around the area or drove him into New York. They became friendly. About 2:30 one January morning in 1986, Russo returned to the hotel, where he also lived, and was told that Joe had been looking for him. When he called, DiMaggio asked him to come to his suite. "He had the blues, and he wanted to talk," Russo said. "At first, he just sat there quietly for several minutes, and then he said, 'You know, everyone talks about how beautiful Marilyn Monroe was, and she was, but people don't remember my first wife, Dorothy Arnold. She was just as beautiful. I used to run around a lot when I was married to her. I was crazy, fucking around.'"

Russo recalled that DiMaggio talked about how the Kennedys "ruined" Marilyn. "That's the word he used, 'ruined,' and about how Sinatra ruined her. 'I'll never talk to him as long as I live,' he said about Frank. He said there had been a lot of lies written about Marilyn. I told him he should write a book to straighten it all out. 'Maybe one day, I will,' he said. I told him the trouble was that he married two girls who were his opposite; they wanted publicity and craved the limelight, but he tried to avoid it. You made the same mistake twice." Joe replied, "You know, Rocky, you are absolutely right."

The two men sat there alternating between conversation and silence until 11:00 A.M. Rocky got up and left. He had been there for eight hours.

"I knew him for about three years," Russo said, "and that was the only time he talked about Marilyn, except for one morning in the hotel coffee shop. He had a magazine in front of him that had a story about Marilyn. He was angry about it. 'Lies, Rocky. Lies. There's always lies about her.' He didn't say anything else, though."

It is amazing to me that Joe would have had that conversation. Anyone who knew him, including former teammates, business associates, and longtime friends, were made aware that there would be no discussion of Marilyn. That included his granddaughters, and even Vanassa, whom he adored. "Those are my memories," he declared, and that would end the questions. The unwritten rule was, if he brought up the subject, listen and ask or say nothing. Nachio was exempt because he was a witness to the love affair. Joe Jr. was, too, because Marilyn was part of his life. DiMaggio spoke of Marilyn to Martha Lee in their quiet moments together, and sometimes to Marina, his nephew Joe's wife, on their long flights to Japan. "But, he never talked of his feelings," Marina said. "He just told me of the times he was with her in the hospitals, and things like that."

There were two pictures in the living room of DiMaggio's Beach Street home: a small framed painting of Marilyn's face, and on the opposite wall, a full-length portrait of Joe in a double-breasted blue suit. To Sam Spear, the subjects seemed to be gazing admiringly across the room at each other, day and night. Spear remembered driving Joe through San Francisco when the song "I've Got a Crush on You" came on the radio. "That was Marilyn's favorite song," DiMaggio volunteered. Funny he should say that. The song's title also told the story of Joe's feelings about Marilyn.

9

JOE AND THE PRESIDENTS

THE SECOND GAME OF THE 1936 World Series was played at the Polo Grounds, just across the Harlem River from Yankee Stadium. President Franklin D. Roosevelt was in the stands, and he would be staying until the last out, even though the Yankees were so far ahead and the game was out of reach for the New York Giants.

Possibly, Roosevelt held to the theory that you never leave a game until the last out. More likely, he didn't want to disrupt the game. It was a major production to get the president out of the ballpark because his legs had been paralyzed by polio years earlier. So, FDR had to arrive and depart in his car, which was brought into the park through the center-field exit. The players had been told to stay on the field after the last out and until the president left the park. The fans, too, were asked to remain in their seats.

There were two out in the bottom of the ninth inning when Hank Lieber of the Giants sent a long drive to center field, which in the Polo Grounds was like an endless void. DiMaggio, as usual, was playing shallow. When he saw where the ball was headed, he turned and in his easy-looking stride, loped toward deep left-center field. DiMaggio told me there was nothing easy about it. "I went tear-assing after that ball. After about 50 yards I turned around and put up my glove, and it's a good thing I did, because that ball would have hit me in the nose," he said.

His momentum carried him up the first few steps to the visitors' clubhouse, which was connected to the Giants' clubhouse, and the two formed a green wooden bridge over the center-field exit. DiMaggio would have continued up the remaining steps into the Yankees locker room except for the orders the players had been given to remain on the field until the president had gone, and DiMaggio always followed orders. It was a wonderful presence of mind for a rookie whose catch had ended a game in his first World Series.

Joe's recollection of that play was so vivid because of what happened afterward. The president's convertible circled the field as it headed for the exit, and the fans stood to give Roosevelt an ovation. DiMaggio stood at attention and felt his heart thumping as the president approached. "He took off his hat and waved it, then smiled at me and said, 'nice catch,'" DiMaggio said. "It was the biggest thrill I ever had, and I never forgot it."

Just about a month later, the twenty-one-year-old DiMaggio cast his first presidential vote, and it went to FDR, who was running against Alf Landon. Roosevelt was one of the few Democratic presidential candidates ever to receive DiMaggio's vote. The last may have been Lyndon Johnson. As he got older and richer, Joe's political views were closer to the Republican philosophy, especially when it came to taxation. He complained the Democrats were spenders and taxers, words he obviously picked up from Republican campaign statements on TV and in the newspapers. He said they spent too much of his money on things he didn't care for. After establishing himself as a Florida resident, though, he voted for Governor Lawton Chiles and Senator Bob Graham, both of whom were Democrats. He knew them, and he liked them, but most important, they were good to "his" hospital.

◆ ◆ ◆

Roosevelt was the first president DiMaggio saw, and he met all the others up to and including Clinton. He visited them all in the White House, except Clinton, because he despised the man he called "Slick Willie" and "the greatest liar of the century."

In fact, after having agreed to accept an honorary degree from George Washington University, DiMaggio changed his mind when he learned that the commencement ceremony would be held on the White House grounds. He gave some other reason, but the truth was that he was concerned Clinton might know he was there and wander over.

DiMaggio felt the man was immoral and a liar. "Look, I can see his nose growing," Joe would say as he watched Clinton make a speech or hold a news conference, and he watched most of those. Joe formed his opinion from the hours he spent watching C-SPAN, CNN, MSNBC, and the various news commentary shows. He also studiously read *The New York Times*, including the editorial and op-ed pages. He would cut out editorials and columns that hit a sympathetic note.

The *Times* was DiMaggio's favorite newspaper, but he was furious at the attention given to the president and Hillary. "They must own a piece of the paper," he joked.

He was particularly upset with the stories of Clinton's alleged sexual adventures, especially with Monica Lewinsky. An outraged DiMaggio referred to her as "that teenage girl," though she was in her mid-twenties. He would comment, "How would he feel if his daughter was in that situation?"

Joe was amazed and distressed at Clinton's popularity, especially with people whose opinion DiMaggio respected. "This guy is so slick and smooth that even on his way to jail the majority would still vote for him," DiMaggio said. He attributed that to Clinton's ability to articulate his case. "Maybe the most convincing speaker of all time," he conceded, "especially when it comes to making people feel sorry for him when he's in trouble."

DiMaggio's strong dislike of Clinton was the reason he doggedly snubbed the president whenever he had the chance. The most notable example was at the Time Warner dinner at Radio City Music Hall in New York, celebrating *Time* magazine's seventy-fifth anniversary. Invitations went out to people who played a prominent role in our society during those three-quarters of a century, including athletes, actors, statesmen, and politicians. Being on *Time*'s cover was one criterion. Joe accomplished that more than once.

When Joe arrived at the Music Hall, he learned he was to be seated with the president. "No, sir," he snapped. "Either I sit somewhere else, or I'm not staying." Joe had invited Dr. Positano as his guest. Among the foot surgeon's other patients was Henry Kissinger, another of *Time*'s cover boys. DiMaggio and Kissinger knew each other since meeting in Positano's office, and the doctor was able to arrange for Joe to join the secretary and his wife, Nancy, at their table. Clinton may have been looking forward to table talk with DiMaggio, but Joe took particular pleasure in disappointing him. He wanted to avoid giving the impression that they were friends, which he felt could get Clinton some votes.

Joe flew back to Florida, and when I met him at Fort Lauderdale airport, he told me what had happened. I asked what he would have done had the Time Warner people insisted he sit with Clinton. "I would have left," he said. And I had no doubt that's exactly what he would have done.

DiMaggio's next chance to brush off Clinton came in Baltimore on the night Cal Ripken of the Orioles broke Lou Gehrig's long-standing record for consecutive games played. Orioles owner Peter Angelos invited Joe to sit in his box along with Hall of Famer Frank Robinson and some others. The president was in the adjoining box, and he and DiMaggio could see each other through the plexiglass. A presidential aide approached Joe and said Clinton would like him to come in and shake hands. Joe told the emissary that he had met Clinton previously and the two had shaken hands then. "Once is enough," Joe said. What he didn't tell the aide was that the meeting had taken place years before Clinton became president. Joe later told me that he had figured that the fellow would be back because "Clinton never gives up." Sure enough, the aide returned and told DiMaggio that the president had invited him to his box to watch the game at his side. Joe sent back the message that he was sitting with friends and would have invited Clinton to join them, but there was no room. I chose to watch that game on television back home because I had a hunch there would be a confrontation, and I wanted no part of that.

DiMaggio was not responsible for the next snub. I was. DiMaggio was gravely ill in Memorial Regional Hospital following his surgery in 1998 when I was told the White House was calling. Clinton had asked to speak with DiMaggio. The hospital said it could provide a portable telephone for the conversation, but I declined. At this point, DiMaggio had a tube in his throat and was heavily sedated and extremely weak. I conveyed this to someone on the hospital's public relations staff, and was told DiMaggio didn't have to talk, just listen. I felt the hospital PR people and possibly the White House would tape the president's remarks and make them public. I knew that would really upset Joe.

As DiMaggio's health surrogate, I was empowered to make the decision, and I did. There would be no phone call. My reasoning was that when Joe was healthy he wouldn't speak with Clinton, so he certainly wouldn't do it under those circumstances.

The day after DiMaggio died, I received a letter from the White House, datelined Tegucigalpa, Honduras, and addressed to "the family of Joe DiMaggio." Clinton said that he and Hillary were saddened to learn of Joe's death. He wrote: "There are some athletes whose character and achievement transcend the world of sports and enter the world of legend. Joe DiMaggio was one of these."

The letter went on to note DiMaggio's "power and consistency at the plate, his speed on the base paths, and his virtual flawless performance in the outfield." It also mentioned his 56-game streak and his appearance in ten World Series during his thirteen-year career. "But it was more than Joe DiMaggio's impressive statistics that captured the hearts of his fellow Americans," Clinton continued. "He was a gentleman both on and off the field, a man who handled adulation and adversity with equal grace, a patriot who gave up three prime seasons in his baseball career to serve his nation in the army during World War II. . . . Joe's death is a great loss for the millions of us who so loved and admired him."

I couldn't help wonder what DiMaggio would have said about that letter. I imagine it would have been some cynical putdown about political motives.

Joe's dislike of Hillary Clinton was nearly as great as his feeling about her husband, although at times he would shake his head and say he felt sorry for her. Before she announced her candidacy for the U.S. Senate from New York, he expected her to seek some elective office. When she called the Joe DiMaggio Children's Hospital, saying she would be in south Florida and would like to tour the facility, he vetoed that idea. "All she's doing is looking for votes," he said. "Tell her to get them somewhere else." When he heard that she might run for Senate against Rudy Giuliani, he fretted that she might be elected.

Joe was a big Giuliani fan, and the feeling was mutual. DiMaggio would speak of how Giuliani had cleaned up New York, referring to both street cleaning and crime. That Giuliani was an enthusiastic and knowledgeable Yankees fan added to DiMaggio's fondness for him. Joe made it a point to shake his hand and talk with him whenever he saw the mayor at Yankee Stadium. I wonder what he would have said about the reports of Giuliani's adulterous behavior that came to light after Joe died. As disappointed as he would have been, he would have found positive things to say about Giuliani's effectiveness as mayor, even before the attack on the World Trade Center.

◆ ◆ ◆

Bill Clinton was not the only occupant of the White House who received a brush-off from DiMaggio. Ronald Reagan was another, and Joe liked him. It happened in July 1994, long after Reagan had left office. We were in Los Angeles for a sports dinner to benefit the Cedars of Lebanon-Sinai Hospital. After the affair, we went to Chasens, which was very popular with the Hollywood crowd. I asked Joe, "Did you ever eat here?" "All the time, with Marilyn," he said.

I noticed a couple of Secret Service men in a corner of the place. With those earpieces, who could miss them? They were there because Reagan and his wife, Nancy, were in the place having dinner. "Joe, there's President Reagan," I said. DiMaggio had played golf with Reagan a few times, starting back when Reagan was governor of California, and DiMaggio had been invited to the White House by the Reagans for a state dinner to honor Soviet leader Mikhail Gorbachev. But Joe didn't react to the former president being in the restaurant.

Reagan got to his feet and was shouting, "Joe, hey, Joe." DiMaggio only briefly glanced at him and responded, "Hi, how are you doing?" Joe didn't even walk to their table, just 8 to 10 feet away. I wanted so much to shake Reagan's hand, but I couldn't do that if Joe didn't, and Joe didn't. That was DiMaggio protocol. We were at a table with six other people, including my wife, Stephanie, and some hospital executives with their wives. Joe sat there quietly, speaking only to me, and ignoring everyone else. His silence was embarrassing.

People at the table would ask him a question, trying to draw him into a conversation, and he would respond with a one-word answer. I don't know what put him in that mood. Maybe it was his recollection of being in the restaurant forty years earlier with Marilyn, or maybe it was his memory of a night he spent at her bedside at Cedars of Lebanon in 1954. They were already divorced by then, but she called him to say she was having pains from a gynecological problem that plagued her for years, and said she needed to get to a hospital. He took her and stayed with her through the night. He didn't say what was bothering him that night in Chasens, but he was not in a good mood.

DiMaggio continued to ignore the Reagans, who were looking at us and smiling. He knew how badly I wanted to meet the former president. I thought that maybe he would go to the men's room and I would accompany him, as I had done hundreds of times. Joe usually made several trips to the men's room during dinner, but that night, he didn't budge from the table. Then, I thought I would go to the men's room and detour to the Reagan's table. But I visualized the Secret Service guys rushing to intercept me. Joe could get away with that, but not I.

The only time the frown left DiMaggio's face was when he spotted attorney F. Lee Bailey wandering around with a drink in his hand and apparently several in his belly. "Come on over," he said. Bailey did, but Joe never asked him to sit down and their conversation took place with Bailey on his feet throughout.

The Reagans finished their dinner and came to our table. They pulled up two chairs and joined us, and I made the introductions, this is so and so, this is so and so's wife. The former president was interested in talking only with DiMaggio. He recalled the time Joe was at the Gorbachev dinner. "Remember that ball I signed for you and got Gorbachev to sign it?" DiMaggio remembered it well. He had been on a select list of about 120 people invited to a state dinner honoring Gorbachev and his wife, Raisa. The Soviet leader was in Washington for a top-level meeting with the president. Reagan, who once had been a sportscaster, was a big Joe D. fan, in addition to having been in the same golfing foursome, which likely was why Joe received the invitation to that state dinner.

DiMaggio, very much informed about world affairs and politics, was honored to be invited to that state dinner, and he flew up from Florida. En route to the White House, DiMaggio's baseball-thinking process kicked in. He realized he would have a rare opportunity to get the autographs of two world leaders. Others might have thought of trying to get the signatures on a program or a napkin; not Joe DiMaggio. He thought of a baseball.

It was tricky enough to find an official American League baseball on a December evening in Washington, which didn't even have a big league team. Getting the ball signed would be that much trickier. Joe put the ball in his overcoat pocket and told the woman at the coat-check counter to put his coat where she could get at it in a hurry.

DiMaggio told Joe Durso, a longtime sportswriter for *The New York Times* and author of *Joe DiMaggio: The Last American Knight*, that when he approached Reagan on the receiving line, he said, "Mr. President, I'd like to get your autograph on a baseball." He said Reagan smiled, and so did Gorbachev when an interpreter told him what DiMaggio had said. Reagan had introduced him to the Soviet leader as "one of our greatest baseball players."

Joe kept thinking about that ball in his coat pocket and worried about his chances. Good fortune was with him when he was seated next to the president's daughter, Maureen. They had met some years earlier, and he felt comfortable asking her advice on how to get his ball autographed. She told him to leave the ball at the office of the chief of the marine ushers, and say the ball was for her, which he did.

The next time DiMaggio saw that ball was the following morning on CNN. It was in Reagan's hand on a telecast of the president's meeting with Gorbachev. Joe told Durso that Maureen later sent him the ball, which had the signatures of the two world leaders.

Then, perhaps for the first time, DiMaggio knew exactly how a fan felt after getting his autograph on a ball. "You know, Morris, it's a double signing," DiMaggio told me, and he laughed. Two or more signatures on a ball was a no-no as far as we were concerned. For years he wouldn't sign a ball if it already had another signature on it. In fact, double signings were specifically forbidden in our memorabilia show contracts until 1996, when he relented.

Joe really prized that Reagan-Gorbachev ball. He eventually removed it from his vault at a Bowery Savings Bank branch and gave it to his granddaughter Paula. That night at Chasens, years later, Joe told Reagan in detail what he went through to get the signatures. "I followed protocol," DiMaggio said. "I always do." "You sure did," Reagan said.

By now, my wife was having a conversation with Nancy Reagan, a very charming woman. "I love your name so much that we named our second daughter Nancy," Stephanie said. When the Reagans got up to go, fifteen minutes later, Stephanie kissed Nancy on the cheek and I finally got to shake the president's hand, a major perk for being Joe's schlepper in Los Angeles for four days.

The next day we went to Dodger Stadium, and when DiMaggio and I came out of the clubhouse locker room, Stephanie was telling Nancy Sinatra, "I love your name so much that we named our second daughter Nancy," the very same words she had used with Nancy Reagan. Joe broke up laughing and asked me, "How many daughters do you have named Nancy?" It was the only time I saw him laugh or smile during the four days in Los Angeles, though he was paid very well for the trip.

◆ ◆ ◆

One of DiMaggio's memorable visits to the White House came during the Eisenhower administration, when he was invited to an event with several other sports stars. Joe arrived by cab, entered the grounds, and was on his way to the entrance when a group of tourists intercepted him. One asked for an autograph, and DiMaggio obliged. That was a mistake, because the others got in line with pen and paper in hand, and before long Joe was in danger of being late for his appointment, something he never did. Then, he heard, "Hey, Joe, how about me, can I have your autograph?" He looked up. It was Ike, on the steps waiting to greet him. The president had been there for five or ten minutes watching DiMaggio signing for the fans, and no one realized he was there.

Another visit to 1600 Pennsylvania Avenue gave Joe the opportunity to act as peacemaker. That was in 1969. Richard Nixon was president and DiMaggio was in the nation's capital for the All-Star Game. Naturally, he was among those invited to a presidential reception. So was his former buddy, Toots Shor. New York's most famous saloonkeeper arrived early and promptly bellied up to one of the bars set up in the room. He soon visited the other bar and bounced from one to the other until he was a little wobbly and well on his way to being an obnoxious drunk, not an unusual role for him. By then, a reception line had formed for the guests to shake hands with the president. Among those on the line were Ewing Kauffman, owner of the Kansas City Royals, and his wife. Shor shouldered his way in front of Mrs. Kauffman, and Mr. Kauffman chided him for doing it. Shor pushed the Royals owner, and the elderly Mr. Kauffman pushed back.

DiMaggio was next in line, chatting with Cleveland sportswriter Hal Lebovitz, and he knew he had to act quickly to keep the scene from getting uglier. Lebovitz said DiMaggio grabbed Shor from behind and calmed him with some "sweet talk." DiMaggio had long since soured on Shor as a friend, but Toots still was in awe of Joe and allowed himself to be walked out of the room quietly, or as quietly as Shor could be. His peacemaking duties accomplished, Joe rejoined Lebovitz in the line. Hal remembered the reception DiMaggio got from Nixon, who was a serious sports fan. "He knew all of Joe's important statistics and recited them. He was like an adoring kid seeking an autograph."

Another presidential baseball fan who received a DiMaggio-signed baseball was on the opposite end of the political spectrum from Nixon. A friend of Dr. Positano's was going to Cuba to meet President Fidel Castro, and he asked the doctor to try to get Joe to sign a ball for the Cuban leader. Why not, Joe reasoned. "Castro was a pitcher, he's a baseball fan, and this isn't political." Still, Joe was cautious when it came to what he wrote on the ball. "I don't want him to get too comfortable with me," he said. When a newspaper printed the story about the signed ball for Castro, there was some grumbling in Miami's Cuban community. DiMaggio was worried that there might be demonstrations when he next went to the city for stone crabs. There were none.

Joe was dead by the time George W. Bush was elected president, but he knew him when he was governor of Texas and, before that, owner of the Texas Rangers. DiMaggio met him at a dinner when we went to Arlington, Texas, for the All-Star Game, and they chatted. "He looks just like his father, doesn't he," Joe remarked. "That resemblance is really something."

After George W. became president, he said that among his prized possessions was a ball autographed by Joe DiMaggio and Ted Williams, which probably was one that had been given to his dad, the first President George Bush, by the two Hall of Fame outfielders.

In 1991, the elder George Bush hosted DiMaggio and Williams at the White House for a reception honoring the two baseball legends, and the next day they flew with Bush on Air Force One to Toronto for the All-Star Game. DiMaggio was awed by his first trip in the presidential plane. When he came home he described in detail what it looked like inside and the reception that greeted them at the airport.

Before DiMaggio and Williams went to the White House, Bush's chief of staff called Joe and told him that the president intended to award the both of them the Presidential Medal of Freedom, the highest honor a civilian can receive and ranking second only to the Congressional Medal of Honor. Joe could barely contain his glee when he was able to reply, "Please thank the president, but I already have one." DiMaggio had been so honored by President Ford in January 1977. The accompanying citation said, in part, "Joe DiMaggio stands tall among the ranks of genuine American heroes. Known and revered around the world as the 'Yankee Clipper,' he contributed many years of style and splendid ability to the sport. His character and grace both on and off the playing field have been a continuing source of inspiration to Americans of all ages." Along with the citation and the medal, a five-pointed star set on a red pentagon and delivered in a walnut presentation case, DiMaggio received a silver miniature medal, a silver lapel emblem, and detailed instructions on how the medal was to be worn. DiMaggio, of course, also let Williams know that he already had been awarded the Medal of Freedom, and he recorded in his diary that Ted responded that they were now even when it came to medals.

DiMaggio also played golf with the elder Bush and his son, Jeb, the governor of Florida. Joe turned sportswriter of sorts after he played with the two Bushes and Arnold Palmer at the Deering Bay Golf Club. "Bush's tee shot (on the first hole) was driven into the water, as well as my first shot," DiMaggio wrote in his diary. "Our second balls found dry ground. . . . We made some good shots and some bad ones, that is the president and me. Palmer and Jeb Bush hit the ball super. The president's game was understandably off, as well as mine. I don't play too much, with my arthritis giving me fits, and the president told me that he, too, has not played too much at this point." The former president also told Joe he was a Red Sox fan, and while they were playing golf, he recalled a couple of games between Boston and New York. In one of them, Joe's brother Dom had made a spectacular catch, and Bush brought that up. DiMaggio asked me later, "How come everybody always remembers that?"

Joe would never get involved in the politics of a presidential election, or any election, for that matter. No more extreme example of that was the Bush-Clinton campaign. He had visited Bush at the White House, flown on Air Force One with him, played golf with him, and had a friendly relationship. Clinton, on the other hand, was an anathema to DiMaggio, and Joe refused to shake hands with him. Yet, DiMaggio turned down a $4 million appearance fee from the Republican Party to join Williams for a television appearance with Bush on the Sunday night before the election. "I don't get involved in politics," was his explanation.

10

THE JOE DIMAGGIO CHILDREN'S HOSPITAL

PEOPLE FOREVER WERE TRYING to name things for Joe, from buildings to pomodoro sauce. Someone even had the bright idea of designating a Manhattan intersection, Fifth Avenue and 56th Street, as DiMaggio Way. Fifth Avenue would be for the number 5 on his Yankees uniform jersey, and 56 for his 56-game hitting streak. DiMaggio laughed when he first heard about it, but he rejected the request for his permission with the explanation that the idea was too political.

He also vetoed a plan to erect a Joe DiMaggio statue in New York's Central Park. "What about Eleanor Roosevelt?" he wondered. "There should be a statue of her, not me. She did more than I ever did. Can you imagine the complaints from all the women's groups if I have a statue and she doesn't." That may not have been the only reason. *Malocchio*, the evil eye, presented a potential danger, he confided in his friend, Mario Faustini. Statues are for people who are dead, DiMaggio said, and he didn't want to tempt fate. He made an exception for the National Italian-American Sports Hall of Fame and agreed to allow a bronze statue to be made for the facility, then in Arlington Heights, Illinois. DiMaggio let himself be talked into it because, after all, he was the Hall's first inductee, but that's not to say he didn't worry about it. In this case, *malocchio* had nothing to do with it. He was concerned that miniature replicas of the statue might be made and wind up in knickknack stores, but the hall's director, George Randazzo, guaranteed that would not happen.

After DiMaggio's death in 1999, the battle to attach his name to public places took on particular controversy in his hometown of San Francisco. As the executor and trustee of his estate, I took it as a serious duty to protect the Joe DiMaggio name, just as Joe himself did throughout his life. Three days after he died, the *San Francisco Examiner* ran a front-page story outlining suggestions from fans for an appropriate memorial to the city's favorite son. Among the local landmarks mentioned as possibilities were the San Francisco International Airport and the San Francisco–Oakland Bay Bridge. These two, along with a rundown playground in North Beach, were among the ten suggestions sent to me by Gavin Newsom of the San Francisco Board of Supervisors. Naturally, I picked the airport and bridge to head the list.

Several times Joe had rejected offers to name facilities in his hometown for him, because he considered them inappropriate and politically motivated. "Everything in San Francisco is politics," he said, "and I want nothing to do with it." He always insisted that I protect his name after he was gone, and that's what I attempted to do when the city politicians decided to name the North Beach playground for Joe. His granddaughters were strongly against the idea, and I knew Joe would be too.

In the end, we dropped our court fight once the city assured us that the playground and adjoining swimming pool would be refurbished and that the city would drop its plans to charge admission to the pool. For years to come, the children of North Beach in San Francisco will be reminded of the legacy of one of its greatest citizens.

◆ ◆ ◆

Perhaps the most significant example of Joe making an exception to the use of his name was for a children's hospital in Hollywood,

Florida. Not only did that decision eventually give DiMaggio a great deal of pleasure, but as the years went on, he said that having his name on the Joe DiMaggio Children's Hospital meant more to him than being elected to baseball's Hall of Fame "It's easier getting into Cooperstown," he said. "Not too many ballplayers have hospitals named for them." No, not even Babe Ruth or Lou Gehrig.

Incidentally, Joe was not a big booster of the shrine in Cooperstown. He thought it was too much of a commercial venture, and he did not send many mementos of his career there. What was there, including an old-style outfielder's glove and a bat, was in a corner of a showcase devoted mostly to Gehrig's artifacts. DiMaggio would be pleased to be so closely associated with his legendary teammate. DiMaggio's plaque at the Hall of Fame noted the record hitting streak first among his accomplishments. Among the other feats mentioned was that he hit two home runs in one inning as a rookie and hit three home runs in a single game three times.

The request to name the pediatric facility for Joe came in June 1992 in a letter from Frank Sacco, chief executive officer of the South Broward Hospital District. It must have made an impression on DiMaggio because he read the letter three times before giving his usual answer. "I do not like to give my name out for anything, Morris," he said. "Somehow, they always find a way to commercialize it and abuse my name. I don't want my name ever being abused." I had heard that song before, but because he had read the letter with more than his usual lack of interest, I saw a chance to go a little further.

"So what, even if they do commercialize your name? It's a good hospital. If using your name somehow puts the hospital in position to save the life of one child, it would outweigh anything that could possibly hurt your name," I said. I also explained that I could draft an agreement that would prevent the hospital from using his name for any purpose without his permission, such as putting it on items sold in the gift shop or in press releases. He agreed to meet with

Sacco. The first question Joe had for him was, "What do you want from me?" Sacco told him, "Your name, and be assured that we will never embarrass it."

Sacco's jurisdiction included three hospitals and a nursing home, and one of them, Memorial Regional Hospital in Holly-wood, was expanding its pediatric unit. The hospital had been sending youngsters who required surgery to Miami Children's Hospital, and were paying the bills for those whose parents had no health insurance and were indigent. Surgeons, anesthesiologists, and nurses had to be paid, operating room expenses had to be covered, and the Miami facility was unable to absorb the costs. About twenty patients a year were in that category. At Sacco's recommendation, Memorial decided that instead of paying Miami Children's Hospital, it would hire a pediatric surgeon of its own.

That decision inspired a further growth of the children's unit. Cancer treatment and orthopedic surgery were added, and soon the fifty beds that were located on a single floor of an older building were no longer enough. Sacco told DiMaggio the pediatric section was ready to play an even bigger and better role in the community, but he said that would require a more prominent identity and a greater fundraising effort. That's where DiMaggio would come in. Joe listened intently to this explanation, and he had more questions than I had ever heard him ask about any subject.

Why name the hospital for a ballplayer rather than someone like Jonas Salk, who had developed the polio vaccine, or some other scientist who had made a notable contribution to saving children's lives?

"Kids and sports, especially baseball, go together," was Sacco's answer. "It's a natural word association."

Why select Joe DiMaggio, who had been retired for more than forty years, before even most of the parents of the potential patients were born? Because Joe's image was squeaky clean. Unlike some other sports heroes, DiMaggio's name was not tainted by scandal,

The photo that began a long friendship. Joe DiMaggio gave me this signed photo at our first meeting, on Febuary 1, 1983. That breakfast meeting lasted nearly five hours, and the friendship lasted for sixteen years. *Author's Collection*

At the opening of the Ted Williams Museum in Florida, I had the distinct pleasure of being surrounded by a triumvirate of baseball icons: Stan Musial (far left), DiMaggio, and Williams (far right). *Author's Collection*

Phil Rizzuto (center) played shortstop in front of DiMaggio for ten years, from 1941 to 1951, during which time the Yankees captured six World Championships. *Author's Collection*

Former heavyweight champion Muhammad Ali was a favorite of DiMaggio's, who was a big boxing fan. They met at the dedication ceremony for the Ted Williams Museum. Williams, as usual, eschewed a necktie; DiMaggio was never without one. *Author's Collection*

One of DiMaggio's many presidential meetings came in 1991 with President George Herbert Walker Bush, when DiMaggio and Ted Williams (center) were honored at the White House. Bush then flew the two baseball greats aboard *Air Force One* to the All-Star Game in Toronto. *Author's Collection*

DiMaggio talks baseball with George W. Bush, then governor of Texas, at the
1995 All-Star Game at the Ballpark in Arlington in Texas. DiMaggio regarded
Bush, formerly part-owner of the Texas Rangers ball club, as a knowledgeable
baseball man. *Author's Collection*

Mayor Rudy Giuliani of New York congratulates DiMaggio on his speech at the Lotos Club, where DiMaggio was honored in 1995. Giuliani often said that DiMaggio was his hero, and the mayor said, "I was surprised when DiMaggio told me that I was his hero." *Author's Collection*

DiMaggio, who dropped out of high school for lack of interest, took delight in the honorary degree he received from Columbia University. He was also honored by New York University and Florida International University. *Author's Collection*

While Joe always made it a priority to protect the use of his name, he made an exception when it came to the Joe DiMaggio Children's Hospital. He believed that his affiliation would help further the hospital's mission to offer affordable health care to all families. Here Joe cradles an infant in the neonatal unit. *Author's Collection*

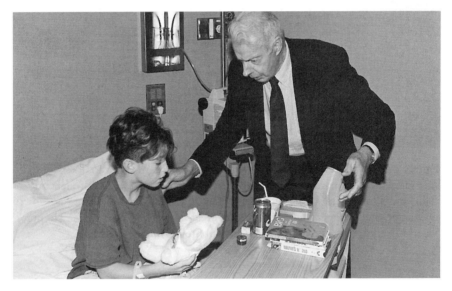

Joe took an active role in the hospital named for him. He made frequent visits, bringing gifts and chatting with the young patients and their families. He was always greeted enthusiastically by the youngsters, who knew he once was a famous ballplayer. *Author's Collection*

Joe spent countless hours autographing memorabilia in the conference room of my law office in Hollywood, Florida. We had it down to a routine, including the can of Diet Coke by his side. *Author's Collection*

Fans would flock to the DiMaggio table at card and memorabilia shows. In this case, the "fan" is Hall of Fame catcher Johnny Bench, who was also signing autographs at the show. *Author's Collection*

DiMaggio made memorabilia industry history in August 1993, when he signed 1,941 bats for nearly $4 million. The signing took place at the Hillerich & Bradsby Bat Company facility. *Courtesy H & B Bat Company*

Joe DiMaggio responds to the cheers from the capacity crowd at Yankee Stadium on Joe DiMaggio Day on September 27, 1998. He holds aloft the eight replica World Series rings given to him by Yankees owner George Steinbrenner to replace those that were stolen. It was DiMaggio's last appearance at the Stadium. *AP/WideWorld Photos*

Joe DiMaggio's casket is carried from the Saints Peter and Paul Church in San Francisco, following the funeral on March 11, 1999. I was one of the pallbearers (front left), along with Joe Nachio, Joe T. DiMaggio, Roger Stein, Joe DiMaggio Jr., and Jim Hamra. *AP/Wide World Photos*

We had a hard time locating Joe DiMaggio Jr. (right) to bring him to his father's funeral. He was living his preferred "hobo life" in a rural northern California town. Joe Jr. died just five months after his father, at age fifty-seven. *AP/Wide World Photos*

there were no DUIs, no drugs, no paternity suits, and since he was seventy-seven, there was unlikely to be any problem.

What got DiMaggio's attention was Sacco's statement that the Miami hospital would not admit poor kids from our area for surgery unless Memorial Hospital paid their bills. He told Sacco that if he did agree to the use of his name, it would be with the understanding that no child would be denied treatment because his parents were unable to pay. "No problem," Sacco told him. "That's the way we operate now." Joe wanted it in writing. He suggested the slogan, "Whether rich or poor, no child will ever be turned away." Corny, maybe, but those words are now part of the hospital's credo and appear in the lobby, the elevators, and in its promotional material.

DiMaggio learned of many cases where the pledge he sought had opened the doors for youngsters to be treated, but none pleased him more than a letter he received from a Hollywood couple whose two-year-old son, Joey, was seriously ill with what the parents described as flu-like symptoms. The father wrote that because of a recent job change, there was a three-day gap in insurance coverage for his family. That proved to be a major problem when he called three other area hospitals. Since Joey was not a trauma victim, the parents were told they would have to pay the emergency room fee and at least $1,000 before the boy could be admitted. The father, a police officer, said when he called the pediatric emergency room at the Joe DiMaggio Children's Hospital, he was told to bring in his son immediately and not to worry about the money. The father went on to extol the ER physician who determined that Joey had a brain tumor, which was removed within hours. The youngster was in a coma for eleven days, and was still in the hospital when the parents wrote glowingly of the care and treatment their son was receiving. "You can be proud of this institution that bears your name," the father said, and Joe indeed was, especially that the lack of finances was not a problem when the boy was admitted. Unfortunately, this particular story did not have a happy ending. Joey died two years later.

The admission policy was only one aspect that DiMaggio quizzed Sacco about. Joe also asked about the staff and medical facilities that were available. Typically, Joe took nothing for granted. "He came out here, he walked through the hospital, he checked things out, and he checked us out to make sure we were legitimate," Sacco said.

◆ ◆ ◆

Joe's fondness for the city of Hollywood, Florida, also played a part in his decision. Though he was strictly a New York and San Francisco type of guy, he enjoyed the environment and the people in the smaller city, south of Fort Lauderdale and north of Miami. There was a sizeable Italian-American population and that meant good Italian restaurants. The mayor was Mara Giulianti and he liked her. DiMaggio was a popular figure in the area, and he enjoyed the horn-beeping salutes he would get when people recognized him. When he lived at the Holiday Inn in the town, his appearance at the lobby or the coffee shop was a major happening. The middle-aged guys usually had a recollection about seeing DiMaggio do something special in a game, and he would listen patiently to a story he may have heard many times.

Harland McPhun Jr., the bell captain and concierge, knew when to come to the rescue and get Joe on his way. "If he stopped for a minute, that was it, a crowd gathered. He was very polite, but sometimes, if he had an appointment, he just kept going until he got out the door. Once, a couple was coming in for their wedding reception. The bride spotted Mr. DiMaggio but the groom was saying 'No, it can't be,' and he went over and asked 'Are you Joe DiMaggio?' The next thing I saw was Joe posing with his arms around the bride and groom, and he told the groom, 'Loosen up.'

The fellow was standing there, his mouth open. He couldn't believe what was happening."

DiMaggio's popularity was evident in the enthusiasm that followed Sacco's recommendation for naming the hospital in his honor. The hospital district's board and Broward County's political leaders gave their unanimous approval. The dedication ceremony on September 17, 1992, drew a huge crowd and was a major event in south Florida, one that Joe never forgot. He made a speech in which he spoke about how touched he was to have the hospital named for him, and he said he regarded what went on in the hospital as his responsibility. He ended by turning to Sacco and saying, "Mr. Sacco, I will be watching you." Most of the audience chuckled, but Joe didn't. He was very serious.

I searched the crowd that day for an anonymous young lady who I believed may have been responsible for DiMaggio's association with the hospital. Early in 1992, an attractive blonde woman in her twenties approached Joe and me as we were leaving a restaurant after lunch. She asked DiMaggio to autograph a baseball cap, which she told him would be sold at Memorial Hospital's annual fundraising auction. I'm sure she had no idea that in those days DiMaggio would not autograph baseball caps. Maybe it was her naive enthusiasm or maybe it was because the cap had a Memorial Hospital logo rather than a baseball team's, but Joe made an exception and he signed the cap. It didn't hurt that she was blonde. DiMaggio was ever the skeptic, though. When she walked away, he said, "I'll bet it's for her boyfriend."

He was wrong. The cap did turn up at the auction, and the excitement it generated that night may have inspired the idea that Joe DiMaggio's name was just what the hospital needed.

A day before the dedication ceremony I drove him to the hospital in my van which had a "DIMAG 5" license plate and a customized rear spoiler on which was painted "The Yankee Clipper" and a No. 5 logo. Joe gave me permission to do this, and I know he took delight in seeing the reaction of people who spotted him being driven around Hollywood. He knew it brought out the boy in me, and he loved it. He always referred to it as the "Clipper Mobile."

As we approached the hospital, I saw something that gave me goose bumps. A huge sign reading "Joe DiMaggio Children's Hospital" was being hoisted to the top of the building. I pulled to the curb and parked and we sat there for nearly two hours, watching that sign go up. "Look at that, Joe! This is your legacy to your family and your heritage." Joe was not one for sentimentality, even at moments like that. He pointed his finger at me, and said, "Forget about my heritage, Morris. You better protect my name when I am alive *and* when I am not here someday." He was not letting down his guard even then.

I learned that the hospital had rejected a multimillion-dollar offer from someone who wanted the pediatric facility named for him. Sacco, who Joe called the commander in chief, had realized that DiMaggio's national recognition would mean much more over the long run. How right he was. It didn't take long for the power of DiMaggio's name to become apparent. Dr. Joel Martin, who was on the hospital's staff, told me that one of his patients, an elderly man with a heavy Italian accent, had asked him if the name on the sign was the same "DiMaggio who was the Italian baseball player." When he was told that it was indeed the very same Joe DiMaggio, the man wrote a check for $1,500 for the hospital. On his next visit, the man handed Martin another check, for $5,000. Martin sent both checks to our office. DiMaggio was so pleased, he wanted to meet the guy, who was also named Joe. Arrangements were made for lunch at the hospital, where DiMaggio had a special fondness for the linguini and pomodoro sauce. The two toured the hospital together, including the neonatal unit, and then sat down to a pasta lunch. The other Joe, speaking in Italian, discussed the pros and cons of various pasta sauces and the best way of cooking various pastas. I wasn't sure DiMaggio understood everything, but he nodded and smiled as if he did. When they had finished eating, the man took out his checkbook and wrote a third check, this one for six figures. "Take this. This is for you," he said, as he attempted to hand the check to DiMaggio. Joe put his two hands in front of him. "You've got the wrong guy," he said. "Please give it to Frank Sacco."

Joe did not consider himself a fundraiser, and he was passive in that role, but still effective. A friend at the Presidio Club in San Francisco asked him to sign some baseballs, and to show her appreciation, she sent a check of more than $1,000 to the hospital. There were many similar donations from people who wanted to show their affection for DiMaggio. Joe wanted every contributor to get a thank-you letter, so I asked the hospital to send us a copy of each note so Joe could see them. That lasted only a few months until Joe finally was satisfied those letters were going out as a matter of form, or more likely, he got weary of going through the stacks that piled up in his office. I finally told the hospital, "Enough already, Joe believes you."

◆ ◆ ◆

The hospital's major fundraising event was the weekend-long Memorial Classic. It started Friday night with a silent auction and cocktail reception, followed by the Legends Game for retired ball players on Saturday night, and a golf tournament on Monday. Joe showed up at all of them. He would tell some of his baseball stories at the reception, throw out the ceremonial first pitch, make a speech at the game, and play in the golf tournament.

DiMaggio became so involved in the weekend that he would invite his celebrity friends to play in "my tournament" and "my game." He enjoyed the ball game because it gave him a chance to see his old buddies like Phil Rizzuto, Stan Musial, and Ralph

Branca, and mingle with celebrities like Tom Selleck, Michael Bolton, and Senator Robert Graham. Cal Ripken also showed up, and we had a nice chat over a sumptuous clubhouse buffet sent by the hospital. DiMaggio sat in the dugout at old Yankee Stadium in Fort Lauderdale schmoozing with the players during batting practice. After making a pre-game speech at home plate, he would climb up to the antiquated press box to watch the game with the local media. Anticipating a post-game crush, I would start trying to get him out of the press box in the fifth inning, but he usually stayed until the ninth. His departure would set off an awesome ovation as he walked through the stands with a police escort. He would stop to shake hands and thank people for coming to the game.

Joe's last tournament was in February 1998, and although he was aching and bent with arthritis and a degenerating disc in his vertebrae, he played the full eighteen holes. He couldn't let on to his friends and admirers that he was slowing down. Jim Hamra, his grandson, caught a glimpse of Joe in an unguarded moment on a golf course when pain and age seemed to have overtaken him. Suddenly, Joe realized that his granddaughter Paula and some others were watching him. He straightened up, and it was as if he had instantly shed ten years.

Joe was alert for any attempt to politicize the Memorial Classic event because he was aware that Joe Reilly, then the chief fundraiser for the hospital, was close with people in the Democratic Party. So, when Senator Graham, a Democrat, was invited to a game, but not Senator Connie Mack Jr., a Republican, DiMaggio was furious. He made sure Graham was not permitted into the room where celebrities were photographed and interviewed.

Reilly's attempts to get publicity for political figures through the hospital was one of the reasons DiMaggio didn't like the guy. He complained constantly about Reilly's appearance, especially the way he dressed. "He doesn't look like an executive of a hospital like this should look." DiMaggio's disdain for Reilly intensified when Joe learned that the hospital gift shop was selling a T-shirt bearing a likeness of Joe taking his trademark swing. Our contract specifically barred the sale of such items without DiMaggio's permission. I tried to placate him by pointing out that the money would benefit the kids in the hospital. Joe said I was missing the point. "People are going to think I am making money from the sale of the T-shirts because my logo is on it." Reilly finally put one over on DiMaggio, nearly three years after his death. Two of the people Joe despised the most, Bill Clinton and Richard Ben Cramer, were invited to the hospital's 2002 Legends weekend. How I wished Joe could have walked in and seen them. Reilly would have been bolted to the wall by the DiMaggio stare.

◆ ◆ ◆

Joe's involvement gave a tremendous boost to the hospital's fundraising. Before the hospital was named for him, about $150,000 came in during that Memorial Classic weekend. At his death, the figure was approaching $1 million for the weekend. DiMaggio's involvement did wonders for the entire fundraising effort. Even after his death, the children's hospital was attracting more than $2.5 million a year in donations. Before DiMaggio's participation, the annual contribution was less than $500,000.

I was surprised when Joe accepted an invitation to attend a Comic Relief concert at Bayfront Park in Miami, but when I learned that a $100,000 contribution was being made to the hospital, I understood why he was willing to participate. Anything for his hospital, and he really enjoyed himself at the black-tie dinner that followed. A lot of ballplayers were there, and he had a chance to talk with his favorite current fighter, Evander Holyfield, who had been dethroned as heavyweight champion by Riddick Bowe. "Don't let it get you down," DiMaggio told him.

"You'll get the title back. And as far as I'm concerned, you're still the champ."

It was at that concert that he began a friendship with Michael Bolton. DiMaggio even agreed to umpire a game of the Bolton Bombers when the singer's touring softball team was in California. He once gave Bolton, who played third base on the team, a batting tip. "You have to get under a softball, Michael. Hit it up in the air." A couple of hours later, I received a cell phone call from Bolton. He was disappointed that he couldn't locate Joe, who had gone to dinner. "Tell him I hit a home run," he said excitedly from the dugout. "My first!"

A lot of money from the Bayfront Park concert was directed to a part of the facility that DiMaggio was very proud of, the "Visitor's Clubhouse." Located directly across the street from the children's hospital, the seventeen-room facility is a place where parents and siblings of the long-term pediatric patients can stay for free so they can be with the ailing child during hospitalization. It looks like a first-rate motel, and has a fully equipped kitchen where meals can be prepared so families can eat together, as well as a laundry room with washers and dryers. The idea is to keep the family together and in a home-like environment during an especially trying time. Bolton was on the board of the foundation that supports the facility, and together with DiMaggio, he helped attract benefactors. The George Steinbrenner Foundation sponsored one of the rooms in the Visitor's Clubhouse.

After DiMaggio died, major leaguer Jeff Conine became a major force in the facility and took over as sponsor of the Memorial celebrity golf tournament, which raised more than $1 million in 2001. DiMaggio helped get Conine involved in that project and the hospital, which wasn't hard after Conine toured the hospital with him. "Joe's way with the kids is what impressed me about his dedication to the hospital," Conine said. "It was obvious that he cared about them, and they related to him, although most of them probably weren't quite sure who he was, except they knew that he was famous."

"I know he had a reputation for being tough to get along with, although I never saw that part of him, but with those kids, he was the nicest, friendliest man. I have wonderful memories of him and the kids in the hospital." Conine wound up with a special bat I had donated to the hospital. It was a commemorative bat from the Marlins' first home game and was signed by DiMaggio.

DiMaggio would visit the hospital at least twice a month. He always felt comfortable with kids and would stop and talk with them on his tours. It wasn't just "how are you feeling?" He really got involved, inquiring of the boys about whether they played baseball and how they did in games. He would see a doll or a stuffed animal in a child's room and would use that as an opening for a conversation. The nurses prepared the young patients for his visits, and as he walked along the halls, they would shout, "Joe DiMaggio, Joe DiMaggio."

His dedication to the children in the hospital was never more apparent than an afternoon when he was interrupted while signing memorabilia in my office. Someone in the hospital called to say that the parents of a terminal patient were asking if Joe could be found because their son was asking to see him. The caller said if Joe were to come, he should do it quickly because the boy did not have much time. We shot over there, and Joe went into the room where the parents were with their son, who was about ten years old. A couple of minutes later, Joe came out, his face drained of its color. "The kid died," he said. "My God, Morris, he died just as I walked into the room." I had never seen Joe that shaken. He had seen GIs die during his visits in hospitals in Vietnam and Korea, but never a youngster. "I consoled his parents, but there was nothing I could do for the boy. He died just as I got there."

At Christmastime, before leaving for San Francisco to be with his grandchildren, Joe would go through the hospital pushing a shopping cart filled with teddy bears, going into each room to hand out the bears and speak with the children, many of who were desperately ill. I remember accompanying DiMaggio and Governor Lawton Chiles on one of those Christmastime tours, and Chiles was amazed at the ease with which DiMaggio talked with the patients. "He has such wonderful rapport with those children," Chiles said. "Frankly, I found it difficult at times because some of them were so ill. Joe managed to keep positive, and I could see he had a fine time." On one of the visits, a kid suddenly threw a baseball at DiMaggio. It surprised him, but as startled as he was and as old as he was, he still had the quick reflexes to make a basket catch. Then, laughing like a kid, he tossed the ball back to the youngster. DiMaggio's love was Marilyn Monroe, but his weakness was children, especially those who were having a hard time with life.

◆ ◆ ◆

Joe had another opportunity to champion the underdog in 1997, when he was asked to play the role of Joe DiMaggio in a movie called *The First of May*. The film told the story of a foster child whose young life was strife ridden, so much so that when I saw the script, I wondered if the kid's story reminded Joe of Marilyn Monroe bouncing from one foster home to another. It was a low-budget project, starring Julie Harris and Mickey Rooney, and was filmed in Deland, Florida. When producer-director Paul Sirmons was driving us from the airport, I mentioned that Joe had recently broken a couple of ribs. "Morris, don't make a big deal out of it," DiMaggio said. Sirmons said under the circumstances, he would understand if Joe wanted to back out. Joe wouldn't hear of that. What would the real actors think? "The show must go on," he declared.

For days, rain held up the shooting of the scene in which Joe was to talk with the youngster, played by Dan Byrd. This meant a costly delay for the shoestring operating budget. Finally, it was decided they would do the scene under the covered stands at Stetson University. As the cameras rolled, Joe sat down with the forlorn youngster and asked, "Rained out?" The reply was, "Worse, struck out." DiMaggio, who rarely struck out, explained that Babe Ruth, best known for hitting 714 homers, struck out 1,330 times between those homers. Joe said some people consider Ruth the greatest hitter ever. When the boy said that his new foster dad told him that "Joe D. something" was the greatest hitter, Joe responded, "Your foster dad sounds like a very smart man." DiMaggio wound up giving the boy some batting tips, and he got a hit.

DiMaggio worked for the Screen Actor's Guild minimum of $248, and he didn't want to take it. "He told me he did it to help the foster kids," Sirmons said. "When I read how avaricious DiMaggio was supposed to be, I thought that whoever wrote that didn't know the real Joe DiMaggio."

The first time Joe saw the film, he critiqued himself by saying, "You, know, I wasn't bad." *The First of May* never gained wide distribution, but it won several film festival awards in Europe.

◆ ◆ ◆

At the hospital, after the youngsters, Joe's favorite was the chef. He always managed to get into the kitchen for a conversation. Invariably, he stayed for lunch. "How about some linguini?" he asked. "Not too al dente," he instructed. "Pomodori, OK? No garlic, but onions are all right." He would tell anyone who would listen that there were a lot of upscale Italian restaurants that didn't have linguini as good as that chef made, with Joe's helpful advice, of course.

The hospital's colorful and cheery decor has a baseball motif, and was designed to eliminate, or least minimize, the fear with which the young patients came into the hospital. The lobby resembles a stadium entrance, highlighted by a brightly colored mural of a ballpark and a couple of seats from Chicago's Wrigley Field. Stepping on one of the bases painted on the floor set off a broadcast of a baseball game.

The place came to look like a baseball museum with showcases of memorabilia, including autographed balls, uniform jerseys, bats, plus scores of photos and posters. Much of the collection came from my office and home, donated by my family. Included among the rare items is a bat signed by DiMaggio in 1992, a year before he broke his self-imposed restriction on signing bats. The inscription he wrote made the bat really special: "To all the children at the Joe DiMaggio Children's Hospital, for a speedy recovery." The date inscribed on the bat, 9/17/92, marked the dedication of the wing. The collection of baseballs in the hospital's showcases would give memorabilia collectors weak knees and sweaty palms; in one small area are baseballs bearing the autographs of Ted Williams, Stan Musial, Nolan Ryan, Reggie Jackson, Muhammad Ali, and a former Yale player, George Bush. One ball has a rare double signature, Bob Feller and Brooks Robinson.

Among the photos displayed was one of the 1936 World Champion Yankees, Joe's favorite team. There were photos of DiMaggio and Casey Stengel and Joe with Mickey Mantle. There was even a 1940s photo of Joe, wearing pajamas and sitting in a hospital wheelchair, surrounded by kids, taken after one of his heel operations.

After taking an elevator to an upper floor, the first thing a child approaching the admissions desk would likely see is a miniature train, whose track tours the entire unit, including the restrooms. The section even has its own kid-friendly emergency room, so youngsters don't have to wait in the sometimes scary environment of a regular ER.

Ironically, the first patient treated in the emergency room was Joe's great-granddaughter Kendahl Stein. His four great-grandchildren and their parents were being shown around the hospital when Kendahl developed an earache, the product of a water-borne ear infection, and a doctor who was accompanying the tour took care of her.

◆ ◆ ◆

More than 35,000 children are treated in the Joe DiMaggio Children's Hospital each year, and admissions each year exceed 6,000. It has become one of the best children's hospitals in the country, especially in pediatric oncology and cardiac and orthopedic surgery. The number of beds has more than tripled, to over 150, including a 41-bed newborn care unit. Patients, including those of the neonatal intensive care unit, are brought to the hospital by plane, helicopter, and ambulance from hospitals throughout southern Florida and from Caribbean islands as far away as Jamaica.

Joe would be proud to see how the hospital has grown since his death, but I'm grateful that he was still around when a waitress interrupted our breakfast one morning to tell us about her grandson. The five-year-old was in Joe DiMaggio Children's Hospital for major surgery, and she had visited him the night before the operation. He must have seen the concern on her face because the boy told her, "Don't worry, grandma. Joe DiMaggio is taking care of me."

11

FAREWELL TO
YANKEE STADIUM

SEPTEMBER 1998—the baseball season was coming to an end, and so was Joe DiMaggio's life. He would be gone before the start of the 1999 season. Joe had been feeling poorly for months, and was troubled by a cough.

The last weekend of September was to be a busy one, culminating with Joe DiMaggio Day at Yankee Stadium. George Steinbrenner and the top administrators in his Yankees organization may have been puzzled why I was pressing so hard for that date, but I couldn't tell them how worried I was about Joe's health and concerned that time might be running out for a farewell tribute. DiMaggio, too, was beginning to realize that he was in deep trouble. "Forget about the lab reports. I feel lousy. There is something really wrong." I knew that a white spot had been detected on one of his lungs.

Joe had previously committed to fly to Chicago to be honored by the National Italian-American Sports Hall of Fame on Saturday, September 26, before a gathering of 1,200 people at a black-tie dinner, and he was determined to make the trip. Joe was the organization's first inductee, in 1978, and he made a special effort each year to attend the dinner and make a speech. Not only did he have feelings of kinship with other athletes of Italian background, he also was pleased that the organization was dedicated to helping needy students go to college, although he did complain that too much money was being spent on the new building and more should go to the scholarships.

He had another reason for being at the 1998 gathering, which was to feature a groundbreaking for the organization's new head-quarters and Hall of Fame at the corner of Taylor Street and Bishop at the center of Chicago's historic Italian neighborhood. Across the street, in a park being named Piazza DiMaggio, a ceremony would mark the relocation of a life-sized bronze statue of DiMaggio taking his famed cut at the ball. The statue and the headquarters had been in suburban Arlington Heights. The statue was refurbished for its move to the city, and Joe was eager to see what it looked like.

The long weekend began with dinner Thursday night with about a dozen men from the Italian-American community and Tommy Lasorda. DiMaggio liked the former Dodgers manager, though he was annoyed at his constant pleas for Joe to autograph baseballs. Lasorda would say he needed a couple "for a charity," and then show up with a dozen or more that needed signing. Lasorda made no secret of his admiration for Joe. "If you said to God, 'Create someone who was what a baseball player should be, with all of the great attributes,' God would have created Joe DiMaggio. And he did." As usual, Lasorda entertained at dinner that night with his baseball stories, filled with Tommy's favorite four-letter adjective. There was a separate room for the men's wives or girlfriends. That dinner was for men only, a tribute to DiMaggio as *La Bella Figura*.

It reminded me of a dinner some years earlier in Eastchester, New York, in honor of Joe's birthday. The setting was Alex and Henry's Roman Gardens, owned by Joe's friends Mario Faustini and Nat Recine. It was an assembly of eight guys, all dressed in their finest, all but two Italian, and one woman, Martha Lee, who sat next to Joe. The men were honoring one of the greatest sons of Sicily of their generation. Course after course of Italian cuisine was paraded to our table, and no one's wine glass was allowed to remain even half empty for long. The final touch was a delicious and expensive birthday cake, which had been air-expressed from Italy. There were gifts befitting a man of Joe D.'s stature, and he opened each with a huge smile on his face. There was a succession of toasts and speeches. Barry Halper chose the occasion to speak of the Mafia. He was an expert on that, but only from books. He probably had read every tome on the subject, and on and on he went, as DiMaggio grimaced and fidgeted. Finally, Joe put an end to it. "Barry, that's enough for one night," he said. "Give someone else a chance."

The evening ended well after midnight on a funny note. Plagued by the combination of a lack of streetlights and a lot of fog, we got lost on the back roads of Westchester County in our search for the parkway back to New York. Finally, we spotted a man walking on the side of the road and pulled over. The inside light went on when Halper opened the door and the guy peered in. "Geezus! Hi Mr. Halper. Hey, it's Joe DiMaggio!" The guy we stopped for directions at 1 A.M. in the middle of nowhere was the chief groundskeeper at Yankee Stadium.

Unlike that night in suburban New York, when Joe was healthy and happy, in Chicago he was feeling the effects of his illness—he had a 102-degree fever—and was exhausted by the time the evening ended. That's when he was told he would be picked up early the next morning for a 7:00 A.M. appearance at the Chicago Board of Trade, where he would ring the opening bell. The weary DiMaggio was in no mood to hear that. "Do you know the difference between eighty-four and forty-eight? I'm eighty-four," he snapped. But, DiMaggio never backed off from a commitment, and he was ready when the car picked us up early Friday morning.

His first stop at the Chicago Board of Trade was the imposing Board Room, where he was to have breakfast with the organization's executives and some major traders, the most powerful money people in Chicago. Everyone had been warned not to ask DiMaggio for autographs, to avoid any chance of aggravating him so early in the morning, and especially before his ceremonial chore. "Give him some breathing room," was the directive. When Joe concluded his remarks and people got up to head for the trading floor, DiMaggio asked, "Would anyone like an autograph?" Baseballs, ticket stubs, and baseball cards came out of jacket and trouser pockets where they had been stuffed in the hope that an opportunity would present itself. The hunch paid off for these giants of Midwest finance, and they lined up to get Joe's signature.

When George Randazzo, head of the Italian-American Hall of Fame, saw that DiMaggio was in a good mood, he decided that it would be a wonderful souvenir for those who sat with him at the front table to have Joe's autograph on their place cards, so he gathered up the cards. DiMaggio had this thing about Randazzo. He gave George a hard time at every opportunity in their twenty-year relationship, never mind how hard Randazzo worked to assure that life went smoothly for Joe when he came to Chicago. The harassment bothered Randazzo, but because he had been such a big DiMaggio fan all his life, he took it in stride and kept trying to please him. Randazzo put the place cards in front of DiMaggio and Joe began to sign them: the president of the Board of Trade, the chairman, the Illinois secretary of state, and others influential enough to be at table number one. Then, he came to Randazzo's card. Joe looked at it and announced, "The train stops here." He never signed it. "What could I say?" Randazzo asked in telling the story.

Chairman Pat Arbor escorted Joe to the floor of the exchange, where the hundreds of traders gathering for the start of the day's business gave him a thunderous ovation. It was the practice to hit the bell once with a gavel to signal the start of trading, but not on this day. Joe was handed a baseball bat, and he whacked the bell four or five times. Each smack was followed by shouts and applause from the traders. They were having a good time, and so was DiMaggio. Joe was to speak from a balcony overlooking the floor, but getting up there was not easy. The traders and employees jostled each other to shake his hand or pat him on the back as Joe waded through the shouting crowd. Finally, we got to the staircase leading to the balcony; it was obvious that DiMaggio would need help getting up. Lasorda took him under one arm and I took him under the other.

Joe told his audience that although the market had been bad for weeks, to take heart because this day it would be better. He was right. The Dow actually did go up. When the cheering stopped and trading began for the day, Arbor checked his watch. DiMaggio had set another record. Trading began twenty minutes late. No one, not President Clinton, not Mikhail Gorbachev, nor any other celebrity, had kept the traders from their frantic buying and selling for that long.

◆ ◆ ◆

Frank Sacco, head of the DiMaggio Children's Hospital, had come to Chicago to speak at the dedication ceremony on Saturday and at the dinner that night. The three of us returned to the hotel after the Board of Trade so that Joe could rest, but he caught a whiff of corned beef and cabbage coming from an Irish pub in the Hilton, and it revived his long-dormant appetite. He dug in with gusto and knocked off the entire plate of meat, potatoes, carrots, and cabbage. It was his biggest meal in five or six months, and he felt so good, he put off a nap and the three of us talked for hours. He was almost like the old Joe D.—but not for long. It was all downhill after what I came to come to regard as his "last meal."

With all that meat and potatoes under his belt, DiMaggio planned to spend Friday evening in his room watching television. He changed his plans, however, when he was invited to what he was told would be a small private dinner at Carmichaels, where the specialties were steak and pasta. Jerry Colangelo, owner of the Phoenix Suns of the National Basketball Association and baseball's Arizona Diamondbacks, would be there. DiMaggio liked him. "He did all right for a kid coming out of the poorest neighborhood in Chicago Heights," Joe said. NBA coach Mike Fratello would also be there, along with Lasorda and "a couple of other guys." The steak was said to be fantastic. A limousine would pick us up. It sounded good to both of us. DiMaggio said, "OK, we're going." The truth be known, the promise of good food always was a bigger lure for him than who would be at the dinner.

When we walked into the restaurant, about ninety people were there waiting for us, and a microphone had been set up for speeches. "For crying out loud," Joe muttered. "What the hell is going on here?" He felt he had been suckered into another public appearance he didn't want to make; he had a big day and night in front of him the following day. "Let's go," he said, but I managed to talk him out of leaving by saying it would be an insult to Colangelo, Lasorda, and his Italian heritage.

On the stage in the restaurant dining room was a framed Yankees No. 5 jersey with DiMaggio's autograph. It was donated by memorabilia dealer Jerry Romolt, and it was being presented to Colangelo in appreciation for his fundraising efforts on behalf of the National Italian-American Sports Hall of Fame. Colangelo led a group of businessmen in raising more than $5 million for the building. There was also a story to that shirt. It was one of the more than 300 that DiMaggio had signed in my office but which Romolt and his helpers had ruined by folding and putting them in plastic bags too soon, while the ink was still wet. The signatures had run in the Florida humidity. Romolt was determined to salvage at least one shirt, possibly with the idea of using it to get a healthy tax deduction by donating it to a charitable organization. So, he asked Joe to sign the back of the shirt "to test if the ink would run again." Only the autographed back was exposed in the frame. "Is that really Joe's autograph?" Colangelo asked me. I assured him it was, but I didn't have the heart to tell him not to remove it from the frame, or he would see its ruined front. "Romolt would cheat his own mother," said DiMaggio when he realized what was happening. "He will get punished someday by the Higher Up for all his conniving."

At the dinner, DiMaggio was seated between Lasorda and me. The place was filled with cigar smoke, which made him even more unhappy. He said all he wanted to eat was soup and pasta. When he tasted the soup, it was cold. By then he was really angry and vowed to "get that goddamned waitress." When the pasta came, it too was cold. "I'm out of here, Morris. Let's go," and he pushed me to get up. I was caught in the middle. Joe was my man, but I felt sorry for Randazzo, who had put together the three-day event.

"Joe, you can't disappoint these people," I said. "Think of your heritage."

"Screw my heritage. They're killing each other every day," he said. "I'm out of here. Let's go." He tried to get up but he couldn't. He made a second try. "Tommy, help me," he said to Lasorda. Tommy took him under one arm. I hesitated to take him under the other arm, because it would look like we were dragging him out. DiMaggio was too proud to leave like that. The way Lasorda was holding him made it look like two buddies walking out arm-in-arm.

Just as we reached the lobby, an elderly Italian woman was coming through the door with her grandson. "Mamma mia, it's Joe DiMaggio," she said. Joe was exhausted, and with Lasorda's help, he plopped into a chair in the lobby. "Shake hands with the great Joe DiMaggio," the grandma urged the boy, and she asked Joe to give the youngster an autograph. Joe, tired as he was, talked with the boy, asking him his name so he could personalize the autograph. "I couldn't believe what was happening," Randazzo recalled. "Ten minutes earlier, he was so mad he was insulting everyone around him, and now he was sitting there, talking with the kid while everyone is saying, 'Let's go, Joe. We've got to go.'"

Joe and I went back to the Hilton and had some cantaloupe and melon and a couple of frankfurters in the coffee shop. We talked for about two hours and Joe was calmed down by the time he went to bed.

◆ ◆ ◆

The day before the ceremony at the new park and transplanted statue, Randazzo received a call from Mayor Richard M. Daley's office saying that the mayor had to fly out of Chicago at 10:00 A.M. to address the U.S. Conference of Mayors in Oregon. So, unless the ceremony was rescheduled for 9:00 A.M., instead of 1:00 P.M., Daley would not be able to make it. Randazzo explained to a mayor's aide that as much as his organization wanted Daley to be there, it wouldn't be fair to an ailing eighty-four-year-old DiMaggio to ask him to get up so early after a second straight late night.

"Thirty minutes later, the phone rang and it was Mayor Daley," Randazzo said. "He said he wanted so badly to be with DiMaggio that he would get out of his speaking commitment if we could assure him he could leave the ceremony by 1:30. He had two other requests: that he be seated next to DiMaggio and that his photographers get the best locations for the hall's groundbreaking. I told him we were so delighted to have him there, and because of all the city had done for the community, including giving two parcels of land for the park, we would do anything he wanted." Had Joe known about this political tradeoff, especially with a Clinton Democrat like Daley, we would have left for New York a day early.

On Saturday morning we headed to Chicago's Little Italy for the ceremony. The mayor and DiMaggio were seated side by side on folding chairs, and they talked of the days when Daley's father, Richard J., was Chicago's mayor. Joe knew the elder Daley, and his wife, "Sis." When Joe came to Chicago in the old days, he and his friend, Bears quarterback Sid Luckman, would have dinner with Daley.

The morning of the dedication was sunny and extremely hot, and as the speeches droned on, I could see DiMaggio getting more uncomfortable. Randazzo kept bringing him bottled water. Joe's face was flushed and sweat ran down his forehead. I was afraid he wasn't going to make it, so I urged Sacco to shorten his speech, in which he lavishly praised DiMaggio for his contribution to American culture as a sports legend and his dedication to the health care and education of all children.

Joe was concerned about the speech he was going deliver at the unveiling of the statue. In retrospect, I realized he may have seen the occasion as his farewell to Chicago, one of his favorite cities, and his friends in that Italian group. I helped him with the speech on the plane and in the hotel. Finally, he had it down the way he wanted it. As he got up to speak under the hot sun, I was worried if he could get through it, looking as distressed as he did.

Several hundred people, young and old, were gathered there, the older ones no doubt remembering the pride he had brought to that neighborhood in his heyday. In some of their homes, their immigrant fathers would demand to know daily, "How Giuseppe do today?" And then they would toast the news, good or bad, with a glass of homemade red wine. There were fond memories of trips to Comiskey Park to watch Joltin' Joe jolt the White Sox, even though some had to take two trolleys and the elevated line to get there.

"My father would take all his kids and he would say, 'we are going to see the greatest Italian.'" Randazzo remembered. "He didn't say greatest Italian ballplayer, just greatest Italian."

Now, they were watching DiMaggio struggle to the microphone. A dozen neighborhood kids in baseball uniforms, the grandsons and great-grandsons of those who had taken pride in DiMaggio's talent half a century earlier, surrounded his bronze likeness planted on a marble base, and the wraps were taken off. Joe smiled, but he was also apprehensive about tempting the evil eye—statues were for people who were dead. But, he looked at the faces of his admiring public, and as I had seen DiMaggio do so many times when it came time to play to his audience, he gained strength and shook off whatever was troubling him. His arthritic back straightened, and for as long as it took him to deliver his speech, he was in top form. He thanked the mayor and the city for the honor, and with a twinkle in his eye he added, "The people in Chicago have been very good to me, especially the White Sox pitching staff."

When he finished, the limo pulled up, escorted by about a dozen Chicago police on motorcycles. DiMaggio was helped to the car, while police kept the huge crowd back on either side of the limo. When the kids began to chant, "Joe D., Joe D.," DiMaggio went around the police, walked into the group, and began to sign baseballs people had brought with them. "Here's a guy who was sick, as it turned out, he was dying of cancer, and he went out of his way to sign autographs," Randazzo said. "He was so weak they had to lift him into the car." That was Joe. During his career, he played when he was hurt, and he would not surrender to pain or illness. He also was a great showman, and he was determined to live up to his image in front of those youngsters and their parents.

The night before, Randazzo had witnessed a completely different DiMaggio. Domenick DiFrisco, an executive with the public relations firm Burson-Marsteller and an ardent DiMaggio fan since Joe played, had written a very laudatory piece about DiMaggio. He told of his first visit to Yankee Stadium in 1938 with his father and friends from his Bronx neighborhood. "I was a kid clutching my Italian flag and waving it gleefully whenever No. 5

took his position in center field or at the plate." DiFrisco said it was a matter of ethnic pride because Joe came along at a time Italian communities all over America were "beginning to lift themselves beyond the organ grinder, stiletto image."

"I have to have it," Joe said when he saw a copy of the article. At the Friday night dinner, DiFrisco approached DiMaggio with a photo and asked him to sign it. "Get that out of here," DiMaggio demanded. Randazzo explained to the heartbroken DiFrisco that it was not the right time to approach DiMaggio. "I just can't believe he did that to me," DiFrisco said. "I mean, I loved that guy." Neither knew, of course, that DiMaggio was burning with fever that night.

The big dinner Saturday night was at the Hilton, where DiMaggio was ensconced in the presidential penthouse suite. There was a helipad right outside the door. The suite was so big Joe couldn't find the master bedroom, so he slept in one of the smaller ones.

When the affair was about to start, Bob Allegrini, a Hilton executive and a member of the dinner committee, went to the penthouse to escort DiMaggio to the ballroom. When DiMaggio opened the door, Allegrini told him he had come to bring him to the dinner. "You tell Randazzo. . . ." Allegrini never heard what message DiMaggio had for Randazzo, because DiMaggio slammed the door. What set Joe off was that he and I were working on his speech when Allegrini rang the bell, and DiMaggio was frantically trying to get it finished before going to the ballroom.

Lasorda was the master of ceremonies again at the dinner. Joe was given the seat of honor next to Lasorda, and as usual, I sat next to Joe. Jerry Colangelo was also at our table. DiMaggio and I were the only ones not wearing tuxedos. Either he hadn't been told, or more likely, he forgot that the event was black tie, so he showed up at the formal dinner wearing a blue blazer and black pants. There was no way I was going to let him be the only one without a tux, so I left mine hanging in the hotel closet, and I, too, wore my blue blazer.

Speaker after speaker was called to the microphone, with a lavish introduction by Lasorda, who threw his arms around each man. A lot of warm Italian hugging and kissing went on that night, but Joe did not get involved. Maybe it was because of his aching back, or maybe hugging and kissing wasn't his style, but he avoided any chance of an embrace by not making eye contact with the would-be huggers.

At one point, Joe got up from the table and disappeared. "He's in the kitchen," someone said. Allegrini went back there and found a smiling DiMaggio posing for pictures with the kitchen help and signing autographs for them. "Can't a guy take a leak?" was his reply when asked why he had left the table. A waiter had told him the nearest men's room was in the kitchen and invited him to use it. He got an enthusiastic reception from the cooks, waiters, helpers, and busboys, many of who were big baseball fans. It was not unusual for DiMaggio to head for the kitchen during or after a dinner. Not only did he use it as a route for a quick exit, but he enjoyed the banter with the staff. Plus, he was curious about how those big kitchens were set up. Maybe it reminded him of his days in Joe DiMaggio's Grotto.

The tribute to DiMaggio began with a film clip of him singing in the movie *Manhattan Merry-Go-Round*. That was followed by a video montage of DiMaggio baseball action, with a musical background of Dean Martin singing "Return to Me." Martin was Marilyn's costar in the ill-fated *Something's Got to Give*, and I wondered if Joe was thinking about that as he heard Dino sing. "You know that stuff about him drinking a lot is all made up. It's an act. He's not much of a drinker," Joe told me. "And his real name is Crocetti, like my old teammate, except Frankie spelled his name with an 's'." When the video ended, DiMaggio was introduced as the Yankee Clipper, and the crowd rose to its feet to cheer him.

The noise rocked the room, and Joe loved every minute of it. As DiMaggio approached the stage, Lasorda set himself up for that hug, but Joe sidestepped past him.

Joe made a brief speech, which he limited to an expression of gratitude for his reception in Chicago, one baseball story, and a sentence that said, "George Randazzo really had me working for three days." George leaned over and whispered to his wife, "You can't ever do anything right with him." But he was pleased that Joe had at last recognized him.

It was after 1 A.M. when Joe got back to his suite. I reminded him we were scheduled to leave O'Hare on a 5:30 A.M. flight to New York, and I suggested we meet in his suite, which adjoined my room, at 4:30 A.M. (Even with six bedrooms in Joe's suite, I opted for a separate accommodation because I was in no mood to cater to him or hear his criticism of the event.) At 3:30, Joe called my room from the lobby and complained that I was late. I reminded him of the time we had agreed to meet. He seemed a little confused, and then realized that he had never changed his watch from Eastern time. I jumped in and out of the shower and joined him in the lobby in thirty minutes.

Arising early usually didn't bother DiMaggio. He would think nothing of getting up at four in the morning to catch an early flight, even into his eighties. Yet, he was very conscious of the hours he slept, so much so that he often recorded in his diary the time he went to sleep and when he awakened. For more than the last twelve years of his life, he was troubled by insomnia, so he began to rate his sleep. "Not too good a night's sleep," or "up at 5 A.M., slept fair," or "Morris called and woke me up at 8:15 A.M. Did not sleep well and it was one of the few times that I got a little sleep after I awakened much earlier."

Randazzo had stayed up all night to be sure DiMaggio left on time, and he made sure the chauffeur who would take us to the airport stayed up as well and was ready when DiMaggio left for the airport. "Joe kept reminding me all weekend that he had to be at Yankee Stadium at noon Sunday," George said. "When he got off the elevator in the lobby and headed for the door, he stopped and pinched my cheeks and said, 'George, you did it again.' That meant more to me than anything else. It was the last time I ever saw him."

When we left the hotel in those predawn hours, two businessmen in their late sixties got into the limousine to ride with us. They weren't leaving town, but they had arranged to get into the car, just for the chance to talk with their boyhood hero. Unusual? I didn't think so, because I remembered getting up before dawn more than fifteen years earlier to meet DiMaggio for the first time.

◆ ◆ ◆

As our plane headed east from Chicago to New York, we rewrote the speech Joe was to give at Yankee Stadium. When he complained that he couldn't read my writing, I took out a blue Sharpie pen and very slowly printed the words in large capital letters.

Steinbrenner's chauffeur picked us up at LaGuardia Airport, and as we rode to Manhattan, Joe asked how big a crowd would be at the game. The driver said it was a sellout, more than 56,000. Then Joe asked how many tickets had been sold before the announcement that it would be Joe DiMaggio Day. "About 18,000." Joe was delighted to hear that. We got to Dick Burke's apartment, where Joe was staying, at about nine o'clock, and two hours later, Steinbrenner's chauffeur was back to take us to the Stadium. Joe was in uniform—blue suit, white shirt, and red tie. He wasn't feeling well, which was apparent, because he was unsteady on his feet and his face was ashen. He had only two hours of sleep, if that much, and his only nourishment had been some dry cereal and a banana on the plane. After a cup of coffee in Steinbrenner's box, we headed to the Yankees dugout for the start of what was to be a disastrous afternoon for Joe.

It was past noon and a big crowd was beginning to fill the Stadium for the final game of the regular season. The Yanks were far ahead in the standings (they would finish with 114 victories), and they were playing the lowly Tampa Bay Devil Rays, but the announcement that DiMaggio would be honored created a big demand for tickets. The stadium was packed.

In what was to be his Yankee Stadium farewell, DiMaggio was driven in a golf cart under the stands to the old Yankees' bullpen in right-center field from where, according to the plan, he would emerge in a white convertible Thunderbird and circle the field. I waited in the dugout so that when he finished his tour, I could take him up to Steinbrenner's box to watch the game. About twenty minutes after Joe had left in the golf cart, Debbie Tyman, a Yankees vice president for marketing who was running the event, received a phone call from stadium security. DiMaggio was very upset about something and was about to leave the stadium through a back exit. "You better get out there and try to stop him," Tyman told me. Since no golf cart was available, there was only one way to get there quickly. I dashed out of the dugout, went along the edge of the infield, and across the outfield. I heard cheering from the crowd. I looked around, and since there was no one else on the field, I realized the cheers were for me. A television camera captured my dash, too, and my grandson, Monty Joe, back home in Florida, saw me.

When I finally got to the old bullpen, DiMaggio was standing by an exit, sweat running down his pallid face, very much in distress. "This guy Steinbrenner has a helluva nerve keeping me sitting in that hot sun waiting for the place to fill up," he fumed. "I don't need this crap. I want to get out of here." Steinbrenner, of course, had nothing to do with the foul-up. He had a genuine affection for Joe and was going all out to honor him with a tribute that would be memorable not only to DiMaggio but to all those who had turned out for the occasion. Joe's outburst was a product of his physical discomfort in the broiling sun and, though none of us knew it then, the cancerous tumor that was growing in his lung. Joe sincerely liked Steinbrenner, and he acknowledged that George had brought him back into the Yankees organization after years of being neglected.

I'm a speedy talker, but I knew I had to talk faster and more convincingly than I ever had before to keep the afternoon from becoming one of the most infamous events in the history of Yankee Stadium. It would be front page in the Sunday papers in New York: "DiMaggio Storms Out of Stadium Tribute."

First, I appealed to DiMaggio's love for the fans, and reminded him that all those people had come to the park to honor him. Then, as the clincher, I reminded him about the World Series rings. Steinbrenner had ordered replicas of the eight rings that had been stolen from his hotel room, and these were to be presented to him at home plate along with the Yankees championship rings from 1978 and 1998. The only ring that DiMaggio had, of the nine his Yankee teams had won, was the 1936 ring from his rookie year, with the team he regarded as the greatest of his career and "the best bunch of guys I ever met." The presentation was to have been a secret, but I had told him on the plane from Chicago to lift his spirits, and I reminded him of the presentation to keep him from leaving.

As we talked, I could hear cheers from the crowd as highlights of Joe's career were being shown on the huge video screen above us. I took Joe out of the hot sun and someone gave us a pitcher of ice water, from which he eagerly drank. This cooled him off, and he was ready to go on with the ceremony. Once again, in the DiMaggio tradition, when the spotlight turned on him, he responded. The crowd roared as DiMaggio came into view in the white T-bird, and as the car circled the field toward third base, 56,000 people rose to their feet and cheered him. His discomfort, his aching back, and all his other physical woes were forgotten. He waved both arms, reached out to shake some outstretched hands, and had a big smile on his face. The car stopped every so often as if to let the moment linger. DiMaggio, the showman, was at his best, not displaying even a hint that he was ill and that minutes earlier he was about to leave in a huff. He could hear the fans shouting, "We love you, Joe." "Thank you, Joe." Once again, this was his Yankee Stadium, and these were his fans.

Among those eagerly awaiting the celebration was Seymour Levy, a senior art director at a New York advertising firm. Levy had been a fan of the Yankees and of DiMaggio since he was nine years old, despite growing up in the Canarsie section of Brooklyn, deep in the heart of Dodgers country. He meticulously kept a record in a notebook of the 56-game hitting streak, and he marked each day of the streak on the kitchen calendar. As a GI in Korea, Levy had just missed seeing DiMaggio there, and he was determined not to miss him at the Stadium. As soon as he heard there would be a Joe DiMaggio Day, he told his wife, Irene, that they were going. The Yankees had clinched their division and were playing only the Devil Rays, but, said Levy, "I wasn't going to see the game. I was going to honor Joe DiMaggio and be part of the celebration."

The Levys found seats in the upper deck behind third base, and Seymour brought along his camera and binoculars. "He looked great," Levy said, as he recalled DiMaggio's stirring tour of the stadium in the convertible. "He was waving and smiling at the crowd. Everybody was standing and cheering and waving back at him. What a great moment! I'll never forget it." Levy and his wife, along with everyone else in the stadium, jumped to their feet when venerable public address announcer Bob Sheppard, as he had done so often, introduced DiMaggio in the eloquent tones that had become as much a part of Yankee Stadium as the monuments beyond the outfield and the distinctive facade above the grand-stand: "The Yankee Clipper, Joe DiMaggio."

Joe, accompanied by Yankees manager Joe Torre, walked from the dugout to home plate, where Rizzuto was to present him with the World Series rings and where a representative of the commissioner's office would give him one of the Joe DiMaggio game-day balls Rawlings made to commemorate the occasion. Joe had thought for days about the speech he would make. He had worked on it almost to the last minute before we went to the stadium, and it included a mention of the World Series rings. I am certain DiMaggio saw this as his goodbye to the fans and to Yankee Stadium. He wanted it to be something for which he would be remembered, just as an ailing Lou Gehrig was for his farewell remarks. In fact, Joe not only patterned his speech after Gehrig's, he used its most memorable words. He had me call the head groundskeeper to find out the exact wording on Gehrig's monument.

In the end, nobody heard Joe's speech, which he had worked on so carefully. DiMaggio's failure to address his fans puzzled and upset Levy, who complained to his wife, "What happened to the speech? I can't believe he didn't say a word. All these people came out expecting to hear him and to display their feelings toward him, and he didn't say anything." Levy recalled that he felt let down, as if a potentially historic moment had evaporated before it happened. "He just walked back to the dugout. I was shocked." Like virtually everyone else in the park, the Levys didn't know that DiMaggio's farewell speech was not heard *because the microphone didn't work.* When Joe realized what was happening, he was so embarrassed and angry that he was near tears. Rizzuto came out to home plate and handed him the World Series rings, shook his hand, and the two old Yankee teammates walked away, leaving the offending microphone standing useless and alone at home plate. I could see DiMaggio's face getting red with anger. In our years together, this was the angriest I had ever seen him. He handed me the rings and tore into Debbie Tyman, the Yankees marketing vice president, with a verbal outburst the likes of which I had never heard from him. Some ballplayers warming up near the dugout stopped to see who was getting bawled out like that. It was embarrassing. Tyman burst into tears and fled to her office. Steinbrenner told me he sent her home.

Joe was so weakened and aching from the ordeal that he could not make it from the dugout to the elevator to Steinbrenner's box. He got no further than a bench less than halfway to the elevator, and he sat down. He was easy prey for the media people, who zeroed in for interviews. He was in no mood for banter, but in no shape to escape. So, he submitted to what proved to be the final interview of his career, indeed of his life.

We eventually made it to Steinbrenner's skybox, but DiMaggio was in no mood to watch the game. Instead, he had a steak luncheon at a conference table inside the suite with Metropolitan Opera singer Robert Merrill, who sang the national anthem before the game; Phil Rizzuto and his wife, Cora; and Barry Halper, who never gave up trying to get back in DiMaggio's good graces. Halper sat next to Joe, hoping to get a crumb of conversation, but Joe ignored him. We were joined later by Dr. Rock Positano, whom I had phoned and suggested he come to the park and get the weary DiMaggio. Unfortunately for Rock, he had rushed to the stadium in his weekend-afternoon casual look—black jeans and a black T-shirt—and thereby violated DiMaggio's dress code. Joe shooed his buddy out of Steinbrenner's box to a grandstand seat behind it. I felt sorry for Rock, and I sat with him most of the time. Our chief topic was how Halper had acquired those stolen World Series rings. We agreed that Halper should have given the real mementos that had been stolen back to Joe, so it would not have been necessary for Steinbrenner to order the replicas.

For much of the afternoon I found myself trying to calm Joe and siphon off some of his anger. I told him he should be understanding of Tyman, who probably felt at least as bad as he did. He would not be placated. He told me how that was to have been the most important speech of his life. He wanted to thank his fans and tell them how much they meant to him. "Now," he said, "I will never get that chance." DiMaggio usually never actually read a speech. He kept it in his pocket as a "security blanket," but he spoke from his memory what was on the paper. Not this time, though. He told me en route to the Stadium, "I'm going to read this one because every word is important. It's history." (He told me the same thing before he delivered the speech when Cal Ripken broke Gehrig's consecutive game record.)

I kept that Yankee Stadium farewell speech that was so important to him, yet was never heard. It read:

> Thank you for your very kind ovation. I want to thank the Yankee organization for the beautiful gesture of replacing my World Series rings, and the Commissioner's office for authorizing the special baseball bearing my name, No. 5 and swing to be used in today's ball game. Hopefully, there will be a lot of home runs hit today for you to catch in the stands.
>
> My teammate Lou Gehrig, one of the greatest baseball players of all time, said it almost sixty years ago at Yankee Stadium, and I want all of you to know that I am also the luckiest man on the face of the earth to be here today and to have had the opportunity to play for the greatest franchise in sports history, the New York Yankees. New York, thank you for the best thirteen years of my life. God bless you all.

◆ ◆ ◆

After the game, I was flying back to Florida, and Joe wanted to go with me. But he was in no condition to make the trip that day. Positano drove him back to the apartment where Joe was staying, and I headed for the airport.

Joe and Positano had dinner that night at Bravo Gianni, a well-appointed, fashionable restaurant on East 63rd Street in Manhattan. It was one of Joe's favorites when he was in New York and in the mood for pasta.

"There was a special DiMaggio table in there, and when Gianni knew Joe was in town, that was his table, automatically reserved for him whether or not he came in," Positano said. "It was perfect for Joe, off to the side. He could see everyone who came into the room, but they could not necessarily see him." That night, Joe wanted to see or talk with no one. He had some soup and pasta, and he left with Positano. Rock said it was apparent that Joe was very ill, and he tried to convince him to go to a hospital. "He was reclining on the back seat, and telling me he was exhausted and all he needed was a good night's sleep," Positano recalled. "I felt it was more serious."

"When I get home, I have an appointment with my doctor," DiMaggio said.

The next morning, Joe said goodbye to Positano and New York. He would never see either again.

12

---•---

FATAL ILLNESS

DiMaggio knew something was wrong with him as early as May 1998. He felt washed out and weak, and he had lost his celebrated appetite. He would go to dinner thinking of steak, shrimp, or lobster, but he stopped eating after a bowl of soup. Sometimes, he managed to get through a plate of pasta, but not very often. He rationalized that maybe it was normal for an eighty-three-year-old man not to be as hungry as he had been in his youth, but he was concerned that he was coughing a lot and spitting up greenish phlegm and blood. That wasn't normal, no matter what age.

When he looked for a reason for his feeling weak, he said it could have been caused by the adjustment of his pacemaker in mid-March. To explain the cough, he went back much further in his life, to those three packs a day he smoked during his playing days. This wasn't the first time Joe had been coughing up blood. It had also happened in late 1992, and he wrote about it in his diary on December 31: "A year of ups and downs, but [I] pulled through OK. My travels don't get less, my arthritis doesn't get any better, and I still pay visits to doctors for checkups—especially after I was spitting up blood—and got a clean bill, as my lungs were a little infected due to a cold." Apparently, the problem was more serious than that, because he was put on a medication that he had to start taking on New Year's Day in 1993 and continue "for seven days a month for four months."

Whatever the cause, he began to spit blood again a few months later while on a business trip to Rome. At 4:30 one morning, he called his doctor in Miami and was told not to be alarmed, that the blood probably was a lingering effect of a recent siege of bronchitis. Still, Joe was so worried that he cut short his stay, leaving his sponsors to explain to the media that he had a cold. Some Italian newspapers erroneously reported that he was in the hospital. DiMaggio was upset by that, and concerned that his family would think the worst. He flew home to Miami and immediately went to a hospital for X-rays. The news that time was positive. No serious problem was detected.

That was not the case in August 1998, when the persistent cough sent him to Dr. Aaron Neuhaus, a pulmonary specialist, who discovered a white spot on the X-ray. Further diagnostic procedures detected a bacterium, which suggested tuberculosis. Joe was put on antibiotics. A few days later, a chest CAT scan discovered something that doctors felt could be pneumonia, so more antibiotics were prescribed. These were huge pills, which Joe complained could choke a horse. He was switched to another medication, and he stayed on that for a while. By mid-September it was apparent that Joe was not getting better, and his weight loss was becoming noticeable. He had dropped twenty pounds. That's when I suggested to Steinbrenner that if he planned to honor DiMaggio, it would be wise to do it before the season ran out.

After the celebrations in Chicago for the National Italian-American Sports Hall of Fame and the Joe DiMaggio Day at Yankee Stadium, Joe arrived back in Florida on Monday, and the following day, Dr. Neuhaus put him through further tests at Memorial Hospital, aimed at examining cells taken from the bronchial tubes. Two days later, I was paged at lunch by my office and told to call DiMaggio at home. "It was an emergency," I was told. Joe said Neuhaus had wanted to meet with us at his office, but Joe told him he was about to leave for a business lunch. He convinced the doctor to let him know the results of the tests over the telephone. The news was terrible. DiMaggio had lung cancer. My heart sank when he told me that. I said I would be right there, to be with him. "No, Morris. I'm just about to go out the door for my lunch appointment and a steam bath." How could he go about his day after getting that news? I was too shaken to do anything, but Joe DiMaggio never called off an appointment.

The next day, Joe and I talked with Dr. Earl Barron, a cardiologist and internist who was DiMaggio's primary doctor, about what came next. "Basically, you either resect the tumor or irradiate it," Barron told us. Try to cut it out or burn it out. The surgeon, Luis Asanza, agreed that those were the options, and his recommendation was: "Joe, let's take it out. I'll go bam, bam, bam, and you're on the golf course in ten days." The operation wasn't performed that quickly, however, because Asanza was out of town for a week at a seminar. "Wait for him—he's the best," advised hospital chief Frank Sacco.

Late in the afternoon of October 12, I drove Joe to Memorial Regional Hospital. He was admitted for the surgery, although there may be no record of a Joseph P. DiMaggio on the admission list. He insisted on his identity being kept secret, and I agreed that was a good idea. A couple of years earlier, he had checked into a hospital in Miami for eye surgery as "Paul DiMaggio." One of America's most recognizable people thought that might hide his identity. He got no further than the elevator before someone shouted, "Hey, it's Joe DiMaggio!"

About an hour after he arrived at Memorial Regional, a tray of hospital food was brought into the room. He looked at the presurgical meal and shook his head. "Boy, could I go for a hot dog," he said. That was my cue. I went to the cafeteria and brought back two grilled franks, baked beans, apple pie, ice cream, and a cup of decaf coffee. What could be more American than hot dogs and apple pie? A nurse looked at the tray and shook her head but smiled. Since the surgery was more than twelve hours away, let him enjoy himself. He did.

I must have looked concerned, because Joe said to me, "Hey, I'm going to make it through. There are still gloves to do." At one time DiMaggio would not autograph bats, caps, jerseys, or gloves. By October 1998, only gloves remained unsigned. He always wanted to hold something back for the future.

I stayed in the room with him all night, waiting for dawn when he would be prepped and wheeled to surgery. I walked alongside him as far as they would let me. He was sedated, but he knew what was happening. Suddenly, he pulled the sheet over his face. "Joe, there is absolutely no one else in the corridor to see you at 5:30 on a Tuesday morning," I said. "The paparazzi are always around," he replied. The orderly who was pushing the gurney laughed, thinking DiMaggio was joking. He wasn't. In his mind, he could see some photographer leaping out from behind a door to snap his picture while being wheeled to the operating room.

I learned later about something that had happened to him under similar circumstances in 1949. A botched operation for a heel spur after the 1948 season was giving him trouble the following spring training. He felt some pain in the opening exhibition games, and it got worse while the Yankees were barnstorming in Texas. The ache in his foot grew so intolerable he was flown from Dallas to see Dr. George Bennett, a foot surgeon, at Johns Hopkins in Baltimore. DiMaggio arrived around midnight, and he was in such pain he couldn't walk. He was put on a gurney and wheeled through what seemed to be an empty corridor. Suddenly, around the corner came the press, writers, and photographers, and the flash bulbs went off—ping, ping, ping. "Lay off, fellas, please lay off," he pleaded. "You're driving me batty."

Now, almost fifty years later, that scene flashed back as he headed for another operation. But this time his privacy would be respected, because the media had no idea he was even in the hospital, and it was "his hospital."

I sat in the lounge outside the operating room, praying and hoping. DiMaggio had taken all possibilities into consideration in the instructions he gave me the night before. If all the cancer wasn't removed, I must tell no one, and he emphasized, "I said no one." If the surgery was successful, and there was no spread of the disease, I was to call his granddaughters, but in a way not to alarm them. "This is exactly what you must tell them," he said. "Paula, good news. The operation was successful and there is no cancer." He actually had me repeat it so there would be no mistake. He told me if the malignancy was not completely removed, "Make up some story until I have a chance to talk to them." He didn't want his grandchildren to be worried.

Another reason he wanted to keep news of the operation from getting out was that the Yankees were on their way to another World Series, and he didn't want his illness to detract from their achievement. A team player to the end. He had been disturbed when Mickey Mantle called a news conference in Dallas before the 1995 All-Star Game in nearby Arlington to announce that he had liver cancer. "He could have waited until after the game," DiMaggio said.

When Asanza finally came out of the operating room, he didn't have to say anything to me. His expression and sad shake of his head told me what I didn't want to hear. For the first time, I realized that Joe might not make it. Still, I didn't want to believe it. I said to myself, "We will beat this, and I will do whatever it takes, even if I have to walk away from my law practice." It was a very emotional time in my life. The surgeon told me the tumor had been removed, but the cancer had spread into the carina node. A growth in that location is virtually impossible to get out without sacrificing the whole lung and part of the other. The noninvolved left lung was weak and eventually would collapse.

Tubes to aid his breathing were put into his mouth, and soon a tracheotomy would be done. IV tubes stuck into his arms carried fluids giving him nourishment and sedation. I spent hours looking at him in his semi-comatose state, his mouth open, eyes half-closed and unaware where he was or what was happening. This man I had idolized since my childhood, this man who had been the most celebrated baseball player of his time, this American icon, now was a helpless old man teetering on the delicate line between life and death.

Three days after the operation, I arrived at Joe's room at 5:00 A.M. and found the bed freshly made and empty. My first reaction was that he had died and no one called me. I rushed through the intensive care unit to find a nurse, and as I passed one room I saw DiMaggio in a chair watching television. "Hi, Mr. Engelberg, good morning," a nurse cheerily greeted me. "How do you like Mr. DiMaggio's new room?"

Barron was astonished at how well DiMaggio had recovered from such a major operation. "He was tremendous," the doctor said. "I looked at this guy sitting up, and I said, 'this is a piece of cake.' I figured he would be home in a week, so I went on a vacation I had planned. My brother, Howard [a cardiologist], would look in on him. No problem, or so I thought."

The Yankees were to open the World Series against the San Diego Padres on October 18 in New York, and George Steinbrenner, unaware of how ill DiMaggio was, wanted Joe to throw out the ceremonial first pitch. DiMaggio was in no shape to get beyond four feet from his hospital bed, let alone walk onto the field at Yankee Stadium. I told Steinbrenner that Joe had infectious pneumonia and not to count on him being there. Instead, Sammy Sosa, who had hit 66 home runs for the Chicago Cubs that year, did the honors.

Joe had appointed me his health surrogate, which I considered a great honor, since he had a brother, a son, granddaughters and their husbands, and friends going back sixty years. Along with the honor he had given me, though, came the terrifying responsibility for approving decisions on medical procedures that could kill him or keep him alive. As an attorney, I had drafted hundreds of powers of attorney and health surrogate designations without ever realizing how tough an assignment that can be, especially for a celebrity like DiMaggio.

The weight Joe had put on my shoulders all seemed worth it when Neuhaus told me what happened when he had awakened DiMaggio in the recovery room. Joe opened his eyes and rasped in a strange sounding voice, "Where the hell is Morris? Get Morris!" He didn't ask for his brother or any of his other relatives or cronies. He wanted me in there. It was me that he entrusted to make the life and death decisions.

The first opportunity for that came on a Sunday, six days after the operation. I had been at his bedside from nine in the morning until noon, and I was on my way home when I was paged by Neuhaus and told to return to the hospital in a hurry. When I got back, I learned that DiMaggio's right lung was collapsing and excess fluid had accumulated in the other. I had to sign a consent form to have it drained. Joe was put back on the respirator.

I realized I had to finally tell Joe's granddaughters how ill he was so they could fly to Florida for a possible farewell meeting. So, Paula and Kathie were the first ones I told of his serious condition. The fewer people who knew, the fewer chances for leaks.

I was being naive, though. Hospital personnel were gossiping about the famous patient, and it didn't take long for the local media to find out. Reporters began to phone or show up at the hospital. I gave orders that no information was to be given out, not that any was available outside the circle of doctors and nurses directly involved in his care. When the switchboard operators said they could not confirm that DiMaggio was a patient, they were telling the truth, because he was not listed in the register of admissions.

News that DiMaggio was hospitalized reached the Associated Press in New York, and I received a phone call from Marv Schneider on the sports desk there. Schneider asked, "Is it true that DiMaggio has lung cancer?" It was a question I had dreaded; yet I knew it was bound to come. Joe had once told me never to lie to the press because eventually the truth will come out and I would be branded a liar. Still, I had promised Joe I would tell no one he had cancer. What to do? "I can't discuss his illness," I said. Schneider persisted and told me it was just a matter of time before the media learned the facts; there was just no way to keep news secret for long about someone like DiMaggio.

"I'll tell you this, he will die of pneumonia before he dies of cancer," I said. "Are you saying he has pneumonia?" Schneider pressed. I repeated what I had said about pneumonia killing him before cancer, which is what Neuhaus and Barron had told me. DiMaggio did have pneumonia in the area where the cancer had been removed, which was not unusual, I was told. That's the way I resolved my problem. I didn't lie; I evaded the truth.

◆ ◆ ◆

When the AP reported the news of DiMaggio's illness, the media dam burst. Reporters and camera crews stormed the hospital and my office from all over south Florida. The parking lots at both places were jammed with cars and TV trucks. Phone calls came in from all over the country and from overseas. DiMaggio's worst fears had been realized. The media circus had begun. Never had I been involved in such activity. My law practice dealt with the bland world of wills, probates, and trust funds. Now, I was in the center of a major news event and had to deal with some people who were more expert at eliciting answers than a prosecuting attorney in a courtroom. Some were creeps, like the San Francisco reporter who warned me that if I didn't tell him what DiMaggio's illness was, he would report that Joe was suffering from AIDS. "Write whatever you want," I said, "but you better be right, because if you're not, you and your newspaper will be hit with the biggest lawsuit in journalism history."

Evading the truth, as I had done, soon opened the door for outright lies, and I felt bad about that. But I was so determined to obey Joe's admonition to keep his condition private, that I made up stories. I put my reputation second to his wishes.

A reporter asked me, "Is Joe looking forward to the World Series?" I answered, "He's very excited. All pumped up." "What's his prediction?" "Yankees in four," I said. The truth was, DiMaggio was so sedated he had no idea the Series was even starting. The prediction was mine, and it proved correct. Once the Series began, I was asked if Joe was watching the games. I said we were watching together. The truth was, he was out of it, and I watched while he slept.

"How's his appetite?" "It's getting better. He's eating pizza, Chinese food, and corned beef sandwiches while he watches the games." To support my stories, I would arrive an hour before the game and march past the gathered media carrying empty pizza boxes and empty containers from Chinese restaurants.

By that time, Joe was battling something else, what Barron called "hospitalitis," an organic medical syndrome that affects some older patients. He was out of touch with reality, babbling, and combative. He tried to rip out the tracheotomy tube and IVs, and he waived his arms around, once hitting a young nurse and tossing her halfway across the room. A psychiatrist, Rick Levine, was brought in to deal with that problem, and he added another medication to those Joe already was being given.

A security guard sat outside DiMaggio's room twenty-four hours a day. The media was relentless. Reporters were in the parking lots

and the cafeteria trying to speak with nurses, orderlies, or cleaning people and learn what was going on behind that closed door.
Answering the inquiries from newspapers, magazines, TV, and
radio was taking up four or five hours of my day. Another six or
seven hours were spent in Joe's room. There weren't enough hours
in a day to do that and still fulfill my obligations as a lawyer. I
would get to my office at 2:00 A.M., go over the paperwork from
the previous day, and then head for the hospital at 5:00 A.M. I
barely had time to return phone calls from my clients. Fortunately, these were longtime clients and they understood. "Anytime you
want to be my health surrogate, I'll put you in instead of my wife,"
one of them joked.

My arrival at the hospital each morning began a routine for
Joe. The nurses tried to wake him as soon as I arrived because
they felt he was sleeping too much. "He's in a deep sleep, don't
wake him," I said the first time. "No, the doctors want him alert
as much as possible." So I turned on the TV set and started to
talk to him. "You're going to have a good day, today. You're going
to be out of here in a couple of weeks." The nurses called me a
cheerleader, and one doctor said I reminded him of Knute
Rockne giving a pep talk to his Notre Dame football teams. I
must have been convincing because the staff, too, would tell Joe
he would be home before long.

"We've got a lot of work to do, the paperwork is backing up," I
would tell him. "A tremendous amount of paperwork." He loved
that word. Before he got sick, he would call me and he would say,
"Morris, we have much paperwork today?" I would say, "lots and
lots of it, too much." He couldn't wait to get to my office to spend
hours going through the "paperwork," most of it having to do with
offers of endorsements or public appearances. So, when I mentioned the word in the hospital, he was up and ready to listen. I
used every key word of our sixteen years together to try to inspire
him in those morning wake-ups. The visits were aimed at inspir-

ing Joe, but they depressed me, especially when I grasped his out-stretched right hand, which he held out limply. When I first shook that hand in 1983, I could feel the powerful grip he still had, and I thought, "I bet he could still swing a pretty mean bat." The hand that I shook in the hospital room made me think of the line from Simon and Garfunkel's "Mrs. Robinson": "Where have you gone, Joe DiMaggio?"

◆ ◆ ◆

A new kind of problem greeted me at 5:30 one morning. Dom DiMaggio, Joe's only surviving sibling, was sitting in the security guard's chair outside Joe's room. When he saw me, he got up, looking as if he had just been called out on a third strike with the bases loaded. His jaw was clenched and he aimed an armor-piercing angry stare right at me. Dom had cajoled and threatened his way past the guard, walked into the room, and saw how badly his sleeping brother looked. "I demand to know what is going on with my brother," he said. "The newspapers are saying he has can-cer." Dom understandably was embarrassed because his friend and former teammate "Teddy" Williams and Stan Musial had called him to ask about Joe, and Dom didn't know what to say.

Joe and Dom were estranged and hadn't spoken to each other for years. Their sibling rivalry could be traced back to when they were kids, but they had a reasonably friendly relationship when both were playing in the American League. I had tried on occasion to reconcile the two brothers, but Joe was not interested.

In the hospital that morning, Dom was shouting at me and warning that he was going to sue me for not releasing the infor-mation about his brother's condition. He ranted and raved that he had powerful friends who were judges and could destroy me, that he would have me disbarred. I wondered, if he were so concerned about his brother's health, why he had waited so long to visit.

Dom lived about an hour away, north on I-95, near Boynton Beach. He said the traffic was horrendous, a refrain that he repeated every day I saw him during Joe's illness.

I explained to Dom that Joe had instructed me to tell no one of his illness, and as his attorney, I had to respect his wishes. "You're no lawyer. You are a phony, a liar, and a control freak," he shouted. I decided that if Dom had a right to know that Joe had cancer, then Frank Sacco, the hospital chief, would have to tell him. I couldn't ignore my promise to Joe. It was a matter of an attorney-client relationship, and I was obliged to follow his instructions. So, Dom went to Sacco's office, where he learned the bad news. After that, Dom and his wife, Emily, visited Joe two or three times a week. I was almost hoping they would stay away. Their visits often were disruptive because the two, mostly Emily, complained incessantly about the doctors, the staff, and the facilities. They wanted Joe moved to another hospital. I remember the first time Dom came into the room while his brother was awake. He peeked in first, very cautiously, as if he wasn't sure what kind of a reception he would get. But he didn't have to worry. Joe was mildly sedated and too tired to be angry.

◆ ◆ ◆

On a mid-November day, about a month after his surgery, DiMaggio's condition suddenly and rapidly deteriorated. Barron told me that a virulent bacterial infection that resisted most antibiotics was in his lung. The doctor called it a major crisis, and he notified Dom that the next six to twelve hours were extremely critical. I had a feeling that Joe's time was running out. Someone else in the ICU must have thought so, too, because a priest was called, and he showed up to ask if he was needed to give DiMaggio last rites.

Not familiar with what this involved, I asked the nurses what they would do if Joe were their father. I worried that if the priest went into Joe's room and began to prepare for the sacrament, Joe might be so shaken he would have a heart attack. On the other hand, I knew he was serious about his Catholicism, and if I did not let the priest perform the ritual, and Joe died, I would feel I had not properly respected Joe's religious beliefs. That would rightfully open me to criticism, especially as a Jew, and I would be accused of doing the wrong thing. It was a tough call, but I decided that heading off a possible panic by Joe was more important. I relayed this reasoning to the priest, who was standing outside the ICU door, and a nurse said he was very understanding. The priest looked at me, nodded, and walked away. It was one of the most agonizing decisions I had to make during Joe's hospitalization.

The doctors finally found two antibiotics that began to battle the bacterial infection, but these caused another problem, because the medications were killing the so-called good bacteria in his bowel. That had to be dealt with. "It's a nightmare," Barron told me. "A pulmonary infection and a serious problem in his bowel." Looking back at it later, Barron said, "That's when we thought he was going to die."

An infectious disease specialist, Dr. Nelson Zide, came through as a hero. He noticed that DiMaggio's urine was not turning red, as it should because he was being treated with the antibiotic Rifampin. That meant the medication being administered through a nasogastric tube was not being absorbed by DiMaggio's system. So, the method of delivery was switched to an intravenous tube, and the results were seen with the first dose. DiMaggio's temperature dropped the next day, his white blood cell count came down, and Joe perked up. Joltin' Joe had survived another crisis.

By then, a gastroenterologist and a neurologist joined the medical team treating DiMaggio. Sam Winn, his ophthalmologist, had been treating Joe in the hospital, and so was urologist Joel Martin. Joe was still on a respirator.

◆ ◆ ◆

November 25, 1998, was DiMaggio's eighty-fourth birthday, and I arranged for a small celebration. I invited Barron and the other doctors and nurses who were usually there before 8:00 A.M. Joe's granddaughters and great-grandchildren were there, and I asked Dom and Emily to come. As the guests arrived, Joe was watching one of those early-morning news shows on television, when suddenly he gasped and his facial expression was one of panic. A scrawl appeared under the picture on the television saying that Joe DiMaggio had suffered a major heart attack.

Joe grabbed my arm. It was difficult for him to speak through the "trache" tube, but his eyes said, "What the hell is going on?" I assured him that he had not had a heart attack, but I said that until we tell the public and his fans that he had cancer, we could expect more phony stories like that.

I had been feeding Joe optimistic prognoses, which were really overly optimistic, because I didn't want him to be depressed. I would always get a smile from him when I told him he would throw out the first pitch at Yankee Stadium on April 9. Steinbrenner had invited him.

I pressed my argument to release the truth about his illness, and he grabbed my hand, letting me know it was time to lift the restriction he had placed on me. That's what I had been waiting for, and before he could change his mind, I told him I would be back soon with the birthday cake. I gathered Barron, Paula, Kathie, Dom, Emily, and Joe Nachio in a conference room for what proved to be a heated meeting. I told them that as DiMaggio's health surrogate, I had the right to make the decision on how the public would be informed about his illness. But since I was not a family member, I was reluctant to do that if they were opposed.

Emily, referred to regularly by Joe as a "highfalutin social butterfly," said that DiMaggio's granddaughters should not be involved in any decision since they were adopted into the family and not his natural grandchildren. Paula and Kathie were shocked and visibly upset by that, and I was angry. I knew how much Joe loved them, and how much they loved Joe. Barron interrupted to say that in Florida adopted children have the same standing as biological children. Nachio said that I, and no one else, had earned the right to make that decision, and he noted that Joe assigned that right to me in writing. I appreciated this support from the man Joe considered his oldest and dearest friend. Nachio would say, "No, Morris, you are his dearest friend. I am only an abused spouse."

I recommended that Barron hold a news conference to announce that Joe had lung cancer and discuss the details of the illness. Before he did that, however, I made the doctor available for an interview with Marv Schneider. I had promised that when I was free to release the full details, the AP would be the first to know. In a matter of minutes, the whole world knew.

The news that DiMaggio had a cancerous lung tumor removed and had survived complications that brought him near death set off another torrent of daily media calls to my office. "Did he have a good day? Did he have a bad day? Is he improving? Is he regressing?" It reached the point where emotionally and physically, I no longer could deal with the questions from the media. Rick Levine, the psychiatrist on the medical team, recommended that I hand off the task to someone else. Barron agreed to field the media calls, as if he didn't have enough to do. He is another hero of this story.

Barron was born in Cleveland and described himself as "an extremely avid Indians fan." He grew up complaining about the Yankees winning year after year. DiMaggio was the ultimate enemy of his youth, and he was stunned when I asked him to take on Joe as a patient.

On DiMaggio's first visit to Barron's office, the doctor let Joe know right from the start that, as an Indians fan, he was a confirmed Yankees hater, and that included DiMaggio. "When you played, the Yankees ruined every chance the Indians ever had at the pennant, except in 1948, and we had to win 111 games that year to do it. I want to tell you up front, I rooted against you." After listening to Barron talk like that for twenty minutes, DiMaggio cupped his hand over his mouth and, in a stage whisper, asked me, "Do you think I'm safe here?"

Barron had heard how tough a customer DiMaggio could be, but was surprised to find that that wasn't true in this case. "He was like any other patient when he came for an examination or treatment. He would do whatever I told him," Barron said. "We had a nice rapport. I would get on him sometimes about the Indians ending his 56-game hitting streak in Cleveland with Kenny Keltner's great plays at third base. It was the only way I could get back at the Yankees."

Actually, whatever Barron knew about the streak was from what he had read. He was born the year DiMaggio went on that epic run through the American League. But the ending, in Cleveland's Municipal Stadium, is part of sports lore in the city by the lake, passed on from generation to generation. "The extent of DiMaggio's celebrity never really hit me until his final illness," Barron said. "It was like nothing in my life, like nothing I ever expected. It was incredible."

Barron's updates on DiMaggio's status showed up on television and in newspapers around the world. Friends would call and say, "I read about you in the *Jerusalem Post*."

DiMaggio's condition improved in early December; at least the infection was controlled and he was breathing easier, although he was still dependent on the respirator. As he started to feel a little stronger, he had visitors. His nephew, Joe T. DiMaggio, flew down from San Francisco, and restaurateur Mario Faustini came from New York. Joe knew Faustini for about a dozen years and would call on him to pick him up at the airport. Their conversations ranged from the preparation of shrimp and pasta to the good old days in New York, including those glorious days when Joe played. "I was a rabid Yankees fan in those years, and would have given my right arm just to shake Joe DiMaggio's hand," Faustini said. He met DiMaggio through John Arcadia, a retired postal employee, who would come into Faustini's restaurant, Alex and Henry's, and talk about how he drove DiMaggio around New York. Then, one day, Arcadia drove him to the establishment in Eastchester and announced, "This is Joe DiMaggio." DiMaggio had lunch and, as they say, that was the start of a beautiful friendship.

Then Steinbrenner came to visit at the hospital. Joe had really looked forward to seeing him. The Yankees owner took a cab from the airport to my office and I drove him to the hospital. He said he was nervous about seeing Joe so ill, especially after hearing he had lost so much weight. Steinbrenner didn't know what to expect. Joe prepared for his meeting. He was propped up in bed and had a baseball in his hand. He had asked for the trache tube to be removed so he could talk.

Steinbrenner filled him in on what was happening. "I'm going to keep Bernie Williams, no matter what it costs me. I'm going to bring another World Series back to New York, two in a row. [The Yanks had recently swept the Padres in four games.] Say, that was a pretty good deal I made, Wells for Clemens." Joe didn't agree. "I don't know about that," DiMaggio said. "Wells is some pitcher." Steinbrenner, though, was ready to argue for Roger Clemens. "Joe, he's the Michael Jordan of baseball." DiMaggio wasn't convinced. Joe liked David Wells. "As a big Yankees fan, he knows about Babe Ruth," Joe said. "He even has a gut like Babe." Joe also believed it was important for the Yankees to have a good left-hander, because southpaws tended to be very effective at Yankee Stadium. The Yankees' success and Clemens' sixth career Cy Young Award, however, proved that the Boss did make a good trade, a very good one. Steinbrenner eventually did get Wells back, in 2002, when he signed the pitcher as a free agent. Wells himself was awed by DiMaggio as a Yankees legend. "It would give me goosebumps talking to him," he said.

The visit with Steinbrenner was a tonic for DiMaggio's morale. He talked about it for days. He also asked to see Martha Lee, and the visit was one she will never forget. He took the tube out of his throat so he could speak. He said hello and asked how her girls were doing. "I was biting my lip to keep from crying," she said. "Just seeing him looking like that, so white, brought back the pain of my father dying. We hugged and I kissed him on the cheek and told him that I loved him. I knew this was goodbye."

◆ ◆ ◆

Around this time, DiMaggio began to vent about his brother, though never when anyone else was in the room. Joe asked the nurse and the security guard to take a break for a couple of minutes, and he told me to close the door. He said he was concerned that Dom would try to hurt Paula and Kathie financially. "He's looking to inherit my estate," Joe said. "He discussed my will with me, and he has no right to do that."

Joe asked me one day if Dom was "OK financially." I assured him that Dom was a millionaire, many times over, and I knew that from comments Dom had made to me about details of a "second to die" life insurance policy. Joe was disturbed that Dom was trying to cut into his granddaughters' inheritance, so much so that one day, when the granddaughters were in the room, Joe grabbed my tie and rasped, "You better take care of my baby," pointing to Paula.

On the morning of December 11, Dom and Emily arrived in the hospital with Dr. Arthur Skarin, a prominent cancer specialist from Boston. Joe's brother and sister-in-law wanted the doctor to review the charts and records of DiMaggio's treatment. Dom was seeking to move Joe out of Memorial Hospital to a facility that he and his wife would choose. I saw that as a move for Dom and Emily to take over Joe's health care, whatever life he had left, and his estate. He had no legal right to move Joe to another facility, and I thought such a move would be an outrageous insult to the doctors and staff who had been treating DiMaggio for two months in Joe's hospital.

Barron disagreed. "Dom had never even heard of me, and must be saying to himself, 'I've got my brother's life in this guy's hands. Maybe we should check into it.' I can put myself in Dom's place. If it were my brother, and he was in Podunk somewhere, and someone was taking care of him whom I had never heard of, I would fly in someone to take a look, also. I honestly did not feel that this was a personal affront, or that it was denigrating in any way. In fact, I think it was probably an appropriate thing to do under the circumstance."

Barron said Dom had called and asked his permission to bring in a consultant. "I've been a doctor for more than thirty-five years, and one thing you never say is 'no' to that request," Barron told me. "The fact is, I thought it was a terrific idea, and I told Dom that I would cooperate in every way."

Barron prepared a three-page summary of what had transpired in the two months and made available charts and other data that might be useful. Skarin, from Brigham Hospital in Boston and professor of oncology at the Harvard Medical School, reviewed the material and discussed the case with Barron.

Dom sat in on the discussion, and Skarin told him, "Everything is being done exactly the way it should be. I can't conceive of it being done any differently. He's doing a good job. Your brother, unfortunately, has an incurable illness. He is not a candidate for radiation," which is what Barron and his team at Memorial had determined.

On the same day of the consultation with the Boston doctor, DiMaggio had another setback. Barron and Neuhaus advised me that Joe's chances of making it through the day were less than five percent. He had another bacterial infection, his vital signs were deteriorating and he was struggling to breathe. The doctors recommended that the respirator be turned off and Joe be allowed to die in peace. Given that advice, I asked the doctors to meet with all of us—me, Joe's granddaughters, Dom, Emily, Nachio, and Dr. Skarin. Dom announced that he would be in charge of the funeral, which would be held in the family's parish church in San Francisco. Paula asked me not to fight him on that, with the hope, "eventually, he will go away."

Several years earlier, when I was drafting Joe's will, I asked him the standard question about where he wanted to be buried and what funeral arrangements he had made. Joe refused to answer, but parried my question with, "What are you trying to do, bury me already?" He had always been uncomfortable talking about his mortality, as if not to tempt the fates.

After the meeting, Dom, Emily, Nachio, and I went for lunch at the Deli Den. We sat in "Joe's Booth," which had a "Yankee Legends" poster on the wall to mark it as something special. My purpose in having lunch with Dom and Emily was to try and close the chasm between us at this very emotional time. Nachio was the buffer because he had a good relationship with Dom. When the check came, I reached for it, and so did Dom. "Let's flip for it," he said, which is something I never heard from his brother. The closest Joe ever came was a tentative offer to pay the tip, "You need a deuce or a fin?"

At Nachio's suggestion, we returned to the hospital to be there when Joe died. I wanted to say goodbye to my friend. I went to his bedside. His eyes were closed, and I wasn't sure he even heard me, but I said, "Joe, today is December 11th, and you can't die on the same date as my father." My father had died in 1939. I also reminded him of his commitment to the Yankees to throw out the first ball at the Stadium on April 9. "If you can hear me, squeeze my hand." I felt his fingers closing around my hand. Barron said it could have been just a reaction to feeling someone squeezing his hand. "No," I insisted. "He heard what I said." Convinced that he had heard me, I repeated several times, "Joe, you are not going to die on me today."

Tears rolled down my cheeks as I left the hospital with Nachio and went home to pack for the trip to San Francisco and the funeral. Paula and Kathie already were on their way to San Francisco after a tearful goodbye. Five hours after I left the hospital, late in the afternoon, Barron called, but not with the news I dreaded. Earl told me that Joe was out of bed, and sitting in a chair reading a newspaper. Miracles do happen—and this one took place with the help of another antibiotic that killed the latest infection. By then, I was ready to be admitted to the hospital as Joe's roommate. Joe's psychiatrist and other doctors again warned me that it was time to take a break from my vigil, or I would indeed be next to Joe. "The hell with them," I thought. "I'm not going to miss a minute," even though sometimes all I could do was stare at him while he slept.

◆ ◆ ◆

Barron, meanwhile, was learning about dealing with a media frenzy. He had taken the burden off my hands, and later told me he never in his worst nightmare had ever been so overwhelmed. "In the middle of the night, the doorbell rang and I opened the door. There was a TV camera crew. The lights went on, and a microphone was stuck in my face. 'Could we ask you a couple of questions?' It happened two or three times. I agreed to hold a press conference and that was a mob scene, with reporters, TV trucks, boom microphones, cameras, and a helicopter hovering over my parking lot. Someone on a cruise ship in the Caribbean told me they saw a video clip of the scene on the ship's television. It was seen in Europe, and probably Asia. The interest in DiMaggio's condition was phenomenal.

"There was this talented reporter, Liz Cho, on Channel 10. She was bright, she asked the right questions, and she was gorgeous. She was the reason I watched that station. I got a call from Channel 10 asking for an interview, and I said, 'Only if I'm interviewed by Liz Cho.' The news director or someone there told me that Liz was on another assignment. 'Too, bad,' I said, 'That's the way it goes.' Half an hour later, she was at my office door."

There weren't too many bright spots. "I was overwhelmed," Barron said. "I had never dealt with anything even resembling that. Morris advised me, 'Just tell the truth.' Dom told me, 'Be honest, and you can't go wrong.' So, I told the truth. I was honest. Then, Dom said to me, "How can you say things like that in public?' I said, 'You told me to be honest, now you're telling me I was too honest.'"

To answer the daily question of "How is he today?" Barron would say, "From zero to ten. I would say. . . ." But that created problems, especially with Dom, who got on Barron for that. After all, Earl was not a public relations expert. Nor was I, of course, so it was a situation of the blind leading the blind.

It got so bad that Barron couldn't even tend to his medical practice. We decided that the only thing that would get him off the hook was to say that Joe told him not to give out any information. Joe hadn't really said anything. "He was incoherent," Barron said. "He couldn't have said a word. It was all fabricated, but it got my ass out of a sling. It was an impossible situation. I couldn't live my life." Barron told me, "Morris, you owe me." I asked him what he would like, and he replied, "A bat." I worked him the same way Joe had tantalized Nachio with his request, and like Nachio, Barron got his bat after DiMaggio's death. Joe would have gone along with that, I believe, because he would have admired the doctor's loyalty and dedication.

A few days into the new year, Barron, Dr. Joel Martin, and I walked into DiMaggio's room just before 7:00 A.M. and were greeted with his broad smile. He pointed to his heart and then took my hand and put it over his chest. I could feel his heart beating. I couldn't tell whether he was telling me he felt good, to support his argument that he should be going home, or expressing concern that he may have suffered a heart attack. Barron assured Joe that his heart was all right. The rest of the news was good, too. The pneumonia had been successfully dealt with, his fever had disappeared, and his blood pressure was normal.

That is not to say there were no problems. The hospital psychosis was one of them. Although Barron assured me that mental problems were not unusual for elderly patients who had been hospitalized for a long time, it was disturbing to see Joe affected by it. He complained to nurses and doctors that I had not been to visit him in three or four weeks, when I had been there every day, with the exception of Christmas when his family was with him. When I told Joe that Paula would be visiting him, he asked who she was. He thought one of the nurses was his wife, although he hadn't been married in forty-five years and the nurse looked nothing like Marilyn Monroe. He playfully pinched her cheek. Such behavior was completely out of character for DiMaggio, who did not believe in a public display of emotion of any kind.

Dom was in the room one afternoon watching an NFL playoff game with Joe, and Joe again brought up the subject of wanting to go home. About the only thing Dom DiMaggio and I agreed on was that Joe should not die in a hospital. Dom wanted his brother out, the sooner the better. In fact, he wanted him out of Memorial the day he found out Joe was in there. But it was made clear that Joe would not leave the hospital until the medical team said he could. That subject had been discussed for some time by the doctors and staff. Sacco was among those who felt it might be better for DiMaggio to stay in the hospital, where he could get more efficient terminal care. But Joe really wanted to go home. He loved that house and the setting on the Intracoastal Waterway. I kept telling him, "Anytime now, any day, we're almost there."

There was concern that if Dom knew when Joe was going to leave the hospital, he would tell his friends, a lot of whom were former baseball players who still kept in touch with some sports-writers. The doctors feared that the departure would then become a media event, which could be too much of a strain on Joe's psy-chological state.

Dom questioned nurses and doctors trying to learn the day his brother would leave the hospital, but he didn't know until I called him twenty minutes before we rolled Joe down a secure corridor and out of a rear door at about 9:00 A.M. on January 19. In an effort to hide his identity, Joe wore dark glasses and his face was covered with a towel. But his famous nose protruded, and I told him, "Lefty Gomez was right. With that schnozz, you could never go anywhere incognito." He was put in a Joe DiMaggio Children's Hospital ambulance that looked like a van. Knowing how much he had insisted on secrecy when he entered the hospital, I was deter-mined that Joe would leave the place the same way. The Allied command that planned D-Day could not have tended to the details with any more any caution than I did. The planning and execution paid off, because there was no media and no excite-ment, and DiMaggio made a quick and uneventful departure. I had kept my promise that he would go home. It was my only vic-tory in those terrible ninety-nine days.

As we rolled along Hollywood Boulevard, I told him, "This is no hearse, Joe, right? I told you, you would get out of there alive, and go home, and that's what you're doing, going home!" Maybe I convinced him with that dramatic performance in the ambulance that he would go on living, but I didn't fool myself. I knew he was going home to die.

13

THE FINAL DAYS

HOME WAS WHERE DIMAGGIO WANTED TO BE, and he made that very clear every day during his final weeks in the hospital. "Get them to let me go home," was his refrain. The house on Waterside Lane in Harbor Islands was DiMaggio's first real home in years, and despite his fondness for hotel living, he had grown to like his handsome place on the water.

There were times in the hospital that he told me he had given up on ever going home. I tried to boost his sagging spirits by promising him that before long we would be out on the dock behind his house, watching the boats cruise by. Also, like the old days, we soon would be sitting in our golf cart reading *The New York Times* and picking apart the news, Joe offering his latest views on the status of major league baseball. That got a smile from him.

When I was able to tell him the exact day he would be leaving the hospital for home, he shocked me when he asked, "Morris, where is my home?" He also asked where I lived; obviously he had forgotten that our homes were separated only by a narrow street, a street he had crossed at least two or three times a day for years. Barron again assured me that such mental lapses were not unusual under the circumstances. He was optimistic that Joe would snap out of it once he got home.

The interior of his pink stucco house was reconfigured to make Joe as comfortable as possible during whatever time he had left. A hospital bed was set up in the downstairs den along with a $3,500 neuro-chair that was large and comfortable and could be easily adjusted into a variety of positions. The doctors said it was essential that he get out of bed as often as possible, and that chair was where he was moved. He was wheeled outside, where he could watch the pleasure craft glide by.

"Basically, what we did was move a complete hospital intensive care unit into DiMaggio's house," Barron said, "with a respirator and all the IV apparatus for feeding and medicating him." ICU nurses and respiratory therapists were on duty around the clock. They clearly were excited to be taking care of so famous a personality, and DiMaggio was treated tenderly and with respect.

Dejan Pesut, a dark-haired man in his mid-forties, was brought in to be the security officer, grocery shopper, cook, and Mr. Fix-it for minor repairs around the house. He also helped the nurses tend to DiMaggio's personal care, moved him when necessary, and kept him company while he watched television. Pesut, who was a muscular 5-foot-10, had been doing similar work for twenty years in south Florida for people wealthier but not nearly as prominent as DiMaggio. He was told that when he sat with Joe outdoors, behind the house, he should be on the alert for any news photographer who might show up across the Intracoastal with a telephoto lens on his camera. DiMaggio always had an aversion to being caught off-guard by a photographer, and I wanted to be sure that no photo of a sickly looking American hero showed up on the front page of one of those tasteless tabloids that delights in embarrassing ailing celebrities.

What shocked me the most when we took Joe home from the hospital was how thin his legs had become. These once-powerful limbs of a well-conditioned athlete had atrophied to the size of a wrist, and the loose skin hung in flaps. Embarrassed for DiMaggio, who always prided himself on his trim physique, I wanted to be sure no outsider ever saw that sight. We shielded the view by planting eight ficus trees on the edge of the yard. Those trees are now in my yard, and every time I look at them, it brings back memories of sitting in the backyard with Joe.

Since image was everything to DiMaggio, Pesut and the nurses kept him as well groomed as he had been since he was a teenage rookie for the San Francisco Seals. He always had a clean shave, neatly trimmed hair, and manicured nails. Gourmet meals were prepared for him, although not always eaten. Pesut was born in Croatia, close enough to northern Italy that he insisted he knew how to cook Italian style.

Though Joe's appetite never returned to what it had been before he got sick, he didn't lose his taste for Western movies, so we stocked his room with an ample library, including some tapes he had already seen three or four times. Boxing, especially heavyweight fights, was another of Joe's favorite TV pastimes, so I bought some videos of famous fights, which he enjoyed watching. Joe Louis was his first real boxing hero, and DiMaggio saw several of Louis' fights, including his first bout with Billy Conn. It took place at the Polo Grounds in New York on June 18, 1941, one month into DiMaggio's monumental hitting streak. Joe D. created a stir, as he always did, when he was spotted walking to his seat. It was like watching the "wave," which became popular at sporting events in the 1980s and 1990s; fans rose to their feet cheering and encouraging him to keep hitting, and soon nearly everyone was standing. He always had good seats, because New York's number one ticket broker, George Solotaire, was with him most of the time.

Boxing historian and writer Bert Sugar said DiMaggio was a genuine and knowledgeable fight fan, and unlike a lot of other celebrities, he didn't go to be seen, but rather to see. Sugar was covering a Gerry Cooney heavyweight fight in the late 1970s at the Cow Palace in San Francisco when he saw DiMaggio sitting by himself, in seclusion in the back of the arena. "You know, I like my privacy," was his explanation.

I was with Joe for the first Roberto Duran–Hector Camacho fight at the Atlantic City Convention Center in 1996. We were in the third row, but Sugar thought that was too far back for Joe DiMaggio, so he got us to ringside. Donald Trump, who was co-promoting the card, was on the other side of the ring with Shaquille O'Neal. He sent someone to Joe with an invitation to join them. "These are great seats," Joe said to Sugar. "Is it all right if I continue to sit here?" When Bert assured him that we could, he sent word to Trump that he was sitting with friends, and if Donald wanted to join us, he would have to bring his own chair. That was Joe's attempt at humor.

"Actually, DiMaggio was a sports fan," Sugar said. "He liked to talk about boxing, football, baseball, or whatever, and he had an unbelievable memory. He would correct me if I was wrong, and I consider myself a historian." Among the more recent heavyweight champions, Evander Holyfield was his favorite, although he also had a high opinion of George Foreman. Mike Tyson, to him, was a bum. He watched tapes of their fights during those long days and nights in bed.

◆ ◆ ◆

The get-well cards and letters flowed into DiMaggio's Harbor Islands home in amazing numbers every day, many of them addressed to, simply, "Joe DiMaggio, Hollywood, Florida." They came from former major leaguers, politicians, and others celebrities. Mostly, though, there were stacks and stacks of mail from fans. The man had not played baseball in nearly half a century, yet he still had all those fans out there who had read or heard reports of his illness and wrote so touchingly of their affection. It was truly amazing. I was astounded at how many cards came from Japan, Italy, and South America. Among the more unusual letters was one from a gentleman in the South who wondered if Joe might be his father. He explained that his mother, who was of Italian descent, had been a Yankees fan, and had spent a lot of time with Joe. "Apparently, she had quite a thing for Mr. DiMaggio." This fellow also said he bore a "striking resemblance" to DiMaggio, and he sent along a picture for Joe to see. He asked Joe to respond if he remembered being in that town nearly fifty years earlier. Poor Joe wasn't quite sure where he was at that very moment in Florida.

Nevertheless, Barron's prediction about Joe's mental state getting better when he got home proved to be true. He still wasn't near to what he had been before his hospital stay, but there was some improvement. We were told to motivate him, to keep him busy so his mind would be alert. Before his illness, Joe would appear at my office eager to put his signature on photos, baseballs, and whatever else needed signing. "Let me practice signing my autograph again," he said from his bed. He tried laboriously to do that, but his efforts had only faint resemblance to his famous signature. "How about trying it on a baseball," a nurse suggested. Well, there were 10,000 baseballs in his living room. Those were part of the Yankee Clipper Enterprises' allotment of the Rawlings commemorative balls used at Joe DiMaggio Day the previous September. It was the payment to Joe for allowing a facsimile of his signature and an image of his famous swing to be put on those balls.

"You up for signing some baseballs?" I asked. His smile, the sudden sparkle in his eyes, and the nod of his head were his answer. Cheered on by applause from two of his grandchildren, the nurses, my office manager Rita Sokoloff, and me, Joe made a gallant try. Rita had been present at virtually all the signings that took place in my office, so her presence at his bedside that day added a familiar note to the scene. DiMaggio at least felt that he was back in business by signing baseballs. But it was a sad sight to see. The man who at one time would sign more than 300 baseballs in an hour with a perfect script, could not sign more than eight or nine before leaning over in pain and exhaustion. The signature was small, shaky and barely legible, a far cry from the carefully crafted autograph he had made famous. The therapy did not have the result we had hoped for. Over the ten days or so, he signed 90 to 100 baseballs, of which 68 were sold by his estate and the rest given to his grandchildren, friends, and Rita. I donated three of them to the Joe DiMaggio Children's Hospital, Xaverian High School in Brooklyn, and the National Italian-American Sports Hall of Fame.

During this time, DiMaggio actually got up and took some steps, with Pesut's help, of course, but I took heart from that. He passed up the feeding tube one evening for some chopped lobster that was rubbed on his lips. I saw that as another hopeful sign. But, Barron brought me back to painful reality. "Moishe, he ain't going to make it," he said, using my Hebrew name to indicate he was speaking as my friend and giving me the *emeth*, the truth.

A cousin of mine, Joey Fishof, is an Orthodox rabbi, and he told me he had offered a special healing prayer for Joe in his synagogue; I wondered if he had ever done that before for someone who wasn't Jewish. "When it comes to Joe DiMaggio," he said, "I can make an exception." The rabbi was a longtime Yankees fan, and he had met DiMaggio at my daughter Laurie's wedding, and as he explained to me, Orthodox Jews do indeed pray for those of other faiths.

While I knew Dr. Barron was right, and it was just a matter of time, I was grateful for the improvement in Joe's condition, if only temporary. It gave us a chance to watch some more fights together on TV, and to sit in his backyard and talk. He could take that trache tube out for twenty minutes, and he saved that time for our talks, the memory of which I will cherish for the rest of my life. It dawned on me that this dying man was trying to lessen my sorrow and heartache. He realized how much a part of my family life he had become, and he knew I was suffering because of his illness.

We talked about his grandchildren and great-grandchildren. He said, "You know what I feel bad about? That I won't see my great-grandkids grow up." "Don't be so morbid, Joe," I replied. "I expect you to be around for your ninetieth birthday. In fact, I've already made plans for that party, and you better be there." He laughed at that and reached out to grab my hand.

Other than that remark, DiMaggio never expressed regrets about dying or any fear of death. In fact, he seemed to be waiting for it with anticipation. We were sitting outside one evening when he looked up at the star-filled sky and said, "Morris, soon Marilyn and I will be together again, up there." He said that a couple of times, but the first time I heard it I froze. I didn't know what to say. Nachio was there once when Joe repeated the comment, and he said, "You have a while to go, Joe. There's no need for a center fielder up there just yet."

One afternoon, DiMaggio showed he could still throw a baseball pretty well. Certainly not as far nor as fast as he once did from the far reaches of Yankee Stadium, but considering that he was eighty-four and threw sidearm while propped up in bed, it wasn't a bad toss. Anger propelled the ball, anger at his brother Dom. Scott DiStefano called to say he had been to a memorabilia show where the commemorative baseballs from DiMaggio's farewell appearance at Yankee Stadium were being offered for sale at $54 each by B&J Collectibles. Although these bore a facsimile of his signature and a likeness of the patented DiMaggio swing, the signature in ink was not Joe's, but Dom's. I ordered two of those baseballs and they were shipped to me overnight. B&J Collectibles was not our friend. In fact, Joe was suing the company because it owed Yankee Clipper Enterprises nearly half a million dollars for default on a contract involving a batch of baseballs. In Joe's view, Bill Rodman, the head of B&J Collectibles, was the lowest of the low among memorabilia dealers, not only because of his business practices, but because of the coarse way in which he conducted his private life. DiMaggio was also in the process of suing Rodman's company over alleged forgeries. DiMaggio rarely used vulgar language; it was not his style. But he frequently used the word "asshole" when talking about Rodman. "How was your flight?" he would ask when DiStefano arrived in Florida with memorabilia for Joe to sign. The next question was, "When are you going to leave that asshole Rodman?"

Joe was furious not only because Dom had made a deal with Rodman, but also because his brother had signed a ball from the Joe DiMaggio Day tribute, and did so while Joe was in the hospital. DiMaggio had refused requests to add his signature to Mickey Mantle and Cal Ripken commemorative balls out of respect for those players. Yet, his own brother had not shown him the same consideration, especially at a time Joe was desperately ill. Just looking at Dom's signature on that ball infuriated Joe. Possibly, he thought of their childhood, when Joe felt Dom was always trying to "one-up" his older brother. Dom told New York *Daily News* columnists George Rush and Joanna Molloy that if he signed any of those balls, "It must have been a stray one." Or, how about two or three or ten, or more?

I wondered what would happen on Dom's first visit after that incident. He had been coming to see his brother at least twice a week since Joe returned home. But when Dom showed up after the ball throwing, nothing happened. Joe was either too weak or too sedated. Actually, he rarely, if ever, reacted to Dom's arrival. Generally, when someone walked into the room, he reached out an arm in greeting and smiled. But not to Dom. Nachio and I rated two outstretched arms.

If that ball-throwing incident was one of the low points of Joe's stay at home, one of the high points was a second visit from Steinbrenner. The first, while he was in the hospital, had buoyed DiMaggio's spirits for days. Joe asked me to keep him informed of what the Yankees were doing in the off-season, and I read him the details of the Wells-for-Clemens deal. DiMaggio wondered what the addition of Clemens would do to the Yankees payroll, and I read him a newspaper story saying the Yankees would be paying $80 million to $85 million in 1999. Joe made an unsuccessful attempt at a slow whistle and shook his head in wonder. So, he and the Boss had plenty to talk about when the Yankees owner arrived on March 2.

Steinbrenner called frequently to find out how Joe was doing, and he told me that he would like to say goodbye in person before DiMaggio died. When it became apparent that Joe was failing, I called Steinbrenner and told him the time had arrived for his farewell visit. The Yankees owner was aware by then of Joe's wishes for a small, private funeral, and he felt it was important to say goodbye while Joe was alive. When I let DiMaggio know that the Boss was coming, his face brightened with a smile of delight.

"Don't get so excited," I said. "With that payroll he already has, he's not going to offer you one of those big contracts."

Joe got out of bed for the occasion, put on a fresh open-collar white shirt and sat in that special chair, his legs covered with a blanket. He also asked the respiratory attendant to remove the trache tube so he could talk with Steinbrenner. About a week earlier, DiMaggio began to experience severe stomach cramps and I could see from his grimaces and the way he would suddenly double over, that the spasms were troubling him the day Steinbrenner visited.

When he came to see Joe in the hospital, George told him the assignment of throwing out the Opening Day first pitch was his again, if he wanted it. So, the nurses created a sign reading, "Our Goal: Yankee Stadium, April 9, 1999," and it was hung in the den, facing DiMaggio's bed. Next to it was a replica of the sign put up above the West Side Highway along the Hudson River in New York: "Joe DiMaggio Highway."

It was gut wrenching watching and listening as Steinbrenner spoke with DiMaggio under those circumstances. It is never easy to talk with a dying man, but there he was, one of baseball's most powerful owners, an unabashed longtime DiMaggio admirer, speaking from his heart for the last time with one of the greatest Yankees of them all. Steinbrenner, wearing a blazer, white shirt and tie, and dark slacks, stood in front of DiMaggio's chair. I felt privileged to be there and thought this was something that should be taped and kept in baseball archives so future generations could hear it, like Lou Gehrig's farewell speech and Babe Ruth's good-bye to Yankee Stadium.

Often maligned as being gruff and uncaring, Steinbrenner told DiMaggio how much he had meant to him and the Yankees. He said as a teenager in Cleveland, he had joined other youngsters in going to the railroad yards to watch the Yankees' train come in. The boys scrambled to carry the players' suitcases to the team bus, and Steinbrenner said he always went for the luggage tagged with DiMaggio's No. 5. He told Joe that, more often than not, he won out. Joe smiled weakly and held out his arm, in a poignant gesture of thanks. Hoping to lighten the mood, Steinbrenner told DiMaggio that when he was ready to come out of retirement, he would be welcome to talk contract terms. Joe chuckled, "You know what those guys are getting today?" Steinbrenner replied, "You would own the team." Joe smiled again—he may have thought of the reply he gave when I had asked him, if he were still playing, what he would say to Steinbrenner to begin negotiations. "Hi, partner," was what Joe said at the time, with a hearty laugh. Now, though, he was in no mood to laugh, as a spasm of pain had him clutching his stomach.

George, making a supreme effort to keep smiling, told Joe to do some arm exercises so he would be ready to throw out the first ball at Yankee Stadium, which was about five weeks away. He repeated what he had told Joe in the hospital, "The ball is yours forever, and you will be throwing it out for many years to come."

Steinbrenner got a chuckle out of the story about DiMaggio seeing a bulletin announcing his death scrawl across the TV screen two months earlier. It was late January, and Joe and I were watching television, switching back and forth between a Western video we had rented and an awards presentation on which Joe was to be mentioned. Suddenly, there it was, the report of DiMaggio's demise. A technician at NBC had pushed the wrong button. Joe, after recovering from his initial shock, was angry. "Joe, if you're dead, then I must be in heaven with you," I said. The man who made the error, Timothy York, apologized the next day in a letter to Joe.

Finally, it came time to say goodbye. DiMaggio reached out and shook Steinbrenner's hand. George hurried for the door, attempting to get out of the room before emotion overcame him. He just made it. George broke into uncontrolled tears as soon as he got outside. I invited him to come across the street to my home for something to eat before heading back. He declined, saying the way his stomach was churning, he doubted if he could keep anything down. He sat in silence as I drove him back to my office where a driver was waiting to take him to the airport. Steinbrenner shook my hand and hugged me. "I hope we can be friends after Joe is gone," he said. The sadness still was etched on his face as he was driven off.

He apparently remained depressed for days, so much so that New York sportswriters wrote about how unusually subdued Steinbrenner was that week. He never even showed up to see Clemens make his exhibition-season debut as a Yankee. The writers, of course, had no way of knowing what had put the Boss in that mood.

◆ ◆ ◆

After I saw how much enjoyment DiMaggio got out of his visit with Steinbrenner, I asked him if I could invite some of his close friends to visit. He smiled and nodded that it was OK. My first call was to Rock Positano. The New York foot surgeon has been likened to a big teddy bear, and he was very emotional when it came to DiMaggio. He always ended a conversation with him by saying, "Joe, I love you." I told Rock that Joe was dying and that now was the time for him to come and say goodbye. Positano began to cry and said that as much as he would like to see Joe one more time, he didn't feel he could handle the scene emotionally. His decision upset DiMaggio's granddaughters and Nachio, who felt his visit would have cheered Joe when he needed support the most. But knowing Positano, I think he made the correct decision. An emotional meltdown in front of Joe would have been devastating for the patient and the doctor.

There were others who never showed up, either at the hospital or at Joe's house, once they heard that DiMaggio was on his way out. Those were the guys who used to go out of their way to take him to dinner at expensive restaurants and give him gifts. What they wanted in return was his signature on a piece of memorabilia or a book. There was one guy in particular, a flamboyant big-time insurance executive from Miami. Nothing was too good for Joe as far as he was concerned. He would send his chauffeur to drive DiMaggio to some fine restaurants in Miami, and he would fly to New York to meet Joe and take him to dinner. But DiMaggio caught on when, after dinner at the Forge restaurant, the fellow asked him to autograph six copies of the Joe DiMaggio Albums, a bound, hardcover collection of newspaper articles and photos. "With my signature, those books will go for $850 for the set of two," Joe figured. "That's $5,100 for a $40 meal. Does he think I'm stupid?" DiMaggio didn't talk to him for six months.

Barry Halper wanted to say goodbye, but was rebuffed by Joe. Halper called my office several times to ask when he could visit, but Joe was explicit, in fact, angry, about his desire not to see him. "Oh, no, not him. Not him! Definitely not him," and he would wave his hand in a brush off gesture. Halper blamed me for blocking his visit, but he was wrong; it was DiMaggio. In addition to his general displeasure with Halper's attempts to take advantage of their friendship to make money, Joe was convinced that Halper would disclose details of his visit and the gravity of Joe's condition to the New York tabloids. He was certain that Halper was the source of news leaks during his illness, most of which were inaccurate.

Joe's resentment toward Halper had escalated to the point that DiMaggio would go out of his way to avoid shaking hands with him. One of Barry's friends implored me to intervene and ask Joe to shake hands because he said Halper was desperately ill and didn't want to take Joe's enmity to the grave with him. DiMaggio finally relented and shook hands, only because he took pity on Halper's supposed impending date with death, and he didn't want that on his conscience. As it turned out, Halper outlived Joe, but Joe died without mending the breach between the two.

◆ ◆ ◆

When Joe's condition started deteriorating dramatically and he began to get those abdominal pains, I made the inevitable decision with Dom, Paula, and Kathie to bring in an outfit called Hospice, whose function is to make a terminal patient's final days as comfortable and pain-free as possible. Ever since those terrible days in October, when Joe was wavering between life and death, I had been resisting the recommendations of Dom and the doctors, including Barron, to let DiMaggio go with dignity. "Turn off the respirator and let nature take its course," they said. I said to myself, "Screw dignity. Where there's life, there's hope." Joe was a warrior, and I pledged to Nachio that I would not turn off the machines until after Joe's last breath. From that time, he lived about five months more.

In January, when we were preparing to take Joe home, I created a furor among doctors and nurses when I talked about revoking the "do not resuscitate" order. No nurse would work in the house unless there was such an order, because they felt its absence would open them to a personal liability suit. I gave in on that, and during the first week in March, I faced reality by calling in Javier Ribe, a registered nurse with Hospice whose task was to help DiMaggio die with dignity.

Ribe visited the house every day to check how much closer DiMaggio had moved toward death. We were advised that when Joe did pass on, Javier was to be paged, no matter what time of day or night. He would come to the house and contact the funeral director and the medical examiner. Ribe assured Paula, Kathie, and me that Joe would have no pain in his remaining time.

When it was increasingly apparent that Joe's life was in its final days, Dom and Joe's granddaughters called a priest to give Joe his last rites.

I kept reminding Joe that HBO had a boxing show on Saturday night, and I tried to get him interested in what was happening so that he would have something to look forward to. David Reed, the only member of the U.S. boxing team to win a gold medal at the 1996 games, was fighting for the WBA super-welterweight title against Laurent Boudouani, but Joe was more likely to be interested in the heavyweight match that preceded the feature bout. Lou Savarese was fighting someone named Mount Whitaker. DiMaggio enjoyed seeing heavyweights slam each other around. When I arrived at his house, however, Joe seemed disconnected from what was going on. He was looking straight ahead, staring into space, and sucking on an ice cube. Pesut came to join us as the bouts began.

Joe was propped up in bed, but his eyes were closed. I made some comments about what the fighters were doing in the ring, and when I glanced at him, his eyes had not opened. That was unusual because DiMaggio usually got right into the action on the screen, sometimes with some caustic comments. Savarese won his fight, and Reed's fight came on, but Joe never awakened. Even a knockdown by Whitaker in the sixth round failed to arouse him. I left before the second bout ended, and before I went, I told Joe that the next day was my birthday, and that my daughters and grandsons were coming to my home for a celebration dinner. I promised I would bring him a Deli Den plate of whitefish, tuna fish salad, salmon salad, and sliced turkey, everything he liked. I said goodnight, but there was no response. His eyes remained closed. I had a feeling of dread that Joe was about to leave us. I lay in bed that night praying that he would make it through at least the next twenty-four hours. I did not want to lose him on my birthday.

My first thought on awakening that next morning was that I hadn't received a phone call during the night, and I was grateful for that. But at 10:00 A.M. the phone rang. I was told by one of the attendants in DiMaggio's home that Joe's time indeed was short, and he likely would be gone before sundown.

My first reaction was to call Nachio in Panama to tell him he had better hurry, but he was already getting ready to fly up. He had called a day or two earlier and spoke with a nurse to ask about Joe's condition. When DiMaggio heard that Nachio was on the phone, he asked to speak with him. That was the last conversation between the old buddies. "I could barely make out what he was saying, but he asked me where I was," Nachio recalled. "I told him I was in Panama but I would be there the next day to see him." When the brief conversation was over, Pesut asked DiMaggio who had been on the phone. "That was my most loyal friend," Joe replied. Nachio was touched to hear that. "You know, Joe was never one to exalt anyone."

Those two had quite a relationship. For nearly sixty years, they loved and argued with each other. There were times one wasn't speaking to the other. DiMaggio picked on Nachio terribly. His refusal to sign a bat for his old buddy was the most extreme example, but there were others. He would give Nachio his money to hold, then count it when he got back and complain that $20 was missing. They would squabble over who ate all the bread from the basket at lunch or dinner. I was having breakfast with them during one of their tiffs. Joe didn't talk to Nachio, but I did. Later, DiMaggio complained to me that I liked Nachio better than him, like a kid. When Nachio was in south Florida, Joe would hang around the office waiting for his call. "You know him, he's going to want to have dinner with me. He'll be disappointed if I don't." Actually, it was DiMaggio who would be disappointed. Joe was far closer to Nachio than he was to Dom.

When I arrived at DiMaggio's house that Sunday morning, Dom was at his brother's bedside, sitting on a leather sofa about 10 feet away discussing funeral arrangements as if Joe already was dead. Again, I made a strong effort to control my temper, not wishing to make DiMaggio's final hours any more trying than they had to be. I told Dom that because Joe was in a coma did not mean he could not hear what was being said. Dom looked at me with confusion and anger. He left shortly after noon, heading for a lunch he had planned, dressed in a jacket and tie. I thought that strange since his last surviving brother was about to die and he was off somewhere, doing business as usual.

Early in the afternoon, my family gathered to celebrate my fifty-ninth birthday. At 4:30, Nachio arrived and we went across the street to Joe's house. When Nachio saw what Joe's unconscious body looked like, he sobbed uncontrollably. Nachio by then looked a lot like Dom, and he often was mistaken for him when he was with Joe. It was ironic that as Joe was dying, Nachio was with him, but his brother was not. Nachio did not share my view about Dom; at least, he did not want to say anything disparaging about the younger DiMaggio, with whom he was friendly. About Joe's problems with his brother, Nachio could never figure out the cause. "I never asked Dominic. I never asked Joe. It was none of my business," he said.

We sat with Joe for better than three hours, and I could see that Nachio was tired. I suggested that he go to his apartment in Hallandale, about 2 miles away, and I promised I would call him when Joe passed.

It was after eleven o'clock when Ribe announced that Joe had only moments to live. To me, it became a race between death and the clock. I didn't want my dear friend to die on my birthday. Hold on for less than an hour. Was that too much to ask? I took Joe's hand in mine, and, as I had done in the hospital on the anniversary of my father's death, begged him to fight off the angel of death. It was my last pep talk to him, a futile attempt to keep him from giving up. But there was no response. He lay perfectly still, breathing deeply, with no indication that he even heard me.

At about fifteen minutes to midnight, I took DiMaggio's 1936 World Series ring off my finger and attempted to put it on his finger. He had given me the ring when he entered the hospital in October and asked me to wear it for safekeeping. I learned that he had done the same thing a few years earlier when he went into the hospital for replacement of a battery in his pacemaker. Just before he was wheeled into the operating room, he gave Rita the ring to hold for him. That time, he got it back before the day was over. Several times while he was in the hospital, I attempted to put it back on his hand, but his fingers had become swollen and the ring would not go on. In those final minutes, I again was having trouble putting that cherished souvenir of his first World Series on his finger. I was determined that he would die with that ring where he had worn it all those years. I looked around the room for Vaseline, and when I couldn't find it, I ran across the street and got a jar from my home. I managed to get the ring barely over a knuckle, but it was on his finger. (Erroneous reports claimed that I was struggling to get Joe's ring *off* his finger as he was dying. In truth, it wasn't on his finger that night until I put it there.)

I kept watching the two hands on the clock moving toward midnight, and finally, March 7 became March 8. My birthday had passed, and Joe was still alive. Ribe took hold of one of DiMaggio's hands, and Kathie and I held the other. Jim Hamra, Paula's husband, was crying; since Joe's hands were being held, he grasped DiMaggio's feet. Joe was still breathing, and then came a moment that sent a shiver through my body. The trache tube was out of his throat, and in that strange voice in which he spoke over the last months of his life, Joe said, "I'll finally get to see Marilyn again."

"Did he say what I think he said?" Ribe asked me. "He sure did," I replied. Yes, he did, and we all heard it. Moments later, at 12:12 A.M., he was gone. I took the World Series ring from his finger, wiped off the Vaseline and put it back on my finger. I bent down and kissed his forehead. "I can never thank you enough, Joe, but thanks for everything." I walked away from the bed, and for the first time since the ordeal began, I burst into tears. His long battle was over. The Yankee Clipper, one of America's most revered sports heroes and my best friend, was dead. I told myself something I had told the survivors of my clients many times over the years: "At least he isn't suffering anymore."

Someone had removed Joe's bridgework. It was a funny time to remember such a thing, but once he had forgotten those teeth and we had to rush them by FedEx to New York. After that, one of the last things Rita would ask him whenever she drove him to the airport was, "Do you have your teeth, Mr. D.?" This time, Mr. D. had his teeth when he made his final journey, but the partial was then taken from his mouth, wrapped in a tissue and deposited in a medical waste bag. I asked a nurse to retrieve them, and I walked outside to the edge of his dock, where I tossed them into the Intracoastal Waterway. I was determined that Joe D.'s false teeth would not meet the same fate as Ty Cobb's dentures. Halper had sold them at auction for just under $7,500 to a woman from Old Forge, Pennsylvania, who wanted to give them to her dentist father as a gift.

◆ ◆ ◆

The funeral home sent a white van, rather than a hearse, to retrieve Joe's body. I had called the Harbor Islands gatehouse and told them oxygen was being delivered. The idea was to keep news of DiMaggio's death from getting out until later in the morning. I was in no shape, emotionally or physically, to deal with a predawn media frenzy. I cried again as I walked to the security gate when I began to come to grips with the fact that the man I had wished was my father had indeed died. It was no terrible dream. I had never mourned for my real father because I wasn't born when he died. But, now I could mourn. Kathie, Jim, and I sat watching as a couple of guys from the funeral home placed Joe in a black body bag. The last thing we saw as the zipper closed over his cleanly shaven face was that famous nose, pointed toward the ceiling.

I prepared a news release about 4:30 in the morning. As I had promised, it would go to the Associated Press, and the wire service would relay it to newspapers and the electronic media all over the world. At 7:45, it was faxed to Marv Schneider's home. By 8:00 A.M., TV and radio stations were airing the bulletin: "The Associated Press is reporting that Joe DiMaggio has died."

Looking back at those final moments—and I did a great deal of that when I awakened in the middle of the night during the weeks that followed—I was consoled that Joe died peacefully. He went the way he lived his life and played baseball: with dignity and with class, *La Bella Figura* to the very end. He had a clean shave, his hair was combed, and his nails were manicured. The French doors facing the Intracoastal were open, and a cool breeze was blowing in.

14

REST IN PEACE

JOE DiMAGGIO'S DEATH SHOWED how much of an impact he had on American culture. His passing came as no surprise, yet it was one of the year's top news stories. The first bulletin was beamed down from the AP satellite as morning newspapers in the western United States and afternoon papers in the rest of the country were being printed. Presses were stopped, something that doesn't happen very often anymore, and the story was headlined on page one. Television stations rushed to the air with videotapes of DiMaggio career highlights, which had been ready since Joe was hospitalized in October. Newspapers across the country clicked into their computer banks where stories and photos had been stored, waiting for his death, and those were used in special sections the following day. Also, on the following Tuesday, DiMaggio's death was front-page news in Japan, Latin America, and parts of Europe. "Joe DiMaggio was famous in Italy even before Marilyn Monroe," Luciano Pavarotti declared.

Flags were lowered to half-staff on buildings throughout metropolitan New York, in the San Francisco Bay Area, and at baseball training camps in Florida and Arizona. Those who asked why were told, "Joe DiMaggio died." Only the very young had to ask, "Who's he?" Memorial bouquets were tossed into the bay at Martinez, California, where the DiMaggio story in America began and where Joe was born.

Steinbrenner issued a statement of grief on behalf of the Yankees, in which he recalled that during his farewell visit a week earlier he told Joe that they were counting on him to throw out the first ball on Opening Day. "It was the class and dignity with which he led his life that made him part of all of us," Steinbrenner said. "I will forever cherish the close association and friendship we shared over the years."

◆ ◆ ◆

Dom had made it clear for months, even while Joe was alive and in the same room, that he and Emily would be in charge of the funeral, and that the Mass would be held in San Francisco. The two insisted that DiMaggio's body be flown to California in the baseball commissioner's plane. That presented a potential problem because Paula and Kathie were determined to carry through on their grandfather's wish that his funeral be low-key and that only the family be there, with the exceptions of Nachio and me. Commissioner Bud Selig had to be made aware of the family's wishes, even if his plane was to be used as a transcontinental hearse.

How could Selig, for whom DiMaggio had little regard, be at the funeral when the doors were closed to such friends as George Steinbrenner, Phil Rizzuto, Yogi Berra, and Reggie Jackson? An obvious solution would have been to defy Joe's wishes and open the funeral to all, but I was determined not to let that happen. When I expressed my concern, Dom assured me that Selig would not be there.

Whenever DiMaggio went to San Francisco from Miami or New York, he flew on American Airlines, and the airline's executives wanted one of their jets to carry his body home for the last time. Steinbrenner offered the Yankees' jet, but it would have been too small to accommodate the coffin and those of us who would accompany the body. The commissioner's plane also was too small, so Major League Baseball chartered a plane, and Joe's body was flown on that, accompanied by Dom, Emily, Selig, and I believe, American League President Gene Budig.

"Let's not make an issue of it," Paula said. "Let Dom have his day." I wasn't quite sure what Dom and Emily had in mind for San Francisco, so I thought it would be prudent to have some legal backing for my position as the personal representative of DiMaggio's estate. Jerald Cantor, then my law partner, had Miami judge Mel Grossman issue letters of administration appointing me, just hours after Joe died. It was a highly unusual procedure, but one I thought necessary if I were to carry out Joe's wishes about his funeral in the face of potential opposition from Dom and Emily. I had those documents with me when I flew west with Nachio at my side. Poor Nachio wept throughout the trip, although he took consolation from having kept his promise to Joe. "I said I would be there to see him and say goodbye, and I made it."

Nachio was determined to find Joe Jr. and make sure he was at the funeral, as a "fitting tribute and a mark of respect for his father." I knew it was going to be tough tracking down this eccentric fifty-seven-year-old. He was virtually a street person and had roamed from one temporary sleeping place to another in the Bay Area. He had made no effort to contact his father in the hospital. Did he know his father had surgery? Just about everyone else in America did. After his dad was taken home, I got a phone call from Junior, wanting to know how his dad was doing. I told him about Joe's illness, that his father was stable at the time, but that he was not likely to survive much longer.

"Just give my regards to my father and tell him that I love him," Junior said. When I asked if he wanted to come and visit, he said, "I'll get back to you." I never heard from him again. Had he learned that his father was dead? "If he hasn't, we'll find him and tell him," Nachio said.

First, though, there was the matter of the funeral. DiMaggio's granddaughters and I were kept in the dark about that. A good way to find out was to go to the Halsted N. Gray-Carew and English Funeral Home in San Francisco. When we got there, we were told that the funeral director was having a private meeting with Dom and Emily, and we were to wait in the lobby. I informed the man who gave us those instructions that if I didn't see his boss, I was ready to move the funeral elsewhere. That got us into the meeting. I told the funeral director that my approval was needed for all funeral expenses. I was the guy that would sign the check, or not sign it. That got his attention. At that point especially, I was thankful for Judge Grossman giving me the power I had requested.

Problem No. 1: Dom wanted his brother in an open casket. Nachio emphatically spoke out against that, saying that Joe certainly would have rejected such a suggestion. "As long as he looks OK, why not?" Dom asked. I told the funeral director, "The casket will be closed." How could anyone even consider an open coffin for so private a man as Joe DiMaggio?

Problem No. 2: Dom said that professional pallbearers would be used because they were all tall and their well-groomed appearance made them more suitable for the occasion. That was a new one on me—"good-looking pallbearers." What was he planning, a wedding, a fashion show, or a funeral? And besides, what were we, ugly ducklings? I am 6-foot-5; DiMaggio's grandsons are both 6-footers; Nachio was DiMaggio's oldest friend; Joe T. DiMaggio was a close nephew; and Joe Jr., if we could find him, deserved to have the honor as his father's only child. "That's who the pallbearers will be," I informed the funeral director.

Problem No. 3: Emily announced that, after the funeral, there would be a repast at Bobby Rubino's Place for Ribs. A rib joint? "You must be kidding," I said. "No, it's a tradition in the DiMaggio family," Dom informed me. "After Mae's funeral, and after Marie's funeral, we all went to Bobby Rubino's." The restaurant was on historic ground in the DiMaggio family. At that very location, the famous DiMaggio restaurant was founded in 1937, and it flourished there for decades, drawing tourists from around the nation. It was there that Joe posed in a chef's hat with a huge grin on his face over a big pot of boiling water, cooking spaghetti during his disastrous 1938 holdout. But Joe had been forced to sell his interest in the restaurant to Dom so that he could meet Dorothy Arnold's financial demands at their divorce. Joe was hurt that his brother bought him out, as Dom had done with his other brothers, rather than lend him the money. Dom said the restaurant buyout was not the cause of the hard feelings his brother had about him. "It had to do with an appearance that I did not make at one of his charitable functions." The restaurant eventually was demolished, and the rib place franchise was built on the land, still owned by Dom DiMaggio. I wondered what memories that old restaurant site would have had for Joe if he had been alive. (Of course, if he had been alive, there would be no need to go to Bobby Rubino's.)

Problem No. 4: We had to find Joe Jr. so that he could be at the funeral, and hopefully as a pallbearer. "You're wasting your time," said his uncle. "He's nothing more than a bum, and he won't come." I replied, "It's not your choice, Dominic. It will be the last gift Joe Nachio and I give to our friend, Joe DiMaggio."

Nachio and I left, but I was too angry to say goodbye to Dom and Emily. If they considered me an ill-mannered, pushy guy from Brooklyn, so be it. I was good enough for Joe to empower as executor of his estate, and I had the legal backing of a Florida judge. That was good enough for me.

We set out in search of Joe's only offspring, with the help of still another Joe DiMaggio, Big Joe's nephew and Junior's cousin. He and his wife, Marina, had been Big Joe's primary link to his son, but by this point they saw Joe Jr. only now and then as he drifted around the Bay Area. When we left the funeral home, Joe spent about two hours on the telephone trying to track down his cousin, calling a succession of taverns and friends, before he picked up a possible lead. We drove a couple of hours out of San Francisco, and even today, I'm not sure where we went, but it was somewhere around Pittsburg, California. Junior had left his humble quarters in the back of the abandoned truck and headed for the hills when he was being hounded for interviews about his father during Joe's hospitalization. On the drive along major highways that took us into a rural area, nephew Joe T. wasn't very encouraging. "You're wasting your time," he said. "Even if we find him, he won't be happy to see you. He's not going to cooperate." He said that Joe Jr. was bright and well-spoken, but he had his moods, and right now he was angry with his older cousin and Marina. He warned me that Junior was a con man.

"You find him, I'll take care of the rest," Nachio said. He and Junior had a long history, dating back to the days when Nachio took him by the hand and walked him back to his mother's hotel in New York after he had visited his father's apartment in the Ely-see Hotel. It was Nachio who took Little Joe to Yankee Stadium to visit his father on the field and in the locker room before games. When Joey went to Lawrenceville for prep school, Nachio drove Big Joe to visit him. Though they hadn't seen each other in many years, Nachio was confident about the reception he would get from Little Joe.

The address we had been given turned out to be a ramshackle house in need of paint and repairs. Out front was an old Cadillac that had similar needs. A man wearing a tank top in the 45-degree chill was hovering around the front of the car, and another man, also wearing a tank top, was working under the dashboard. Grease and grime covered his neck, shoulders, arms, and legs. Nachio and I were wearing black suits, no doubt inspiring suspicions that we were federal agents. The guy under the dashboard was the man we were looking for.

Nachio got out of our car and approached the Cadillac. "Hey, it's me, Joe Nachio—Panama Joe," Nachio shouted. Joe Jr. eased himself out of the car. What a sight! Unkempt gray hair tied in a pony tail, not a tooth in his mouth, and a face caked with dirt. "Uncle Joe!" he exclaimed. He put his arms around Nachio's shoulders until he realized how dirty his arms were, and he quickly withdrew them. The two went into the house, where Nachio told Junior that his father had died and that I was a friend of his dad's who had come to tell him about his inheritance. He said that I was the only man his father had trusted, and that he could, too.

Nachio signaled for me to come into the house. A putrid sour smell in the kitchen was overpowering. There were a lot of empty beer bottles around, but little furniture, and a couple of kids ran around in diapers.

Nachio introduced me to Junior. There were not enough chairs, so I sat on the floor, looking incongruous in my suit. I explained to Joe Jr. that his father had made me his trustee, and that under the terms of the will, he would get at least $20,000 a year from a trust created by his father's will, to be paid in installments of about $1,666 a month. Junior had a question, "Is that before or after taxes?" His father would have been proud. Joe Jr. was living on welfare and food stamps, but still concerned about the bite from the IRS. I told him that I had the authority to go into the principal if he needed more money.

Joe looked at Nachio as if to seek additional assurance about me. Nachio told him, "Junior, you can trust this man with your life." Joe Jr. shook my hand and put an arm around me. It was an emotional moment for me. I had been hearing about Joe Jr. for many years, and whenever I tried to give DiMaggio advice about a reconciliation, he would reply, "Butt out. My boy is a bum." But his remark would be softened by the disclaimer, "But, he's a good boy."

I told Junior I would try to do for him what his father wanted to do, but for some reason couldn't bring himself to do. "Your father really loved you, I hope you know that," I said. "I loved my father very much," he told me. Nachio interrupted to say, "Joey, it's time you reconciled with your father. Out of respect for him, we would like you to come to his funeral on Thursday." Junior assured us, "I'll be there." Nachio wondered if Joe Jr. had any clothes to wear to the funeral. "Just the ones I'm wearing," he answered. Jeans, a tank top, and thong sandals were hardly suitable attire for a pallbearer. Nachio gave him four $100 bills and told him to get a black suit and whatever else he needed. His father's oldest friend also said he would pay for his transportation to and from the funeral. Joe Jr. expressed his thanks and asked what time he should show up. He had more than a full day to buy what he needed and get cleaned up.

On the way back to San Francisco, we told Junior's cousin and his wife what had taken place. They gave each other knowing glances, and Joe T. said that although the man was his first cousin and he liked him, he was sure that Junior would not show up at the funeral. He told Nachio that he had just been conned out of $400. "He's a manipulator." I guess it was wishful thinking on my part, because I had known Joe Jr. for only twenty-five minutes, but I said, "My money is on Junior. He'll be there." Nachio replied, "If I lost the $400, it was worth the try."

Junior was a major concern as I tried to sleep that night. What if his cousin was right and Junior was a no-show? I worried if he did show up, what his reaction would be when he saw his ex-wife, Sue, the two daughters he hadn't seen in years, and their children, his grandchildren, whom he had never seen. Would he do an about face, and head out the door at his own father's funeral? I was also nervous about how he would dress for this final tribute to his father; would he look like the aged hippie I had seen, wearing a tank top, faded jeans, and thong sandals?

◆ ◆ ◆

Nachio and I decided to get to the funeral home at eight o'clock, an hour early, and a wise decision that proved to be. Fifteen minutes behind us, forty-five minutes early, Joe Jr. arrived in a white stretch limousine. He rolled down the tinted window of the limo, held out a scrubbed, manicured hand, and gave me a hearty handshake. When he stepped onto the sidewalk, I breathed another sigh of relief. Nachio's money had been well spent. Junior was wearing a three-button, well-tailored black suit with cuffed trousers, white shirt, a conservative tie, and a pair of shiny new shoes that, while not the Allen-Edmonds brand his father and I favored, were perfectly acceptable. He looked indeed like a successful son of Yale, *albeit* one with a ponytail.

My concerns about his reunion with family members also evaporated. Nachio and I stayed close in case he decided to bolt for the door. That was unnecessary. Although he hadn't seen most of his relatives for ten years, he hugged and kissed them as if there had been no gap in their relationship.

Jim Hamra told me later that I wasn't the only one impressed at how Junior handled himself at the funeral home. Jim was, too. "He stood there, off to the side of the room, shoulders back, head up, studying the people as if he was figuring out who he knew, and who he didn't know," Hamra recalled. "He then worked the room, hugging some people, shaking hands with some, and he seemed completely at ease."

Among those in the room were Selig and Budig, there at Dom's invitation, in complete disregard of his promise that only family members would be at the funeral. I was upset that Selig and Budig were there, while Joe DiMaggio's friends were not. I was chatting with Nachio and Joe Jr. when Dom approached and told me that the commissioner and American League president would like to meet me. "I have no interest in meeting them," I said. "They shouldn't be here, and you told me that they would not be here." Dom said he felt obligated to invite Selig and Budig because they had all flown together on the chartered plane that brought the coffin to San Francisco. I reminded him of his promise, but he shrugged and walked away.

Junior chuckled and said, "Now, I know why my father loved you. He would have said the same thing in the same situation." Dom insisted in a *Daily News* interview two months later that there was "no deal." I guess it just happened that way.

Selig, in a statement issued by his office in New York, said of Joe, "I idolized him from afar as a youngster growing up in Milwaukee. In later years being with him was an event, bringing on an air of excitement, anticipation, and joy."

Junior, Nachio, and I were put into the same limousine for the ride to the church, along with Junior's ex-wife and her new husband. I had never met Sue and I asked Junior in a whisper who she was. "My ex-wife," he whispered back. I was shocked and thought the arrangement was a risky one since Sue and Joe Jr. had not parted amicably. I had a feeling that Junior might have left the car and walked to the church had he not been wedged between Nachio and me. But, he and Sue spoke cordially, and they had a pleasant conversation later in the hour-long ride to the cemetery.

The funeral Mass was held at Saints Peter and Paul, the huge North Beach parish church the DiMaggio family had attended, and the setting for Joe's frenetic wedding with Dorothy Arnold in 1939. The mood was much more subdued on a sunny springlike day sixty years later. In contrast to the mob that jammed Washington Square and choked traffic for a glimpse of the biggest wedding North Beach had ever seen, only about 200 people were there to see the funeral cortege pull up. About sixty family members filed into the old twin-spired building as the church bells tolled their mournful message that a funeral was about to take place.

As I helped carry the casket up the steps and into the church, the unusual aspect of that moment struck me. I, who grew up in an Orthodox Jewish home, studied in a yeshiva, and in those days wore a yarmulke wherever I went, now had the distinction of being a pallbearer at a Roman Catholic funeral Mass. Joe would have smiled at that. He had performed an important role at my grandson Harrison's ritual circumcision, and he had come to Sabbath eve dinners at my mother's home, where I traditionally recited Kiddush, the prayer over wine that precedes the meal. "I didn't know you were that religious," he said on his first visit. I told him that I had been very religious at one time, but had become less observant. Joe, who regarded himself a practicing Catholic, respected prayers and the people who said them, no matter the religion. Many of the important people in his life were Jewish, going back to the first friends he made in New York, Joe Gould, George Solotaire, and Bernie Kamber.

I thought of that when Father Armand Oliveri recited the 23rd Psalm, "The Lord is my shepherd." I had heard many rabbis deliver those comforting words at Jewish funerals. Father Oliveri, who grew up with DiMaggio in North Beach, celebrated the Mass along with the church pastor, Father David Purdy. Emily and Dom obviously had a strong influence on the rest of the one-hour service, which included scripture readings by their son and daughter and by DiMaggio's granddaughter Kathie. Dom delivered the eulogy, which he seemed to use as a catharsis to make himself feel better. He talked of Joe being a lonely, unhappy man, one who never had a lifetime companion, and that he had to involve himself in a children's hospital to assuage his loneliness. Were it not for Nachio, I would have walked out of the service at that point; that's how incensed I was that Joe was being portrayed as a recluse to be pitied. I chastised myself for allowing his brother to deliver the eulogy.

"I was put in charge of the funeral," Dom said later. "I was given that privilege, not much more. I think I did a pretty good job."

Getting the casket down the steps was much harder than carrying it up, and the six of us strained to hold onto it. When we reached the sidewalk, I could hear polite, restrained applause from those in Washington Square. I had managed to maintain my composure until then, but after helping push the coffin into the hearse, the tears came involuntarily. I kissed the top of the brown casket and said, "Joe, I love you."

A yellow rose had been placed on a step in front of the church with a hand-printed note that read, "Grazie, Joe. North Beach." A gray-haired woman held up cardboard on which she had mounted a photograph of Joe and Marilyn.

As we drove off, I looked out the window of the limo. Old men and women from the Italian neighborhood, many of whom as kids may have known Joe, stood by the curb. Some of the men took off their hats, women waved farewell at the hearse, and a couple of younger men saluted. Among those watching was Margaret Mann, who was struck by a typically North Beach sight as the mourners left the church: "About forty of San Francisco's notorious flock of exotic escapee parrots, blue, red and green, flew raucously through the street and into the park across the street. It was stunning."

Carl Nolte, among those from the *San Francisco Chronicle* covering the funeral, wrote: "In New York, the funeral of a legend would have been an Event. In Los Angeles, it would have been Showtime. But in San Francisco, it was as dignified as DiMaggio himself."

After we left, some of the people went into the church. Among them was Rocco Boschetti, a man in his late seventies who knew DiMaggio from the neighborhood, and who had met him again in Hawaii during World War II. The old timer had a photo of that unexpected reunion, DiMaggio with his arm around Boschetti, who was in the merchant marine at the time. Boschetti remembered that the following day, DiMaggio had hit that tape-measure home run against Pee Wee Reese's navy team. "I lost a good friend," he told a reporter in the church. "I said a prayer."

A police escort led the hearse and procession of cars through North Beach, where Joe and his brothers had grown up, and into the Marina neighborhood, passing the Beach Street home where DiMaggios had lived since Joe purchased it for his parents. Our destination was suburban Colma, where the buried and entombed outnumber the living. There, in a hilltop mausoleum overlooking the Holy Cross Catholic Cemetery, Giuseppe and Rosalie DiMaggio were among the 40,000 entombed in the crypts that line the walls, ceiling to floor. Joe's casket was put there, temporarily, and later moved to its eternal resting place under a tree in a single tomb. The sight has become a cemetery landmark. On either side of the crypt were huge flower urns, made of stone and filled with flowering plants. In addition to Joe's name and the dates of his birth and death, the stone in front of the tomb, bears the message, "Grace, Dignity and Elegance personified." During a typical week, visitors left remembrances against the front of the crypt, including flowers, American flags, photos of DiMaggio, baseballs, and even bats.

If Joe had known what it was going to cost, he might have fought death even longer than he did. He was still alive when the estate bought the site and the crypt, and when I saw what it cost, I thought, "If he ever survives, then I'm dead." Dom was running the funeral and the interment, and Paula, who was getting the bulk of the estate, told me not to fight him on that. I, as executor, followed her wishes. "Keep him happy," she said. "Give him a purpose in life."

I explained to Paula that while funeral expenses were deductible, the IRS requires that these be "reasonable." I spent about seven hours researching cases to determine what was considered a reasonable expenditure.

After the funeral, something happened that I did not consider reasonable, either esthetically or financially. The post-funeral repast at Bobby Rubino's was an insult to Joe's memory. The buffet was limited to what was said to be sliced turkey, but which looked like it came from a compressed loaf of something that may or may not have been alive at one time, with bowls of iceberg lettuce, tomatoes, and coleslaw. Paula and Kathie wondered, since this was called a "place for ribs," where were the ribs? Eventually, these were brought out and served to each person one at a time. The bar was closed after an hour. The estate of Joe DiMaggio was presented with a bill for more than $6,200, which came to about $100 a person for a $3.95 buffet. I did what Joe would have done. I refused to pay it. He would have left in a huff long before the ribs were doled out. It was not Joe's kind of a place, and he no doubt would have muttered to me about someone as "highfalutin" as Emily selecting that joint. I could hear Joe saying, "Well, Dom did it again. He took care of his tenant. Morris, don't pay the bill." He would have pointed out that Dom still owned the building.

◆ ◆ ◆

The first thing I did upon returning to the hotel was to call Dr. Positano in New York. "What we need is a New York tribute to Joe," I told him, and I knew he had the class and the clout to do it. On his request, I sent him a letter, on behalf of the estate, authorizing him to make the arrangements. A memorial service at St. Patrick's Cathedral, to be followed by a repast at a more suitable place than the one in San Francisco, is what I wanted, and Positano came through in grand style. This time, there would be no spareribs.

St. Patrick's, across Fifth Avenue from Rockefeller Center, had become known as the Yankees' church. The imposing cathedral was the setting for the funerals of Babe Ruth and Billy Martin and for a memorial service for Roger Maris. Positano recalled that when DiMaggio was in town on Sundays, he occasionally would insist that they go to St. Patrick's together. Positano said that DiMaggio would lecture him: "You were raised a Catholic, and

you raised your family Catholic, so you have to set a good example." Rock told him there were several small churches off the beat-
en track in New York that drew scant congregations on Sunday, so
his appearance would be unnoticed. But, Joe wanted St. Pat's,
even though he risked creating a stir.

One Sunday, Joe told him, "Don't worry, Doc. I'll show you
how we'll fool them." Positano said, "He put on a pair of sunglasses, and we walked into a side entrance at St. Pat's on 50th
Street. He made me lead the way—he always did that when we
went into a place—and we sat in a pew. There was a noticeable
buzz and people turned to look in our direction. Joe stared straight
ahead. Cardinal John O'Connor was on the altar when we tiptoed
in, and later, in his homily, he said, 'I am so delighted and honored
that we have with us at today's Mass an American legend, Mr. Joe
DiMaggio.'" People applauded and stood up so they could see the
great hero. "I have to hand it to you, Joe, that's a great disguise,"
Doc told him. "You really fooled them."

"There's a part of the Mass called the Peace of Christ, when
you turn to the person nearest you and shake their hand. The
priest who was celebrating the Mass asked the people to offer a
sign of peace to their neighbor. Joe shook my hand and said, 'The
peace of Christ to you, Doc,' and I said, 'The peace of Christ to
you, Joe.' Then a man came to our pew, put out his hand and said,
'The peace of Christ to you, Mr. DiMaggio.' Joe hesitated, but
shook the man's hand and responded, 'The peace of Christ to
you.' The guy then pulled out a photo and asked Joe to autograph
it. Joe's jaw set, and you could see he was angry, but when he
looked at the picture he smiled and said, 'I don't think the Pope
would like me signing across his face.'"

For their grandfather's service, Paula and Kathie wanted
Michael Bolton, Joe's friend from the Legends Game in Florida,
to sing "Amazing Grace" or "Ave Maria" at the service, but Cardinal O'Connor rejected the idea. I tried unsuccessfully to get the

cardinal to reconsider. The cardinal's aides asked me to submit four names as candidates to speak during the service. I requested Kissinger, former Governor Mario Cuomo, Mayor Rudolph Giuliani, and Bobby Brown. The cardinal turned down Giuliani, Kissinger, and Cuomo, which would have left Brown as the only speaker. There was an exchange of faxes between the cardinal and me, and I managed to get the OK for Giuliani to speak. DiMaggio respected the mayor's knowledge of baseball and regarded him as a genuine Yankees fan. They had some intense baseball discussions whenever they met at Yankee Stadium. Giuliani, like me, was a Brooklyn kid who rooted for the Yankees because of DiMaggio. His father and uncle were big DiMaggio boosters, and although the family lived only about a mile from Ebbets Field, young Rudy was taken on the long subway ride to the Bronx to see the men in pinstripes play. Years later, when he was mayor of New York, he was surprised at a Columbus Day parade to learn that DiMaggio had asked to have lunch with him because he considered Giuliani to be a hero. "Me, a hero to DiMaggio, who was my hero all my life?" Giuliani was fond of telling people. "The reason I was his hero, he said, was because I helped to throw the Mafia out of New York." (I wasn't there, so I don't know what Joe told Giuliani, but in all the years I knew DiMaggio, I never once heard him use the word "Mafia." Sometimes, he would call them "wise guys," and he would flatten the tip of his nose in the New York gesture that invariably went with that description.)

Before the service, Cardinal O'Connor walked up to the front row where I was seated and asked, "Which one is Engelberg?" "I am," I said. He smiled and offered me a handshake. He also shook his head as if to say, "You're a tough negotiator." I considered that an honor, especially since I was able eventually to get Giuiliani approved.

The memorial service at St. Patrick's was held on April 23. On the previous day, the *Daily News* ran a story saying that I had barred Steinbrenner and people from the Yankees organization from the service. There was absolutely no truth to it. In fact, I was looking forward to seeing George because I felt bad that he was excluded from the funeral. Joe sincerely loved the man. Where the *News* got that malicious story, I had no idea, but I faulted the newspaper for not checking it out before publishing it—that's basic journalism. It seemed that someone on the staff had his own agenda, and basic journalism be damned.

As I was about to walk up the front steps of the cathedral, I saw Steinbrenner. Uh-oh. What would be his reaction? George spotted me the same time I saw him. As we approached each other, he laughed, reached out for a handshake and hugged me. I should have known that Steinbrenner was too astute and knew me well enough to spot a lie when he read one.

A huge crowd filled the cathedral for the service. Steinbrenner sat in a pew that also included the unlikely pair of Henry Kissinger and Yogi Berra. Rizzuto was there, so were Woody Allen, who was a big DiMaggio fan, and Michael Bolton. To me the most surprising of those in the cathedral was my cousin, Rabbi Fishof, wearing his skullcap and a thoughtful expression. This was the first time he had ever been in a church. When I asked him what he was doing there, he replied, "Sharing a piece of American history." Like so many others, he was drawn by his affection for the Yankees and his admiration for DiMaggio.

Giuliani spoke from the altar and told of the pride DiMaggio's success had brought to Italian-Americans, a theme echoed in other cities around the country. The mayor also recalled the first big league game he saw, the Red Sox against the Yankees at the Stadium. "Each team had a center fielder named DiMaggio, and I thought that was strange," Giuliani said. Dom was seated several four rows behind me, thankfully, and not with Joe's granddaughters and their husbands. Emily was not there.

Bobby Brown's remarks created a stir in the cathedral, which I am sure was unintentional. The cardinal, in his homily, explained that the event was not a Mass, but a prayer service. "Mr. DiMaggio made two mistakes during his lifetime, and his soul now is in purgatory between heaven and hell," O'Connor said. "We are here to pray that his soul goes to heaven." The Cardinal apparently was referring to DiMaggio's divorce and remarriage. Brown began his remarks by saying, "I am sure that Joe DiMaggio is in heaven today." Although I never spoke with him about it, I am sure Bobby had his speech prepared long before he went to the altar that morning and had no desire to get into an ecclesiastical debate with His Eminence.

Cardinal O'Connor recalled the Sunday Mass when he had noted DiMaggio's presence in the cathedral, and said that Joe was "greeted with wild applause." At the end of the service, the Cardinal asked for a farewell salute to Joe's memory. Everyone rose and DiMaggio got a standing ovation that reverberated through the huge cathedral.

What a sight it was on 51st Street as we walked the one long block to a reception at Le Cirque in the Palace Hotel on Madison Avenue. Police lined the sidewalk as Kissinger, Giuliani, Steinbrenner, Berra, Rizzuto, Bolton, and the others walked by. Talk about stopping traffic, even in blasé New York! Noticeable by his absence from that procession was brother Dom. I thought he probably went, instead, to a Bobby Rubino's.

Le Cirque is an elegant restaurant. Joe would have looked it over and remarked, "A very nice place." After the touching memorial in the awe-inspiring cathedral, this was the setting I had in mind for New York's goodbye to Joe DiMaggio. He himself often said, "No place does it up as well as New York," and he was right again.

Positano, microphone in hand, went from person to person in the restaurant for personal stories about DiMaggio. Kissinger told about asking DiMaggio if he wanted an autographed baseball from him. "Not really," Joe replied. "I can't understand what you write." Steinbrenner remembered a day in the 1980s when DiMaggio came to his suite to pick up three World Series tickets he had requested. The Yankees owner was tied up with a phone call in his office and Joe waited in the reception room, but not for long. After three minutes, DiMaggio angrily stormed out. George called him the next day and located him on the golf course. "He hung up on me," Steinbrenner recalled. The following day, Joe returned to the Stadium in a better mood. But he rejected Steinbrenner's invitation to join a party that was underway. saying he "didn't want to intrude."

Rizzuto told of how, when he joined the Yankees, he was so in awe of Joe, he watched him shave, comb his hair, knot his tie. "Joe probably thought I was gay."

I told how Joe delighted in teasing me by never referring to me in public as his friend. At dinner with a small group, I was his dear friend; in his home and mine, I was his dear friend; but at a card show or a personal appearance, with thousands of people around, it was, "meet my lawyer," or "meet my adviser," or "meet my financial consultant." My feeling was that by doing that he was displaying his power, showing the world that he was being represented by a professional, not a friend. On the plane coming to New York from Chicago for his farewell to Yankee Stadium, I said, "Joe, I'm your friend, so please just once introduce me in public as your friend." He laughed.

In Steinbrenner's crowded private box that afternoon in 1998, DiMaggio spotted Joe Pepitone. "Hey, Peppie, come over here and say hello. I want you to meet someone," DiMaggio said. "This is it," I thought, "I'll finally get the introduction I am so eagerly awaiting." I was wrong. Joe said, "Peppie, you know my main man, Morris?"

◆ ◆ ◆

I was back at Yankee Stadium on April 25, 1999, under much different circumstances. Joe again was being honored, but this time it was a memorial tribute. A monument to DiMaggio's memory was being unveiled in hallowed Monument Park, beyond the outfield fences.

A crowd of 52,000 was at the Stadium on that sunny Sunday for a game with the Toronto Blue Jays. Some of the fans had traveled part of the way along the Joe DiMaggio Highway. A portion of the West Side Highway had officially been renamed that morning. New York's Governor George Pataki had wanted to rename the Major Deegan Highway, which runs past Yankee Stadium, for Joe, but Giuliani knew that DiMaggio preferred the West Side Highway, and he stood firm in that. As Joe would have wanted, I backed up the mayor in a strongly worded letter to the governor.

The monument unveiling ceremony was held before the game. It was a fitting tribute to one of the greatest Yankees of them all, and was well orchestrated by Steinbrenner. "No. 5 is alive in our hearts," read one of the signs displayed by fans. "Joe D. Now and Always," said another.

The thrill of being introduced from the Yankees dugout was diminished by the reason for the ceremony, but it was without a doubt an emotional day. As I stood on the dugout steps waiting for that moment, I looked up into the upper deck behind home plate and then behind first base, and I thought of the days when I sat up there with my uncles waiting for the games to start. I had fantasized then about charging out of the dugout onto that famed field, and now I was about to do it. Six of DiMaggio's teammates from the 1951 Yankees participated in the ceremony: Rizzuto, Berra, Whitey Ford, Gil McDougald, Hank Bauer, and Jerry Coleman. Paula and Kathie represented the family. Again, Dom was not there. Bob Sheppard, whose deep, rich voice had told millions of fans through the years that Joe DiMaggio was playing center field, did it again that day. He recited the starting lineups of Joe's final game, Game 6 of the 1951 World Series.

Cardinal O'Connor delivered the invocation, Rizzuto made a speech, and Paul Simon, standing in center field, brought the crowd to its feet and sent a chill through me when he sang those famous lyrics: "Where have you gone, Joe DiMaggio? A nation turns its lonely eyes to you."

According to the script, Berra and Rizzuto were to pull the cover from the monument, but something went awry, and when that didn't happen, Paula and Kathie did it. The bronze plaque on the 5-foot-high granite stone had a portrait of Joe, under which were the words: "Joseph Paul DiMaggio The Yankee Clipper." His lifetime batting average was listed, along with the years he was the league's MVP and the years he won batting titles. There was an epitaph that read: "A baseball legend and an American icon. He has passed but he will never leave us."

Until that day, there were four monuments out there, to Babe Ruth, Lou Gehrig, Mickey Mantle, and manager Miller Huggins. With Joe DiMaggio, there were five.

I left Yankee Stadium that day with a lonely feeling. Joe was not with me, as he had been so often during the last sixteen years. I thought about the day I would see him again. He would introduce me to Marilyn and say to her, "This is my friend Morris."

BIBLIOGRAPHY

Allen, Maury. *Where Have You Gone, Joe DiMaggio? The Story of America's Last Hero.* New York: Dutton, 1975.

Appel, Marty. *Now Pitching for the Yankees: Spinning the News for Mickey, Billy, and George.* Kingston, N.Y.: Total/Sports Illustrated, 2001.

Cramer, Richard Ben. *Joe DiMaggio: The Hero's Life.* New York: Simon and Schuster, 2000.

DiMaggio, Joe. *Lucky to Be a Yankee.* New York: Grossett and Dunlap, 1947.

DiMaggio, Joe, and Richard Whittingham. *The DiMaggio Albums: Selections from Public and Private Collections Celebrating the Baseball Career of Joe DiMaggio.* New York: Putnam's, 1989.

Durso, Joseph. *DiMaggio: The Last American Knight.* Boston: Little, Brown and Company, 1995.

Frommer, Harvey. *The New York Yankee Encyclopedia.* New York: MacMillan, 1997.

Johnson, Dick, and Glen Stout. *DiMaggio: An Illustrated Life.* New York: Walker and Company, 1995.

Kahn, Roger. *Joe & Marilyn: A Memory of Love.* New York: Morrow, 1986.

Leaming, Barbara. *Marilyn Monroe.* New York: Crown Publishers, 1998.

Pepitone, Lena, and William Stadiem. *Marilyn Monroe Confidential: An Intimate Personal Account.* New York: Simon and Schuster, 1979.

Slatzer, Robert F. *The Life and Curious Death of Marilyn Monroe.* New York: Pinnacle House, 1974.

Spoto, Donald. *Marilyn Monroe: The Biography.* New York: Harper Collins, 1993.

Summers, Anthony. *Goddess: The Secret Lives of Marilyn Monroe.* Boston: G. K. Hall, 1985.

Taraborelli, J. Randy. *Sinatra: Behind the Legend.* New Jersey: Rose Books, Inc., Carol Publishing Group, 1997.

Wolfe, Donald H. *The Last Days of Marilyn Monroe.* New York: Morrow, 1998.

INDEX